GENERATION XBOX

How Videogames Invaded Hollywood

JAMIE RUSSELL

YELLOW ANT

Published by Yellow Ant

First published in Great Britain in 2012 by

Yellow Ant
65 Southover High Street, Lewes,
East Sussex, BN7 1JA

www.yellowantmedia.com

Cover by Matt Hobbs of Rumpus Graphics
Typeset by Yellow Ant

ISBN 978-0-9565072-4-2

For Louise, Isobel and Alice, my three muses - with all my love

And in tribute to two inspirational women:
Morag Grisotti (1914-2012) and Doreen Whitehouse.

CONTENTS

The End of the Beginning

"[Videogames] are genuine narrative forms and we would have to be very stupid not to be immersed in and understand [them].... In the next 10 years, I see a huge shift whether we like it or not. It's going to take you either by surprise or you're going to be there to do it. It's going to be like going from silent films to sound. There are going to be a lot of us that cannot do the talkies because we are not familiar with the form. I think it's urgent that you get familiar with them. The art direction, soundscapes and immersive environments in videogames are as good, if not superior to, most movies. I'm not talking about Kieslowski or Bergman. I'm talking about most movies. They are far more advanced and far smarter about it, so I think it's something we all can learn from and it's urgent that we do."
Guillermo Del Toro, director of Hellboy and Pan's Labyrinth, speaking in 2006

"We see games as being an emergent art form, that will eventually supplant or challenge movies,"
Dan Houser, co-founder of Rockstar Games, creators
of the Grand Theft Auto series, speaking in 2008

It was almost finished before it started...

On Thursday 22 September 1983, a fleet of 18-wheel trucks rolled out of a non-descript manufacturing plant in El Paso. They trundled through the streets in a single column, engines groaning as they eased onto Route 54 and headed north. Their cargo? Millions of Atari VCS cartridges including *E.T. The Extra-Terrestrial*, the most hyped game in the company's history. Their destination? A landfill site in Alamogordo, New Mexico.

Arriving in the desert dump in the mid-morning heat, the trucks emptied their once precious loads. Millions of black plastic cartridges, none much bigger than a cigarette packet, scattered into the dust. Each bore an artist's impression of the wrinkled prune face of E.T., the alien star of Steven Spielberg's blockbuster movie. A few minutes later, they were flattened and crushed into a mangled mess of twisted plastic, microchips and torn labels.

Among the debris were computer hardware, game cartridges and other leftovers from Atari's bloated inventory. "We're covering them with garbage and then with dirt," said Ed Moore, one of the waste management employees on duty on that tragic but historic day. "I've been crushing them as fast as they dropped them off the trucks with my Caterpillar. It's kind of sad." Chances are Ed wasn't a gamer; probably his kids were. But maybe he felt moved - like so many moviegoers had been - by that alien face as it stared plaintively up at him from the abandoned cartridges.

Spielberg had designed his extra-terrestrial for maximum emotional effect superimposing, so the story goes, Albert Einstein's eyes onto a picture of a five-day old baby. Here in the New Mexico desert that ancient-yet-vulnerable visage still tugged at the heart strings. But there was no Elliott to save E.T. this time. There was just Ed; and he had a job to do. He threw his Caterpillar into first and drove forward again. He couldn't hear the sound of cracking plastic over the throbbing chug of the machine's engine.

When Ed was finished what was left of the mangled cartridges was scooped into a landfill pit. Then came the cement. A thick layer was poured over the crushed remains to prevent any salvageable pieces being looted. Even still, by the weekend, there were reports that rescued *E.T.* and *Pac-Man* cartridges were being hawked around local stores. Despite the dump's no-scavengers policy - and a security guard who'd been specially hired at Atari's request - a few carts had escaped the cull. The rest weren't so lucky.

Ed chugged his Caterpillar across the dump and repeated the process over and over again. Each truckload cost Atari $300 to $500 to dispose of but the real price paid by the fledgling videogame industry ran into the millions. The VCS 2600 game of *E.T. - The Extra-Terrestrial*, the brainchild of Steven Spielberg and Atari, poisoned Hollywood's love affair with gaming overnight and crashed the nascent business itself. Since 1983, the story of the buried Atari cartridges has become enshrined in videogame lore. Although contemporary reports in the New York Times and Alamogordo Daily News detailed the dumping, Atari never officially confirmed events. Manny Gerard, former co-chief operating officer for Atari's owners Warner Communications, concedes it was probably true - a simple matter of waste disposal rather than some dirty corporate secret. "There was overproduction because everybody thought E.T. [the game] was going to be the greatest thing in the world. At some point you realise you're better off just destroying them than trying to sell them at 5¢ to some guy who's going to come and take them away."

Armchair historians of the 8-bit videogame era remain fascinated by the desert burial. On the internet, a group of true believers even hatched half-baked plans to excavate the site in the hope of discovering archaeological relics from videogaming's early history. As one poster put it on an ongoing AtariAge.com forum thread that has been running since 2005 - the legend of the buried *E.T.* cartridges is the videogame industry's "grassy knoll".

If it had been a different cartridge that had been buried, would the interest be so acute? Probably not. The Great Mass Burial of E.T. resonates because it marked the Icarus-like fall of Atari and the early videogame industry itself. But most of all it stands as potent image of the troubled, on-off love affair between videogames and Hollywood that continues even today.

Back in 1983 Atari was owned by Warner Communications, the parent company of the venerable movie studio Warner Bros. Atari had been hailed as the future of the entertainment industry. Games like *Pong* and *Asteroids* were supposed to end America's obsession with movies forever. It didn't quite work out like that. *E.T.*, one of the earliest attempts to translate a blockbuster movie into a blockbuster game, fell flat on the prune face of its eponymous alien. Warner Communications' stock nosedived and Atari, which had once generated more revenue than Warner Bros. Studios, suddenly became a millstone around the conglomerate's neck. The major motion picture studios rejoiced. They had fretted that videogames would eclipse them. Now they watched as the bogeyman they had feared was unmasked as nothing more than a paper tiger.

In that brief moment between 1981 and 1983, though, the seeds of a much bigger cultural shift were sown. The studios believed that games were simply ancillary products to sell alongside T-shirts, lunch boxes and action figures. They were wrong. The medium had the potential to become Hollywood's inspiration, imitator and ultimately its bête noir.

While the major motion picture studios have spent most of the last 30 years lazily trying to co-opt videogames, the videogame industry itself has been evolving into a real competitor in the entertainment business. From *Dragon's Lair* to *Night Trap* to *Grand Theft Auto III*, *Uncharted 2: Among Thieves* and *Heavy Rain*, videogames have been offering players increasingly immersive, cinematic experiences. At each point on that journey you can bet someone, somewhere dropped their joystick or gamepad and said: "Hey, it looks just like a movie!"

What I call Generation Xbox - the 13- to 34-year-olds who lived through the era of Sony PlayStations and Microsoft Xboxes - were born into a world where videogames were already a viable storytelling medium.

They don't need convincing that games can be more exciting, addictive and involving than movies.

In the last couple of years alone, they've been fired at while crossing the favela rooftops of Rio de Janeiro in *Call of Duty: Modern Warfare 2*; they've played a father trying to bond with an estranged son in *Heavy Rain*; they've munched hotdogs in Liberty City in *Grand Theft Auto IV*; they've chased murderers through the mean streets of *L.A. Noire*. Why would they want to watch a movie when they can play inside one?

Generation Xbox knows that the once solid boundary between games and movies has become a permeable membrane. They use their Xbox 360s and PS3s to watch Netflix movies. They create their own machinima videos out of the latest first-person shooters. They're more likely to have a poster of Niko Bellic from *Grand Theft Auto IV* on their bedroom wall than Travis Bickle from *Taxi Driver* or Tony Montana from *Scarface*.

No niche market, Generation Xbox is now the predominant force in the entertainment industry and Hollywood is frightened by how its core audience is changing. As always, the numbers tell their own story. In 2010, according to figures from IHS Screen Digest, the US videogame sector was worth $15 billion, compared to US movie ticket sales of $9.6 billion. Although adding in US DVD, Blu-ray, video-on-demand and digital sales (another $14 billion) suggests the battle hasn't been lost yet, it's clear that Hollywood is right to be concerned about interactive entertainment. We're all gamers now: even the White House, after President Obama's election, has a Nintendo Wii.

No wonder Bobby Kotick, chief executive of leading game publisher Activision-Blizzard has predicted that videogames have the potential to "eclipse" both film and television by 2014. As the head of an interactive entertainment empire that stretches across the multi-billion dollar *Tony Hawk*, *Guitar Hero*, *World of Warcraft* and *Call of Duty* franchises, you wouldn't want to bet against his take on the market.

When *Call of Duty: Modern Warfare 2* was released in November 2009 it took $1 billion in its first 10 weeks, pushing it into the same billionaire league as blockbuster movies such as *Titanic*, *The Lord of the Rings: The Return of the King*, *The Dark Knight* and, of course, *Avatar*. Twelve months later, as cinema attendance in the US hit record lows, *Call of Duty: Black Ops* took $360 million on its first day of release - five times more than the biggest Hollywood movie opening and 15 times more than the fastest-selling CD. It made entertainment history, making more money in 24 hours than any movie, album or book... ever.

In November 2011, *Call of Duty: Modern Warfare 3* broke those records all over again and helped push the franchise's total sales beyond the box office takings of the *Star Wars* and *The Lord of the Rings* movie series.

In response, movies are starting to look more and more like games. From *Tron* to *The Matrix* to *Inception* to *Tron: Legacy*, the aesthetics of videogames' virtual worlds have infiltrated cinema. *Pirates of the Caribbean* may be based on a Disney theme park ride but it owes an indirect debt to LucasArts's *The Secret of Monkey Island* too. Zack Snyder's *Sucker Punch* is littered with gaming references from its clockwork German soldiers (who have the same glowing eyes as *Killzone 2*'s helghasts) to its heroines' stiletto-heeled *Bayonetta* chic. *Avatar* recycles the space marine imagery of *Halo* (itself inspired by James Cameron's *Aliens*) to wow non-gaming audiences. Even arthouse movies aren't immune. *Oldboy*'s famous set-piece, a long-take corridor sequence, has its hero fighting off thugs as he progresses from left to right as if in a side-scrolling beat 'em up. Jacques Audiard's *A Prophet* captures the down-at-heel ambience and mission structure of a *Grand Theft Auto* game. The visual lexicon of videogames has invaded pop culture.

Meanwhile, today's blockbuster filmmakers are using digital tools to craft imaginary worlds out of nothing but bits and bytes. Digital cinema is blurring the line between videogames and filmmaking. High-end directors - like Steven Spielberg, Peter Jackson and Robert Zemeckis - now spend as much time crafting immersive but non-existent worlds as game designers. Technology has reached the point where, for instance, *Resident Evil 5*'s African set zombie apocalypse uses exactly the same virtual camera set-up as the billion-dollar game-changer, *Avatar*.

Generation Xbox tells the story of how we got to this point - and where we might go from here. It's the story of how two very different industries began competing for the same audience's screen time; and how Hollywood has been scared and simultaneously seduced by its upstart, interactive competitor.

Technology's relentless progress raises important questions over the nature of narrative in a medium that's interactive. In all the excitement, it's easy to forget that videogames are still in their infancy. The novel has had several centuries to develop its strategies for storytelling. Cinema has had over a century to evolve and it standardised its format of choice (35mm film) early on. Videogames, in contrast, are an art-form forever in flux, where each new technological leap makes the last benchmark redundant. Only 35 years separate *Pong* from *BioShock*, but in technological and artistic terms it's like comparing the "still motion" of the 16,000-year-old Palaeolithic cave paintings at Lascaux with *The Bourne Supremacy*.

Imagine if Henry Fielding, Leo Tolstoy or even Dan Brown had been forced to build a new language and a new printing method from scratch every time they wanted to publish a story. Or if D.W. Griffiths, Orson Welles and Martin Scorsese had to upgrade the movie camera every time they planned a new film. The art of storytelling would inevitably be stunted by the focus on technology rather than art.

From that perspective, it's no wonder that videogaming has looked to cinema for help. Jordan Mechner, the game designer who created the *Prince of Persia* game franchise and wrote the screenplay for the 2010 Disney movie produced by Jerry Bruckheimer, believes videogames are an art form with a cultural inferiority complex. "If you want to make an interesting analogy, it's with film itself," he says. "At the turn of the 19th-century, when film was a fairground attraction, you dropped a nickel in the machine, turned the crank and you could see the early silent films on the Kinetoscope. That wasn't seen as the beginning of a new art form that would one day be as legitimate as stage-plays or novels. It was looked at, at best, as a harmless amusement - which is how videogames were seen in the days of *Space Invaders* or *Asteroids*. You dropped a coin in the slot and were entertained for a few minutes."

Just as film repudiated its carnival beginnings by turning to theatre and novels for inspiration and instant artistic legitimacy, videogames have leaned on cinema as they have evolved from simple diversions into a medium in which it's possible to tell stories. When Mechner created *Prince of Persia* in 1989 he sent a two-minute demo of the game on VHS tape to NYU Film School. "They responded very kindly that this was very interesting, but they were look-ing for applicants who had a body of work to demonstrate an interest in film as opposed to computer games," he remembers. Almost two decades later, when Mechner and Jerry Bruckheimer shopped the *Prince of Persia* movie around the Hollywood studios, they took a demo reel of videogame footage from the 2008 *Prince of Persia: The Sands of Time* videogame with them to present to studio executives. Clearly much had changed in the intervening period - both in terms of videogames themselves, and the perception of them.

Even still, the videogame is a medium that's in the process of finding its storytelling feet and working out what it can do that cinema can't. Yet as the medium becomes more confident and daring, the world's best filmmakers - James Cameron, Peter Jackson and Guillermo del Toro - are paying attention and getting involved. Others, like Steven Spielberg and George Lucas, saw its potential early on and have had played an often unacknowledged role in guiding games towards their present form.

Generation Xbox tells the story of how videogames invaded Hollywood and the men (and it was mostly men) who masterminded it. It's a story full of creative frustrations, litigation and moments of genius. It begins with Spielberg choking on dope fumes in the anarchic offices of Atari in the 1980s; then continues through Disney's fury over the *Dragon's Lair* coin-op; and Bob Hoskins drinking to stay sane while shooting *Super Mario Bros.*

Along the way we'll also hear about the Watergate-era journalist who tried to reinvent TV; CAA's role in building bridges between the two industries; the aborted *Halo* movie; the videogame technology that made *Avatar* possible; and the future of game-movie convergence currently being mapped by companies like Ubisoft, Warner Bros and Valve. It's a story of bearded programmers, evangelical inventors, duplicitous producers and egotistical movie stars. In short, it's a story that's never been told before.

It's been almost 30 years since that mass videogame grave in the New Mexico desert was filled-in and concreted over. But the ghosts of that era still haven't been laid to rest. There are still many questions to answer: have videogames changed the movie business? Has Hollywood sowed the seeds of its own destruction by helping the game industry? What does a truly interactive movie look like? What can Hollywood and videogames learn from each other? And is the game-movie convergence creating a truly new art form?

What happens next is going to define the entertainment landscape of the 21st century. You only need to look at *Avatar* to see the truth of that statement. James Cameron's immersive sci-fi epic didn't simply ape videogame aesthetics; it also marked the crossover point between film, videogames and 3D CGI. From *The Matrix* to *300*, *District 9*, *Inception* and *Scott Pilgrim Vs The World*, filmgoers are getting used to emerging from the movie theatre and saying: "Hey, it looked just like a videogame!"

Only one thing is certain. As movies and games from *Avatar* to *Heavy Rain* redefine the frontiers of both mediums, it's obvious that the future of entertainment is changing for everybody, forever. Are you ready to play?

CHAPTER 1

E.T. Phones Home

"There isn't a company in the US at the moment that isn't hoping to get into videogames. You hear it the whole time: 'We're in the meat packing business, but my son's hoping to start a videogames division.' Yes there is a danger that movies are going to end up being expensive commercials for videogames. The whole thing is moving so fast it's crazy."

Tron director Steven Lisberger, October 1982

When he was 19, Howard Scott Warshaw had an epiphany. It wasn't the traditional vision of burning bushes or dancing angels. Instead, Warshaw's epiphany involved several tanks, some rolling terrain and a complex piece of calculus. Sitting in a theoretical mathematics class at Tulane University in New Orleans in the autumn of 1976, the young kid from Scotch Plains, New Jersey suddenly realised that the mathematical formula chalked up on the blackboard behind the lecturer was more than just an abstract equation. It could be used to build a great game.

The revelation was weird not least of all because Warshaw didn't consider himself a gamer. Sure he played. Back in 1976 everyone under the age of 25 knew what a videogame was, even if they didn't know the difference between an Apple I computer and a Californian navel orange. In the bars around college campuses you couldn't buy a pitcher of beer without being enticed to drop a quarter into a coin-operated videogame cabinet like *Breakout* or *Night Driver*. Ever since Atari's revolutionary table tennis coin-op *Pong* was unveiled in 1972, videogames had been hoovering up the loose change of a whole generation. Jukeboxes and old-fashioned pinball machines stood gathering dust.

So Warshaw played. Truth was, though, he preferred puzzles and card games like Pan to joysticks and fire buttons. He wouldn't be truly blown away by a videogame until he spotted *Space Invaders* in Blimpie's, a sandwich shop, a couple of years later ("I walked up. I played one game. I said this is going to be big! This is going to wipe pinball out! I mean, it was great. I had no idea I would ever have anything to do with it, but I just knew this was it.") In 1976 he hadn't even learned to program a computer and he certainly didn't envisage a career making games.

Sitting in that calculus class, though, he had a sudden rush of blood to the head. The mathematical equation on the blackboard could be used, he reckoned, to minimise the amount of information you'd need to communicate between players. Suddenly, the world receded and time and space contracted into a single, concise vision of data transfer. In the empty air in front of him Warshaw saw a rolling battlefield stretch out with realistic hills and valleys dotted with tanks.

"For some reason this whole interactive, real-time game sort of came to me in my mind before I'd really even thought about videogames," he says. "I don't even know why I knew or understood the variables that needed to be maximised or minimised or taken care of. I just did. There was some aspect of it that was just inherently a part of me." Advanced calculus suddenly made sense to him in a way it never had before. It was just a shame that the hardware didn't yet exist to turn his epiphany into a reality.

Some people are cursed by seriousness. Warshaw wasn't one of them. He didn't fit the cliché of the nerdy computer programmer. Instead he was a merry prankster, a '60s child adrift in the brave new world of the microprocessor. "He was the kind of guy who wants to see how much fun he can have and still get into heaven," said Rob Fulop, one of the programmers who'd later work with him at Atari. In Warshaw's eyes, life was like a can of soda. The more you shook things up, the more explosively interesting it became. No one, he decided, ever got anywhere by being bored. And Warshaw's boredom threshold was pretty low, as he discovered when he joined Hewlett-Packard.

Back in 1980 getting a job at HP was what any bright young kid with a Masters in computer engineering was supposed to dream about. Arriving at the company's Cupertino offices, Warshaw soon found himself working on data communications systems. It wasn't long before he realised what a mistake he'd made. The programming tasks were dull and Warshaw's temperament wasn't suited to it.

Nor was he suited to the straight-laced corporate environment. With his wild-eyed hippie look and weird clothes - his favourite being a joke "tuxedo" T-shirt - he soon marked himself as the odd man out among the tweed suits, elbow patches and pocket protectors of his peers.

Rebelling against the stuffy corporate set-up, he'd goof off. His offenses were minor league stuff. He used to customise his noise mufflers with long strands of listing markers; he'd kill the boredom by holding computer game championships from *Star Trek* to *Yahtzee*. "It sounds passé today," he says, but in 1979 [at HP] this was very unusual."

One HP colleague found his antics so hilarious that he started coming home and telling his wife his stock of "Howard stories". To his surprise she was deeply unimpressed. She worked at Atari - where no one batted an eye at a man climbing along the walls or programmers hosting marijuana parties in the ladies toilets. Warshaw's japes seemed minor league in comparison.

When he heard about Atari's relaxed work environment, Warshaw applied for the next programming job that came up at the company's offices in Sunnyvale, California. His interviewers, initially suspicious of anyone who came from straight-laced Hewlett-Packard, turned him down. They were worried that he wouldn't fit into the zany environment. Warshaw begged, pleaded and even offered to take a 20% salary cut. He knew deep down that he wanted to make videogames not packet switching software. But most of all, he wanted to play. And in the summer of 1981, Atari was the most playful place on the planet.

* * *

Atari was founded by Nolan Bushnell and his business partner Ted Dabney on 27 June 1972. Bushnell was a 29-year-old entrepreneur who'd studied electrical engineering at the University of Utah and had learned his sales patter on the midway at Lagoon Amusement Park outside Salt Lake City. He'd taken the job to pay his tuition fees after blowing all his savings on an unfortunate poker hand at the end of his sophomore year. He was that kind of student.

Good luck followed bad. On the midway Bushnell had discovered that he had a natural talent when it came to rounding up punters for the ball toss booth. Smooth-talking his customers into parting with their quarters to knock down milk bottles came easily to him - and a more perfect preparation for his future role as America's chief games master couldn't be imagined. Atari would effectively recreate the midway in the videogame arcade, coin-op cabinets luring the same punters to part with the same quarters. The only difference was that the sales pitch and the games themselves were electronic.

Bushnell had first glimpsed the power of videogames as a student in the computer science labs at the University of Utah. In the 1960s hulking, refrigerator-sized computers like the PDP-1 were unlikely tools for playing games. That didn't stop enterprising MIT student Steve Russell from coding *Spacewar!*, one of the first videogames. It began as a hobbyist's experiment featuring spaceships battling against the backdrop of deep space. When Bushnell came across the game, though, the budding entrepreneur realised he was glimpsing the future of entertainment.

It took him over a decade to realise his student dream of releasing a coin-operated videogame for the public to play. After several false starts he co-founded Atari, named after a move from the ancient Japanese strategy game Go where the term was used as a warning from one player to another that they were about to capture a counter. It was appropriate. Bushnell's new company, committed to bringing videogames to the American public, would capture the imagination of an entire generation: Atari!

The company's first success came with *Pong*, a coin-op videogame designed by Al Alcorn, one of Atari's earliest employees. *Spacewar!* was written by computer programmers for their peers - undergraduate scientists and engineers who would salivate over the game's intergalactic setting and knowingly appreciate the Newtonian physics that drove the spaceships around the gravitational pull of a distant sun. For the average man in the street, though, it was all geek to them. *Pong* was much more accessible. The digital logic chips inside the cabinet created something intimately familiar to anyone of any age or education, a simple game of table tennis. Two players controlled paddles to bat a ball around the screen from left to right. Each time bat hit ball there was a satisfying "pong" sound.

What Bushnell liked about the game, he later explained, was that it was "so simple that any drunk in a bar could play [it]". From the moment *Pong* first debuted, as a prototype placed in Andy Capp's Tavern in Sunnyvale, the game was an instant success. Its instructions were simple: "Avoid missing ball for high score". It could have been Atari's motto. Over the next few years, the company went from strength to strength, hitting each and every ball that came its way right out of the park. *Pong*'s success bolstered Atari's coffers and inspired a flood of imitators. In its first year in the amusement arcade cabinet business the company made $3.2 million. Bushnell was lauded as "King Pong" by Newsweek. "We've created a whole new market," he boasted.

Bushnell's competitors soon realised what was happening - and amusement companies like Williams, Taito and Bally-Midway grasped Atari's revolution of the arcade business. By the start of the 1980s the arcade industry had produced a core of instant classics including Taito's *Space Invaders*, Williams' *Defender* and Atari's *Asteroids*. Yet, the real story of Atari didn't lie in the video arcades and college bars where curious gamers huddled around coin-op cabinets. It was in people's homes.

In 1975 Atari burst into the living room videogame market with a home version of *Pong*. It was one of several simple home videogame consoles - most structured around bat and ball game concepts - that would vie for dominance in the ensuing years. Although it was a huge success Bushnell instinctively knew that video tennis was just a fad. What he needed was a machine that would bring the variety of the arcade into the home by allowing users to play more than one game. His idea was codenamed "Stella" and it would eventually hit shelves as the Video Computer System, or VCS 2600 in the autumn of 1977. The genius lay in the business model. Consumers wouldn't just buy the VCS and forget about it. Once they'd purchased the unit, they'd be enticed to buy more and more games. Over the next few years, Atari's gamble would prove a runaway success. The sleek, black VCS would change the face of American pop culture forever.

In the summer of 1976, before the VCS 2600's release, though, there was just one problem: Atari had run out of money. Convinced that his new iteration of the videogame fad would secure Atari's long-term future, Bushnell proposed selling the business on. He knew from his time on the carnival midway what the first rule of winning was: quit while you're ahead. With the VCS blueprints on the design board, he began to court the major media companies.

There's no degree course for entrepreneurship. There's not even a checklist of requirements. But if you were to draw up such a list, a sixth sense for predicting social change before it actually occurs would definitely be near the top. Few people realised what the arrival of the microprocessor in the early 1970s would mean for the entertainment industry. Bushnell did, though. These little rectangles of silicon with their metal pin legs resembled tiny scarab beetles. The ancient Egyptians believed that the scarab god Khepri pushed the sun through the sky like a beetle rolling its dung ball; Bushnell believed the microprocessor beckoned a new dawn too.

The stalwarts of the American entertainment industry were less visionary. Atari approached both Disney and MCA, who owned Universal Studios. Neither took the bait. Disney's lack of vision particularly disappointed Bushnell. As a young college grad he'd applied to work at Uncle Walt's company, convinced that the bastion of the American entertainment industry would be the place to foster the coming computer revolution. He was wrong. Disney had rejected his application - apparently, they didn't hire fresh-faced graduates until they'd earned some proper experience. Now they rejected Atari's approaches in much the same off-hand way; Bushnell believed it was monumentally short-sighted of them.

Ultimately it was Warner Communications that stepped in to buy Atari. The media conglomerate, with an interest in music, publishing, comics, toys, baseball and movies (the latter through the venerable Hollywood studio Warner Bros.), clearly understood the revenue potential of the videogame. To them it was just another entertainment property to be exploited. What they didn't get - at least not at first - was how valuable it could be for their movie division.

According to legend, Warner Communications' chief executive Steve Ross first recognised the impact of videogames on American pop culture in the summer of 1975. On a trip with his kids to Disneyland, Ross was shocked to realise that they were more interested in spending all day in the arcade beside Space Mountain than chasing Mickey and Goofy down Main Street. The lure was the *Indy 800* arcade machine.

Designed for eight-players, the *Indy 800* cabinet was fitted with steering wheels and pedals arranged around a table monitor. Mirrors reflected the action from the screen overhead for spectators to watch. It was thrillingly competitive. Ross couldn't get his kids off the machine. He couldn't get himself off it either. Hooked on the game, he even looked into getting a personal machine shipped to his apartment (it proved too bulky).

The experience was an eye-opener. Ross, head of one of America's biggest entertainment conglomerates, intimately grasped the power of videogames during that summer vacation. Not even the joys of Disneyland could tempt his kids away from this arcade game. Right then he guessed how profitable the videogame industry could be for Warner Communications and even jotted down the name of the coin-op cabinet's manufacturer: Atari Inc.

A few months later a memo arrived on Ross's desk from Manny Gerard, a former Wall Street entertainment industry analyst who'd been hired to search out worthwhile new acquisitions for the Warner Communications fold. Gerard had come across Atari and thought it would be an interesting gamble. Ross didn't need much convincing. Over four months in 1976, Warner and Atari negotiated a $28 million deal.

In truth, no one at Warner quite understood exactly what they were buying or how it was going to impact on their other media concerns. "When I first heard about Atari," says Gerard, "I was told it was a 'technology-based entertainment company'. I had no idea what the hell they were talking about but I went out to Los Gatos, which is where they were based then, and I saw Atari. At that meeting they showed me the beginnings of the VCS 2600. They called it 'Stella' and the game they played on it they called 'Polish Tank'. It was a gag, an engineers' gag, because all the tanks went backwards or something. Looking at it, I understood intuitively that a cartridge-based game system was a big deal. So I wrote a memo and I said, 'I have seen the future and it's called Stella'."

Already a player in the toy industry - the conglomerate owned Knickerbocker Toys - Warner's executives believed that Atari would be a good fit and give them access to a high-tech, growth sector. "In the Warner 1976 annual report we wrote a piece which was prophetic," recalls Gerard. "We saw these electronic games as part of a long progression of games starting with stones and going to wood and plastic and so on. It was going to be a big part of the toy market. That was why we initially bought Atari; the motivation, at that point, had nothing to do with the movie business."

The VCS launched in December 1977 and, after a shaky start, it became apparent that it was more than just a toy. Atari, the "technology-based entertainment company" that Gerard had been so impressed by, was revolutionising the entertainment industry itself. A new paradigm was emerging in the living room and the company's early advertising drew clear battle lines between old and new mediums. "Don't watch TV tonight," they instructed, "play it!" The rallying cry was anathema to the more traditional media companies. Telling consumers not to watch TV? Using the TV for something other than watching *Happy Days* or *Starsky and Hutch*? Were these Silicon Valley types mad? Apparently so...

The revolution started as a fad but slowly snowballed into a phenomenon. Between 1977 and 1981 the Atari VCS - and competitors like the Magnavox Odyssey[2] and the Mattel Intellivision - invaded American leisure time. The razors and blades business model proved lucrative. The consoles continued to generate revenue long after the initial hardware purchase. Since the average VCS game cartridge retailed at around $30, and manufactured for less than $10, Atari's coffers swelled as the bucks poured in. The initial VCS line-up of nine titles quickly doubled then tripled, then tripled again. Staying in suddenly became cool. The Woodstock generation, as Time magazine memorably put it, was morphing into the Atari generation.

Warner had little understanding of the business they'd entered. It was too new, too undisciplined. In literal terms there was an incredible cultural clash as this small, free-wheeling company was subsumed into the Warner corporate hierarchy. When Bushnell met the Warner suits he turned up in a T-shirt with the slogan "I love to fuck". Beyond mere sartorial taste there was also a shift of emphasis. "The biggest difference," Bushnell told historian Tristan Donovan, "was a marketing-centric versus an engineering-centric company."

For Warner's executives, the question would ultimately boil down into a simple business proposition: how they could use the VCS to buoy up their other subsidiaries? The years of Atari's spectacular rise from 1974 to 1982 were also the era of *Jaws, Star Wars, Superman* and *Raiders of the Lost Ark* - big-budget, high-profit blockbusters that turned the motion picture business on its head. The blockbuster paradigm had already rewritten the Hollywood rulebook, making ancillary profits from merchandising and licensing deals hugely lucrative. *Star Wars* had led the charge, George Lucas's phenomenally successful sci-fi movie selling more T-shirts, bedspreads, lunchboxes and plastic toys than movie tickets and generating millions in revenue.

Warner knew how to work that kind of cross-marketing magic too. In December 1978, Warner Bros. released *Superman* in 700 movie theatres across the US. Based on a comic book owned by Warner subsidiary D.C. Comics, *Superman* was a manufactured marketing event involving $300 million of books, toys, T-shirts and lunchboxes and bubble gum cards. It wasn't just a movie, it was "Supermania". Every subsidiary of Warner was expected to ride the licensing gravy train. "The theory was that the movie would be the engine driving the train," explains Bud Rosenthal who was the movie's international marketing coordinator, "and that all of the products of the other divisions would benefit from the success of the film." With Atari now part of the Warner stable, it became part of this strategy.

From its beginnings, Atari had never been in the habit of creating licensed games based on movies. Bushnell had seen the potential early on but had remained wary of committing large chunks of cash to the strategy. In 1975 he'd tried to secure a license for *Jaws*, convinced it would make a great arcade game. Universal had turned him down. Ever the maverick, he went ahead with an unofficial coin-op called *Shark JAWS* anyway. Reaping the benefits of his education on the carnival midway, Bushnell made sure that the coin-op cabinet rendered the first word in a font so small most players assumed the game was simply called *Jaws*.

Fearing possible legal action from Universal, Atari set up a front company called Horror Games to release the cabinet. Players controlled a scuba diver collecting fish and avoiding the carnivorous attentions of a Great White.

Somewhat surprisingly, Universal never complained - either because they saw the early coin-op as a flea on an elephant's backside or because they simply didn't know it existed. "It was such a tasteless game. It was all about swimmers being eaten by sharks," recalls Bushnell. "It wasn't a success. I think if it had been successful I would have heard something [from Universal]. But it wasn't. The nice thing about failures is that they die quietly." After its unimpressive release, he gave up on the idea.

With the *Superman* movie in production it would have made sense for Warner to have pushed the title via Atari. But in reality the two *Superman* games that were produced - an Atari VCS title and a pinball machine - weren't at the forefront of the marketing campaign. "Our efforts with Atari were limited to point of sale materials for their products," says Rosenthal.

"I think it's pretty clear that they stumbled in to it," explains John Dunn, the VCS software engineer who coded the *Superman* game. "The only reason someone picked up the phone [to call Atari] is because of the recent acquisition by Warner, and they were trying to maximise a new asset. My guess is the marketing genius behind the videogame/movie tie-in was an unknown bean-counter checking off a list."

Over in Atari's pinball division, designer Steve Ritchie and his colleague Eugene Jarvis had a similar experience. Ritchie initially approached his bosses about the potential of a *Superman* pinball game. "We figured that with all the big picture corporate synergies and such, this would be a slamdunk," recalls Jarvis. "Unfortunately we got no support from Warner's D.C. Comics division, and they demanded a massive advance and royalty which Bushnell and the Atari brass rejected."

Frustrated, the team released the game in a test location under the title "Rockstar" and ditched all Superman references from its cabinet. Even without its super-powers it proved a hit and Warner realised their mistake and granted Atari the license. Released in March 1979, a few months after the movie, it shipped around 3,500 units. For Atari, a minor player in the pinball market, it was a big success. "In terms of convergence the experience with *Superman* pinball was an eye-opener to me," says Bushnell. "It was actually worth the royalty." Ritchie, however, remains unconvinced. He believes the game succeeded because it played well, not because of the tie-in. "While I know in my heart what actually made *Superman* [the pinball machine] their bestseller, its success will likely be attributed to the value of the license," he says. "It is not a true assessment of what occurred."

It wasn't just the pinball division who were unconvinced by the new emphasis on marketing and synergy. When Atari's VCS programmers were told that Warner wanted them to make tie-in games based on Hollywood movies, they practically rebelled. Used to creating their own, highly personal titles they weren't happy about relinquishing creative control to a marketing agenda. "Pretty much all the programmers jeered at it," recalls Dunn of the *Superman* license. "They were saying, 'Oh I'm not gonna do that sort of thing'. They viewed it as prostituting themselves."

The programmers' suspicions were right. Warner weren't interested in games or art, they simply wanted a product they could stamp *Superman*'s logo on. Programmer Warren Robinett was originally asked to code the game but refused (he was busy working on his classic *Adventure* at the time). Dunn, a big Man of Steel fan from childhood, was press-ganged into accepting the job instead. To encourage him, Robinett offered him some code from *Adventure* to speed things along.

The VCS *Superman* game did its best to bring The Man of Steel to the 8-bit VCS console when it was released a few weeks after the movie's opening. Players controlled Superman as he traversed Metropolis and tried to foil Lex Luthor's bombing campaign by air-dropping his evil henchmen into the city's jail. There were nice touches: you changed from Clark Kent to Superman by stepping into a phone booth; and Lois Lane wandered the city offering kisses to Supes that would recharge his strength after he was exposed to Kryptonite. "*Superman* was a real landmark for VCS games," says Jarvis. "You had the sense of a huge world of Metropolis that you were moving around. You could even take the subway. Obviously the graphics were rudimentary by today's standards, but it was a massive creative leap from the *Pong* and *Space Invaders* clones of the era."

Given the graphical limitations of the VCS 2600 it was no surprise that the game bore little resemblance to the movie. As a result it became the object of derision among some of the VCS engineers. "We called it Stupidman," remembers Atari programmer Rob Fulop. "It didn't feel like Superman. It was a little 8-bit, one-colour graphic character, so you didn't feel like it was The Man of Steel. Nothing about who Superman was translated into the game."

Not even the box art was inspired. Instead of Christopher Reeve's face there was just a bland drawing of Superman from the D.C. Comics flying through space. It sold modestly well and proved, if nothing else, that slapping

Superman's distinctive image on a VCS cartridge was an easy way of making consumers part with their cash.

Bushnell got to attend the *Superman* movie premiere on the back of Atari's involvement: "It was great fun. Us guys in Silicon Valley didn't usually get to go to premieres. That was a real Hollywood thing." Yet it would be a good three years before the floodgates for similar games based on movies were opened.

Around the same time as *Superman*, Bushnell left Atari eased out by the Warner board. He was replaced by Ray Kassar, a former textile manufacturing executive with a Harvard MBA. Like the rest of Warner's executives Kassar knew next to nothing about videogames. An autocratic businessman with a taste for fine clothes and fine wines, he was considered a safe pair of hands from a corporate point of view. Under his tenure, Atari began to make licensed movie games, although Kassar concedes it was more by accident than design. "When you talk about strategy," he says, "this wasn't Atari's big, main focus." The company's success was based on games that had no movie connection whatsoever. Instead, the push was coming from Hollywood itself. "The studios were all trying to find a way to get Atari to make [games] out of one of their products. They were in desperation mode. They assumed that videogames could overtake movies."

Atari's profits didn't necessarily need Hollywood's help. With the VCS sweeping America the company was in rude health. By December 1981, Atari was making more money than Warner Bros. Studios itself - a revelation that would send shockwaves through the entertainment industry. For Warner Communications, the Sunnyvale technology company turned out to be the goose that laid the golden eggs. Tragically, the corporate suits would eventually wring the lucrative but fragile creature's neck - although not before young VCS programmer Howard Scott Warshaw went all the way to Hollywood.

* * *

When Howard Scott Warshaw arrived at Atari for his first day of work on 11 January 1981, America was welcoming in a new decade. Ronald Reagan was about to be inaugurated into his first term in the White House, promising "an era of national renewal". A few minutes later, 52 US hostages being held in Iran would be freed. The future, it seemed, was arriving ahead of schedule. As if to prove that fact, the first DeLorean DMC-12, a high-tech, high-performance sports car, rolled off the assembly line the next day, its distinctive gull-winged doors and stainless steel body panels were supposedly a sneak preview of 21st century design.

America may have been changing, yet at Atari many things were still the same as they ever were. Although Bushnell's departure in 1978 had left the company in completely in the hands of Warner's buttoned-down executives, the old ways were hard to change. As a company Atari had always had a reputation for hedonism, ever since the early days of *Pong* when the production line was staffed by bikers and long-haired dropouts who smoked joints as they assembled the videogame cabinets and shot up heroin in the bathrooms on their breaks. Bushnell, larger than life and no virgin when it came to the joys of partying, knew how to keep his management staff happy too. Friday nights came with kegs of beer. Board meetings were held in hot tubs. It was a house of games staffed by people who liked to play.

Even though Bushnell had been gone for a couple of years when Warshaw arrived on that January morning, Atari's programmers still had a reputation for raising hell. A clear split had cleaved the company in two. The straight-laced management and marketing suits led by Kassar were frequently left dumbfounded by the bad behaviour of the programmers. It was a clash between creatives and corporates, two alien cultures that needed each other to survive but whose relationship was perpetually strained.

"The marketing department had never played a videogame," says Fulop. "Marketing thought the programmers were lazy, the programmers thought marketing was stupid. We didn't like them, they didn't like us." It went all the way to the top. Kassar famously dismissed Atari's engineers and programmers as "high-strung prima donnas". In revenge they dubbed him the "towel czar", a nod to his textile industry background.

Warshaw, fresh from Hewlett-Packard and eager to get to it, had a handle on the situation by his first afternoon. Sharing an office with programmers Rob Zdybel and Tod Frye, he was quickly inducted into Atari's unique work environment. "At the end of my first day I was reading in the office and Tod blows into the room, shuts the door, looks at me and says, 'I'm going to smoke a joint in here, so if you don't want to be around that you'd better take off.'" Warshaw had come prepared and pulled out his own joint, a secret weapon he'd brought along to ingratiate himself among his new colleagues. Frye stared at it and said: "No offense but mine is really good stuff." He lit it and they got stoned. OK Toto, Warshaw told himself, we're definitely not at Hewlett-Packard any more.

Drugs were common currency among the Atari coders. Management considered the place a human zoo of nerds, hackers and geeks - whacked out hippie throwbacks who'd swapped peace 'n' love for microprocessors and ROM sets. Warshaw's prized tuxedo T-shirt didn't seem out of place at all. Indeed, if anything, it seemed rather tame.

He certainly had to try hard to beat some of the more memorable stunts the programmers pulled. Frye entered Atari legend after developing a technique for literally climbing the walls. Discovering that the prefab corridors of the company's Sunnyvale offices were narrow enough for him to place a foot on each wall, Frye managed to traverse the hallways suspended five foot off the ground with his legs spread like a human spider. The party trick - destined to be known as the "sprinkler lobotomy" - ended with a visit to the E.R. when he cut his head open on a ceiling water sprinkler during a hasty dismount.

It wasn't just Frye. The rest of the programming team were equally wild. The office intercom would regularly crackle to announce meetings of the MRB, Marijuana Review Board, in the ladies' lavatory. Female security guards were enticed to romp naked in the workout room's hot-tub. When Warshaw decided, on a whim, to shave half his moustache off on one side of his face and half his beard off on the other, no one paid him much attention. What else would one expect in a company where the core business was playing games? Atari was like *National Lampoon's Animal House* for computer science geeks. "We really thought of our job as thinking up whacked out shit and just doing crazy things," recalls Warshaw.

The high-jinks took their toll and there were numerous casualties. Programmers were sectioned; relationships collapsed; one stoned engineer became convinced he was waiting with Jimi Hendrix for an audience with the Pope. Warshaw himself suffered his fair share of emotional turmoil too. When he arrived at Atari he was married to his first wife; on leaving four years later, he was divorcing his second. Atari's high-intensity, high-stimulus work environment put a strain on every home.

The boisterous creativity of the play was matched by the creativity of the games themselves. Atari was a hothouse environment and the blooms it produced were legion. VCS games like *Missile Command*, *Joust*, *Adventure* and *Combat* would be lasered into the memories of a whole generation of players who spent hours blasting monsters and aliens, solving puzzles and performing tricky jumps. While many games were ports or conversions of popular coin-op machines, a fair few suggested the artistic talent of the programmers behind them.

Forging a new industry and perhaps even a new artistic medium, Atari's programmers were true pioneers. There were few touchstones for what a game could be, how it should play, or what it should be about. The programmers were single-handedly creating them as they stumbled forwards. These stoned, whacked out engineers-cum-artists armed with their logic analysers were the avant-garde of the fledgling medium. "We were like renegade Picassos," Warshaw later claimed, "involved in the pioneering of a new kind of technology."

His first published game was *Yar's Revenge* which debuted in 1981. Despite its outlandish premise - you played a buzzing, space-faring house fly attacking an alien base - it was brilliantly addictive and sold over one million copies. Across the board, VCS software sales were soaring and Atari was flooded with cash. A lot of cash.

With Atari's profits dwarfing those of Warner Bros. Studios, there were serious concerns in recession-battered Hollywood that Warner Communications might stop making movies altogether. The movie industry - then suffering a crisis of confidence as blockbuster costs spiralled, films like *Heaven's Gate* and *Reds* flopped, and the new home video market struggled to find its feet - watched nervously. "In the 35 years I've been in the business, business has never been more dead," Martin Baum of Creative Artists Agency told the New York Times. Videogames, it seemed, had the potential to wipe cinema out.

Official figures comparing the two industries profits made for painful reading. According to Variety and Play Meter Magazine, the movie business made $2.7 billion in 1980 while amusement arcades took $7.2 billion. Videogame revenue from coin-op cabinets was so strong that Midway were coining in $8.1 million a week from *Pac-Man* in 1980 according to RePlay, the arcade trade magazine. Those figures made *Pac-Man* more profitable than the year's record-breaking movie blockbuster, Warner Bros.' sequel *Superman II*.

"Hollywood," The Montreal Gazette gloated, "does not need this news". Add in the numbers from the Atari VCS - nearing $2 billion per year in 1979 - and it was clear that the movie studios were significantly lagging behind in terms of dollar income from films. In 1981, in a desperate attempt to protect themselves, movie theatre chains began installing arcade machines in their lobbies to try and cash in on the new craze.

The schadenfreude was palpable. "There just isn't that much to really make you want to go to the movies these days," complained Midway's sales director Larry Berke, talking his book. "Things like *Raiders of the Lost Ark* and *Superman II* will make money. They're exciting. But how many other movies are like that? A game is always exciting. And what does it cost to see a movie today? $4.50 per person? For $4.50 you can go to an arcade and the whole family can play." Nolan Bushnell, then retired from Atari, also weighed into the debate. "Videogames, per se, are becoming as popular a form of entertainment as movies," he decided. "That's hard to prove, but the collective pocketbook of the children of America is a finite resource."

Aware of just how far and wide the videogame craze was spreading, some Hollywood distributors tried to cash in. Several movies were released between 1982 and 1984 that spoke directly to the Atari generation. Leading the pack was Disney's *Tron* - more on which in the next chapter - but there was also the Cold War thriller *WarGames*, which featured Matthew Broderick as a computer hacker who almost triggers World War III after hacking into a military computer and mistaking it for a videogame developer's software catalogue.

Universal were particularly astute when it came to appreciating the changing tastes of the youth audience. In 1983, portmanteau horror movie *Nightmares* featured a story about a demonic coin-op cabinet that sucks Emilio Estevez into a virtual prison. The moral? Beware those evil videogames... (and stick to movies instead, presumably). The following year, the studio released another movie which put a more heroic spin on the coin-op craze. *The Last Starfighter* (1984) centred on a teenager (Lance Guest) who is whisked into space to fight in an intergalactic war after he hits the top spot on an arcade cabinet's high score table. It turns out the arcade machine is really a recruitment tool for an alien space squadron. Sadly, Atari's planned tie-in coin-op never materialised.

Having built bridges with Atari, Universal tried once more to forge synergy with *Cloak & Dagger*, a pioneering movie-videogame marketing cross-promotion that was plagued by disaster. The 1984 movie, a loose remake of *The Window* (1949) which Universal owned the rights to, was headlined by Henry Thomas, the child star of Spielberg's *E.T. the Extraterrestrial*. He was chased by secret agents after discovering aeronautical plans hidden inside a game cartridge for the Atari 5200 console.

Screenwriter Tom Holland and film editor Andrew London recall the relationship between Universal and Atari being far from fruitful. "I honestly remember Universal being generally clueless," says London. "I flew with [producer Allan Carr] to Atari's headquarters but I don't think Universal had any sense of exploiting and marketing the game." It didn't help that both sides of the equation were caught in regime change: the planned Atari 5200 conversion of the *Cloak & Dagger* coin-op was shelved after the 1983 videogame crash; and the movie suffered after the executive who green-lit it left Universal just before its release.

Creating synergy was more difficult than it looked. Yet it was obvious that at least some studio executives saw the rise of the Atari Generation as something to be concerned about - and also as a potential market for videogame-related movies. It was a form of cross-marketing that, as we'll see, would elude the studios until the '90s. In the early 1980s, the real money lay in licensing movies for games. When Atari hatched a deal with Lucasfilm - announced in the summer of 1982 - the first proper licensed movie games began to appear.

* * *

The first time Howard Scott Warshaw met Steven Spielberg he took a copy of his bestselling game *Yar's Revenge* with him. He also told Spielberg his pet theory about how the bearded director wasn't human - he was actually an alien from outer space. In August 1981, the two men were sitting together in Spielberg's luxurious office at Universal Studios, an Aladdin's Cave crossed with a toy shop that was packed with games, gizmos and gadgets.

Atari had struck a secret deal with Lucasfilm to license the *Raiders of the Lost Ark* movie for the VCS and Warshaw had flown down directly from the Sunnyvale offices early that August morning for an informal job interview. Spielberg, who by this time had already made *Jaws, Close Encounters of the Third Kind* and *Raiders* and was prepping *E.T.*, listened to the programmer's opening spiel and nodded.

Warshaw took it as a good sign and continued by outlining his alien thesis, jumping off the couch in Spielberg's office as his excitable mouth ran away with him. "[He was] a frustrated stand-up comedian. He wanted to be more into show business than software engineering," said Warshaw's colleague Dave Staugas. "He had stars in his eyes," concurs Jewel Savadelis, Atari's marketing director for the Home-Video Division at the time. With Spielberg a captive audience, Warshaw was in his element.

"Look Steven, I know why you're here."

"Excuse me?"

"I said, I know why you're here. Everyone thinks that when aliens show up on Earth they're going to arrive in a spaceship going 'Hi, here we are'. But when we really discover the aliens, we're going to discover that you're already among us."

"Um, OK..."

"If you're smart enough to get here and understand our culture, you're smart enough to know what paranoid jerks we humans are. You're going to have to prepare us to accept you. So I believe that you, Steven Spielberg, are part of an advance team sent to Earth. You're the production arm and you're making all these movies about how aliens are really friendly. The rest of your team are the marketing arm. They're making sure these movies are seen all around the world to get everybody on the planet in a positive state of mind of first contact. I figure we're coming very close to that window when it's time to meet the aliens. It's very exciting..."

Spielberg smiled that patented grin of his and the deal was done. Warshaw was granted permission to code a tie-in game to 1981's hottest summer movie *Raiders of the Lost Ark*. His zany charm had worked wonders. "Howard Scott Warshaw," Spielberg would later claim, "is a certifiable genius".

It was a heady time for the kid from Scotch Plains, New Jersey. Before the *Raiders of the Lost Ark* game, no one at Atari had ever rubbed shoulders with Hollywood royalty. And Spielberg was as close to being a true blue blood as the movie industry got.

For his part, the bearded director was equally smitten with the videogaming world. His interest had first been snagged after dropping a quarter into a *Pong* cabinet in the early '70s. "I was making *Jaws* and living on Martha's Vineyard," he later recalled. "Somebody plugged in a coin-op game called *Pong* at the merry-go-round in Oak Bluffs. I remember Richard Dreyfuss and I, playing *Pong* together, got hooked. After shooting every day we'd come back and unwind by playing *Pong.* That got me into the whole videogaming world." For the director of *Jaws*, Atari's *Pong* coin-op was "the Woodstock of videogaming".

Spielberg and Warshaw had plenty in common - more than enough to forge a cordial working partnership. They shared the same childlike view of the world; they both sported bushy beards; they were both geeks. They hit it off instantly. The coming "synergy" between games and movies was no longer just a simple matter of licensing. A creative and personal bridge had been built between the two industries. Atari dug Spielberg and Spielberg dug Atari. "It was like we were being validated in what we were doing," says Warshaw.

Still, it was obvious enough which industry was the dominant partner in the relationship. On the morning that Warshaw flew down from San Jose to Spielberg's office at Universal he was informed that the director was running late. Five hours late, to be exact. In terms of putting the young upstart programmer in his place - whether deliberate or not - it couldn't have been bettered. But Warshaw, ever the adventure-seeker, decided to seize the opportunity. Faced with the prospect of sitting in the director's office all day or wandering around Los Angeles, he instead decided to live out every movie fan's dream. "Do you mind if I have a look around the studio?" he asked Spielberg's receptionist.

The next five hours were a blast. Warshaw wandered the warren of alleyways of the Universal back-lot like a star-struck kid, sticking his nose into everything he could find. Without a pass he had to dodge security guards but he still managed to rack up some impressive memories: he snuck onto the sets of various TV shows and ate lunch in the commissary surrounded by extras in costume. For a young programmer obsessed with movies it was a fabulous adventure.

Warshaw, always first in line when Atari's staff block-booked seats at the local movie theatre for films like *Dragonslayer* or *Krull*, had to pinch himself. Here he was breathing the same rarefied air that had produced *Dracula, Winchester '73, Psycho, Spartacus* and *Jaws*.

Despite his movie mania, Warshaw had his doubts about the *Raiders of the Lost Ark* project. Conventional wisdom among Atari programmers held that the idea of combining movies and games was fairly ludicrous. The marketing suits, unconcerned by the niceties of programming or engineering, naturally loved the concept. From their perspective, putting a recognisable brand name on a game could only lead to greater sales - although that myth was soon to be dispelled.

"It started purely as a marketing manoeuvre," Warshaw says. "The idea was we'll do a game and the movie will carry the sale, just like people think today. It was the same principle. But for the programmers, the idea of taking something like the VCS and making something that relates to the movie in any way was a tough call. I mean, none of us really bought the idea that we were really representing the movie with the game. I sure tried though."

When Atari's management first floated the idea of a *Raiders* game it prompted a lot of soul-searching among the VCS programmers. *Superman* had laid the ground for what many saw as an inevitable shift. Kassar and his management team were keen to exploit the licensing potential of videogames. Atari's new chief executive never played games himself but was convinced that a profitable movie would yield equally profitable VCS cartridges. It was simply a matter of branding.

For the people tasked with turning a movie into a game, however, there were questions that needed to be answered. What exactly was the relationship between games and movies supposed to be? It was fairly obvious to Atari's programmers that games were an active medium, interactive even. Movies, in comparison, were a passive experience. You watched a movie to be swept away by a narrative and led by the filmmakers - you couldn't wait to see what would happen to Indy next. When you played a game, it was different. You were desperate to see what you got to do next.

One only had to look at the primitive capacity of the VCS to understand just how impossible the idea of a movie-game seemed in 1981. How could you bring Harrison Ford's Indy character to life on a machine that only had 128 bytes of RAM and no frame buffer? You couldn't come anywhere close to replicating the movie experience. With his customary ebullience, Warshaw wasn't about to be cowed by the limitations of hardware, though.

In *Raiders*, he pushed the envelope by deciding that the best way to approach the movie was to reduce it to its most rudimentary action components. You could then recreate them in broad gameplay strokes. The hope, he decided, was that the player's basic desire to engage with the fantasy would carry them past the blocky VCS sprites. Firing the player's imagination was the key.

True to his reputation as a natural extrovert, Warshaw decided he needed props to suspend his own disbelief. He trawled the sex shops of the San Francisco Bay Area looking for a decent bullwhip. All he could find were "marital aids". They weren't quite manly enough for Indy. He eventually chanced upon a 10-foot-long bullwhip in a leather working shop on Olvera Street in LA. Over the next few months he'd prowl the corridors of Atari, cracking the whip while wearing a fedora. The whip, he claimed, was for R&D - research and discipline. The programmer spent a good chunk of that autumn sneaking up behind unsuspecting marketing and management suits and letting loose with his new toy. The sound of leather slapping leather was as loud as a gunshot.

Squeezing *Raiders* into the 8k of ROM that each VCS cartridge now had available was no joking matter, however. Quickly rejecting suggestions that he should adapt Spielberg's movie into a simple "one-screen" game - something like Indy fighting off waves of Nazis and snakes, *Space Invaders* style - Warshaw wanted to be more ambitious. If a game was going to echo a movie, it had to have scope. And if it was going to riff on *Raiders* it had to be exciting. The answer, he decided, was to make an adventure puzzle game.

Back in 1979 Warren Robinett's VCS game *Adventure*, a sprawling outing inspired by *Dungeons & Dragons*, had established the graphical action-adventure genre. It made a lot out of very little: your avatar was a bland, cursor-like square; the game's dragons looked more like mutant chickens than scaly lizards. But its innovation lay in presenting players with a large game space to explore. It was a true virtual world, despite its rudimentary graphics, that was full of keys, chalices, bridges and item-stealing bats.

Warshaw wanted to create a similarly ambitious world. But he was also determined to go much further. His Indy was a proper character - a stick man in a fedora, admittedly, but still an improvement over Robinett's simple dot. *Raiders* also tried hard to echo the movie it was based on. It opened with a surprisingly authentic burst of John Williams's distinctive theme tune and took its cue from the movie's settings. The quest to find the Ark took Indy through a Cairo market, a thieves' den and a secret map room. There were encounters with sheiks and snakes and players could pick up and use various objects including grenades, parachutes and, of course, Indy's trademark bullwhip. With so many items to use, Warshaw was forced to innovate. The second joystick operated the player's inventory. It was a pretty radical bit of control design.

The poverty of the graphics was compensated for by the richness of the imaginative play that the game encouraged. Visiting the Cairo market and buying a magic flute from the traders unleashed a clichéd burst of "The Streets of Cairo" from the TV speakers; it also made Indy invulnerable to snakes. Opening a parachute after falling off one of the mesas saved you from sudden death and revealed hidden rooms. At times the game's ambition far outstripped the hardware. How would players know that the circling pixel dot that surrounded Indy while he stood on top of the mesas was supposed to be a grappling hook? In many ways, though, the abstract graphics only added to the enigmatic nature of the game's puzzle element.

When Atari's marketing department saw the finished product they insisted that the manual contain spoilers giving the player tips and hints. Warshaw was aghast but in truth the game would have proved impossible without them. No player could have guessed the right screen to drop a hand grenade on to blow open a wall leading into the Temple of the Ancients. Since it was one of the first puzzles players had to solve, it was likely that most would have given up at the first hurdle. Even with the tips, *Raiders* generated a huge community of stumped players who swapped stories and strategies. In the days before internet walkthroughs, that kind of "meta-gaming" was still something of a novelty and it helped the mystique of *Raiders* immensely. The game teased you with secrets waiting to be unlocked - and in that respect it captured the thrill of the movie perfectly.

Whether or not it lived up to Atari's marketing hype was debatable. "*Raiders of the Lost Ark* starring YOU!" was how the original press ads described the game, adding "It doesn't matter who you are - when you play Atari's sensational *Raiders of the Lost Ark* cartridge, you're transformed into Indiana Jones, one of the great swashbuckling heroes of all time!" Atari spent a fortune on a 30-second TV ad that juxtaposed in-game footage with clips of Harrison Ford running from that famous boulder (which didn't actually feature in the game). "It's diabolically difficult, it's mysterious, it's never the same twice and it's only from Atari!" thundered the sales pitch. Placed side-by-side with the movie itself, though, the limits of the VCS's graphics were hard to ignore.

Raiders was released in November 1982, almost eighteen months after the movie had first hit cinema screens. The VCS cartridge sold well and cemented Warshaw's reputation as one of Atari's bright young things. By January 1983 it had reached number five on Billboard's weekly Top 15 Video Games chart, selling over a million copies. It succeeded in part because the videogaming audience was desperate to relive the movie - even in crude 8-bit terms. In today's world of movies-on-demand, DVD, Blu-ray and illegal camcorder torrents, it's hard to remember that there was a time when movie fans didn't have immediate access to films that had ended their theatrical run. *Raiders of the Lost Ark* hit US cinemas in June 1981 but wasn't released on Betamax and VHS videotape until the autumn of 1983. For Indy aficionados, the VCS game was a means of keeping memories of the movie alive in the interim.

When Spielberg saw a 15-minute play-through at the Atari booth at the Consumer Electronics Show in the winter of 1982, his verdict was succinct. "Gee Howard," he said, "it's just like a movie". The programmer beamed. "It was one of the most validating moments of my entire life: Oh my God, I make a game and Spielberg thinks it's like a movie!"

Raiders sold well, although it bore little comparison with the VCS versions of *Pac-Man* (around seven million) or *Missile Command* (around two-and-a-half million). Its success was tempered by the fact that the marketing department had overspent on advertising. Costly TV and press ads, combined with the whopping licensing fee Atari paid to Lucasfilm, didn't translate into healthy profits. Nor did it help that Atari over-cranked the production line and produced more *Raiders* cartridges than there was actually demand for. In 1984

Kenneth Lim, an analyst for San Jose market research firm Dataquest, claimed that Atari "sunk literally millions of dollars into ad campaigns for [*Raiders*] and overproduced by an incredible margin, five to 10 times what was sold". Despite hitting the bestseller charts, the numbers behind the game didn't add up.

"In the beginning we would pay say 3% in royalties to license a title," recalls Jewel Savadelis, former marketing director for the VCS division. "But as there started to be competition for licensing games from companies like Mattel and Coleco, the price began to go up. When it came to licensing titles like *Raiders of the Lost Ark*, the industry was at a stage where you had to pay 10 to 12% and who knows what other goodies - a fixed advertising dollar would have to be put behind a game. There was a frenzy about 'We've got to grab it, it could be a good game, blah, blah, blah'. Licensing fees were paid that were unreasonable in light of the number of games that could be sold. It was a case of 'We've paid x million dollars up front without a line of code being written. So what happens now?'"

Clearly, Warshaw wasn't the only person at Atari with stars in his eyes. "Upper management were interested in a title like *Raiders* because of the Hollywood connection," says Savadelis. "It's easy to get caught up in all of that and there were bragging rights attached [to securing those licenses]. There was a lot of excitement over *Raiders* and frustration when the expectations weren't met."

Despite the downside, *Raiders* was one of the key titles - along with Atari's earlier *Superman* and Parker Brothers' million-selling *The Empire Strikes Back* (released in May 1982) - that laid the framework for the licensed videogame. The high-profile advertising splurge that accompanied *Raiders*' release convinced many that the videogame industry was nipping the heels of Hollywood. Gaming suddenly seemed more dynamic and ambitious than an off-shoot of the toy industry had any right to be.

Spielberg, with his finger forever on the pulse of suburban American pop culture, believed that Atari was a pioneer in a lucrative and exciting field. He visited the company's Sunnyvale offices a couple of times, sweeping into the compound in a fleet of limos that carried his sprawling entourage. Meetings were held with the Atari top brass. Then the excitement really began as they walked a few hundred yards from the executive building to the development labs.

It was always a red letter day when Spielberg came. For the VCS programmers he wasn't simply the hottest movie director in the world. He was also the man who was validating their work. Having someone of Spielberg's stature professing an interest in Atari and its games was priceless, like being sprinkled with fairy dust.

Two photographs from the period capture the mood. The first shows Warshaw shaking hands with Spielberg and presenting him with a personalised copy of the *Raiders* cartridge (when loaded, the inventory display was emblazoned with the legend: "Steven"). The smiles are jovial, the handshake warm. The second shows Atari's employees lined up for an impromptu group shot with the visiting director who stands among them - a geek like them yet clearly not one of them. One Atari employee peeps over his shoulder, almost completely dwarfed by him. It was something the whole of Atari could relate to.

Although Los Angeles was only 400 miles away, for most Atari employees the white letters of the Hollywood sign might as well have been on the moon. The relationship between the two industries was a one-way street. Programmers never went to Hollywood. They were engineers, not equals. There was only one exception to that rule: Warshaw.

* * *

As 1982 unfolded, it wasn't just Spielberg who was intrigued by the videogame industry. That summer the whole of Hollywood seemed to be waking up to the fact that a major shift in pop culture was underway. Every studio wanted a piece of it. "The implications for the entertainment industry are enormous," claimed journalist Aljean Harmetz in the New York Times in 1982 as the momentum reached critical mass. "Hollywood has already plunged into the field by licensing its successful movies to game manufacturers. Most movie studios have also started divisions to create and design games."

The licensing frenzy was unstoppable. "[Videogame companies] have licensed everything that moves, crawls, or tunnels beneath the earth," said an exasperated Bill Kunkel, executive editor of Electronic Games magazine. "You have to wonder how tenuous the connection will between the game and the movie *Marathon Man*. What are you going to do? Present a videogame root canal?"

There was certainly big money to be made and Warner chief Steve Ross's early decision to buy Atari began to look like a shrewd and prescient move. The media corporation had taken pole position in a highly profitable industry years before its rivals woke up to the potential of interactive entertainment.

"1982 was the year the alarm bells started to ring at the studios," recalls Frank O'Connell, a former Mattel employee who set-up Fox Video Games. "When I first talked to Twentieth Century Fox, the rise of videogames wasn't even on their screens. They were much more worried about videocassettes and cable and all the other stuff at the time. It's one of those things, the thing that kills you is the thing you never see coming. Progressively, though, they saw the huge amount of consumer money and time pouring into games. They got very concerned. Definitely very, very concerned."

O'Connell met with Twentieth Century Fox's owner, Denver oilman turned media mogul Marvin Davis, in January 1982. He outlined his vision of interactive entertainment to the studio boss. "The first words out of Marvin's mouth were: 'What on earth is interactive entertainment?' So I started to describe to him, here's the videogame business and interactivity and here's where it's heading. It's going to be huge and some day there'll be interactive movies. I told him his properties would be very valuable in terms of developing games. They're popular, they're well-known, the stories are there and we know how to generate interactivity. What I'm really after isn't just your money, I told him, I'm after the interactive licensing rights for all of your properties."

Davis took the weekend to think about it. The following Monday he signed a $5 million deal that turned O'Connell's Santa Clara start-up Elite Capital Partners into Fox Video Games. In the following months the company's programmers would turn out titles based on *M*A*S*H*, *Porky's*, *Alien* and other Fox movie properties. The beauty of the model, as far as O'Connell and the studios were concerned, was that it traded on brand awareness. "If you developed a game yourself that nobody knew anything about you were starting at ground zero," O'Connell says. "But if you had a known property you had a very distinct advantage in terms of getting the shelf space and cutting your advertising and promotion costs. With television and movie properties you already knew everything about their strengths and who they appealed to."

It was a pattern that was being repeated across the major studios during 1982. Paramount, whose parent company Gulf & Western now owned arcade game manufacturer Sega, started to look at ways of using its Home Video distribution network to shift console games. In June 1982, Universal announced that they were looking into games based on *Jaws* and *E.T.* through their new MCA Video Games division. It was the entertainment industry's equivalent of the scramble for Africa. Even food manufacturer Quaker Oats dabbled, buying US Games in the summer of 1982 and releasing a VCS game based on the Fox-Warner Bros. disaster movie *Towering Inferno*.

"Hollywood is cashing in on the videogame boom," claimed Aljean Harmetz in another of her New York Times articles. "Each studio is aiming its laser guns and space ships down a different path but all share at least one goal - replacing games titled *Pac-Man*, *Defender*, *Berzerk* and *Frogger* with games called *Jaws*, *9 to 5*, *Star Wars* and *Star Trek*." Clearly it was marketing, not games designers, who were now calling the shots as the big corporations entered the market.

Against this backdrop, Warshaw was scheduled for his second meeting with Steven Spielberg in the summer of 1982. In a sign of how much things had changed, this time he was flown down to Los Angeles on a private Learjet. The limo trip from the airport to Universal Studios was even better. The car was fitted with a TV, a mini-bar and a sink. It even had a car phone... pretty jaw-dropping back in the pre-cell phone dark ages of 1982. This, Warshaw thought to himself, is what it feels like to be a high roller.

He wondered what everyone back at Atari would make of it when he told them. Many of the Atari programmers were becoming used to being rich. Ever since Atari's chief executive Ray Kassar had been prevailed upon to introduce royalty payments for the VCS programmers, the consumer division's programmers had been force fed cash. Tod Frye, who Warshaw had shared a joint with on his first day at Atari, was the first to benefit from the new deal. His work porting arcade hit *Pac-Man* to the VCS earned him a million dollars in royalties. He immodestly pinned a photocopy of his first cheque to his office door.

As the limo purred through the palm-tree lined streets of Burbank, Warshaw stared out the tinted windows. He realised he'd entered a truly different league. He was taking videogames to Hollywood. He was on first-name terms with Steven Spielberg. He was driving in a limo with its own sink. His thoughts were interrupted by the grumpy mumblings of Skip Paul, Atari's chief legal counsel, who was sharing the limo with him. The lawyer had just tried the hand sink and discovered that it didn't have any running water. Please, thought Warshaw, never let me get that jaded.

This time Spielberg wasn't late for the meeting where they were going to discuss a videogame based on *E.T. The Extraterrestrial*. Warshaw felt like a movie star. Here was Spielberg asking for his participation in the project by name. Outside on the street, kids would come up to Warshaw and ask him to sign their VCS cartridges of *Raiders* or *Yar's*. He was earning huge money, he was doing a lot of drugs and he was having a ball. "It totally blew my head WIDE OPEN!" he says. "America was the *Pac-Man* nation. The zeitgeist was *Pac-Man* running around eating dots. Whenever you told people what you did for a living, they'd get really excited. It was like being an astronaut in the '60s. You were in the centre of this place where everyone's dreams and imagination and attention were focused."

E.T. was the peak of the madness, the moment that the Hollywood dreams of both Atari and Warshaw turned sour. The deal was struck in the summer of 1982 by Steve Ross, head of Warner Communications, with Spielberg and Universal. It had to do with more than just videogames. Ross was well aware of the political capital in the movie industry of luring Spielberg away from Universal, the company that had launched his career. Creating connections between the hot director and Warner Bros. was something Ross was trying to forge by using Atari as a pretext. "He wanted Spielberg to make more movies for Warner," says Atari's then chief executive Ray Kassar. "There were a lot of favours being given to Spielberg". Videogames - and Spielberg's passion for them - were the carrot in a much bigger seduction strategy.

It helped that Spielberg and Ross were neighbours. "I think of Steve as a six-foot three-inch *E.T.*," said the director. He certainly was friendly. As Connie Bruck details in her book *Master of the Game* on Ross and the creation of Time Warner, the Warner boss was a generous suitor. When Ross wanted Spielberg to live near him in the East Hamptons, he convinced an elderly neighbour to sell her house to the filmmaker. When Spielberg's girlfriend Kathleen Carey befriended a nine-year-old boy with special needs, Ross sent a Christmas present of TVs, VCRs and toys to the orphanage ("He was like a Frank Capra movie," the filmmaker joked). When Spielberg told him he was planning to shoot *Indiana Jones and the Temple of Doom* in India, Ross sourced prints for five movies set in India that Spielberg had never seen - even though *Raiders* was being made for one of Warner Bros.' competitors.

It was obvious that Ross was courting Spielberg; although whether it was genuine affection or a predatory business interest (or, perhaps, both) was uncertain. "I had been told, 'Watch out for Steve Ross he is only being your friend so you'll make movies for Warner Brothers'," Spielberg said, according to Bruck. Could the Atari deal have simply been another gift to woo him? Quite possibly.

For his part, Spielberg apparently always believed that the relationship wasn't fuelled by an agenda - but it's worth noting that the director eventually did come over to Warner Bros. for a brief spell. Among the films he made for the studio was *The Color Purple*. It was nominated for 11 Oscars.

Whatever the truth about Ross's agenda, the details of the *E.T.*-Atari deal were certainly unusual. Sid Sheinberg, chairman at MCA/Universal and Spielberg's mentor since his debut as a TV director, had originally been in talks with console maker Coleco about an *E.T.* licensing deal. Eager to stall the negotiations, Atari sent Skip Paul to visit him. He offered Sheinberg a $1 million fee and 7% royalties. It was more than Atari had ever paid for a license and it was actually a pretty robust deal. By the beginning of 1983 the industry standard for game-movie licensing was around $1 million to $5 million per title. Sheinberg didn't agree, however.

"I was thrown out of Sid's office," Paul recalled to Bruck. "Then I was told that the deal had been done over a weekend, at East Hampton, between Steve and Steven - and that was for $23 million. I thought, 'Yes, I understand the $1 million. But what is the other $22 million for? It must be for some other reason'." Perhaps it was simply a sweetener, part of a bigger game of chess in which Warner's head attempted to lure Spielberg to Warner Bros. Or perhaps it was indicative of the monumental arrogance that was infecting Warner and Atari as the videogame sector boomed.

Certainly Atari was used to throwing money around. Stories in Silicon Valley about Atari's lavish spending were common currency. It was acting less like a technology company and more like a Hollywood studio. There were parties where $30,000 plates of chilled shrimp were piled high. Kassar says he was constantly being pressured by Ross to purchase a Gulfstream IV or a private helicopter; apparently, Ross wanted the vehicles for his own use and was hoping to put their expense on Atari's operating statement.

"[At Atari's height] we represented 40% of Warner's operating profits and 50% of its volume," says Kassar proudly. "We were the fastest growing company in the world [...] When I got there Atari was doing $75 million and losing about $15 million. Years later were doing about $3 billion and our profits were off the chart." In that context, paying a guaranteed $23 million royalty to gain a foothold with Spielberg might have seemed like a canny loss-leader. As Atari's Skip Paul later told Connie Bruck, "I think it was a brilliant move by Steve Ross. He succeeded in breaking MCA's hold on Spielberg. Steve's viewpoint was, so what if I overpay by $22 million? How can you compare that to the value of a relationship with Spielberg? And I think he was dead right."

Certainly there was a palpable sense that the world was changing. The videogame sector was by now grossing between $8 and $9 billion a year. In comparison theatrical releases of movies were making $3 billion. *Pac-Man* alone took in an estimated $1 billion in quarters in its first 15 months of release. Such ascendancy was Icarus-like - too far, too fast - and videogames would soon crash down to earth. But in 1982 the industry was on the up and arrogance was the order of the day.

Warshaw himself wasn't adverse to the odd bout of hubris either. Riding high from the Learjet flight and the knowledge that he had been personally requested by Spielberg to handle the project, he joked with the director that *E.T.* would be "the game that makes the movie famous". The words would eventually come back to haunt him. The VCS release of *E.T.* wouldn't bring fame, only infamy.

It wasn't Atari's first brush with a bad product. Tod Frye's *Pac-Man* port earlier that year earned the programmer a million dollars in royalties, but it was a pig of a game. Frye claimed he had no love for the coin-op dot-eater and it showed. *Pac-Man* on the VCS bore only a passing resemblance to the Namco game adored by millions. The mazes looked different; *Pac-Man*'s animation wasn't quite right; even the fruit was missing. Worst of all, the visual display was a flickering mess. Atari overproduced the cartridges, convinced that a couple of million people would buy a VCS simply to play the game. *Pac-Man* sold well - despite record complaints and returns - but paradoxically it was also the canary in the coal mine warning of impending danger.

Such a cavalier attitude towards the niceties of game production had become endemic at Atari by the summer of 1982. And *E.T.* was to prove it. As part of the deal with Spielberg, Ross agreed that the game would be out in time for Christmas. He also planned to ship five million copies (the deal was so punishing that Atari needed to sell four million copies simply to break even). When Kassar learned the conditions he was gobsmacked. The turnaround for the game would be five weeks. That was five weeks to design, program and manufacture it. *Raiders*, one of the few points of comparison for such a project, had taken a relatively leisurely ten months from start to finish. Convinced that an *E.T.* game would top the Christmas sales charts, Ross had committed Atari to an impossible task. Fortunately Warshaw was too cocksure to baulk at it. It was a challenge he couldn't resist.

The programmer negotiated good terms for performing such a Herculean feat. He asked for a $169,000 non-refundable advance against royalties (later, at a company meeting, an all-expenses-paid trip to Hawaii was thrown in to his "surprise and delight"). When news of the *E.T.* project leaked to the other VCS programmers at Atari, there were rumblings of discontent from his co-workers. Why was Warshaw getting to hobnob with Spielberg? What made him the go-to-guy for these movie adaptations?

It was typical of a sourness that was beginning to pervade the company. The rock star salaries, fast cars and hard drugs that were flooding the VCS section attracted a lot of jealousy from other divisions and among the programmers themselves. When Frye scored his $1 million royalty for *Pac-Man* someone from the coin-op division scrawled a poster with the legend "Why Frye?". The programmer responded by drawing a horizontal line over the "Why" – rendering the sentence, in logical notation, as "Why not Frye?".

Discontent came to a head during a meeting in the Consumer Division at the end of July 1982. As his co-workers grumbled about the *E.T.* project, Warshaw stood up in front of them all. "I'll tell you what," he announced to the assembled team, "the deadline for this game is September 1st. If anybody else wants to do this game for that deadline, I'll let them have it."

You could have heard a pin drop.

"Anybody wants to do it for that date, just say so..."

Silence.

Nobody spoke up because everybody thought it was impossible. A five-week turnaround for a complete VCS game was utter madness and Warshaw was the only person at Atari with the chutzpah to attempt it. He spent the next month eating, sleeping and dreaming *E.T.*, hunched over an assembler that he took home with him. Working so speedily was a challenge. It was also something Warshaw remembered from his college days: "I think of myself as a very quick person. During exams I wanted to be the first one out of the class. You could freak out the class and ruin the curve by leaving early. It's a great tactic."

Despite all the bluster, though, the whole enterprise was symbolic of just how immune to failure the VCS division had become. Someone should have sounded the alarm - indeed some did. George Kiss, director of software in the VCS division, recalls telling his bosses on the Atari board that *E.T.* was a terrible idea. "There was no way we could produce a good game in that time," he says. "They noted my objection and told me to get on with it".

When Warshaw worked on *Raiders*, Spielberg had shown no interest in the game design at all. With *E.T.* he offered an opinion. Wouldn't it be neat, the director asked the programmer, to do *E.T.* as a *Pac-Man* style character wandering around gobbling Reese's Pieces or something? Warshaw, bumptious to a fault, shrugged off the suggestion. The five-week turnaround didn't dampen his enthusiasm. He hoped to approach the movie's emotional tone.

By September 1st, the game was ready. Taking the bare bones of Spielberg's movie - E.T. needs to phone home - Warshaw had created an action-adventure game out of its domestic drama. The alien wandered suburbia looking for the missing pieces of his intergalactic telephone; he dodged FBI agents and fell - more often than was enjoyable for the player - into pits that he had to levitate out of. As a technical feat of against-the-clock-programming it was a triumph. No one had ever completed a game in just five weeks before. As a game it was utterly, utterly awful.

Frustration dominated the action. It wasn't helped by the game's lonely aesthetic which tried to capture the emotional pull of the movie. It failed miserably. Instead of pathos one was left with a sense of desolate boredom. Not even E.T.'s cute likeness on the title screen could mitigate its dreadfulness. When former Atari engineer Al Alcorn, the creator of *Pong*, saw the game he said he wanted to cry because it was so bad. The first focus groups to play it returned terrible scores. Atari's programmers were unanimous in their belief that the very concept of the movie was wrong for a game. "They said that it was a lovely, sweet movie, and kids like to kill things," recalled Kassar.

The VCS just didn't have the capabilities to do such a sensitive, emotional movie justice. When Atari legal counsel Skip Paul saw the finished product he had helped to license he was aghast. Forget the lack of a working hand sink in the limo, this was something really worth complaining about: "It wasn't a game, it was a thing waddling around on a screen."

Brand awareness worked, though, and by January 1983 the title was in Billboard's Top 15 Video Games chart at number four. Many thought it was proof that Atari's Hollywood obsession could do no wrong. The figures told a different story. E.T. sold around one-and-a-half million copies making Warshaw the only Atari programmer whose games all broke the million mark. The problem was that E.T. shipped more than twice that amount, if not more. For any other title that would have been a problem. However, given the overheads involved in the game's licensing and Spielberg's royalty payment, it turned out to be disastrous. Record numbers of cartridges were returned and Atari was left with a glut of millions of unsold games. A fortune was spent on television and press adverts. Just as with *Raiders* fairly respectable sales figures simply didn't add up on the spreadsheet.

"We don't think it's your fault, Howard."

The first time he heard those words, Warshaw knew something was wrong. Executives and marketing people would stop him in the corridor and tell him, earnestly, that it wasn't his fault. What wasn't his fault? He didn't know. For the programmers, cocooned in their bubble of assemblers and game design on the fly, what happened after the cartridge shipped was out of their sphere of influence. Once the ROMs were pressed and the usual $40,000 bonus cheque cashed it was just a matter of waiting for the royalties to start coming in.

Warshaw knew that *E.T.* had run into problems but he was in denial. Heck, the whole of Atari was in denial about what was happening. "The VCS was this huge gravy train," he remembers. "Nobody wanted it to go away. Nobody wanted to admit that things weren't great. But then they started talking about massive returns of *E.T.*. Things weren't selling. There were big complaints about the game. I started to realise there was a problem."

The problem was bigger than Warshaw and his game. Atari's business model was collapsing under the weight of the company's mismanagement. Easy cash and unstoppable success had gone to everyone's heads. Its inventory was a mess. The over-extended catalogue of software wasn't being properly tracked and returns from retailers were mounting - a new distribution deal in November only infuriated retailers even more. The company was overproducing cartridges in the deluded belief that consumers who hadn't already bought a console would purchase one simply to play games like *E.T.* and *Pac-Man*. Meanwhile Atari's research and development arm had been all but shut down by Kassar. There was little forward thinking, no innovation. The business model had simply been milked dry.

Consumers were beginning to lose patience. Kids parting with $30 for a rubbish *Pac-Man* port had their fingers so badly burned they went on a buying strike. Slapping a movie license like *E.T.* on a cartridge and selling it like a movie with big-spend TV ads didn't solve the problem. In fact it only made it worse. The game's artistic poverty was bad enough. The fact that it tarnished a hit movie loved by millions only raised gamers' ire. Atari's costly Christmas TV ads featuring *E.T.* in a Santa suit said it all. The game that should have been that year's most anticipated Christmas present was simply a turkey. A blockbuster movie didn't guarantee blockbuster game sales, no matter how much money was spent on it.

The problem was bigger than Atari, too. Across the board, videogame manufacturers had flooded the market with product. Quality control had plummeted. *E.T.* was just a high-profile example of a malaise that was affecting the entire videogame industry. At the same time, Hollywood was striking back. Sales of the new videocassette recorder machines doubled between 1982 and 1983. Movies were back in the living room.

As record numbers of the *E.T.* cartridges were returned to Atari, it was easy to lay the blame on a single title. "It's not your fault, Howard" became a mantra among the Atari execs who knew that it was really management and marketing's fault. Avarice and hubris had taken their toll and *E.T.* had been a folly right from the beginning: the five-week schedule; the multi-million dollar payment to Spielberg; the belief that consumers would buy any crap put in front of them. Ironically *E.T.* was proof that games were an artistic medium rather than a merely technical one. Artistry had been sacrificed in the deal and the soulless nature of a lacklustre product was clear for all to see.

"It's not your fault, Howard."

The North American Videogame Crash arrived in 1983 and *E.T.* became the standard-bearer of the slump. Mattel's hardware sales plummeted, its electronics division posting a $201 million deficit in 1983. Activision's software sales plummeted losing $3 to $5 million over three months from August to October. Atari was hit worst of all, the market leader becoming the market loser too. When the company's lower-than-expected fourth quarter figures were released in the winter of 1982, Warner took the hit. The media conglomerate's stock sank "like a runaway elevator", as Time put it, shedding $19 per share - a market valuation loss of $1.3 billion.

In the dark days of 1983, Atari racked up a $536 million loss. The Sunnyvale company became a millstone around Warners' neck. In September 1983, the trucks rolled out from the El Paso manufacturing plant carrying their shipment of unsold Atari inventory to be buried in the desert. It was the end of an era. "Americans are mazed out and shot out. They're tired of videogames," noted Atari's new chairman James J. Morgan in early 1984. "Atari must compete against movies, novels, TV, anything that makes up America's six hours a day of leisure time". Not long afterwards, Warner cut Atari loose, only retaining the coin-op division as a reminder of what had been.

Warshaw never flew on another Learjet. And he never hung out with Spielberg again. By December 1985 he was being profiled in The Los Angeles Times along with several of his Atari programming peers in the aftermath of the collapse. It read like an obituary. The stardom that Warshaw and a handful of others had briefly tasted had died overnight. When the bubble burst the millionaire programmers watched their cash disappear as poor accounting and tax planning taking their toll. "A lot of people handled it well on the way up," Warshaw said mournfully. "But on the way down, the people who were losers became big losers. Some people gave up. People grasped at straws. People became desperate. People believed this was never going to go away. Some people just went crazy. As a group, we were a bunch of screaming babies. We lost our perspective. But to get an industry started like that, you needed a bunch of screaming babies."

As the cash evaporated and the trips to Hollywood became nothing more than treasured memories, Warshaw decided to become a real estate broker. "I expect to make several million in the next five or six years, I hope," he told the reporter from the Los Angeles Times. As the years passed, he'd return to making videogames, dabble in robotics, shoot documentaries and eventually retrain as a psychotherapist. True to his free-wheeling philosophy of life, he chalked the Atari adventure up to experience.

And what an experience it had been. Atari had created the home videogame business. It had pioneered the licensing of movie titles for videogames. And it had challenged the supremacy of Hollywood. The movie studios, burnt by the crash, took stock. Interactive entertainment had both terrified and enthralled them. Videogames had been proved as a source of merchandising revenue. Indeed, games based on movies would continue to be licensed for the VCS and other platforms throughout the dark days of 1983 and 1984 with titles as diverse as *Halloween*, *Star Trek* and *Ghostbusters*.

The general belief was that 8-bit graphics and rudimentary gameplay simply couldn't compete with the reality of the movies themselves. Hollywood, the consensus believed, could offer much richer experiences. But in the middle of the videogame industry's slump, one company would prove otherwise by releasing the most movie-like videogame the arcades had ever seen.

CHAPTER 2

Here Be Dragons

"Dragon's Lair is this summer's hottest new toy: the first arcade game in the United States with a movie-quality image to go along with the action [...] The game has been devouring kids' coins at top speed since it appeared early in July. At Castle Park in Sherman Oaks, Calif., the crowd around Lair grows all day, while a nearby row of Pac-Man games stands empty [...] Said Robert Romano, 10, who waited all day in the crush at Castle Park without getting to play, 'It's the most awesome game I've ever seen in my life.'"

Newsweek, 8 August 1983

Disney was pissed about the dragon. It was hardly surprising. Don Virgil Bluth, a veteran animator with the studio and the one-time heir apparent to Uncle Walt himself, drew some of the best fire-breathing reptiles around. He'd made his mark working on *Pete's Dragon* in 1977, a chipper kid's movie about a boy and his animated dragon. But then things at Disney turned sour.

Bluth had spent his life wanting to work for the company. As a child, growing up in rural Utah, he'd whiled away his mornings and evenings milking the family's herd of twenty-four cows while singing Disney songs. Each Saturday he'd ride the four miles into town from the family farm on horseback and spend his pocket money in the local movie theatre. When he was four he'd seen *Snow White and the Seven Dwarves* and from that moment on, he knew that he would do whatever it took to be part of that magic. He watched and read everything that bore the Disney name. Most of all he learned how to draw in the Disney style. It would be his passport out of rural Utah and into Hollywood.

He first worked in the company's animation department in 1956, not long after his family moved to Santa Monica, California. He was just 18 but skilled enough drawing-wise to be offered a junior position as an "inbetweener" for veteran supervising animator John Lounsbery, working on *Sleeping Beauty*. It enabled him to watch Uncle Walt's company work their magic close-up. After graduating from university and producing theatre musicals, he decided to make animation his career. He returned to Disney in April 1971 to work as an animator on *Robin Hood*. Later, he was promoted to directing animator on

The Rescuers. The veteran animators thought he was a promising talent, an artist with a real appreciation of the company's heritage and the animation styles that went into creating its past glories.

As the years went by, though, Bluth realised with sadness that Disney - the company he loved, the company he had grown up wanting to be a part of - had lost its way. Rudderless since the death of its founder in 1966, the studio was selling out for lower costs. Production values were falling and artistry had become a dirty word. All that mattered, it seemed, was keeping the shareholders happy. Although Mickey Mouse was still the company's figurehead, it was the almighty dollar that really ruled the roost. The magic of Disney's Golden Age - the attention to detail, the artistry and pride that went into films like *Snow White* and *Sleeping Beauty* - was being squandered on second-rate junk like *The Black Cauldron.*

The only choice, Bluth decided, was to make a stand. Together with his colleagues Gary Goldman and John Pomeroy, he set up a studio in his garage. For four-and-a-half years the men worked together, nights and weekends, on a featurette called *Banjo The Woodpile Cat* using whatever materials they could purchase, scrounge or borrow. Their aim was to train themselves in the classical animation techniques that Disney was on the verge of forgetting, all the while still working days at the house that Walt built. It was a passion project - and a costly one too.

"We took our vacation money, our stock options, our savings [to fund the movie]," Bluth later recalled. "We needed an orchestra, so I mortgaged my house for $15,000." When no one at Disney would even look at Banjo, Bluth realised his time at the company was over. He couldn't stand back and watch the art form he loved being bastardised; and he refused to waste all his passion fighting total indifference.

Bluth, a thin, straight-backed man with a warm smile sneaking out from underneath a thick moustache, knew all about the power of schisms. Born a Mormon, he understood what happened when an organisation lost its way. Sometimes a strong figure was needed to restore to old values. Sometimes you had to splinter away from the group to stay true to your convictions.

Bluth was an unlikely rebel, but he was passionate about making the Disney films Disney no longer wanted to make. As his namesake, the Roman poet of *The Aeneid*, had written: fortes fortuna adiuvat ("Fortune favours the bold"). On his 42nd birthday Don Virgil Bluth decided to be bold. Bolstered by the promise of financing from Aurora Productions, he handed in his resignation along with Goldman and Pomeroy. The next day 11 other members of the animation staff joined them. Their departure created headlines in the trade papers, the Wall Street Journal and the New York Times. Within three months a total of 17 animation artists had left the Disney fold.

Disney's management - in particular, company president Ron Miller - was furious: "They were angry with us. There were no hugs and kisses - they were throwing rocks". Production on animated feature *The Fox and the Hound* was thrown into disarray by the mass exodus. Its theatrical release was delayed by six months and Disney stock dropped by 6% on the news of the group's departure. But Bluth and his followers knew the company was big enough to survive without them. The only question was whether or not they themselves could survive without Disney. It didn't help that the split was so acrimonious. "We were called every name in the book, everything from renegades to defectors to traitors, as if we were horrible people."

Bluth was a principled man and the name-calling stung cruelly. But he knew that they had left Disney for the right reasons. It wasn't self-aggrandisement. It wasn't greed. Competition, he hoped, would make the studio he loved grow stronger. A monopoly wasn't healthy for anyone and certainly not the industry itself. "All we were trying to do was promote the art of animation so it would continue to grow."

Don Bluth Productions, an animation studio dedicated to restoring the past glories of Disney's Golden Age, grew out of that decisive action. Four years after the split, the studio would score its first financial success - not with a movie but with a videogame. *Dragon's Lair*, an arcade game released by Cinematronics, would bring classical hand-drawn animation to the video arcade. It would be the best Disney videogame Disney never made. No wonder Bluth's former bosses were dragon green with envy.

* * *

The Talking Car impressed all the ladies. Every time Rick Dyer took a girl out on a date he got the "computer" to ask her what radio station she liked to listen to. None of them could understand how it knew their name. It was just a silly little novelty but it made an impact. Bringing an inanimate object to life could have that effect - something Dyer had discovered as a kid when he'd soldered together a talking cuckoo clock that not only told you the time but would reel off a famous quotation to improve your mind too.

Inventing things came naturally - precociously even - to Dyer. With his piercing blue eyes and neatly clipped moustache, this engineering graduate from California Polytechnic looked like a geeky Tom Selleck. What he lacked in physique he made up for in brains. Indeed, he was never short on ideas. Some worked. Others didn't. But he pursued all of them with the single-mindedness of a mad inventor. An early success came with an electronic horse-racing game he designed that caught the attention of toy company Mattel. It was his first taste of business and he was soon running his own research and development company, Advanced Microcomputer Systems (AMS) out of an office in Diamond Bar, California. The year was 1981.

Dyer wasn't simply an enthusiastic inventor. He was also an entrepreneur who was eager to innovate. While his staff worked on handheld games for toy manufacturer Entex, he continued to develop ideas for a new type of videogame. Looking around at the success of Atari and its competitors, he felt disappointed. Here was a great revolution in the offing and yet the fruits it was bearing were limited, stunted things. The arcade was full of "twitch" games - *Frogger, Defender* and the rest - which were dominated by simple shoot-run-jump mechanics.

Dyer, inspired by text adventure games, wanted to do something that had a story, a real narrative told through words and pictures. He also wanted it to be interactive like Edward Packard's *Choose Your Own Adventure* gamebooks, the fantasy role playing novels that emerged in the late-1970s. The issue was how to get the underpowered computers of the '80s to handle graphics and a sprawling, interactive story. It was a sticking point that seemed insurmountable. Frustrated by the limitations of technology, Dyer designed a mechanical game he called The Fantasy Machine. It might as well have been called The Never Never Machine since it was one of those ideas that stubbornly refused to leave the design lab.

The Fantasy Machine had a long and torturous history. Dyer started work on it back in 1979 in his garage in Pomona, California. The early prototypes were weird contraptions, awkward handheld machines that seemed old-fashioned even back then. Victor Penman, one of the writers Dyer hired to join the staff at AMS in 1981, recalls seeing an early version and being surprised by how mechanical it was. "It was this interesting contraption that ran on servo motors, with a hand illustrated, broad paper strip," he remembers. "At the top there'd be a still, backlit picture and a list of options you could take. You'd press the button and the light would go off and servos would just go CHUG-CHUG-

CHUG and the thing would go back and forth until it came to the next illustrated panel." It was a mechanical version of random access memory, the motors scrolling through a roll of cash register paper to find each new "chapter". In the age of the Atari VCS, this Rube Goldberg device seemed like a technological step backwards, a regression akin to swapping a 35mm movie projector for a zoetrope.

Over time, the concept of The Fantasy Machine evolved. While still creating handheld electronic games for Entex - to keep the company's cash flowing - Dyer tasked his staff with developing an adventure game called *The Lost Woods* that would run on The Fantasy Machine. The main influence was *Dungeons & Dragons*. It was something that Penman was intimately familiar with, since he'd previously owned a shop in Pomona, California that sold role-playing games. He had even run classes for novice players eager to get to grips with the game's esoteric rules and distinctive polyhedral dice. Like the open-ended *Dungeons & Dragons* universe, the goal of *The Lost Woods* was simply to stay alive, exploring a world created in words and images.

Meanwhile, The Fantasy Machine itself was tweaked. Dyer moved from watercolour illustrations to using a film strip in a 35mm projector hooked up to a membrane keyboard. It was a box-like unit about the size of a child's plastic cash register. Players could move from one location to the next and pick up objects and interact with their environment by pressing colour-coded keys. Nobody at AMS was quite sure what they were making. It was a story, yet interactive. It was shot on film, yet it wasn't a moving image. It was low-tech and clunky, a not-quite-videogame. Unsurprisingly, Dyer couldn't find a buyer for it.

No design ever springs fully-formed from the drawing board and the joy of research is the process of discovery that accompanies each reset and accompanying post-mortem. Far from being disheartened by his failure to get The Fantasy Machine functioning properly, Dyer began to rethink the mechanism he was using. He knew he needed something that would offer him random access and he knew that the 512 bytes he was using in his handheld games for Entex wouldn't be nearly big enough to run the kind of adventure he envisioned. He needed a different approach, a new kind of technology. What he needed, he eventually realised, was the laserdisc.

In the early 1980s, as sales of home video-recorders were taking off, laserdisc technology was decidedly futuristic. The shiny discs, about the size of an old-fashioned vinyl LP and with a plastic-coated surface that reflected a full spectrum of colourful light, made the utilitarian black VHS and Betamax cassette tapes look positively prehistoric. MCA had released *Jaws* on its DiscoVision format in 1978 and there was already vague talk in the games industry that laserdiscs would replace ROMs and floppy discs as the standard storage format. But for the majority of consumers, the technology was a total mystery. "No one knew what a laser was," laughed Dyer a few years later. "They would imagine a James Bond movie with a laser beam that cut someone in half!"

In reality, lasers had more uses than simply threatening the crown jewels of MI6's philandering spy. As an integral part of the most advanced storage medium around, they promised to be Dyer's salvation. He needed a system that would let him jump between episodes, offering different outcomes to player's choices. Laserdisc technology offered him exactly that.

While a person reading one of Edward Packard's *Choose Your Own Adventure* books had to skip through pages to find the paragraph that corresponded to their choice, the laserdisc could do it automatically - and with pictures and sound, not just text. It was a technology designed to play movies - high-quality images that outstripped anything you'd find on VCR - and for an engineer who was already experimenting with text and 35mm film, its suitability was immediately obvious. It begged a question, though: if laserdiscs were used for movies, why not produce a game with moving images rather than stills?

At first Dyer had thought about selling his game as an add-on product to existing laserdisc owners. You'd pay for the input equipment and disc needed to play the game and enter a world of adventure. The problem was that laserdisc penetration in American homes was virtually non-existent. There just weren't enough machines to make it a viable business strategy. Frustrated, Dyer knew it was a dead-end. And yet there was something about the idea of using real film footage that he kept returning to. There must be a way to make it work.

In the middle of his deliberations, Dyer took his wife Jan to the cinema to see a new animated feature called *The Secret of N.I.M.H.*. It was the summer of 1982 - the moment when the whole of America seemed to be thinking about videogames. Sitting in the air-conditioned theatre watching this family-friendly story about a pack of intelligent lab rats, Dyer suddenly realised he'd found his solution. When the credits rolled, he waited to see who he needed to call. To his surprise, it wasn't Disney that was behind *The Secret of N.I.M.H.* It was a company called Don Bluth Productions.

* * *

Nobody was naïve enough to think that breaking away from Disney was going to be easy. At Don Bluth Productions' offices in Studio City, the staff felt much like the rebel pilots in *Star Wars*. Disney was like the Death Star, a monolithic force capable of wiping them off the map if it chose to protect its monopoly aggressively. Just like the Death Star, however, Disney had an unexpected weakness. Its Achilles' heel was videogames - although neither Bluth nor even Disney realised it at the time.

In the past, Disney had deliberately resisted the lure of videogames. As early as 1981, the company's president Ron Miller had said he had no intention of taking Disney's much-loved characters into this new arena since, he believed, it was already "too late" to break into the new medium. It was a questionably cautious approach. By the summer of 1982, the studio watched while competitors like Paramount, Universal and Fox carved up the videogame market. And still they didn't step forward and set up their own videogames division. The general sense was that the ship had already sailed.

Synergy, however, works both ways. Disney may not have made its own videogames out of its movies, but in the summer of 1982 it made the first videogame movie: *Tron.* This garish sci-fi adventure was a high-tech outing that combined live-action with computer-generated effects. Directed by fine arts graduate and animator Steve Lisberger, the movie was Disney's attempt to woo the Atari generation.

Lisberger had first played *Pong* at his parents-in-law's house in 1977. Watching his family bat the ball around the screen, the animator suddenly realised that videogames made the tech-head's esoteric world of silicon chips and code assemblers accessible to Joe Public. "It occurred to me that the games, which are so human and silly, were a perfect bridge to the whole world of computer technology," he explained. "Then I started meeting all these computer people; they walk around just like the rest of us, but they spent all their time and energy projecting their will into this other microcosmic world inside the computer. In fact some of them are much more alive inside the computer than they are here. And it came to me to do an electronic *Wizard of Oz* which would show people that what's inside the computer is only an extension of the programmer's personality."

After trying to fund the film independently, Lisberger and producer Donald Kushner struck a deal with Walt Disney Productions to sink $18 million into the movie's visual effects heavy production. It was a brave move by the venerable animation studio, which was then floundering since its films seemed increasingly out of touch with popular taste. *Tron* offered Disney a new lease of life - and a means of reconnecting with audiences - by placing its finger firmly on the nation's pulse.

With over a thousand visual effects shots, the film's high-tech vision of a world inside a computer network tapped directly into the public's fascination with computing and, more importantly, videogames themselves. Lisberger's belief that games were an accessible way of talking about how computers were influencing our lives proved spot on. This wasn't *Bambi*. It was modern, technologically-sophisticated and, most of all, cool: sci-fi fantasy for the post-disco era.

Tron hasn't aged well but in the prehistoric days of 1982, its bold visuals were truly amazing. Blending live action footage with hand-tinted, back-lit scenes and computer-generated imagery, the film's animators created a pulsing, neon-tinged virtual world. It possessed all the precise mathematical beauty of the computer sphere - and much of its barren coldness as it reduced its human characters to pixelated avatars in a clinical universe of bits and bytes. Whether you loved it or hated it, there was no denying that *Tron* was an incredibly important movie. It was one of the first major studio films to fully engage with computer-generated effects and it marked the first, mainstream attempt by filmmakers to connect to the "Pac-Man nation".

Its plot was a high-tech reimagining of *The Wizard of Oz*. Games designer hero Kevin Flynn (Jeff Bridges) gets zapped into the mainframe of the corporate network he's hacking and ends up battling its villainous Master Control Program. Each show-stopping set-piece within the movie plays like a videogame. There's a light-cycle chase where two digital motorbikes zip along a cross-hatched grid performing perfect 90-degree turns. Later we see a gladiatorial Frisbee fight and a CGI tank battle as competing computer subroutines clash.

As a visual spectacle, *Tron* thrives on the immediacy of its action sequences rather than its character interactions. You watch it and want to play it. As Janet Maslin commented in The New York Times, taking her cue from Atari's VCS 2600 adverts, "Though it's certainly very impressive, it may not be the film for you if you haven't played Atari today".

For all its eye-candy visuals, though, *Tron*'s real achievement was in recalibrating the relationship between movie marketing and videogames. Lacking its own standalone videogame division, Disney approached Bally-Midway to design and manufacture an arcade game based on the movie. The result was a popular coin-op containing four interlinked sub-games based on the movie's best action sequences. "When it came to *Tron* we didn't look at Atari or anything like that as an enemy," recalls Jim Garber, who was Disney's vice president of marketing at the time. "We looked at it, in some respects, as an ally. As more people became interested in videogames it was obvious that there was a public that would be interested in this kind of movie."

Released a couple of months before the film hit cinemas, the *Tron* coin-op helped build a huge amount of advance buzz. In the US, a national tournament was held to find the most talented player. Around a hundred regional winners were flown to a championship bout at Madison Square Gardens in New York, where Disney and Bally-Midway had lined up baseball players Willie Mays and Hank Aaron. "We used it as a promotional tool to promote the film in advance [of its release]," says Garber. "It just seemed something very natural to do based upon the storyline of the film, the introduction of the game and licensing partnership we had developed with Bally. It all just fell into place. Disney had always, at that point in time, looked for ways to leverage their business partnerships to the greatest degree possible to generate more exposure for the film so they didn't have to invest so many advertising dollars."

This was marketing synergy at its most cutting-edge and it proved invaluable since *Tron* opened to a surprisingly poor response from the public. Disney was hit hard by the negativity surrounding the film's release and the company's share price shed $2.50. Indeed the company, which had banked on *Tron*'s success, might have made a loss with the film if it weren't for the tie-in videogames.

Momentum flowed out of the arcades and into the movie theatre, boosting ticket sales as players were inspired by the game to see the movie. Such a situation was a clear case of the tail wagging the dog. As one Disney exec put it in the spring of 1983, "I don't think there's any question that movie ticket sales to people who bought or played the videogame *Tron* helped the movie break even. Otherwise, without any game, it would have lost millions".

But it didn't simply stop there: incredibly, the coin-op game actually out-grossed the movie. John Pasierb, Bally-Midway's vice president of engineering who worked on the game, believes the coin-op moved around 30,000 to 40,000 units and earned north of $60 million (more than double the US box office for the movie). "It wasn't a *Space Invaders* or a *Pac-Man* but it was a darn good run," Pasierb says. "I think it affected some people in the movie business when they saw the numbers. It spurred a lot of interest from the studios to really take a long, hard look at the videogame business."

Over at Fox Video Games, company president Frank O'Connell could see that studio executives were now taking games seriously: "I used to kid them in the movie industry saying, 'Maybe you should release the videogame first and then the movie'. *Tron* shifted the whole paradigm."

For Bluth, *Tron* meant something else. It was the film that marked the battleground between himself and Disney - not least of all since it was released just a week after Don Bluth Productions' first feature, *The Secret of N.I.M.H.* There was no shortage of irony that the two films should cross swords at the box office like that. With its cute cartoon rats, *N.I.M.H.* was an old-fashioned movie, the kind of film Disney used to make. *Tron* represented Disney's new era - a world where computer-generated effects apparently mattered more than traditional, 2D cel animation.

Critics loved *The Secret of N.I.M.H.*. Each frame was lavishly, painstakingly rendered and the movie could have been a throwback to the animated features of the '30s and the '40s. Bluth was carrying the torch for Disney at a time when The Walt Disney Company seemed to have lost its way. Film Comment ran an article comparing the two movies entitled "Will The Real Walt Disney Please Stand Up?" which posed, but diplomatically didn't answer, the question: "Where does the future of the animated feature lie - with the futuristic imagery of *Tron* or the meticulous drawings of *N.I.M.H.*?"

Several reviewers believed that Bluth was the winner in this clash. "*The Secret of N.I.M.H.* is not only a wonderful film but an acronymic rebuke to the Disney people at precisely the time that Uncle Walt's heirs are unleashing *Tron*, their own capital-lettered bid for the teenage market," claimed the Minneapolis Star & Tribune. "*N.I.M.H.* seems to be asking: Why have you given up on the family-orientated market?"

It was a question worth asking and the answer came soon enough. *N.I.M.H.* may have received strong reviews but its box office performance was abysmal. Sandwiched between two family movies - *Tron* and *E.T. The Extra-Terrestrial* - it was inevitably overshadowed. Poor marketing by distributor MGM/UA didn't help matters and it never found its family audience. Hailing the past at a time when all eyes of the *Pac-Man* nation were on videogames' future, turned out to be a foolhardy move. Disney, it seemed, had been right all along. Bluth was chasing a long, lost dream.

The Secret of N.I.M.H.'s box office flop was quite possibly the greatest disappointment of Bluth's career. For a big corporation like Disney, such misjudgements could be balanced out across a varied production slate. For a small independent outfit like Don Bluth Productions, *N.I.M.H.*'s failure to break even was colossal. Although work began on a follow-up feature called *East of the Sun, West of the Moon*, the company's investors were spooked. Things came to a head after the animators' union called an industry-wide, 73-day strike to protest against the foreign outsourcing of work on Saturday morning TV cartoons. It wasn't just Disney's animators who were told to man the picket lines. Bluth's staff were asked to leave the building too. Production on the new film ground to a halt and their investors pulled out.

Bluth's hopes of proving that there was life for independent animation beyond the walls of Disney's Sleeping Beauty castle were shattered. Worse still, it looked like the company itself was about to go under. For a while, they managed to limp along on promises and hopes. One notable dead-end was a Japanese-American investor who approached them in late 1982. He claimed to have been badly burned by Disney after they pulled out of a deal to finance his last business proposition - a computerised loom that could produce any design in knit form. It was supposed to dramatically change the apparel design landscape for knitwear and help Disney to shake up movie merchandising in the process.

Finding common ground with the animators over their mutual distrust of Disney, the potential investor told Bluth and his business partners Gary Goldman and John Pomeroy that he admired their work on *The Secret of N.I.M.H.* He also claimed to be in a position to help them. He said he had access to European finance and could find $12 million for their next project. Although Bluth and his team were suspicious of his motives, they were too desperate to look a gift horse in the mouth. After around three months of nerve-wracking phone calls - during which their mysterious benefactor would always promise that he was on the verge of securing their finance - he was revealed as a fraud. In his final phone call to Don Bluth Productions he told Goldman that he had located the funding. It was currently in the form of gold bars buried under a runway at a Swiss airport. Incredulous, the animator hung up the phone. He was convinced that the businessman was "a charlatan, someone to lure us into a ruse that would hopefully ruin us financially".

Sitting in their empty office on Ventura Boulevard in Studio City, after the union had ordered the reluctant animation staff to walk out, Bluth and his business partners were left with little to do except survey the wreckage of their dreams. The excitement of resigning from Disney and forging their own path seemed to have lead to a dead end. Outside the windows, the ever-optimistic California sunshine shone on a sidewalk lined with palm trees that stood tall like proud giraffes. Inside the office, though, the mood was black.

"We were completely depressed," remembers Bluth. "Our story was supposed to have a happy ending. We'd made a picture and we thought it was a good picture and we thought we'd go on to make another and build a studio." They were nearing bankruptcy. Instead of saving the animation industry, it looked like they were about to become its victims. Until the phone rang again...only this time it wasn't another investor but the office of Rick Dyer at AMS. The engineer was calling with a business proposition for Don Bluth Productions.

When the traffic's light, it takes about an hour to drive the 45 miles from Studio City to Diamond Bar, a straight run along Highway 101 through Universal City and West Hollywood and out past Walnut Valley. When Bluth visited the AMS offices in September 1982, though, he might as well have been making a trip to the moon. It certainly was uncharted territory for him and the rest of his team. "We knew nothing about how to put a videogame together," he recalls. "I hadn't been in arcades, I knew nothing about games. I knew *Donkey Kong*." Goldman was equally out of touch: his knowledge of the videogame industry stopped somewhere around *Pong*. At AMS, Dyer invited the artists to surround themselves with microprocessors, circuit boards and engineering flow charts.

The meeting of art and engineering was unlike anything either side had experienced before. Mistaken assumptions were legion, some of them deliberately cultivated as the two companies discussed collaborating together. The fact was that both organisations were feeling the financial pinch. AMS was cash-strapped; Don Bluth Productions was skating on the edge of bankruptcy. Both needed a deal to buy them a little more time. But in a classic example of business poker, neither side knew quite what a crappy hand the other was holding.

From the perspective of the engineers at AMS, Don Bluth Productions seemed like a pretty sophisticated outfit. They'd had a major animated movie in cinemas that summer; they were former Disney employees and Hollywood types. Bluth's team harboured similar misconceptions about AMS. They knew that Dyer had a track record of creating games, most recently a coin-op maze game with a mouthful of a title, *Zzyzzyxx*. They also knew, as everyone did in the summer of 1982, that videogames were big business. You only had to look at Atari's profits to see that. They thought they were getting in on the ground floor of something lucrative.

In many ways Dyer and Bluth had much in common. Both were shy and retiring; both had begun their careers as garage start-ups; and both shared a similar kind of unflinching belief in their passion. What separated them was Dyer's head for business. While Bluth was a relative innocent when it came to matters of finance, Dyer had an entrepreneur's eye for the deal and an intense demeanour. "Dyer made me think of Thomas Edison or Benjamin Franklin," recalls illustrator Tom O'Mary who joined Dyer's later company RDI in 1985 and used to watch his boss wandering the office, holding court as he gripped the lapels of his three-piece suit. "He was completely focused. He could walk down a hall and you knew he wasn't seeing anybody in the hallway, his mind was completely gone [somewhere else]. He truly was looking at something in the future."

Dyer also had a secretive demeanour that bordered on being theatrically enigmatic. "I always thought Rick was a very mysterious kind of guy," recalls Bluth. "He had a look about him when you were talking to him. He wasn't quite looking at you; he would be looking at some vision somewhere. He had a little mystery about him that always intrigued me."

The San Diego engineer had a habit of playing his cards close to his chest. "He always put a lot of effort into presentation," recalls Penman. "For example, we had an area that was an empty warehouse. He put a big sign over the door saying "OFF LIMITS, AUTHORISED PERSONEL ONLY". When potential customers came by he'd make up some story about things going on back there that he couldn't show or tell them about. We also had a recording studio, which we were using once we got involved in the laserdiscs. He'd carpeted everything: the walls, the ceilings, the floors to soundproof it. It looked impressive and when Don Bluth's people came, they obviously thought we had money, which we really didn't." It was the business equivalent of psychological warfare, divorcing perception and reality in the hope of making a couple of bucks look like a couple of million.

The enigma only deepened when Dyer showed them an early prototype of The Fantasy Machine. Neither Bluth nor his partners knew what to make of it. "It was basically a box that had scrolling paper inside it," remembers Goldman. "It was operated by a computer for choices so that you could go back and forth. We thought 'This can't possibly be where we're going'. But that's the way Rick's mind worked." It was only when they heard the story pitch for the laserdisc game and saw some of the early scripts AMS had produced that Bluth began to understand what they could bring to the project. This wasn't a simple game. It was a movie. And Bluth knew all about movies.

The benefits for Don Bluth Productions were immediately obvious. The partnership with AMS not only promised to dig them out of their financial hole, it also offered them a chance to break the animators' union strike that was currently crippling them. The idea of using cel animation in a videogame was so new and unheard of that the Animation Guild, the animators' union, didn't have a clause in the contract about it. That meant Bluth's staff could cross the picket line and get back to work without fearing reprisals. Meanwhile, Dyer talked Bluth through his vision of a coin-op arcade game called *Dragon's Lair* that would use shot-on-film animation on a laserdisc instead of the conventional raster graphics. As he listened, Bluth began to feel he was part of something excitingly new.

He couldn't afford to believe it was anything else. Dyer was offering him a lifeline. In return for the animators creating 20 minutes worth of footage for free, Don Bluth Productions would own a third of a new venture called Starcom, later renamed Magicom. AMS (which itself would later become RDI Video Systems) would handle the engineering side of things and take a third of the profits. Cinematronics, the distributors of the lacklustre *Zzyzzyxx* coin-op, would look after manufacturing and sales and take the final third. Bluth took the deal, and not even the fact that Cinematronics had already filed for Chapter 11 bankruptcy could dampen his enthusiasm. He was desperate, after all. "It was," he decided, "a dinghy to a sinking ship. We didn't have the money to do another movie. We didn't even have the money to do the game!" Fortune hadn't favoured the bold when they had left Disney to make *N.I.M.H.*. In fact, short of breaking their arms and legs with a baseball bat, it couldn't have smiled any less on them. Perhaps their time had finally come?

With plans to reveal three episodes from the game at the Amusement Operators Expo in Chicago in March 1983, Bluth and his team begged and borrowed money from friends and relatives to keep themselves afloat while they worked on the animation. They needed $300,000 to create the necessary sample footage for the Expo. It seemed an impossible sum until Bluth's brother arrived one afternoon with a Safeway grocery bag stuffed with hundreds of dollar bills. They counted it up and it totalled $50,000. As a joke he'd cashed the first payment cheque from a new investor and brought it over in hard currency to cheer the company's spirits. The bank didn't see the funny side. Goldman had to convince the manager that it wasn't the proceeds from a drug deal.

It was time poorly spent since the clock was ticking. The laserdisc craze was already gathering pace. In May 1982, Sega/Paramount had previewed their own laserdisc game called *Astron Belt*, which would be released in Japan and Europe early the following year. A standard shoot-'em-up with fancy visuals, it let players pilot their spaceship through wallpaper backdrops of star-fields and lunar canyons lifted from the Japanese sci-fi B-movie *Message from Space*. Enemy fighters were equally realistic - not computer-generated sprites but digitised footage of the spaceships from the movie. The game's trick was superimposing the player's pixelated ship onto the movie footage stored on the laserdisc. It looked incredibly realistic. Just like playing a movie, in fact.

Since *Astron Belt*'s US release was delayed until the autumn of 1983, Dyer knew there was a limited window of opportunity. *Dragon's Lair* would win few prizes for being second out of the gate. If they were going to unveil a laserdisc game in the States, it had to be the first laserdisc game players had ever seen. Marshalling his staff of thirteen animators, Bluth got to work on Dyer's storyboards, sketching the characters who would become Dirk the Daring, Princess Daphne and Singe the Dragon of the eponymous lair. It took four months, 50,000 drawings and a budget of $1.1 million to produce the animation alone. The rest of the manufacturing process brought the total cost of the cabinet's development up to $3 million. It was a terrifying sum at a time when most coin-ops cost under $200,000 to design, program and manufacture.

Since Sega already had a laserdisc coin-op ready to go, secrecy was the order of the day. At Dyer's somewhat dramatic request, the Don Bluth Productions office was cloaked in mystery. Staff were ordered not to talk about the game to anyone who wasn't working on it - not even their wives and children. To some it seemed like overkill. They were working on a videogame, not a top secret CIA coup. How groundbreaking could a game about a hapless knight's quest to rescue a damsel in distress be? It was typical of Dyer's love of enigma. But it was also a savvy move. They were operating in a highly competitive field and the rewards were high - far higher, in truth, than anyone realised.

* * *

Video arcades have always been gaudy temples dedicated to the sublime mystery of The Eternal Game. They are unruly churches with little reverence, their peace forever disturbed by the sound of missile launches, thundering explosions and a hundred tinkling theme tunes playing simultaneously. Those who come to worship arrive with trembling hands and a pocket full of quarters to be slotted into the collection plates one by one. Cigarette smoke and stale sweat serve as incense; the lure of the high score is the equivalent of a religious ecstasy. As in all temples, the mood is sometimes disturbed by a divine event - a life changing moment when a sinner repents or a faltering soul sees the light. The first people to see *Pong* knew all about that. So did the first players to encounter *Space Invaders* and *Pac-Man*. But *Dragon's Lair* was something else. For many in the summer of 1983, it was gaming's road to Damascus experience.

It was certainly a phenomenon. The moment it debuted, jaws began hitting the floor. An early preview machine, installed at the Malibu Grand Prix theme park in El Monte California in June 1983, stopped traffic on the park's miniature race track. "There were hundreds of people and they were standing there with their mouths open and their eyes dilated just staring at our game," recalled Dyer who was present in the throng. "And when I got up to the machine there were quarters all across the front panel [left by people waiting to play]."

Excited, Dyer called the president of Cinematronics, Jim Pierce. He was in San Diego previewing a second cabinet. "Yes Rick," he confirmed in amazement, "the same thing is happening here." The first outing of *Dragon's Lair* wasn't so much a preview as a showstopper. Nobody who saw the coin-op could believe their eyes. It looked like a Disney movie... and yet it was a game? Conventional wisdom said it couldn't be possible. Up until then videogames were comprised of pixelated spaceships and ravenous Pac-Men. There was nothing life-like about them, nothing cinematic about the games they appeared in either.

Dragon's Lair was something else. When it wasn't being fed with quarters - which, given the demand in those early days, was a rare occurrence - the game would enter its "attract mode". It was like watching a movie trailer. On-screen the bandy-legged, rubber-faced knight Dirk the Daring - the love child of Dick Van Dyke and Wile E. Coyote - would be electrocuted, attacked by bats and burnt alive in molten lava. What you were watching was a Disney-style cartoon. It looked truly incredible: twenty minutes of classical animation, hand-drawn with intricate shading, realistic character movement and all lavishly shot on 35mm film. It was, put simply, an animated movie. And, for the princely sum of 50¢ you could play it. Yes, actually play it. The attract mode wasn't just a demo that was completely different from the game itself. It was the game. You took control of the same clumsy knight and led him through the same movie-quality visuals.

No one had ever seen anything like it in a video arcade before. When the game was released on 1 July 1983, *Dragon's Lair* fever quickly swept the nation. The arcade industry, already struggling as the videogame crash hit Atari and its competitors, couldn't believe their luck. *Dragon's Lair* may not have pulled the market out of its slump, but for a few sweet months it helped it defy gravity and fight against the downward trajectory. Earning between $200 and $400 a day, each *Dragon's Lair* cabinet left arcade managers hefting huge bags of quarters to the bank at the end of each week. According to some estimates the game pulled in $100 million in pocket shrapnel alone during its arcade release.

The machine itself was expensive. A single cabinet cost arcade owners $4,000 - almost double the typical price of a non-laserdisc coin-op - and resulted in *Dragon's Lair* becoming the first arcade game to charge 50¢ a play instead of a single quarter. The price hike was dictated by the technology under the hood. The cabinets, fitted with bulky industrial Pioneer 7820 laserdisc players, were state-of-the-art. The storage space on the laserdiscs could cope with Bluth's rich, high-quality animation while the CPU and ROM chips on the circuit-boards ran the software that Dyer's team had developed to make the movie you watched seem playable.

The end result was like an electronic, cinematic version of the popular *Choose Your Own Adventure* books. As Dirk headed towards the castle to rescue the princess, you nudged him in the right direction. Each animated sequence presented you with a threat and a response: walking across the castle's drawbridge you had to dodge the eyeballed tentacles of a creature that rose up from the moat's murky depths. Joystick and action button had to be pressed in the right sequence at the right moment for Dirk the Daring to escape through the castle's portcullis. Getting it wrong - or just a fraction of a second too late

- delivered a different sequence: Dirk being wrapped in tentacles and plucked from the drawbridge.

In total there were around 40 screens to work through, randomised to add novelty, and they all offered the player a series of fight or flight choices. At each branching point the laserdisc skipped through its store of animated sequences and picked the appropriate consequence to match the player's actions. Stringing together a series of successful moves kept the movie moving; failure meant an early grave. Death was more common than success and the game came with a fiendishly grotesque selection of beautifully animated drownings, disintegrations and deadly pratfalls. Like a slapstick comedian, Dirk suffered all kinds of iniquities. He battled past Mud Men, skeletons, creepy crawlies, giant bats and an obstinate suit of flying horse armour. If he survived the castle's traps, he'd ultimately find the shapely Princess Daphne waiting for him, locked away inside a glass bubble in Singe the Dragon's coin-filled lair. She was a blonde siren with nipples erect enough to hang your coat on - and her design owed more to animator Gary Goldman's Playboy magazine collection than to the chaste Cinderellas and Snow Whites of Disney. In a medium where the primary customers were 12- to 18-year-old boys, she was perfect. Even still, getting to that final screen was no mean feat. It involved spending a lot of coins, almost much treasure as Singe himself guarded.

Part of the attraction of *Dragon's Lair* was that it was as incredible to watch as it was to play. Arcade managers were swamped by demand. The game lured thousands back into the coin-op temples. Some managers took the initiative and presented *Dragon's Lair* as if was a movie: red carpets, chrome stanchions and velour ropes led players up to the machine. Others, including the manager of Captain Video's arcade in Los Angeles, fitted the cabinet with overhead monitors so non-players could watch someone else try their luck. Audiences swelled to such numbers that a few arcades decided to install bleachers for the crowds to sit on. The phenomenon wasn't limited to Los Angeles, either. The New York Post guided readers to the machine installed in Penn Station's arcade, warning them to expect a long wait in line to see what all the fuss was about. In a Boise, Idaho arcade there were reports of patrons taping $5 bills to the machine to reserve their places. "The cozy relationship between Hollywood and videogames has moved a step closer to marriage," wrote veteran industry watcher Aljean Harmetz in The New York Times.

Dragon's Lair posed a huge question: what if videogames could tell stories just as well as cinema? The previous year Spielberg had praised the Atari VCS cartridge of *Raiders of the Lost Ark* with the words "Gee, Howard, it's just like a movie". *Dragon's Lair* was something else. Not just similar to a movie but an actual movie that had been turned into a game. It was an incredible milestone.

* * *

Don Bluth was sitting in the Mikado restaurant on Riverside Drive in North Hollywood when he first realised how pissed off his former employers were. It was the late summer of 1983, a few weeks after *Dragon's Lair* had become a phenomenal success, and Bluth and Gary Goldman had taken their new publicist out to dinner. While the two animators perused the starters menu, the publicist excused herself and headed over to another table. She'd spotted a group of Disney marketing executives dining on the other side of the restaurant and, being a former Disney employee herself, went over to say hello. Little did she realise that she was crossing into hostile territory.

Ten minutes later she scurried back to her seat and took a deep breath, half-serious, half-laughing: "Oh boy, are they mad. They thought they killed you on *The Secret of N.I.M.H.* and now you come out with a videogame and they have no way to stop you because they're not even in that business."

It was, for both Bluth and Goldman, proof of something they'd suspected for a very long time: their sole competitor, the powerful studio that resided in Burbank, had been intent on their destruction ever since they had the temerity to leave. *Dragon's Lair* was one in the eye for Disney, a shot across the bows to the studio. It was also a wake-up call to the entire movie business that videogames were evolving fast.

In the weeks that followed *Dragon's Lair*'s release, Bluth couldn't help taking the odd pot-shot at his former employers. "If Walt Disney was alive today he would probably be in the forefront of the videogame animation business," he told reporters. "Walt was always astute, he always saw opportunities for new things. He saw the value of TV very early. He saw the importance of theme parks. And he'd be right in the front of making animated games and interactive movies today." It was no wonder the Disney marketing suits were furious.

Bluth was gloating. And, in truth, he had every right to. *Dragon's Lair* was a juggernaut. In its first five weeks of release the game generated 7,300 orders at $4,000 per cabinet. By the year's end, Cinematronics had sold 8,000 units totalling around $32 million in sales. In arcade terms, it was an enormous hit. And it far out-grossed the estimated $14 million box office disappointment that was *The Secret of N.I.M.H..* "I couldn't get those kids excited about a little lady mouse," Bluth noted with just a tinge of sadness, "but I sure can get them to come and see this stuff." *Dragon's Lair* became Don Bluth Productions' first smash success, the happy ending that *N.I.M.H.* had failed to give their story. Fortune had finally favoured them.

"That phone call from Rick Dyer was some kind of switch in destiny," says Bluth. "It was something we had no control over. It just happened out of the blue. You can call it luck, you can call it destiny, or whatever it is. If it hadn't been for that call we would probably have given up. What *Dragon's Lair* did for us was make us say, 'Hey, wait a minute, this is a success. Your first movie wasn't, but this is.' The twenty minutes of animation that was in *Dragon's Lair* was so much easier to build than *The Secret of N.I.M.H.* Our self-confidence was restored again. We had been validated as animators by having that successful game."

Soft-spoken Bluth certainly wasn't shy about stamping his authority on both industries. *Dragon's Lair* was, he said, *The Jazz Singer* of the coming Hollywood-videogame convergence. "Classical animation is going to provide the bridge between the arcade and Hollywood," he said. There would be "no more computer-generated dots and sticks. All the current machines will be obsolete". He was also keen to claim videogames for Hollywood: "We're in the visuals market. If the interactives end up becoming the most important part of the electronic game business, then I think they belong in the Hollywood arena, not solely in the engineer's lap where they've existed in the past."

It was ironic that the man who had set out to take Disney back to its roots had instead inadvertently ended up pioneering a new kind of gaming and cinema. No one was quite sure what to call the result. Were they "mini-movies", "participatory movies" or just "animated games"? Whatever they were, in 1983 they looked like they'd strayed onto the movie industry's turf. Even trade paper The Hollywood Reporter picked up the story and ran a piece on it, one that inevitably emphasised the financial aspect: "*Dragon's Lair* is the follow up to the Don Bluth film *The Secret of N.I.M.H.*, which did about $14 million at the box office. In less than one month Bluth has realised nearly four times the estimated rentals of *N.I.M.H.* over the last year. And *N.I.M.H.* has yet to break even."

For many, Bluth's involvement was pivotal and it's telling that as *Dragon's Lair* fever gripped America it was the animator's story - his quitting Disney, his failure with *N.I.M.H.* and his comeback success with a movie-like videogame - that captured journalists' attention. Rather unfairly, Dyer's contribution became something of a footnote.

The laserdisc games that followed *Dragon's Lair* continued to blur the boundary between gaming and cinema. Sega's *Astron Belt*, the coin-op that Dyer had worried about when he first met Bluth, was one of the first. It arrived in the US, after its Japanese outing, licensed by Bally. It was soon followed by Mystlar/Gottlieb's coin-ops *M.A.C.H. 3* and *Us Vs. Them*. All three games parted with the animation of *Dragon's Lair* in favour of using real-life footage of actors, vehicles and backdrops. Stern Electronics' *Cliff Hanger* found a middle ground; its movie footage was recycled straight from Japanese anime series *Lupin III*.

That autumn *Firefox,* an Atari laserdisc coin-op based on the Warner Bros. Clint Eastwood thriller about a stolen fighter jet, proved the point perfectly. Players watched an attract mode that featured dramatic clips from the film. Then they flew their fighter jet over Greenland's ice fields and through mountain valleys in backdrops that were based on assets created for the movie by Hollywood special-effects company Apogee. Eastwood himself recorded additional dialogue especially for the game and Atari's engineers found themselves competing for studio time with Hollywood studio productions.

Warner weren't the only movie company interested in pursuing such crossovers. Universal shot back with a rather lame animated *Dragon's Lair* clone called *Super Don Quix-ote*. Paramount was particularly keen, giving videogame subsidiary Sega access to their film library to search for suitable images for future live-action laserdisc games - although, the resources of a major motion picture company weren't always enough. "We'll never find exactly what we want," complained Sega's chairman David Rosen somewhat peevishly, "so we'll also have to go out and shoot a stock car race for a race game".

Meanwhile, Steven Spielberg's interest was piqued by an ill-fated laserdisc coin-op called *Freedom Fighter,* which used footage from the Japanese anime *Galaxy Express 999*. "*Freedom Fighter* wasn't *Dragon's Lair,* which was a game of memorisation," recalls David Riordan, one of the game's designers. "We actually figured out how to layer these scenes so that if you were like shooting robots in a window or something like that you could put up different sequences. It was actually a real game but in video." Spielberg was particularly interested in pursuing the laserdisc concept and was given one of the 400 or so *Freedom Fighter* cabinets that were produced by its makers.

Word among arcade industry experts was that this new cinematic realism - whether live action footage or animation - was the future of gaming. The new leaders in the field obviously weren't going to argue with that. Bluth's business partner Gary Goldman described *Dragon's Lair* as a "window on the future". It was, he claimed grandly, "a means by which gamers could play movies. Down the road, I think we'll see more film companies approach videogames via their own film productions. Rather than take the character from a film and create the game around it, they will take the movie and at the same time produce a game based on the actual live-action or animation from the film."

Yet, like Dirk's troubled quest, there were traps and disappointments lying in wait. The first murmurings of dissent were heard in the arcades themselves. *Dragon's Lair*'s incredible popularity proved to be little more than a flash in the pan. Within a matter of a few months, both gamers and arcade managers had begun to shun the expensive machines.

Part of the problem was technological: the industrial laserdisc players used inside the cabinets weren't fit for purpose and would frequently malfunction resulting in extended periods of downtime. The cabinets garnered a notorious reputation for being expensive and unreliable and Cinematronics' repairs team wasn't ready to cope with such widespread failures. The issue was compounded by the fact that arcade machines are frequently moved around venues. Unlike conventional coin-ops, the laserdisc machines were bulkier and yet less durable. The laser heads needed to be locked in place before being moved, advice that was largely ignored by the crews that transported the units.

It was an industry-wide problem. "These guys were dropping these things off the back of trucks because they were used to doing that with coin-ops with a motherboard," recalls Riordan. "The arcade owners would call the company and say that it had stopped working. When you went and opened up the cabinet to see what was wrong, the laser was just sitting there in shambles. You'd be like, 'What happened?' They'd say, 'Oh the guy dropped it off the other day...' They meant it literally!"

A simultaneous shortage of laserdisc units meant that repairs were slow. According to one contemporary report: "Until the fever for videodisc games broke out the biggest single order for laserdisc players probably was 10,000 units bought by General Motors from Pioneer Video in the late 1970s. Now, game manufacturers - some small enough to fit into General Motors' glove compartment - are beseeching Pioneer and a handful of other player manufacturers for 1,000 or more units a day." It left many *Dragon's Lair* machines out of action for long periods, frustrating for players and those arcade owners wanting to claw back their expensive $4,000 investments.

Players of the laserdisc games, however, knew that the biggest issue wasn't one of hardware. It was a gameplay flaw. You only needed to drop a few dollars into *Dragon's Lair* to appreciate just how little freedom the game offered you. Its interactivity was fundamentally limited - a case of making a right/wrong, right/left, up/down, fight/flight response to each screen. Dirk wasn't really your avatar and you weren't really in control of him. Rather your input on the joystick and buttons decided whether or not the animated scene would keep playing. Hit the right combination and you'd see Dirk slash, dodge or dash his way to safety. Get it wrong and you'd see a clip of his death.

It was frustrating and it was only made worse by the second or two of temporary "black out" that sometimes occurred between scenes. This was because the laserdisc, spinning at 1,800rpm inside the cabinet, sometimes struggled to find the next section of footage to be played from the 54,000 picture frames it contained. The interruption only underlined the lack of control you had over this supposedly interactive movie.

In retrospect, *Dragon's Lair* was much like being in charge of a railroad switch on an electric train set. The train would move without your input; when it reached a set of points you could send it one way or another or do nothing. During most of its circuit, however, you simply had to sit and watch it run around the rails. Such passivity wasn't what videogaming was about. Increased realism had sacrificed player agency and the disappointment was keenly felt by gamers once the initial shock and awe of *Dragon's Lair*'s visuals had worn off. It was the arcade equivalent of a five-minute wonder. Yet, in those hyped-up five minutes, *Dragon's Lair* caused a media sensation that reverberated all the way into Hollywood itself.

In different circumstances, it's likely that the laserdisc craze could have attracted big name filmmaking talent. *Freedom Fighter* had promised that much and its lead designer David Riordan believes the industry was on the cusp of a revolution. "If they could have figured out how to stabilise laserdiscs in that market place, Steven [Spielberg] would have done one. I know he would have. The only reason he didn't follow up on it was because there was no way to get those boxes to hold up."

George Lucas was similarly vexed. Impressed by *Dragon's Lair* he asked Peter Langston, head of his Lucasfilm Games division to look into the laserdisc's potential as a medium for interactive storytelling in games. "The attraction to movie-makers was obvious," reckons Langston. "Here was a medium that required all their existing skills and offered a further new capability that had only been toyed with previously in movies where the theatre audience would vote towards the end to choose which final reel the projectionist would mount.

"So of course George and Steven, who were big successes, innovative by nature, and probably feeling the nipping-at-their-heels of upcoming innovators, were interested in this new, nearly-cinema medium." The biggest problem was that laserdisc manufacturers weren't mass-producing laserdisc recording tools. Frustrated by the lack of foresight, Lucasfilm abandoned their plans to make laserdisc games.

Yet, the gauntlet had been thrown down. Disney recognised it. So did Lucas and Spielberg. Overnight videogames had evolved from 8-bit sprites to possessing cinema quality animation. It was a wake-up call for many in the movie industry. They'd already seen Atari eating into their profits. Now here was a videogame company actually invading the very medium of film itself. It was a watershed moment. As Goldman puts it, "everyone remembers where they were when they first saw *Dragon's Lair*".

On paper the coin-op's brief but immense success should have made Don Bluth Productions rich. As is often the case with successful innovations, however, the cash didn't quite flow as expected. When Cinematronics returned to Chapter 11 bankruptcy shortly after the game's release they were holding around $12 million in shared profits. A protracted four-and-a-half year legal battle ensued and the release of *Dragon's Lair II: Timewarp* was delayed until 1991. In the meantime, Bluth's team worked on the similar, sci-fi themed *Space Ace* laserdisc coin-op released in 1984. There was even a short-lived *Dragon's Lair* Saturday morning TV cartoon and - quelle surprise - unrealised plans for a movie.

However, *Dragon's Lair* did make Rick Dyer wealthy and in the wake of its success he moved into a mansion in Leucadia, north San Diego County, with a black-bottomed swimming pool, live-in servants and thirteen acres of land. He drove a low-slung Lotus Esprit with the license plate read SPY-1. "He always described himself as a 30-year-old millionaire," recalls Bill Van Workum who joined RDI as a design engineer around the time of *Space Ace*. "Unfortunately, it was one of those cases where he made a lot of money quickly and spent a lot of money too. So it didn't last." Most of Dyer's fortune was blown in an ill-fated attempt to launch a home laserdisc console, the RDI Halcyon in 1985.

For Bluth the success of *Dragon's Lair* meant he could keep the animation staff in their jobs, and eventually make another movie. It wasn't long before the phone was ringing again, this time with an offer from Steven Spielberg to work on what would become the animated feature *An American Tail.* It was the first of 11 animated features Bluth would direct over the next two decades. Despite his success in the videogame world he was eager to get back to Hollywood. He had been away long enough.

Today *Dragon's Lair* stands in the Smithsonian Museum, preserved for posterity alongside *Pong* and *Pac-Man* as a landmark in the evolution of the videogame. It's also something more, a videogame that has a place in the history of cinema too. It's that switchback between the two mediums that allowed the coin-op to transcend its novelty value and the limitations of its interface. It has been ported to dozens of different platforms from the Commodore 64 to the Sega CD and, most recently, the iPhone and iPad.

Dragon's Lair was the first true attempt to take cinema-quality visuals into the videogame sphere. Its phenomenal, if brief, success proved that consumers wanted interactive experiences that looked like movies. Over the next few years, one man would try to deliver that. He would also take gaming into the boardrooms of every studio from Paramount to Disney to New Line.

CHAPTER 3

Welcome to Siliwood

"Hollywood at that point could care less. They saw games back then the way you or I would look at a Speak & Spell or some LeapFrog learning product for tykes today: 'That's nice. We make movies. Kiss our ass.'"

Ken Melville, former Axlon employee

Tom Zito was in his 20s when he ran out of adjectives. A reporter on the Washington Post, he'd carved a niche for himself as one of the paper's bright young things. He joined in 1966, on the same day as Carl Bernstein. They had both applied to be the paper's first rock critic, but it was Zito who got the job.

He spent his time watching The Rolling Stones in concert, writing Elvis's obituary and hanging out with Captain Beefheart. Too much rock 'n' roll would eventually leave him partially deaf. Bernstein, meanwhile, began as the paper's night police reporter. He teamed up with Bob Woodward and exposed the Watergate scandal that toppled President Richard Milhous Nixon. The jury's still out on whether Zito or Bernstein had the most fun.

One day, though, Zito woke up and couldn't face writing another review: "I'd just run out of adjectives." He became a general assignment reporter since even he knew that there was more to life than rock music. The world was a-changing; you only had to look at Silicon Valley to see that. The two Steves - Jobs and Wozniak had launched Apple; a young nerd called Bill Gates was doing great things at Microsoft; and Nolan Bushnell, the man behind Atari, had some skin back in the game with a new company called Axlon. Heading to Silicon Valley in 1978, Zito was excited and intrigued by the brave new world that was being built by engineers and venture capitalists. He met Bushnell, the King of *Pong*, and wrote a profile of him for the New Yorker. He also started work on an unfinished book about the videogame industry. While he was researching it, Bushnell offered him a job in Sunnyvale.

If Atari showed what happened when the inmates took over the asylum, Bushnell's start-up Axlon was like a high-tech toy factory where the kids were in charge of research and development. Play was taken seriously: there was a scary project called Tech Force which involved toy robots that could be controlled via a signal broadcast on kids' TV; there were radio-controlled cars that let you spy on people; stink bombs potent enough to make you cry; and crazy furry things that stuck to walls and did who knew what.

Zito, who was hired as Axlon's vice-president of marketing, took two products to retail: a Hasbro/PlaySkool baby monitor that undercut its Fisher Price rival and sold millions; and a talking teddy called A.G. Bear that ran second place to World of Wonder's Teddy Ruxpin. Despite knowing nothing about marketing, the former reporter quickly won the praise of his new boss. "I liked him," says Bushnell. "Tom was resourceful. He had a good market sense for various things. When you're doing things that are new, resourcefulness is very important. Tom generally had a store of that and could lay his hands on people and things at the right time at the right place. He was an excellent hustler."

Zito might have continued making early learning toys if it weren't for a trip home to New York for Thanksgiving in 1985. Stopping to buy some rolls of film at Willoughby's, a camera shop on 5th Avenue, he noticed something unusual. In a corner of the shop a throng of excited kids were shouting and laughing around a TV set. With his journalist spider-sense tingling, Zito went over and looked over their shoulders. The kids were playing a videogame console, the just-released Nintendo Entertainment System (NES). "When I got back to California I told Nolan about this incredible frenzy I'd seen. I told him if anyone needed to get back into the game business it was him."

The arrival of the NES console pulled the US videogame industry out of its slump in the wake of the 1983/1984 crash. Games were cool again. Within 12 months of its 1985 launch the console was in 1.9 million American homes. By 1988 Nintendo was selling $1.7 billion worth of games, hardware and related licensed merchandise a year in the US. The 8-bit console's titles quickly began to invade American pop culture. Mario, the moustachioed Italian plumber became the new Mickey Mouse thanks to scrolling-platform game *Super Mario Bros*. The videogame market, on life support since Atari imploded, was back in rude health. Bushnell wanted back in.

According to Ken Melville, a former Axlon employee, the aim was to create a "Nintendo Killer" that would smash the Japanese company's grip on the US market. "Nintendo was the god of the universe in 1986," he remembers. "Nobody could touch it. So Axlon hired me and some top game designers to design hardware and software that would use actual video to beat out the crappy

8-bit graphics in the Nintendo engine. And we did." Among the team were Steve Russell, creator of *Spacewar!*; David Crane, co-founder of Activision; Rob Fulop, a former Atari and Imagic programmer; and former Lucasfilm Games programmer Charlie Kellner who'd worked with Melville on the *Freedom Fighter* laserdisc coin-op and was an expert on video codecs.

What could possibly rout Nintendo's cute Disney-esque charm? The answer, Bushnell believed, was a console so powerful it would be able to take videogame visuals to the next level. *Dragon's Lair* had proved that there was a market for videogames that were indistinguishable from movies. What Bushnell planned was essentially *Dragon's Lair* Mark II, a home console that would be able interweave 8-bit sprites and live-action backgrounds. He called the project NEMO (reputedly code for Never Ever Mention Outside).

Bushnell believed there were two ways of adapting the technology for home use. The NEMO console could be hooked up to the cable network and could use footage streamed in real-time as the basis for its games. Or the footage for the game could be recorded onto VHS cassette tapes (saving on expensive ROM cartridges) that NEMO would play like a VCR. His plan was to build a console and a launch line up of ten games that would all be story-based. At least half, if not two-thirds, of them would be animated cartoons much like Don Bluth's coin-op, since editing cartoons for an interactive game was much easier than editing live-action.

What Bushnell had seen in *Dragon's Lair* was a game with a story that offered a cinematic experience. It was something that he hoped to replicate in consumers' living rooms with NEMO. "I liked the idea that you could play a narrative," he says. "If you were pulling it off a cable channel, everybody could sit down at 10 o'clock on a Friday night and start playing. I saw two different marketplaces: one broadcast on a cable channel where at T minus zero everyone would play the same game; the other that you could play later on videocassette." It offered a shift towards the Hollywood exhibition mode: a live premiere on cable TV, followed by an ancillary sales market on VHS where players could replay the game at a time of their choosing.

Zito, a big movie buff, immediately grasped the significance of the project. He'd been president of the Georgetown University film society. He'd attended NYU Film School, where he'd studied in Martin Scorsese's cinematography classes. What he saw in NEMO was the future not just of games and movies but also of America's most popular mass entertainment medium: television. "What I truly believed was that interactive television could be something akin to today's casual gaming," he says. "At the time I really believed that it could be something very, very big." Axlon wasn't just making another games console. It was trying to redefine the gaming market itself. "The direction was to try and go after family entertainment - essentially TV viewers," says Zito's colleague Jim Riley.

Although Bushnell was against the idea, his young protégé lobbied hard for NEMO to have a Hollywood connection during its development between 1986 and 1989. "When I hired Zito to manage the project he was really a big proponent of doing blockbuster titles," Bushnell says. "He loved to wine and dine with the glitterati. But I felt that we should stick to pretty simple games on which you could really keep the budget low. My theory was that you can't even shake hands with anybody in Hollywood without it costing you half a million dollars. So I stayed away from it entirely."

Bushnell bore the scars of Atari. He'd seen how Warner's executives had been seduced by Hollywood and how it had helped derail his former company. He vowed he wouldn't let that happen to Axlon. Zito, though, was convinced that building bridges with Hollywood was a necessary evil. If you were shooting live-action footage, it wasn't much of a leap to tie these NEMO games in with Hollywood movies. It also meant that videogames could cash in on the allure of celebrity and feature movie stars. Forget the stick-man Harrison Ford in the *Raiders of the Lost Ark* Atari VCS game. How about seeing the real Harrison Ford on-screen instead?

Zito had witnessed the power of movie stardom early on. As a young reporter at the Washington Post, he'd watched from the sidelines as the cast and crew of Alan J. Pakula's movie *All the President's Men* arrived to shoot in the newsroom. Half the paper's veteran reporters embarrassed themselves trying to impress Robert Redford and Dustin Hoffman, who were playing Watergate twins Woodward and Bernstein. And when a group of high school kids touring the office saw Redford, they went bat shit crazy, cameras clicking and hormonal hysteria building to fever pitch. "Here's the real Bob Woodward," a reporter told the baying mob, "Don't you want a picture of him?" "No," they replied.

If it hadn't been for a cash shortage, Bushnell might have got his way. But with no money to finance a console launch, Axlon was forced to find an investor. Hasbro, who had been impressed by the company's work on the PlaySkool baby monitor, stepped up. Concerned by the way Nintendo was sucking dollars out of the toy market, Hasbro was keen to get into the videogame business too. They wanted to develop a console that would stand out and NEMO's groundbreaking use of live-action footage seemed perfect. Bushnell's visionary business plan turned their heads: he was predicting the rise of multiplayer gaming, the coming dominance of cable TV and a new kind of interactive entertainment. Hasbro believed they were getting in on the ground-floor of something extremely exciting.

With the toy company onboard, the NEMO project shifted from Axlon to a new company Isix, a Hasbro subsidiary. Barry Alperin, a former New York lawyer, was in charge of the project with Zito as his right-hand man. Bushnell stayed on as an advisor. No longer under Bushnell's thumb, Zito began to push his vision: this new form of interactive TV was perfect for Hollywood. Hasbro were more than receptive to that idea. They already dealt with the studios' licensing departments and a sizeable chunk of their business involved making toys based on movies. If you had a videogame console that could display live actors on-screen, tackling licensed movie properties seemed logical. After all, these games didn't feature computer-generated characters or objects. What you saw and interacted with was 'full motion video' (FMV), pre-recorded TV quality video footage.

Encouraged by Hasbro's receptiveness, Zito began to set up meetings in LA. Yet one question still remained: how would a game based on live-action footage actually work? No one had ever tackled anything like that before. Videogames were mostly either text adventures or shoot 'em ups. The idea of making a game with a cinematic narrative was a puzzle. Solving it would take Zito and his team from environmental theatre in LA to the board rooms of the major motion picture studios.

* * *

The American Legion Post 43 stands at 2035 North Highland Avenue in Hollywood. It's not an easy place to miss. For a start it has a five-ton Howitzer artillery piece parked on the front steps. Then there's the building itself, a solid Art Deco bunker in the Egyptian Revival style adorned with the Stars and Stripes. If Cleopatra and General Patton had been an item, this would have made a decent love nest.

The celebrated building is no stranger to celebrity, either. Over the years, the distinctive bunker has played host to Hollywood talent like Bob Hope and Errol Flynn. But between 1983 and 1994 it was better known to theatregoers as Il Vittoriale - the central location for *Tamara*, a unique play about politics and scandal in '20s Italy. Unlike most conventional theatre, *Tamara* had a brilliant selling point. Staged in the American Legion building, the play asked its audience to follow the actors as they moved from room to room. You didn't simply sit and watch the drama that unfolds as Polish artist Tamara de Lempicka is seduced by Italian poet Gabriele d'Annunzio, you became part of it.

With as many as nine parallels stories running in 13 different rooms over three floors, the audience had to make choices: would you follow mysterious chauffeur Mario? Or were you intrigued by the arch seducer D'Annunzio? Did you want to know the story behind the house's pretty maid, or was the fascist policeman a more interesting character? Depending on what you chose and where you went, you might witness a suicide on the first floor but miss a lesbian tryst that was happening downstairs in the scullery.

Moses Znaimer, the Canadian TV producer who bankrolled the long-running $550,000 production, liked to describe it as "a living movie". Reviewers compared it to a cross between *Dynasty* and Disneyland. The New York Times suggested it was like watching "a movie in which each theatregoer does the editing without ever seeing the rushes".

For the NEMO team, *Tamara* was more than just a play. It was also the blueprint for the kind of movie-videogame they were grappling with. Over the course of a weekend in 1985, Axlon employees Rob Fulop and Jim Riley watched three performances, hoping to piece together its multi-strand plot by repeat attendance. At around $80 a ticket it wasn't cheap, yet the price was worth paying. "It was the first design model that made sense," recalls Fulop. "We decided you could let the user be the camera, just lock a camera down into a room and let people walk in and out of the scene." For Riley, who'd previously worked with laserdisc technology at MCA, the play mirrored the kind of interactive experiences he'd been experimenting with.

Tamara became the basis for a five-minute demo of NEMO's live-action video capabilities called *Scene of the Crime*, co-created by Fulop and Riley. Styled as an Agatha Christie-style whodunit, the demo was a radical re-imagining of what a videogame could be. Instead of moving 8-bit pixels around a screen you were being asked to drive a narrative, each choice leading you to another piece of filmed footage featuring real-life actors. Just as *Tamara* had offered different perspectives on the story, so *Scene of the Crime* jumped between characters and points of view as the player tried to solve the mystery by watching and interacting with video clips.

As far as Hasbro's executives were concerned, they were witnessing the evolution of the industry Atari had started. The console, attached to a VCR that it used to load the data from VHS tapes, looked nothing like the Nintendo NES. And neither did the game it played. "The immediate assumption was that this was a huge leap in videogames," recalls Fulop. "They were like, 'Wow, just imagine videogames with live footage.'" After watching *Scene of the Crime*'s rather adult whodunit plot unfold, Hasbro's suits offered just one instruction: "This is great. Now go and make it for kids". Zito and his team were about to become filmmakers. It was a huge step.

Three months later on a soundstage at GMT Studios in Culver City, the NEMO team watched as a pretty blonde in a lace teddy arranged her hair in a bathroom mirror. As the cameras rolled three monstrously misshapen Quasimodos, kitted out in black boiler suits and pantyhose face masks, limped and shuffled towards her. One of them brandished a strange contraption that looked like a cross between a cattle prod and an oversized dildo. They grab her. She screams. And the machine sucks the blood out of her neck. Director Jim Riley shouts "Cut!" and the crew try not to giggle at the silliness of it all. Somewhere in a cemetery in Golders Green in London, Bram Stoker's corpse turns in its grave.

Night Trap was the first movie-game designed for the NEMO system. Starring actress Dana Plato, famous from hit TV comedy *Diff'rent Strokes*, its live-action footage was shot over three weeks at a privately-owned studio in Culver City, south west of Hollywood. Although it was a videogame, it was essentially a film production: a B-movie horror in which a bunch of pretty young things are picked off by modern day Draculas while spending the weekend in the in the vampire equivalent of a wine distillery.

Investigating the house is Kelli (Plato), an undercover law enforcement agent who's tagged along with the girls. In *Night Trap* the player's job is to act as her off-site back-up, watching the action via the live feeds from surveillance cameras inside the house. Like a shopping mall security guard sitting in front of a bank of monitors, you can switch between viewpoints; and, by hijacking the vampire's security system, you can also trap and capture their black-clad assistants as they try to kill the girls one-by-one.

Riffing on cheesy '80s horror, the screenplay by future Sports Illustrated Group editor Terry McDonell revels in its own ridiculousness. You spend most of the game watching the girls gossip, bicker and strip down to their underwear, while occasionally hitting a button to trap the creatures as they creep around the house. It's not supposed to be taken seriously: press the right button at the right time and you can bash the monsters with sliding bookcases or catapult them out of windows thanks to spring-loaded beds. The funniest bit is when you send them tumbling down a staircase that turns into a slide and deposits them through a hole in the floor. It's pure slapstick.

Yet, at a time when Nintendo fans were helping moustachioed plumber Mario navigate the primary colours of the Mushroom Kingdom and video arcades were filled with the tinkling melody of Magical Sound Shower from the *OutRun* coin-op, *Night Trap* was an incredible departure. This was a movie you could play, a game that told a cinematic narrative complete with actors, close ups, spoken dialogue and sets. No one had ever made a game - or a movie - like it.

What *Night Trap* seemed to promise was an interactive experience where instead of simply passively watching a movie, players would shape its course themselves. Just as *Tamara* asked the audience to edit their own story together out of a series of parallel streaming narratives happening simultaneously, *Night Trap* wanted the player to choose what they saw. Keep watching the living room feed and you might see the house's villainous owners (Jon R. Kamel and Molly Starr) doing some pantomime scheming. But if you did, you might miss the party scene that was going on upstairs, or the chance to catch a couple of creatures limping through the kitchen.

If *Night Trap* had been a movie, it would have been forgettable straight-to-video junk. But as a videogame - a medium in which cinematic storytelling had previously seemed impossible - it was a landmark. Just as text adventures had blurred the boundary between novels and interactivity, *Night Trap* did the same to the line dividing movies from games. Regardless of how it played - and as we'll see, it played very badly - as a concept it was truly breathtaking.

Night Trap was also the birth of what Zito would come to call "Siliwood". Flying from Silicon Valley to Hollywood, the NEMO team were brokering a new kind of convergence. It was a meeting between two industries quite distinct from the movie licensing deals of the Atari VCS era and Howard Scott Warshaw's trip to Universal. Now, games creators were dipping a toe into the world of film production, getting to grips with things like actors, set design, and continuity.

Night Trap's credits said it all. Although it wasn't A-list, the crew was dotted with established Hollywood talent. The cinematographer was Don Burgess, who'd go on to shoot the Oscar-winning *Forrest Gump*, as well as *Spider-Man* and *The Polar Express*. The line producer Donald Klune, whose résumé included *The Man From U.N.C.L.E.* and *Hang 'em High*. The NEMO programmers were rubbing shoulders with people from a completely different industry.

For the actors, the production was equally unusual. Handed an enormous script, the young, largely inexperienced cast were asked to grapple with something no aspiring Hollywood player had ever been involved with before - an interactive narrative. "It was a 250-page script," recalls Deke Anderson, who met a grisly end in the game as one of Kelli's law enforcement colleagues. "I mean 250 pages! Holy cow!"

Few among the cast really understood what they were making. Scenes were shot multiple times with multiple outcomes. One set-up might have actress Debra Parks escaping from her bathroom encounter with the vampires' assistants. The next would have a different slant as the teddy-clad scream queen was captured and blood-sucked because the player failed to rescue her. It was like shooting several different versions of the same story simultaneously. "It really didn't feel like shooting a film," recalls actor Andras Jones, who played one of the vampires. "It felt like being part of an experiment. We knew that it was something that we were unlikely to see for a while and when we did, it would show up in a completely new format. Most films are shot out of sequence but there was even less cohesiveness to what we were doing. It seemed very different."

The actors weren't the only ones being asked to step outside their comfort zones. The programmers were equally challenged as they tried to ensure that they shot enough coverage to cover all the different paths this interactive, branching storyline might take. Continuity and camera lenses were suddenly more important than sprites, control interfaces or processor speeds. Keeping track of the 250-page script - and the eventual editing of the footage to use within the game itself - was a tremendous headache. "I personally didn't think I was making a game anymore," says Fulop, *Night Trap*'s co-creator. "When you make a game you can adjust it as you make it. You're tweaking stuff, moving graphics around. With a movie you can't do that. Once you've shot it, you've got what you've got. As a game designer you had no control once the footage was shot."

After putting the game together, it was obvious that there was one fatal flaw in using "full motion video". The price of using of "real" images was a loss of interactivity. Players may have been looking at real actors but they couldn't control any of them in a traditional sense. You didn't have an avatar to move around the screen. Instead you were just a spectator with limited control. Tap the right button at the right moment and you'd get to watch a different video clip.

This was the curse of *Dragon's Lair* all over again: a game that looked amazing but played badly. Yet despite the downside in terms of interactivity, there was something incredibly seductive about the merger of movies and games. There was an immediacy that came from using live action footage, an immediacy of emotional response that resulted from using real people instead of blocky sprites. For Zito that was the whole point. "There are certain human, gut-reactions that can only be triggered by seeing another human," he'd tell Next Generation magazine several years later. "Real people produce real reactions. And that's what we're after. For example, I could never really care enough about Princess Zelda to spend the 40 hours I needed to spend battling through the forest in order to rescue her."

He was right. When Dana Plato turns straight to camera and talks to you in *Night Trap* there is a frisson of excitement and intimacy that goes far beyond anything that the 'toons in *Dragon's Lair* achieved. Breaking the fourth wall to set up a dialogue between actor and player, FMV draws you into the story much in the same way as *Tamara*'s actors encouraged the audience to become active participants. The use of real actors heightens the tension and works particularly well in the context of *Night Trap*'s horror story. Would we care about Lisa's murder in the bathroom if the screaming blonde was an 8-bit sprite instead of a real actor? Absolutely not.

Seeing real actors on-screen was also something many non-gamers felt comfortable with. According to Riley, it was often the adults who brought children to Hasbro play tests who were most impressed by NEMO. "The parents would bring in their kids to play the games and then go snack on refreshments," he recalls. "But the minute the adults saw real images on the monitors, they'd walk over. We watched fathers dragging the controllers out of the hands of their sons! They were amazed because this wasn't a cartoon, it was TV. They'd say: 'OK, I get it, I can do this - TV is my world. Wow! I can interact with it!'"

This was the revolution that Zito had envisioned early on, a redefinition of television itself for a mass audience of casual gamers. "We were trying to change the definition of a videogame," he says. "[We thought that] if you give people what they're most used to, namely television, and make it interactive you've opened up a much bigger opportunity. [But] that may have been unfounded. In other words it may be that when people watch

TV they don't want to interact with it. They just want to sit on the couch and become mindless."

From Hasbro's perspective, the concept was certainly worth further development although there were already concerns. "We knew it was flawed and we were disappointed by the play experience that was generated by the project," says Barry Alperin, who headed up the project for the toymaker. But since Hasbro had already sunk millions into NEMO's development - setting up an R&D lab in California and flying out to Taiwan to fabricate the chip-sets needed to power the console - the decision was taken to keep on going. The hope was that the problems could be ironed out. Renting sound stages, setting up film crews and hiring actors clearly didn't come cheap. *Night Trap*'s production costs came to $1 million. Although Hasbro was rolling in profits - thanks largely to the dynamic leadership of then chief executive Stephen Hassenfeld - the toy company had its limits. If NEMO was going to continue, they decided, they needed to find a production partner in Hollywood who would be willing to finance future shoots, or a licensor who would let the programmers use footage from an existing movie or TV property.

Zito, who was convinced that NEMO was the beginning of a much bigger revolution in interactive television, was adamant about the next step: they needed to get the major motion picture studios onboard. Hasbro, haemorrhaging cash, was only too happy to agree. NEMO - by now dubbed the Hasbro Control-Vision - was going to Hollywood. But like a naïve, young starlet hoping to be in pictures, NEMO's wide-eyed dreams of fame and fortune would be shattered on the casting couch.

* * *

If you were to compile a list of people in Hollywood who were excited about the advent of full motion video in the mid-1980s, Jane Fonda probably wouldn't be near the top of it. In fact she probably wouldn't even be on it at all. Yet in 1986, she was one of the few people who got what Zito and Hasbro were trying to do.

NEMO's arrival in Hollywood wasn't quite the success that the team had hoped. Hasbro's clout opened doors at all the major studios, many of which already had business relationships with the toy company. Zito talked to everyone from Disney to Viacom. There were meetings with Warner Bros. and The Ladd Company about using the *Police Academy* series as the basis for a game; Orion Pictures were approached about *RoboCop*; New Line were interested in licensing a *Nightmare on Elm Street* game; former Monkee Michael Nesmith was sounded out about doing a series of comedy shorts for the console.

Last, but by no means least, was Jane Fonda. The queen of the '80s VHS exercise tape held a day-long meeting with the NEMO team. Out of everyone the Hasbro developers spoke with, she was the most enthusiastic and could instantly see the appeal of an interactive fitness workout that could be changed on a daily basis instead of following the same old pattern.

"Doing an interactive workout video was a no-brainer," says Fulop. "The thinking was here was Jane Fonda, she's already making the workout videos anyway so she's got the whole production set-up all ready. We'd just go and shoot extra footage." Fonda was astute enough to see that this could be a money-spinner, though, and wasn't about to let a bunch of Silicon Valley geeks waltz into her fitness productions without her pound of flesh. "She thought it was a terrific idea," says Alperin, "but her demands were too great. If I remember correctly, she wanted half the company to allow us to use her stuff. We didn't do it."

In all of this, Zito was having fun. Ever since his time at the Washington Post he'd appreciated the advantage of having a thick and well-thumbed address book. "Tom is one of these guys who's been around and around," says Robocop screenwriter Ed Neumeier who became a close friend after meeting him at Orion Pictures. "If you lifted up a manhole cover in Paris and there was someone down there, you could say: 'Do you know Tom Zito?' And they'd go: 'Tom Zito?! Of course I know him!'"

With Hasbro's funding behind him, Zito was making connections in the movie biz. "Tom liked schmoozing around Hollywood," says Fulop. Melville is more scathing: "All he ever really wanted to do was pose as a Hollywood producer, bang babes and hang with stars."

Zito himself disagrees. "To me it was a necessary evil," he says. "You have to remember I had spent 15 years as a journalist. I'd been around a lot of celebrities. Some people looked at it and saw glamour. I looked at it and saw nightmares." He certainly endured his fair share of hostility while hawking NEMO around the studios. "My fondest memory, and I'm being sarcastic, was meeting with [*Top Gun* producers Jerry] Bruckheimer and [Don] Simpson to talk with them about creating an interactive version of *Top Gun*. Simpson, with great affect said, 'Nobody's going to re-edit one of my fucking movies!'"

Top Gun and Fonda's exercise tapes weren't the only ideas that failed to launch. "In the beginning, Hollywood was very interested in what we were doing," says Riley. "Because we were creating games using real images, the studios believed they could offer more than just a license deal: they could make interactive products using their libraries. We were being wined and dined by all the major studios and networks. It wasn't until they realised that we couldn't just re-edit their existing content that they lost interest."

Among the projects that the NEMO team tried to get off the ground was a *Star Trek* game that was going to recycle footage from the original Paramount TV show and let players take charge of the USS Enterprise. To make the game work, though, the NEMO team needed to shoot additional material of Kirk and Spock critiquing the player's decisions, talking straight to camera. With *Star Trek IV: The Voyage Home* going into production, Hasbro and Paramount tried to thrash out a deal.

All the NEMO team required was a half day on the set of the Enterprise bridge with actors Leonard Nimoy and William Shatner. In the end, though, it proved unworkable. "There was a big discussion over who would serve as 'director' for the few hours we would need on the set of the Enterprise," remembers Fulop. "The issue of 'Who directs Nimoy and Shatner?' came close to a deal-breaker. Obviously nobody on the NEMO team was qualified to interact with let alone direct such 'big names'. If I recall correctly, I think we ended up deciding that either Nimoy or Shatner themselves would serve as the director for our project. But then it turned out from their people that they couldn't agree on which of them would step up into the director's chair!"

It's conceivable that the issue could have been smoothed over if the back room negotiation over the deal hadn't already been floundering. "The economics made a lot of sense but the deal making was always complicated," says Fulop. "It was Hollywood and they were sharks and it was all about who gets the rights. There were big arguments between Hasbro and Paramount and a lot of lawyers just never got the deal done." However, Alperin says there weren't any big legal issues. It was simply that the concept was just too new for the studio.

Star Trek producer Ralph Winter, one of the key people involved in the movie franchise, recalls the actors' backend participation being the sticking point. "They were already feeling left out after the success of *Star Trek II: The Wrath of Khan*, and it didn't make negotiating any easier, especially for something that was so unknown. No one was willing to take a risk - and the studio wasn't willing to push. My memory is that it was interesting, we wanted to help. [We weren't] disdainful or worried about [the NEMO team] encroaching on studio territory - no one knew enough back then. We were intrigued but couldn't make the deals."

The Paramount experience was indicative of the confusion and suspicion that the NEMO team discovered at all the major studios. Miscommunication was the order of the day. "At one point we were in Silicon Valley and we had film directors, film writers, game designers, software programmers, hardware engineers all in the same room," remembers Riley. "I have never seen more confusion. It was a circus of really talented people who all operated in very different languages."

Such problems dominated the meetings with Paramount. The NEMO console's attempt to make filmed footage interactive and non-linear was such a conceptual shift that the studios, never known for being particularly ahead of the curve, struggled to grasp what it meant. NEMO was apparently offering a Copernican revolution. Yet the major studios' initial euphoria over exploiting a potential new revenue stream stalled when they realised just how complicated it was. "When we met Paramount to talk about Star Trek," recalls Riley, "the studio thought 'This is fantastic! We have this library of product, both feature films and television, and now we have a chance to turn it into this wonderful interactive thing.' We said 'We do, but you're going to have to approach it differently from the way you approach your linear material.' They couldn't understand why you couldn't just take the footage and re-cut it to make it interactive. Our response was you can, but it's not going to be very interesting."

It didn't help that the studios were apparently so snobbish about these Silicon Valley upstarts and their Hasbro backers. Toy companies were makers of ancillary products. They were plastics merchants, riding on the coattails of the real, filmmaking talent. That corrosive mentality influenced their take on the NEMO team too.

"People in Hollywood regarded us as kind of like the B-team," says Fulop. "It's like the guys who were making toys out their games; they didn't really consider them an important part of the creative process. The people who make the action figures and the dolls based on these movies don't get to go onto the set and decide what the characters should do. Nobody thought that we should either." As Fulop's colleague Melville puts it: "Hollywood looked at us the way you'd look at an industrial project. A film for a car show or a documentary on manufacturing auto upholstery".

Outside of the Hollywood bubble, there was considerably more interest. Zito flew to England to meet Stanley Kubrick who was quite taken with the idea of creating a movie-game. "He got it," says Zito. "But I think that was Stanley at his best and worst. He was an incredibly smart guy who loved technology and wanted to do everything but then when it came time to do something he was overwhelmed by the immensity of all the opportunities that were available to him. He was, more than most, the greatest example of how this would be a complete nightmare. He would go through so much preparation simply to shoot a single storyline, that if he'd tried to do one of these things, it would have been impossible." Interactive video, with its multiple, branching plot-lines, wasn't a medium suited to an auteur's perfectionism.

Meanwhile, Melville was heavily involved in two more fruitful attempts to generate interest in the NEMO system. His *Make My Video* game, featuring footage from the music video of "Rhythm of Love" by the rock band Yes, suggested it might be possible to use NEMO to showcase interactive music videos (basically an editor that let the user create their own MTV mash-up). He also started work on an FMV game called *Mad Max: Autorama* and flew down to Sydney, Australia for talks with *Mad Max* director George Miller and his producer Doug Mitchell. Both filmmakers were enthusiastic about the project.

"I wrote in Savannah Nix, Scrooloose and Gekko and everybody," recalls Melville. "The interactive script was about 200 pages long, and I had it storyboarded by George's *Mad Max* guy in Hollywood, Ed Verreaux, who's now a major production designer. It looked incredible. George got Mel [Gibson] to sign on, and we were about to get off and running in Oz on what would have been the greatest blockbuster FMV game of all time."

This time, though, the reluctance that ruined the project came from Hasbro not the studios. "Unfortunately, I got all responsible and stuff. I had cleared the *Mad Max* project with Barry Alperin and Steven Hassenfeld at Hasbro, but I thought, 'Wait, do these guys actually realise what the *Mad Max* universe is all about?' They said they did, but I double checked. Turns out most of the Hasbro execs were these old, cigar-chomping dudes in Pawtucket, Rhode Island and they never went to the movies. When they actually saw *Mad Max*, they ran screaming from the project screaming: 'There's like, guns and queers and stuff!' It was a sad ending." According to Melville, the game never got beyond pre-production although Alperin says he has no record of the *Mad Max* discussions and also takes exception at the description of Hasbro's board: "They weren't cigar-chomping old folks but rather young, aggressive individuals". Fulop, however, confirms the existence of the *Mad Mad* storyboards and still has one of the original copies.

The *Mad Max* project highlighted one of the biggest problems with the revolution that NEMO was promising. Videogames were still regarded as kids' toys and Hasbro's involvement didn't do much to dispel that misconception. Yet here they were trying to muscle in on the more adult world of cinema, where real people acted out real situations and where guns, violence and sex were key commodities. Using FMV in videogames had the potential to take them out of the world of toys and into an entirely different realm of media properties. Videogames were growing up, just like the generation that had first started playing them, and no one who wore a suit in Hollywood was quite ready to grapple with what that meant. It was an issue that would come back to haunt Zito, and *Night Trap* in particular, in the years to come.

For the most part, however, NEMO was hamstrung by the suspicion that existed between the two industries. Although the brief laserdisc arcade craze surrounding *Dragon's Lair* had pointed the way towards the use of film footage in games, there wasn't much appetite for it among the studios. They were used to seeing videogames as ancillary products, tie-in marketing promotions. NEMO was offering them a new kind of interactive filmmaking technology, but it was being presented by a toy company.

"There really was a great gulf between Hollywood and San Francisco Palo Alto," says Alperin. "The Hollywood people didn't see the coming impact of videogames. They thought movies were the best and they weren't willing to admit that this was a new form of entertainment that was going to be very important. They just didn't want to get involved. We were talking at the highest levels of studios and we couldn't get them to work with us. They had no understanding of what was going on two or three hours north of them and they thought videogames would go away and just wouldn't impact movies at all."

With hindsight, the studios were right to be wary. What NEMO offered - its vision of interactive TV or playable movie-games - was an awkward marriage of two forms. "I think initially [the studios] thought that interactive movies could be a big new revenue opportunity for them," says Zito. "When they began to think it through, they thought it was more problematic than 'solution-al'. I think they understood the notion that if you can engage an audience in a different way there's some value to that. But nobody, including us really, had figured out some way to do this in a cost effective way or in a way that proved there really was an audience for this."

The underlying problem was that the technology just wasn't watertight enough to convince the conservative studios that they had to be involved in this. The VHS tapes were slow and unreliable. The play mechanics were awkward. "With 20:20 hindsight," says Zito, "what's pretty clear to me is that we had created this oddball curiosity."

Yet NEMO was also the birth of something much bigger, an early step in an evolution that is still playing out. "Going back to NEMO is like looking at the first tools made by humans," suggests Riley, who sees today's interactive services like Google TV as a conceptual cousin of that early attempt to redefine television viewing. "If there's a full circle here, the birth of NEMO was really silly kids playing with trucks in the sandbox compared to what will probably become a real market place in the next five to 10 years."

After completing the *Night Trap* shoot, Hasbro began work on a second project *Sewer Shark*. It boasted a screenplay by Melville and had *Star Wars* visual effects supervisor John Dykstra in the director's chair. His staff from VFX house Apogee collaborated on the shoot. Filmed in Hawaii, the project racked up another couple of million dollars of expenditure for Hasbro on top of the millions that had been spent developing the NEMO console's chip sets.

While *Night Trap* had been ambitious in its attempt to copy *Tamara* by letting the user flit between simultaneous video feeds, *Sewer Shark* narrowed the scope. Narrative storytelling was still a huge part of its appeal but the full motion video element was an adjunct to what was essentially an on-rails shooting gallery. Decision-making was reduced to choosing which tunnel to fly your ship down.

Piloting a "Hole Hawg" ship through the tunnels to blast away bats, scorpions and the odd mutant "zerk", you were regularly yelled at by the actors in straight to camera footage. It was something Fulop jokingly called "In Yo' Face" feedback. It certainly enlivened the repetitive gameplay as memorable characters like Ghost (David Underwood), your aggressive, mad-as-box-of-frogs co-pilot, screamed abuse at you: "Wrong way, retard!"; "Shoot the tubes, Dogmeat!" Even more than *Night Trap* it gave videogames their first taste of what using actors to create flesh-and-blood characters could offer. Today's videogames, with their use of actors and performance capture, can be traced right back to this point in 1988.

Back in Pawtucket, Hasbro's executives were getting nervous. They'd spent around $20 million on the NEMO project and the studios had slammed the doors in their faces. In the meantime, World of Wonder's VHS-based, light gun focused console the Action Max - which was far inferior to the NEMO - had belly flopped on its release in 1987.

After Stephen Hassenfeld, Hasbro's chief executive and NEMO's biggest supporter, died unexpectedly in June 1989, enthusiasm for the console quickly waned. "It just didn't deliver the wow that we were hoping for," says Alperin. "It wasn't satisfying enough to take the next step - which was what I called the $100 million step." With projected manufacturing costs soaring and on-going software problems over the unreliable loading of data from the VHS tapes, Hasbro decided to cut their losses. "They got cold feet," says Fulop. "They took it all the way to the push the big red button stage and then... they didn't push the button."

If they had, would the videogame landscape have changed irrevocably? Possibly. Certainly Nolan Bushnell's original business plan for the NEMO console had envisioned the use of FMV as having a huge financial reward over a projected five-year lifespan. "I believe that if NEMO had seen the light of day, it would have blown everyone's socks off," he says. "It may have had a 10 to 15 year run because there were so many marketing approaches and interesting possibilities. It looked like you could easily get a $30-50 million run from any game title if you had a million NEMOs in the market place."

The impact of that kind of financial success on the Hollywood North-Siliwood convergence that Zito and Hasbro had tried to forge would have arguably been enormous. If NEMO had made it to the marketplace, it's quite possible that even the biggest snobs at the studios would have held their noses, followed the money and embraced Silicon Valley's vision of interactive entertainment much sooner than they did. If that had happened, NEMO might also have made interactive television a reality. An early prototype of the console had captured the imagination of Steve Bornstein, chairman of sport channel ESPN. Zito says ESPN were interested in the box's ability to give TV viewers interactive access to multiple camera angles and statistical information during sports events.

Yet as far as videogames went, the big problem still remained: the interactive element just wasn't interactive enough. The NEMO experiment proved that using live-action footage inevitably sacrificed interactivity, the very core of gameplay. With the NEMO project disbanded, the programmers and games designers began to look for new employment.

Watching from the sidelines in a consultancy role, Bushnell was particularly aggrieved. NEMO had originally been his baby and he blamed - and still blames - his protégé for its failure. "NEMO still kind of pisses me off," says Bushnell. "It was killed by Tom Zito's arrogance."

By refusing to keep the budget low and stay away from live-action filmmaking, Zito's vision caused the NEMO budget to balloon. Says Bushnell: "The problem was, as smart as he was - and Tom Zito's a smart man, don't let me say anything disparaging there - but he had myopia about business. To put a proposal in front of Hasbro where they would have to come up with $150 million to launch the product was, I thought, the height of foolishness. IBM wouldn't green light that project. Hasbro was a big company but it didn't have $150 million to lose. It was just so predictable and unnecessary." Bushnell may be right. Yet without Zito's vision of Siliwood, it's unlikely Hasbro would have financed the project to begin with.

After NEMO was shutdown Zito - ever the hustler - cannily snapped up the underlying rights to the games he'd worked on. He was determined that his first baby-steps into filmmaking wouldn't be lost forever. It turned out to be one of the most astute decisions of his professional life. It didn't matter that he was partially deaf from all the rock 'n' roll he'd listened to at the Washington Post; he could still hear Hollywood's siren call.

* * *

David Riordan was driving around Aspen, Colorado when he first realised the cinematic potential of videogames. Weird thing was he was actually sitting 2,000 miles away in Massachusetts at the time. Hired as a consultant by Lucasfilm in 1980, Riordan spent six months ferreting out new technology that might interest the movie company. He flew up to Canada to meet the creators of the *Tamara* stage-play. He investigated satellite and cable television. He also got a hands-on slot with MIT's *Aspen Movie Map* - a laserdisc simulation of the ski town designed by Nicholas Negroponte's now famous Architectural Machine Group (later renamed the Media Group) and funded with Department of Defense cash.

As he waggled a joystick in Massachusetts and propelled himself through on-screen Aspen, Riordan felt like he'd discovered the missing link between two mediums. "I just remember getting goose bumps. I wasn't sure that driving around Aspen was my idea of entertainment, but I realised that this could be used to make interactive movies. I had always been a games player and I always wanted to make games that were like movies. But when you looked at things like the Atari VCS, the games on it were just bits of light showing some guy swinging on a jungle vine or whatever. They weren't of interest to any of us who had come out of the film business. They were programmers' toys basically."

The Aspen experience would help shape Riordan's games career, although it would take several years before the laserdisc technology he'd seen at MIT was accessible enough to be practical for games. "When I showed George [Lucas] the tape of the machine working, he said something very smart and asked me how much equipment it required. I'd been so smitten by the experience that I really didn't think through the mainframe that was running the laserdisc. In those days a computer had its own floor, it wasn't on your desk. George just went, 'Well, I think it's going to be a while before that becomes home entertainment...!'"

"A while" actually turned out to be only a couple of years. After *Dragon's Lair* proved that these shiny laserdiscs could be immensely profitable, Riordan seized his opportunity. At Atari he worked on an aborted laserdisc project called Playland that was abandoned when the company crashed in 1983. In the aftermath he joined the *Freedom Fighter* team that approached Japanese movie studio Toei Animation about using their film archive to make videogames.

Riordan teamed up with a team of designers, some of whom would later work on NEMO. Among them was Melville who, like Riordan was a refugee from the music business. Riordan, a former musician with the six-man combo Sweet Pain, had scored a hit in the autumn of 1970 co-writing the song Green Eyed Lady for Colorado rockers Sugarloaf. Melville was a bluesman who'd opened for the likes of Cream and The Velvets as a teenager and later graduated to film soundtracks (he co-scored the soundtrack for *Twice Upon a Time*, which George Lucas executive produced). Both turned out to be well-suited to games development.

Their first game together was *Freedom Fighter*, a laserdisc coin-op game based on Toei's anime *Galaxy Express 999*. Riordan and Gary Hare's company Search & Design teamed up with Gaijin Gameco run by Melville with Bill Couturié, a future Oscar-winning documentarian and Hollywood animation director Chuck Swenson. Financing was arranged through George Lucas's lawyer.

What was groundbreaking about *Freedom Fighter* - much like *Dragon's Lair* which had just been released - was the desire to create a playable movie. The issue that raised, though, was one the NEMO team would also face: stories were supposed to be told, not played. "We had no idea what a narrative would look like if you actually asked the audience to step into that world and have some choice," recalls Riordan. Intrigued, he decided to find out. "David has that pure designer steely trap conceptual thing - he can sort of think like a programmer," says Melville. "He worked for weeks and weeks on this insane template of the entire game design of *Freedom Fighter* on an enormous piece of paper. He hauls it out and there's this semi-graphical layout of the entire game that fills half the room, scene by scene, decision point by decision point! Our jaws dropped. It was a true HOLY SHIT! moment. So we bring over the programmer Dick Houston (an Apple Fellow - one of the originals) and Dick scopes it out, all over, carefully, and says, 'Yup, I can program this.'"

Freedom Fighter went far beyond *Dragon's Lair*'s simplistic branching structure. "*Dragon's Lair* was just [Milton Bradley's handheld memory toy] Simon on rails," says Melville. "In our game, you could navigate, and shoot stuff, and strategise around in the world." The finished coin-op was impressive enough to capture the attention of Spielberg. However, as the laserdisc craze ended unexpectedly in the mid-1980s after *Dragon's Lair*'s crash-and-burn trajectory, *Freedom Fighter*'s chances of finding widespread distribution were dashed. It sank into videogame obscurity.

Disheartened, Riordan moved back to the movie biz while Melville graduated to Axlon and the NEMO project. Despite all the hoopla surrounding the first laserdisc coin-ops, their failure rate had proved insurmountable and the vision of making interactive entertainment that could compete with movies seemed like something of a pipe dream. The promise of the Aspen simulation he had seen in MIT's lab seemed to have stalled.

Ultimately, it was a very different kind of movie-game experience that would tempt Riordan back into the realm of interactive entertainment. "I was bemoaning to someone about how I thought it was a lost opportunity and they said, 'Can I show you something?' So they took me to this computer called an Amiga and loaded up Cinemaware's first game *Defender of the Crown*. I just freaked out. The first thing I saw was the classic Cinemaware thing, the princess with big breasts. I remember my wife at the time going: 'What the hell is that?' I was like 'It's a game'. She says: 'It's not like any game, I've ever seen.'"

Mrs Riordan was right. It wasn't just a game. It was a game that was pretending to be a movie and her husband knew immediately that he wanted in on the action. Unlike the laserdisc games he'd originally been interested in, Cinemaware's titles didn't use cartoon animation or full motion video. Instead they relied on the graphical power of the 16-bit Commodore Amiga home computer to create a videogame pastiche of movie genres. They had only a fraction of the visual allure of the abandoned NEMO games or the *Freedom Fighter* coin-op, yet they worked on an interactive level.

Impressed, Riordan dropped Cinemaware's owner Bob Jacob a fan letter. A day later, the phone rang. "Bob said: 'You have this really weird resumé. Come see me because we're looking for people who know how to tell a good story. We're doing movies, but we're just doing them in this videogame form.'"

Cinemaware didn't need a mission statement. Everything you needed to know about the company was in its name: it was dedicated to making games that debuted on the high-end Commodore Amiga home computer that were inspired by, marketed like, and entertained just as thoroughly as movies. Based in Thousand Oaks in Ventura County, California, the developer was small-scale - a mom and pop operation run by husband and wife team Bob and Phyllis Jacob. "Bob Jacob really wanted to make movies instead of computer software when he started," recalled Pat Cook, who was a producer and later head of Product Development at the company. "He thought that melding his storytelling abilities with computers would be a 'backdoor' way into making movies."

When Riordan arrived for an interview he discovered a start-up with boxes all over the floor and no desks, but plenty of cinephile passion. Bob Jacob sat him down and gave him a list of ideas he'd come up with for future games. He had just one question: 'If you had to do a game based on a movie, what would it be?' Riordan scanned the list and tried to think of something original. "I told him that I'd probably do a big bug movie. You could have B-characters, big monsters, it'd be fun. You'd build this little town in the desert and have ants turn up. Bob looked at me and said: 'That's the one I didn't think of...'"

Each title Cinemaware made stuck close to its chosen movie genre: *Defender of the Crown* was a medieval swashbuckler; *King of Chicago* was a '30s gangster epic; *Rocket Ranger* was loaded with the sci-fi charm of Saturday morning serials. The unofficial template for *It Came From The Desert* was *Them!* (1954), the cult Cold War sci-fi movie about gigantic mutant ants. Riordan tweaked the basic premise: in the game, it's a meteor rather than nuclear testing that turns the ants into monsters. But he stayed true to the movie's vibe. The finished result was an interactive narrative experience that was poised somewhere between cinema and videogame.

The action takes place in the California town of Lizard Breath, a desert outpost complete with a buxom, Jane Russell-esque vamp, a stuttering gas station attendant and a local switchblade-carrying bully. It's less an ironic parody of '50s B-movies than a loving pastiche. "We wanted to take the player into that world, not make fun of it from arm's length," recalls Melville who, having left the aborted Hasbro NEMO project, was on-hand to pen the game's playful script. Unlike Melville's earlier work, *It Came From The Desert*'s graphics wouldn't be able to use the grammar of filmed video as *Night Trap* and *Sewer Shark* had done. Instead it deployed familiar genre tropes and constructed an atmospheric B-movie vibe through its story, score and characters.

Acting as director, Riordan decided that the key to the gameplay was drama. Tellingly, he approached the game design as if he was actually directing a movie: he hired a storyboard artist to sketch out locations and characters, while his secretary built a model of Lizard Breath using Plasticville. Most of all, he concentrated on the narrative. Putting the player in the role of a scientist, the game forces you to race against the clock as its three act structure unfolds: investigate strange events by talking to townsfolk; gather evidence to convince the authorities; and eventually lead the National Guard against the ants. Peppering the plot are varied arcade mini-games - crop duster flying, knife-fighting, first person ant battles, and top down ant nest exploration - all woven into the overarching meta-story in what had become already the distinctive Cinemaware style.

"One of the things I insisted on having was a timeline," remembers Riordan, who designed the game to play out in real-time. "Basically it's a narrative device. You can't wait around. If you don't go and do something, even if that something is wrong and you lose, if you just sit and play it cautious, the ants aren't going to stop; they're going to overrun the town." It was a classic dramatic technique and it's no accident that the game's feel - from the gradual reveal of its monsters, right down to the score's ominously insistent chords - is reminiscent of *Jaws*. Events sweep the player along, each new incident keeping the narrative ticking towards the inevitable moment when the ants overrun the town. Respond quickly and decisively to each situation and you may buy enough time to gather evidence, upgrade your pistol to a flamethrower and convince the National Guard to roll out their tanks. It's a situation familiar from the movie itself; but how it unfolds is dependent on the player.

Making such playable movie narratives - even without full motion video - was a leap in the dark for everyone in the Cinemaware team. This was uncharted territory and there was no manual on how to translate a linear, movie narrative into an interactive, branching script where player decisions would produce different outcomes. Most videogames were still level based: shoot six enemies and then graduate to the level to fight eight enemies. Rinse and repeat. Games like *It Came From The Desert* marked a complete departure, inviting you into a graphical environment that was fully-formed and populated by memorable characters. They tried to tell cinematic stories using 16-bit graphics (ironically, *It Came From The Desert* was retooled for the TurboGrafx-16 console in 1992, with full motion video of live actors replacing the Amiga's animated characters and backdrops).

"A lot of Cinemaware's success was to do with branding," explains Riordan. "Bob Jacob had a great talent for that - the way the posters and boxes were designed was just brilliant. But there was also a real love of movies. We tried to get to the heart of what we liked about the movie and celebrate it. We tried to take all the best elements of fun and tension and drama and actually do something that was really an ode to the form rather than just a translation of the movie."

At a time when movie games were lacklustre tie-ins like *Die Hard* or *Rambo III* on the NES, Cinemaware's cinephilia was remarkably fresh and daring. Instead of making throwaway shovelware, they were proving that it was possible to make decent games based on movies. *It Came From The Desert* may be the best licensed movie game nobody ever bothered to secure a license for.

It was hardly surprising, then, that Cinemaware's chutzpah and sumptuous production values would eventually snag the interest of Hollywood players keen to break into gaming. In January 1990, Peter Guber flew down to the upscale, white-bread town of Thousand Oaks, California. Guber was head of Columbia Pictures and had produced the previous year's seminal comic-book blockbuster *Batman* with director Tim Burton. Accompanying him was Mickey Schulhof, chairman of Sony USA, and an entourage of executives. The purpose of their visit was to take a look at Bob Jacob's operation. Word of the start-up software house that was making movie-games out in Thousand Oaks had obviously trickled across to Los Angeles. At the time, Sony was keen on expanding its empire. In the 1980s the company had been traumatised by the VHS-Betamax debacle in which Sony's superior technology lost out to that of its rival Matsushita simply because the VHS format had more movies available. Learning a hard lesson, Sony decided to focus not simply on making platforms but also content. In 1989 the Japanese corporation purchased Columbia Pictures and Tristar Studios as part of an $8 billion investment in Hollywood. It also snapped up CBS Records. The only piece of the puzzle missing was videogames.

As Guber and Schulhof toured the Cinemaware office, they were introduced to Melville. Making the most of the opportunity of giving an impromptu presentation to two of the most powerful men in the entertainment industry, Melville showed them several older NEMO projects he happened to have lying around: the *Sewer Shark* prototype and his *Make My Video* title. "A light bulb went off," he says, "they went gaga over it." Sony's suits were particularly impressed by the *Make My Video* demo. Melville's use of "Rhythm of Love" by Yes was an obvious selling point: "That was what convinced Sony to kick in major bucks. They had a huge backlog of expensive music videos rotting on the shelves and wanted desperately to recycle it all somehow. And this would be their path to that."

Sony's plans to buy Cinemaware would come to nothing. As Riordan explains: "At the last minute the Sony bosses in Japan told Guber they wanted him concentrating on film production and the small size of Cinemaware was just peanuts to them. They passed because they believed they could start their own game groups later on, which is what they did."

Another, separate deal did emerge from the Sony visit to Thousand Oaks, however. After meeting Guber and Schulhof, Melville called up his old Hasbro colleague Tom Zito. By coincidence, Zito's younger brother Bob handled PR for Schulhof and after a few hurried phone calls, Sony's interest in the NEMO products was confirmed. Zito headed to Rhode Island and opened up the warehouse where he'd stored the materials from *Night Trap* and *Sewer Shark* a couple of years earlier. Within a matter of weeks, Zito and Melville founded Digital Pictures and had a development deal with Sony.

Never one to scrimp on bombast, particularly if it helped drum up financing, Zito would declare the arrival of the world's first interactive movie studio. "We are redefining, in some ways, what Hollywood will be about in the 21st century," he would claim. Video was about to come to videogames.

CHAPTER 4

The New Hollywood

"If traditional film is a river, the viewer of that film sits on the bank and watches the water flow by. We want to take that viewer, turn them into a fish and put them down into that river."

Greg Roach, founder of Hyperbole Studios

"All you need to make a movie," said legendary French film director Jean-Luc Godard, "is a girl and a gun." All you need to make a videogame, proved Nolan Bushnell, was a ball and a couple of bats. So what did you need to make an interactive movie? In the early 1990s, it was a question that was on everyone's lips, not least of all the staff at Digital Pictures. The start-up company - initially based in the heart of Silicon Valley in Palo Alto, California - was to become the standard-bearer of a new wave of convergence between games and movies. It was a merger of two industries that would have far reaching consequences for both.

The early 1990s would prove to be a time of breathless, heady excitement as videogames and Hollywood finally got past the awkward shyness of first base and went all the way. Like all teen romances, the results would be messy, histrionic and embarrassing - but also momentous. After all, no one ever forgets their first time.

For Tom Zito, the resurrection of *Night Trap*, *Sewer Shark* and *Make My Video* was one of those incredible events when life completely blindsides you. When he closed the door on the Rhode Island warehouse that stored the leftovers from the failed NEMO project, the former reporter hadn't expected to be reopening it for anything other than nostalgic reasons.

Now here he was in 1990 with a batch of aging products designed for the NEMO that had suddenly become cutting edge all over again. Hollywood's resurgent interest in videogames - largely spurred by tech corporation Sony's entry into the movie business - meant that FMV games were cool. It didn't seem to matter that they weren't particularly good games. It didn't matter that they were largely a niche section of the videogame industry. Because they used live action footage, they made instant sense to anyone from the movie industry. When Sega launched a CD-peripheral for its Genesis console in the US in October 1992, Zito's games showcased the future: multimedia had arrived.

For most videogame players in the autumn 1992, just seeing full motion video on a console like the Sega Mega Drive/Genesis was a mind-blowing sight. Games like *Night Trap* and *Sewer Shark* - neither of which had seen the light of day beyond the walls of Hasbro when they were first created in the 1980s - offered a truly cinematic experience. They had incredible novelty value and brought the kind of interactive movies usually only seen in laserdisc arcade coin-ops like *Dragon's Lair* or *Mad Dog McCree* into the home.

Along with the games, Digital Pictures itself was something of a novelty too. The company's self-assuredness was astounding. No matter what the limitations of their products - and their flaws were numerous - Digital Pictures seemed to be flipping Hollywood the finger. We don't need you, was the company's apparent boast. We can do this without you. Zito revelled in such grandstanding, especially when it came to taking the major motion picture studios down a peg or two. "It's going to be a whole new kind of business. Ultimately, I believe the [videogame] business will be more like traditional Hollywood stuff than what's coming out of Silicon Valley today: some dinky animated guys running around the screen," he told the New York Times in 1993. "We'll be doing interactive game shows, talk shows, dramas, sitcoms."

He was convinced that a revolution was coming to the entertainment industry. It would be one that went far beyond videogame consoles and created interactive television. The videogames were just a means to an end - the birth of a casual gaming market that would let television viewers play games by interacting with live-action footage.

He was also taking revenge on the studios that had slammed doors in his face during the NEMO project. If Hollywood wanted to stick its fingers in its ears and sing "la, la, la", Digital Pictures would simply fund its own movie productions. It would be the world's first interactive film studio. Zito, with his beard and baseball cap embossed with the company's logo, was styling himself as the Spielberg of this New Hollywood.

Moving the company to Sand Hill Road in Menlo Park, California, he nailed his colours to the mast early on. The innocuous sounding address was the hub of Silicon Valley's finance. For any innovative start-up company looking for funds, Sand Hill Road might as well be called Money Street since it is home to the biggest collection of venture capitalists in the world. This is where every dotcom found funding during the tech stocks boom. It's a place where money doesn't just talk, it works for a living too.

Sitting in Digital Pictures' offices surrounded by canvases by Frank Stella and Chuck Close (the building doubled as an art gallery), Zito slowly built an empire. He had plugged into the mainline of Silicon Valley's funding stream and was closely tied to Sony and Sega, two enviable business partners. The symbolism was clear: Zito didn't need Hollywood's old, East Coast financiers to make his movies. He was playing the game his own way. Out in the parking lot, his Jeep's personalised license plates read simply: PIX.

"We really saw this as the New Hollywood," says Digital Pictures animator and artist Josh Solomon. "We'd make digital experiences that would be movies with scripts and actors but where the player could choose their own way of having the experience. Why watch a movie where you can't have any effect over it? Why not be able to come in and put your own stamp on it?" Selling its dream of interactive movies, Digital Pictures quickly became one of the hottest videogame companies around.

The tool that made all this possible was the CD-ROM. Unlike previous storage devices - 3.5" diskettes or the cumbersome VHS tapes NEMO had used - these shiny little compact discs allowed fast access to sounds and images and had an impressive capacity of up to 650 megabytes. In the early '90s, CD-ROMs were revolutionising the PC industry and they were also rolling out into the videogame console market.

When Digital Pictures was first set up, the company began to port the NEMO games to the Super Nintendo Entertainment System which Sony was planning to manufacture a CD-ROM peripheral for. After Sony's deal with Nintendo collapsed in acrimony – an event that would eventually lead to Sony entering the console market as Nintendo's competitor with its PlayStation console in 1994 - Digital Pictures became a developer for Sega and its Mega Drive/Genesis console. Sony retained close ties with Zito by acting as publisher through its Sony Imagesoft label.

Sega pushed FMV hard. The company was already making inroads into the console market with its Genesis console (known as the Sega Mega Drive outside the US), a sexy, jet-black console that was challenging Nintendo's supremacy. Its CD peripheral for the console was a weapon designed to shock and awe consumers. Games like *Night Trap* and *Sewer Shark* were the ammunition. For Digital Pictures the deal was fantastic. These two old games were resurrected from the dead and *Sewer Shark* was bundled with the CD hardware.

It gave the start-up company an incredibly lucrative influx of cash as 1.5 million units of the game were sold overnight.

In technological terms just getting the Sega CD to play video was something of a marvel. Digital Pictures' crack team of coders - including former Atari and Lucasfilm alumnus Charlie Kellner; and Mark Klein, a former Imagic programmer - were able to digitise analogue video by running it through a variety of compression and decompression algorithms. In layman's terms, they made the console handle multiple video streams simultaneously so that clips triggered by the player's in-game choices could be switched between seamlessly. The infamous black screens of *Dragon's Lair*, which occurred as the laser hunted the next piece of footage on the disc, were banished. It was quite a feat and not even the architects of the Sega CD could believe it. When Digital Pictures programmer Ken Soohoo flew out to Japan to demonstrate the company's work, he received incredulous stares. "They just looked at me like I was crazy but also as if we'd done something amazing with their product."

There were compromises for such fast transitions. Digital Pictures faced an arduous task taking colour movie footage and digitizing it into something that could work within the console. The Genesis hadn't been built to run video. It couldn't display FMV in full-screen, nor could it handle more than 16 colours in each region on the screen (and the total universe of colours was only 64!). It meant that video output on the console actually looked terrible, grainy splurges of moving pictures that were ironically far less impressive than the earlier VHS-based NEMO's video had been. Like the gigantic Chuck Close portraits that adorned the company's office building - pixelated, grid-like mosaics of human faces that looked photorealistic from a distance but proved more abstract up close - Digital Pictures' FMV had a strangely surreal feel to it.

"All our video had to be tortured, kicking and screaming, into the most horrifying, blurry, reduced-colour-palette mess imaginable in the Sega CD. I shudder to think about it," says Ken Melville. "The audio, the video, the accessing of data on the slo-o-o-o-w crawling 10k per sec bandwidth CD was all tortuous and disastrous. The limitations presented were enormous."

It didn't seem to matter; at least not at first. For videogame players used to the cartoon worlds of Mario or Sonic the Hedgehog, merely seeing live action footage in a console game was momentous. Sales of games like *Night Trap* were largely based on the novelty value of watching actors like Dana Plato - the real Dana Plato, not a cartoon representation of her - in a videogame in your living room.

By the beginning of 1993, however, Digital Pictures was facing a more serious problem than image quality: a shortage of inventory. After the leftovers from the NEMO period had been reheated, the company needed fresh product. The answer, Zito decided, was to move back into film production and shoot more movies.

Working closely with Sega and publisher Sony Imagesoft, Zito and his team began to flesh out a series of new games that would be released between 1993 and 1994 that included *Ground Zero Texas, Double Switch, Corpse Killer, Prize Fighter* and *Supreme Warrior.* These were the second generation of the company's products, the first interactive movies to be shot under its banner instead of simply salvaged from the NEMO project. If Digital Pictures was going to live up to Zito's bragging and become an interactive movie studio, the fun couldn't really start until someone shouted ACTION!

* * *

Nobody who lives near Los Angeles is impressed by the arrival of a film crew anymore. So the sight of a 100-strong film crew building a fake Mexican bor-der town on a ranch north of the city in the late summer of 1993 passed large-ly unremarked. Nobody paid much attention to the actors either, although the stuntmen wearing bulky sci-fi suits like Cylon rejects from *Battlestar Galactica* were undeniably memorable. But mostly people were unimpressed. It was just another Hollywood movie shoot in the desert: hey ho, that's the price you pay for living near LA.

If they'd dug a little deeper they would have discovered that this movie, called *Ground Zero Texas,* wasn't just another Hollywood production. It was actually the first game in Digital Pictures' attempt to build an interactive movie empire. True, it used an LA crew as its grunts. But its generals weren't studio executives. They were Silicon Valley programmers and games designers who'd suddenly found themselves writing cheques for a multi-million dollar production.

"It certainly felt like a movie," remembers *RoboCop* screenwriter Neumeier who collaborated on the game's story and visited the California location during the 12-day shoot. "If you'd just wandered up you wouldn't have realised that this was for a videogame. It seemed like it was slightly better funded than a Roger Corman movie." With a budget of $3 million, it was the most expensive interactive movie Zito's team had produced.

Directed by Dwight H. Little, whose CV included *Halloween 4: The Return of Michael Myers*, the game was groundbreaking in terms of convergence. So much so that Digital Pictures had to enter into negotiations with the Directors Guild, Screen Actors Guild and Writers Guild before shooting commenced. "They didn't know how to deal with interactive art at all," says Melville. "No idea. It wasn't really an industrial medium, nor a commercial. So we had to pioneer the agreements."

In all honesty, *Ground Zero Texas* isn't a particularly good game. It's essentially a shooting gallery: you play a soldier stationed in a Texas town where shape-shifting aliens called Reticulans have infiltrated the local populace of rednecks. Holed up in a motel room, you're ordered to watch events in the town via four camera feeds. Switching back and forth between the video clips you watch the town's rednecks going about their business while waiting for the aliens to break cover. When they do you blast them with the plasma cannons mounted on each camera.

In terms of its production, however, *Ground Zero Texas* represented a real departure for videogames. Unlike the NEMO era, when Zito and Hasbro had shot *Night Trap* in LA, this title was being made for a console that was already in the marketplace. As such, it garnered a good deal of attention not least of all from the New York Times who sent a reporter on location to write a story about "Movies That Press Buttons". To all intents and purposes, Digital Pictures looked like it was ushering in the beginning of a new chapter in both games and movies. "This Christmas, along with home videogames inspired by Hollywood movies," began the article, "there will be a new type of entertainment: videogames that are Hollywood movies."

That allure - the imitation of Hollywood - was Digital Picture's chief selling point. With their $2 to $3 million budgets, games like *Ground Zero Texas* were lavish affairs at a time when most videogames cost just a third of that. Over the next 18 months, Digital Pictures churned out a succession of games that featured some surprising crossovers between the two industries.

Debbie Harry starred in *Double Switch*, a horror-thriller game directed by Mary Lambert, who was noted among horror aficionados for her Stephen King adaptation *Pet Sematary*. Boxing drama *Prize Fighter* was directed by Ron Stein, the stunt co-ordinator on *Rocky 3* and TV shows like *Wonder Woman* and *Airwolf*. Zombie shooter *Corpse Killer* was directed by John Lafia, who'd cut his teeth on horror movies like *Child's Play 2*. Shoots for the games would take place on exotic locations like Hong Kong or the Caribbean; or on soundstages at Hollywood Center Studios.

From a technological point of view Digital Pictures' products were cutting edge in terms of getting FMV onto the Sega console. In cinematic terms they were B-movies at best, Z-grade trash at worst. It was as if Zito was resurrecting the spirit of the Poverty Row studios of the 1940s. Back then, nickel and dime outfits like Monogram and Republic had churned out cheap horror quickies with Bela Lugosi, vampire bats on string and a variety of other (un)special effects. Digital Pictures' penchant for kung fu, zombie and sci-fi games seemed to be Siliwood's answer to that golden age of clag.

Whatever their shortcomings, though, the point was that these were as much movies as games. Convergence had suddenly happened overnight: Digital Pictures was now creating interactive products out of traditional, analogue cinematic assets. As far as Zito was concerned the business model was a lucrative one. Although there was clearly great risk involved in not having a major studio partner to fall back on, the financial rewards far outweighed any concerns. Funding every aspect of the production allowed Digital Pictures to control the rights and how the end product would be monetised. "It seemed like a business in which you could make a lot of money," says Zito. "In that context, spending $1 million [on a movie shoot] to do what it takes 200 people sitting at computer screens drawing pixels for *John Madden Football* to do seemed pretty rational."

Still, the Siliwood convergence was often awkward. Interactivity was such a new concept that the film crews hired for titles like *Ground Zero Texas* frequently struggled to comprehend what they were getting involved in. Working on these games often felt like shooting three movies in one. Key scenes, like the endings in *Ground Zero Texas*, were shot in different ways to give players a sense that their actions were influencing the narrative. One unsuccessful playthrough might end with a B-52 nuking the town. Or, if you killed too many civilians your superior would punch your lights out and order you onto the next chopper. Add in the various permutations of plot and action - What happens if aliens overrun the town saloon? What happens if you don't save a colleague from an alien attack? - and continuity issues quickly became apparent.

"It was unbelievably complicated because it was non-linear," recalls director John Lafia who worked on *Corpse Killer*, a title that combined live-action footage with miniature work and green screen. "I spent a lot of time with these guys looking at these reams of paper that had diagrams showing the gameplay: if you do this, that and that, that happens. If you do this, this and this, this other thing happens. All the choices of the gameplay were outlined and showed you what kind of footage you had to now shoot. There was an awful lot of figuring out to do in order for this thing to make sense." Bottom line was interactive movies were a bitch to write, shoot end edit.

Ultimately, the responsibility didn't lie with the filmmakers but with the programmers themselves. Soohoo recalls being on the Caribbean location of *Corpse Killer* and having to occasionally step in and tell Lafia that he would have to shoot something in a different way. The demands of interactivity - how the filmed footage would cut together when streamed through the Sega CD - took precedence over everything else. The Hollywood crew watched such exchanges with slack-jaws: no one on-set was supposed to boss the director around, least of all a young, geeky computer programmer. "During the breaks they'd sidle up to me and try to understand if I was wealthy or something," recalls Soohoo wryly. "What was the reason I was able to tell the director what to do?" For some, it was a sign of everything that was unholy in this creative alliance between movies and games.

Gamers tended to agree. The second generation of Digital Pictures games moved further and further away from the ambitious *Tamara* model that had inspired *Night Trap*. Yet the dream of a truly interactive narrative was being stifled by the realities of hardware limitations and gameplay suffered as a result. *Ground Zero Texas* is a good example of all that was wrong with these FMV games. It's a strangely passive experience. Locked away in a distant room you're little more than a chair warmer, hunched over a weapons console and occasionally remote-blasting aliens. For any teenager destined to become a UAV operator, piloting Predator drones across the battlefield in Afghanistan while stationed 7,000 miles away in North Dakota, the game was undoubtedly a good training ground. For everyone else it was simply frustrating. One of the key pleasures of gaming - the freedom to explore an imaginary environment - was consistently denied. Interaction was reduced to simply choosing which video feed to watch and when to shoot that camera's weapons. You didn't even have that much influence over the narrative. Different scenes would play depending on your actions, but you rarely felt you were watching something unique. Indeed, by the time you'd played the game two or three times, the unskippable video clips would be mind numbingly over-familiar.

Just as with NEMO, interactivity was being sacrificed on the altar of full motion video and it was debatable whether the novelty of seeing real-life actors on-screen was any compensation for playing a game so lacking in agency. Neither movies nor games were being served well by Digital Pictures.

Back in the early '90s, though, cynicism was in short supply. It was possible to believe that the problems FMV faced would soon be ironed out. Popular thinking was that the technology required to make it work properly was coming - and coming fast. Faced with a videogame like *Ground Zero Texas* that was using live action footage and that looked like a movie, what movie studio exec would want to bet that FMV was just a passing fad? "The silver disk," warned the New York Times, "may soon eclipse the silver screen."

* * *

Paradigm shifts sometimes occur as a trickle, each new development nudging the consensus towards the appreciation of a position it had never considered before. At other times, though, such shifts arrive as a flood. Between 1990 and 1994, the American entertainment industry found itself deluged by interactive products. The dam broke at the point where Hollywood and Silicon Valley intersected. And the resulting flood was powerful, if somewhat confusing for those unused to swimming in such deep water.

It wasn't just Digital Pictures who were pushing buttons. "Games are part of a rapidly evolving world of interactive amusements so new that nobody knows what to call them," reported Time magazine in September 1993, two months before *Ground Zero Texas* hit shelves. "[Are they] multimedia? Interactive motion pictures? The New Hollywood?"

Time magazine suggested that the two industries – games and movies – were locked in a secretive, passionate tryst: "Both sides talk excitedly about making interactive movies with synthetic actors, of allowing players to take full control of the character's action and even, with the proper equipment, to enter a virtual reality in which they are the character. Over the past 18 months, two groups, one representing Silicon Valley, the other Hollywood have been meeting at trade shows, visiting labs and quietly cross-fertilising." You didn't need a seismograph to sense that something earthshaking was happening.

For the first time ever, the conditions were of the Goldilocks variety. FMV, CD-ROM and improved processor speeds could now display movie-quality images. Meanwhile the information superhighway, as it was still quaintly called back then, focused studio executives' minds on the very future of entertainment. The internet was coming and videogames, which had gone through a remarkable boom and bust in the early '80s, were getting ready to boom again as the cycle came full circle. It was like 1982 all over again only this time, Silicon Valley was no longer an upstart newcomer but a force to be reckoned with.

All over the entertainment industry, particularly in the Bay Area and in Los Angeles, it was possible to plot the spikes on the seismograph. Digital Pictures' was just one aspect in a much bigger evolution that was happening. Nintendo had given the green-light for a movie based on their lucrative *Super Mario Bros.* franchise. Sony was trying to make movie theatres interactive by financing the Interfilm experiment (more on that in a moment). Elsewhere MCA, Universal Studios' parent company, was building ties with VPL Research, a small Silicon Valley company, to investigate virtual reality movies ("vomies") that could play in specially equipped theatres. Lucasfilm and Disneyland teamed up for the "Star Tours" space simulation ride. In specially-designed BattleTech arcades across the US, players could pilot virtual reality mechs and fight each other. Elsewhere, companies like IBM, Microsoft and Time Warner were all exploring different aspects of the new "multimedia" craze.

Intuitively aware of the flow of financing blood that streamed through the entertainment industry even the vampiric talent agencies were alert to the shift that was occurring. Michael Ovitz, head of talent agency CAA, hired AT&T executive VP Robert Kavner to help him chart the multimedia universe. Not to be outdone, rivals ICM and William Morris assigned agents to scout Silicon Valley for talent. "They just sense that there's money here," Zito told Newsweek. The general sense was that interactive entertainment was overtaking the traditional Hollywood movie model in terms of revenue. The entertainment industry was being dragged into the 21st century.

"Hollywood agencies already have the dollar signs of Silicon Valley in their sights," Newsweek claimed in 1994. "The movie business, at a stale $5 billion a year, has begun to overlap with the estimated $9.5 billion-a-year videogame business - an exponentially growing playground that includes CD-ROMs and interactive PC-based games. In one early example, New Line Cinema has struck a deal to make a movie based on the videogame *Mortal Kombat.*" As Amy Harmon in the Los Angeles Times put it, in an article that traced the culture clash between Perrier-sipping agents and the long-haired programmers at id Software, "For multimedia's emerging superstars, are Hollywood's talent agents the 10% solution?"

Interactive entertainment was now so popular and so exciting that the long-awaited marriage between Hollywood and Silicon Valley was beginning to take shape. The guest list was being drawn up and nobody wanted to be left out. Exploratory meetings were being held between both sides on a regular basis.

Daniel Kaufman was an attorney with Palo Alto based law firm Brobeck, Phleger & Harrison. At the time he was representing clients like Spectrum Holobyte (who brought the hit puzzle game *Tetris* to America from the U.S.S.R.) and Humongous Entertainment, which created educational games for kids. He recalls setting up one such exploratory meeting in July 1993. "I met Bill Block who was head of ICM and we thought it would be useful to have a big powwow between these two worlds to see if there was a there there. I was horribly, horribly naïve about how Hollywood works," he recalls. The unlikely meeting threw together Hollywood talent like actor Richard Dreyfuss, director Reginald Hudlin (*House Party*) screenwriter Pen Densham (*Robin Hood: Prince of Thieves*) with representatives from software companies including Spectrum Holobyte, Crystal Dynamics and Activision. "We all sat in this conference room and I don't know what came out of it but it was clear that there was a lot of energy and excitement," Kaufman remembers. "I think people were trying to position themselves as the new agency for multimedia."

Ron Gilbert, the former Lucasfilm Games designer who'd created titles like *Maniac Mansion* and *The Secret of Monkey Island*, was among those present (by that point he was creative director at Humongous Entertainment). "I gave a little talk about games and all I could think about was 'Hey, Richard Dreyfuss is staring at me'," he remembers. From his perspective the meeting was symptomatic of the relationship between the two industries. "Hollywood has always had this on-again off-again love affair with games. They seem to always go 'Wow, look how much money games are making, we should be in that', then they turn their unblinking Eye of Sauron on us."

In the aftermath of the event, Kaufman fielded angry missives from CAA: "They were saying 'Who are you and why are you insulting us?' I remember thinking, I can't possibly be insulting you because I don't even know who you are. They were cross because they saw an article about the meeting in Variety and felt slighted." Nobody wanted to lose their place on the multimedia bandwagon.

Pretty soon, the major studios were no longer content to simply watch from the sidelines. Although they still remembered getting their fingers burnt in the crash that followed Atari's nosedive, this time they were looking at a very different landscape. Videogames were no longer a simple novelty. They were part of a much wider, technological evolution that was happening across the board. Virtual reality, cable TV and the development of the internet all suggested that the high-tech future had arrived. True, the relationship between videogames and the movie studios would ebb and flow through elation and disappointment over the coming years. But it was an old-fashioned, Catholic marriage: from around 1992 onwards, divorce was no longer an option. Technology had reached a tipping point and the studios were longer able to ignore interactive entertainment.

Virtual reality, multimedia, interactive and digital were quickly becoming movie industry buzzwords. In cinemas in 1992 *The Lawnmower Man* captured the zeitgeist, much as *Tron* had a decade before, by wrapping cutting edge computer-generated graphics around a story that tackled virtual reality. In keeping with the schizophrenia of the film industry's love/hate relationship with Silicon Valley, it managed to be both incredibly high-tech while peddling a technophobe agenda. It was a film that ostensibly had nothing to do with videogames and yet it seemed to be pointing towards a future where the interactive world was so immersive videogames would drive us mad. There was little doubt that a cultural upheaval was happening - not just in Hollywood, but across the entertainment landscape as a whole. FMV was part of a much wider trend, a pioneering sense that technology was the new powerhouse driving cinema, games and the much cited, but little understood concept of interactivity. Although Siliwood had many faces, there was one constant: profits. "People used to ask, 'What's the risk of getting into this business?'" an investment analyst told Time in 1993 as the studios viewed videogame revenues with envy. "This year the question is, What's the risk of not getting into the business?"

As the major motion picture studios scrambled once again to seize their piece of the interactive pie, some feared a turf war between games and movies was coming. Noah Falstein, a veteran games designer who had worked at Lucasfilm Games and would later join Digital Pictures, suggests this was at least one factor driving the evolution of FMV. "There was a fear around that time [the early 1990s] that Hollywood was just going to come in and take over game development and games were gradually going to become interactive movies. You'd have real actors and, of course, if you had real actors getting paid millions of dollars, the studios are going to want real film directors with experience handling that. Anyone on the games side would be relegated to a small technical role. There was a surge of trying to gain control and gain some mastery of the whole video production [there was] the sense that a lot of the big studios were opening up game subdivisions and we really thought that they might take over."

Grasping the nettle of film production was one way videogame companies could prevent that from happening. From that perspective, Zito wasn't so much an explorer pushing ahead into new territory as an officer ordering his troops to shore up the defences. Digital Pictures wasn't the only company that was pushing ahead with FMV, although no others could boast such a colourful, outspoken chief executive. While FMV never took over from more conventional sprite-based videogames, it certainly proved a fertile fad. Dozens of titles experimented with live action in a variety of ways.

Margot Kidder and James Earl Jones were among the cast of *Tex Murphy: Under a Killing Moon* (1994), which used FMV in its story about a hardboiled private eye in a dystopian, near-future San Francisco. Oregon-based developer Trilobyte created a polished puzzle game in *The 7th Guest* (1993); Sierra experimented with FMV in *Phantasmagoria* (1995) and *Gabriel Knight II: The Beast Within* (1996). Elsewhere, LucasArts drew on its parent company's movie heritage to create *Star Wars: Rebel Assault II* (1995), a bestselling game that drew in fans by featuring the first live-action footage shot within the *Star Wars* universe since the theatrical release of *Return of the Jedi* in 1983. Meanwhile, the long-standing videogame franchise *Wing Commander* replaced its traditional animated cut-scenes with FMV in *Wing Commander III: Heart of the Tiger* (1994). Among the actors working their way through its particularly cheesy script was former *Star Wars* lead Mark Hamill.

While one of the problems that plagued Digital Pictures games was their inability to expand non-linear storytelling beyond the most simplistic terms, other pioneers in the field saw the opportunity to create truly interactive movies that would challenge the supremacy of conventional movie narrative. The FMV fad's historical importance lies in the way it suggested an alternative kind of videogame: a more adult, less twitch-based entertainment experience that could hold its head up high among its cinematic peers.

Looking back, it was a highly experimental time. "Everyone was inventing in the dark back then," says David Riordan, who had experimented with FMV in the TurboGrafx-CD version of his Cinemaware game *It Came from the Desert*. "We really didn't know what would work and what wouldn't."

Back in 1991, Riordan had watched Cinemaware collapse. The mooted Sony buyout had failed and after a deal with EA also collapsed, the Thousand Oaks company faced bankruptcy. Sad to see the talented production team he'd been working with disbanded, Riordan wondered how he could keep them together after Cinemaware folded. Suddenly, one afternoon, his phone rang.

"I picked it up and this voice says, 'I can make all your dreams come true'. He didn't even say hello..."

The voice belonged to Gordon Stulberg, executive producer of Oscar-nominated musical *A Chorus Line* and former head of Twentieth Century Fox. By 1991 he was in charge of the US division of Philips Interactive Media and overseeing the release of the company's CD-i console. "He was one of the last of the studio moguls," remembers Riordan. Stulberg, who had worked with Riordan's team on a couple of Cinemaware/Philips co-productions, was keen to set up an in-house development unit for the Philips CD-i console, an interactive CD system. Seizing the opportunity, Riordan and his partner David Todd thrashed out a production deal. Stulberg would commit to three projects from their new development team Philips POV: mystery thriller *Voyeur* and two sports titles *Caesar's World of Boxing* and *NFL Hall of Fame Football*. The advantage of the deal for Riordan's Cinemaware refugees was that they could stay in Thousand Oaks with their families. They would also be well outside the corporate sphere of influence in LA.

The Philips CD-i wouldn't exactly turn gaming on its head - poor hardware design and even poorer marketing quickly snuffing out its chances in a marketplace dominated by Nintendo and Sega. Yet at least one CD-i title stood out from the pack and suggested the possible evolution of interactive movies. *Voyeur*, released by Philips POV in 1993, was a mystery thriller loosely based on Alfred Hitchcock's *Rear Window* that offered an intriguing blend of live actors and computer-generated backgrounds. *Voyeur* was representative of the attempt among FMV game designers to broaden the scope of interactive storytelling. Riordan, who had graduated to games from a career in linear media, was not only inspired by Hitchcock. Like so many other designers who were trying to grapple with branching narratives, he recalled watching the stage-play *Tamara*. His aim was to create a game like *Tamara* that had parallel streaming narratives - and also narrative tension.

Tasked with spying on a wealthy American family and gathering evidence for your client, you watch the action in *Voyeur* from an apartment opposite the family's mansion. Armed with espionage devices, you're able to watch and listen in on events inside in the house as they happen... with a catch. You can only watch one room at a time and the multiple storylines inside the house continue in real-time regardless of whether or not you're observing them. With the clock ticking the game plays out in real-time as multiple vignettes happen simultaneously. It's up to the player to decide where to point their high-powered binoculars - just as *Tamara's* audience had to choose which room to enter and which actors to follow and *Night Trap's* players had to choose which video feed to watch. Choose the wrong windows or look too long in one place and you won't gather enough evidence to indict industrialist and presidential hopeful Reed Hawke (played by Robert Culp, star of '60s TV show *I Spy*).

"One of the things we were concerned about as dramatic storytellers was that there was a lack of tension in branching narratives," says Riordan. "You could choose this path and an alien ate you; or that path and an alien didn't eat you. There was nothing pushing the narrative along, there was nothing like in the three-act movie process or five-act television drama."

In comparison, *Tamara* suggested a different way of approaching an interactive title. "*Tamara* got the audience running all over the house. Why? Because we didn't want to miss anything. But the thing was, you were always going to miss a lot. It simply wasn't possible to see everything so you were forced to build a narrative out of incomplete pieces." It was an intriguing gameplay design, not least of all because the experience subtly changed depending on which disgruntled member of the Hawke family hired you.

Voyeur's $750,000 production was also significant. Riordan's team at Philips POV and director Robert Weaver (son of the actor, Dennis Weaver) brokered a deal with Propaganda Films, another Polygram/Philips subsidiary, to provide production services. Propaganda had a strong Hollywood reputation thanks to its music videos and a filmography that included key '90s movies like *Madonna: Truth or Dare*, *Candyman*, and *The Game*. Shot against a green screen, *Voyeur's* high-tech interactive movie-making proved to many industry watchers that Siliwood was very real. Unlike Digital Pictures, which produced its own shoots and hired Hollywood talent on an ad hoc basis, Philips POV's relationship with Propaganda pointed towards a very real kind of collaborative convergence.

As its eye-catching title suggested, *Voyeur* also pushed the boundaries of adult themes in games. An opening sequence lived up to the title's promise with an actress stripping down to stockings and suspenders before tying her S&M partner to a bed. "There were gasps when we showed it to people," recalls Riordan. "But it needed that to set up the game, intrigue players and get them to watch. They thought, 'This is going to be interesting, I'm going to find out what's happening in this house.' It wasn't a bunch of cute little creatures dancing around the screen like most games were; it was something else." *Voyeur* won seven Interactive Academy Awards for design, acting and writing.

Riordan wasn't the only games designer hoping that FMV might counter the adolescent aspect of videogames with a deeper, more resonant style of storytelling. Several other FMV pioneers also believed the format could lead videogames beyond the rather basic dynamics of running, jumping and shooting. Among them was Greg Roach, a Texan writer who began to push the interactive movie towards something more avant-garde through his company Hyperbole Studios.

Roach started out writing short stories and directing plays at the Houston Stages Repertory Theatre. After a bit part as a bad guy in TV show *America's Most Wanted* in 1990, he cashed his cheque and bought an Apple computer and a hypermedia authoring system called Hyperstudio. At first uncertain what to do with the expensive kit, he started to publish a twice-yearly hypermedia journal and released a CD-ROM of *The Madness of Roland*, what he billed the world's first interactive multimedia novel. After that came *The Wrong Side of Town*, a short that the American Film Institute designated the first interactive narrative movie.

Hailed as "The Bard of CD-ROM" and "The Spielberg of Multimedia", Roach then graduated to making more sophisticated interactive experiences including two game/movies that used Apple's multimedia tool QuickTime to straddle the divide between the two forms: *Quantum Gate* and *The Vortex: Quantum Gate II* released in 1993 and 1994 respectively. Set in 2057, the story of *Quantum Gate* follows Drew Griffins, an army medical student sent onto an alien planet to help mine a mineral needed to save Earth from extinction. Layering environments, flashbacks and narrative through multiple video clips, the game tried hard to present a mature slice of sci-fi and followed Drew as he learns the dark secret of Earth's true agenda on the alien planet.

Both *Quantum Gate* and its sequel were built around a patented software tool called VirtualCinema that aimed to immerse players inside the game world by using FMV. They also tried to push the boundaries of games themselves, stripping out conventional game-play mechanics and pushing an evocative narrative that dealt with themes including genocide and ethical crisis. *Quantum Gate* sold over 100,000 copies - quite a feat for a niche CD-ROM title in 1993.

Roach saw interactive movies as an attempt to expand the horizons of gaming. "I was fascinated by using digital video to move beyond simply giving players sweaty palms or throwing a bunch of silly-assed puzzles at them," he explains. "I wanted to move the experience into the realm of real art, where people are affected on a deeper level and understand their own lives and humanity in a deeper way because of their encounter with this artefact of art - that's what theatre, cinema and literature is capable of accomplishing and I always thought interactive media had the capability to take its place among all those other forms."

Hyperbole set out to do exactly that. In case anyone was in any doubt as to its aims, Roach ordered a reproduction of Salvador Dalí's painting *The Hallucinogenic Toreador* to be hung in the company's lobby when they moved from Houston to Seattle. With its array of optical tricks - in which a bull's head, the Spanish flag and the Venus de Milo are layered over one another - Dalí's canvas was a fitting totem. "It was the first thing you saw when you stepped off the elevator," says Roach, "and I'd often ask new hires to meditate on it." Here was a videogame company that didn't just want to make games. It wanted to make art.

The problem was most gamers didn't share Roach's vision. Brought up to expect challenge and complex interactivity, many were frustrated by Hyperbole's arty and cerebral sci-fi movies. They were particularly aggrieved by *Quantum Gate*'s reduction of gameplay to a string of video clips. But for Roach, gaming was less important than storytelling. He was convinced that multimedia offered a new narrative medium - a kind of high-tech indie filmmaking that let him create sci-fi stories at the fraction of the price of trying to do the equivalent for the big screen. The chief problem was his audience. The "players" he needed - the kind of people who been in the front row at the Stages Repertory Theatre back in Houston - just weren't out there.

"A lot of people, the kind of people for whom an 'interactive movie' would be an interesting and compelling experience, didn't look at the computer as an entertainment platform," he says. "You wanted entertainment, you read a book, you went to a cinema, you watched television. You used the computer for spreadsheets and email. The people who did look at the computer as a platform for entertainment were gamers, so they came into the equation primed by a generation of games that were built on the ideas of fast action and deep interactivity. Story? What story? Characters? What characters?"

It was telling that during the course of Hyperbole Studios' troubled relationship with their publisher Media Vision, their patrons recognised that *Quantum Gate* wasn't ticking all the boxes of a mainstream videogame. "They said to us, literally: 'We want more guns and tits in the title'," says Roach. Shortly afterwards, Media Vision collapsed in scandal over insider trading allegations and Hyperbole only just escaped from under the wreckage.

It was Hyperbole's next project that would truly push the boundaries of full motion video. Approached by Twentieth Century Fox Interactive in 1993, Roach was offered the chance to create a game based on *The X-Files* TV series. It was arguably the most sophisticated FMV game ever designed and became what its creator calls "the last hurrah for FMV". It was also a prime example of the creative difficulties facing Siliwood as games designers and studios converged. Development took four years and $6m, a significant investment for Fox. What sold them was Hyperbole's proprietary VirtualCinema system. "It was primarily a media engine," remembers programmer Jason Vandenberghe, "a set of scripting tools to let you do point-and-click adventure games but with full rich media. It was like the Avid editor for games. You didn't have to be a programmer to use it because you could do all the gameplay logic inside the engine, assemble different types of media clips and have them play at different places."

Unlike many FMV games, which often used their live-action footage as nothing more than wallpaper backdrops, *The X-Files* presented you with a universe to explore. Developing the VirtualCinema process to allow full 360 degree film capture, Roach and his team built a game engine that invites players into the filmed footage. Turn left or right and the film - a series of stitched together jpeg images - shifts with you. Turn on a flashlight in a darkened room and the footage on-screen is bathed in a pool of light. "We were really trying to immerse you in the world of *The X-Files*," says Roach. "That was one of our big goals - a movie that you live inside, that wraps completely around your head."

Playing as FBI Agent Craig Willmore (Jordan Lee Williams) you're tasked with tracking down missing colleagues Mulder and Scully (David Duchovny and Gillian Anderson) who've vanished in mid-case. The level of agency is key: you can interrogate supporting characters and employ equipment from lock picks to a trusty Apple Newton PDA. Find a document with a phone number on it and you can call it up. Pull a gun on Assistant Director Skinner (Mitch Pileggi) and he'll be spectacularly unimpressed.

As ever with FMV, the magic was brief. Navigation was clumsy, the FBI field office you begin the game in becoming a frustrating maze as you struggled to move through the narrow corridors - issues of depth perception and a too-small location causing unexpected problems that couldn't be rectified once the footage was shot. It could sometimes take five minutes of twisting and turning to find the exit to a room, truly and utterly disastrous in terms of the suspension of disbelief the game was designed to encourage.

When it worked, though, it was incredibly immersive. For the first time, FMV had fulfilled its promise and had become a halfway house between the passivity of traditional movie and the freedom and immediacy of the kind of virtual reality so many people were daydreaming about in the '90s. Foregrounding character, plot and atmosphere over action, the game appealed to non-gamer fans of *The X-Files* since it was instantly recognisable and familiar to them. However, the emphasis on atmosphere came at the expense of action, something many hardcore gamers - who wanted to play as Mulder and/or Scully - railed against.

"One of the problems with FMV, because of the brittleness of the medium, is creating convincing agency, reflects Roach. "The idea that I can do-fucking-anything, is a real challenge. It's a challenge even in the world of 3D. The verbs in games are very, very basic, physical and crude. The agency in most real time 3D games is expressed in your ability to shoot fucking anything that moves, or blow up a wall and do these kinds of things. It's a rare title, even today, where the agency is expressed along the arc of character development or in verbs that are more focused on emotional or dramatic actions rather than visceral physical run, jump, shoot forms of expression."

For Fox Interactive, the project was unusual and not be repeated. The next game based on the franchise, *The X-Files: Resist or Serve* (2004) developed by Black Ops Entertainment, would be a third-person, 3D affair in the vein of the *Resident Evil* series. It was considerably more conventional although arguably much less striking. For Fox the issue was one of cost. But it was also one of difficulty. Making an FMV game based on a licensed property was an awkward, exhausting process for both studio and developers. It wasn't simply a case of signing off on a game and maybe scheduling a few hours voice work by the actors. It was an invasive, demanding process that required access to cast, crew and assets.

Roach's team certainly found the project exhausting. "Working with a company like Fox is a lot like talking to a person with multiple personality disorder or Alzheimer's," explains the game's director. "They never remember from one minute to the next what they've agreed to. We had to deal with the legal division, marketing department, Fox Interactive, the TV division, and [*X-Files* creator] Chris Carter. Each of them has their own fiefdom and their own veto capacity that only extends so far in certain areas."

Carter was initially wary of the project. "In our first meeting, we sat down with Chris Carter, producer Frank Spotnitz and all the reps from Fox Interactive and a couple of people from my company," recalls Roach. "There were like 15 people in this room. We sit down and the first words out of Chris's mouth were 'What can you do that I can't?' I thought, How the fuck do I answer this without totally blowing it?"

After Roach explained that he wouldn't presume to write an *X-Files* episode but did know how to craft an interactive experience, the atmosphere softened slightly. Still, it remains a telling anecdote about the suspicion in Hollywood circles about the new digital arrivals.

When it came to the first day of shooting, Roach experienced much the same hesitancy from Fox's management. *The X-Files* game was the first FMV title to feature bona fide Hollywood stars in a franchise tied to an ongoing TV series. Back in the '80s when the NEMO team had been trying to sign on Paramount for a *Star Trek* game, the issue of who would direct the talent had been a sticking point. By the mid-1990s, that attitude had softened and Roach was permitted to direct Duchovny and Anderson himself.

That didn't stop all of the top brass from Fox coming down to the set on the first day of shooting to make sure the talent was being well-cared for. "Everyone wanted to be able to see what we were doing," recalls Roach who was more than a little intimidated by the experience. "I remember that first day well. Fuck, it was hardcore." With the budget ticking away at a cost of around $7,000 per minute of shooting, the game designer suddenly found himself in the frontline of convergence. Such suspicions were endemic. Vandenberghe, who'd later work at EA on very different licensed movie games like *007: Everything or Nothing* and *The Lord of the Rings: The Third Age*, reckons it was largely a result of the two industries' different attitudes. "We don't share the same language," he argues. "Hollywood is a culture of personality where people with strong personalities can convince you even if they don't know what the fuck they're talking about. It's Hollywood, they're selling faces. That's what they sell in its 18-foot tall glory. Everything else derives from that. The game industry sells systems. We don't trust those types of personalities. It's an engineering culture where you have to know what you're talking about. You can't be a bullshitter. Those two cultures are incompatible with one another and unless you have someone who can bridge the gap, everything comes to a screeching halt."

While most FMV games failed because they were B-movies, with cheesy acting and low-budget production values, *The X-Files* was the genre's first true blockbuster: a true Hollywood production that used the same assets as the show it's based on.

Released in the summer of 1998, *The X-Files: The Game* sold around a million copies. Partly its success was a case of enviable timing; the movie arrived in cinemas a month later, a fantastic piece of synergy. It was also proof of how well-received the title was among fans of the TV show, many of whom were non-gamers and so happy to ignore the compromises that the title's immersive atmosphere demanded in terms of agency.

It became something of a belated poster child for FMV. "I had a lot of people come to me and say, in various forms, we feel like the concept has been acquitted by *The X-Files* title, we feel like this one knocked it out of the park and proved these weren't just harebrained ideas," says Roach. But by the point it was released, the backlash against FMV was already well-entrenched and 'interactive movie' had become what Roach calls "a dirty word".

Today *The X-Files* stands as one of the last FMV titles and a glimpse of where the technology might have led interactive drama if the games industry hadn't discovered the more dynamic, malleable joys of 3D graphics. In many ways, 3D has FMV to thank. "If it weren't for FMV's realism," Roach suggests, "we might have been more content to settle for the pixelated muddle that used to pass as game graphics. I think you can make the argument that FMV - its plusses and minuses - helped to spur the advancement of real-time 3D. FMV defined the problem that real-time 3D ultimately solved."

In other words, the photorealism of FMV set a benchmark for cinematic, realistic looking game visuals that 3D graphics have been working towards matching ever since. Deeply flawed as it was, *The X-Files* embodied the essential promise of FMV: that you might be able to step into a world you knew and recognised from film and TV and live inside it rather than just blow it up. "Everything old is new again," comments Roach. "In the early '90s there was such a buzz around virtual reality. What's the buzz today? 3D. There's not a lot of difference between 3D, FMV and immersive VR. We're still chasing that idea of being able to truly live in the fantasy."

* * *

If convergence was a seduction between games and movies, it was a highly unusual and often quite schizophrenic one. Far from true love, it was rather like watching Travis Bickle dragging Betsy along to a Times Square porno theatre in *Taxi Driver*. The beautiful blonde agrees at first, flabbergasted by her date's clueless audacity and secretly intrigued to see what lay beyond the salacious marquee advertising a Swedish couples movie. But once she sits down in the stalls surrounded by seedy-looking men gawping at clinical copulation on-screen, she comes to her senses. No amount of popcorn can convince her to stay. Seduction gives way to outright repulsion.

For many watching the fumbling attempts of videogames to entice Hollywood's interest with FMV and CD-ROMs during the '90s, the problem wasn't so much the proposition as the technique. FMV was something of a blunt instrument: impressive to heft but awkward to wield. It was only effective when it hit its target, which wasn't very often. But convergence had many paths and in 1992 a former virtual reality pioneer called Bob Bejan tried a different approach. Instead of making games cinematic, he wanted to make movies game-like.

Bejan, an energetic little man with oversized specs and a highly-caffeinated, scattershot approach to conversation, turned out to be one of the early zealots of Siliwood. By the early '90s he'd already had an eclectic career having moved from Broadway musicals (he had also, incidentally, once been the assistant choreographer on the Los Angeles production of *Tamara*) to singing telegrams to jingle writing and working with the *Teenage Mutant Ninja Turtles* live action show. After the latter firmly established his name he became involved with Virtual Worlds Inc., the company behind the BattleTech virtual reality systems. During his time at Virtual Worlds looking at how interactive technology could power entertainment experiences, he noticed a gap in the cinema exhibition market place. In the early '90s, movie theatre owners were complaining about the state of their business. Ticket sales were down, screens were frequently empty during the daytime and a lot of premium real estate simply wasn't paying its way.

Bejan's solution was one of those ideas so simple that they seem blindingly obvious after someone else has thought of them: why not marry the new technology of the digital revolution with the old technology of cinema and offer audiences a more interactive experience? It would be a modern version of the Kinoautomat, a Czech exhibition at the Montreal World Fair in the '60s that let audiences tour Prague on-screen and vote where to go next using buzzers. Behind the scenes, projectionists on roller skates would quickly cue up the reels of film to respond to the audience's collective decision-making.

After hooking together five laserdisc players and writing the software needed to control their sequencing, Bejan's development team then shot a 20-minute comedy short called *I'm Your Man* in 1992. Made for $370,000 and shot over six days on 16mm film, it was a bumptious if rather threadbare prototype to show what the technology was capable of.

When the first audiences filed into a retrofitted Loews Cinema on 19th Street in New York, they discovered strange, three-button pistol grips on their seats. Hooked up to the computer in the projection booth, the red-orange-green buttons let each audience member vote on which way the narrative would go at regular intervals during the film: which of the three lead characters did you want to follow? Where should our heroine hide when the bad guy comes looking for her? Should our hero run, fight or jump off the roof of a building? After the computer tallied the votes, the laserdisc players in the projection booth whirred into life and played relevant option for the audience.

If Zito's FMV games brought the movies to your home console, Bejan's company Controlled Entropy Entertainment (later renamed Interfilm) was committed to doing the reverse: turning the movie theatre into a giant videogame controller. In terms of convergence it was a Trojan horse strategy that snuck interactivity directly into cinemas. It looked like a movie, it ran in a movie theatre...but it could be played. All the conventions of cinema attendance were swept aside. In the past the most interaction you were likely have in a movie theatre was a quick fumble in the back row. Now you were being given the opportunity to occupy your hands in other ways. It turned movie-going into a truly social event as audience members were encouraged to shout, bicker and even run around the auditorium pressing voting buttons on empty seats. "Generally behave as if you were born in a barn," was the advice. Anything, except sitting passively, was permitted.

With laserdisc technology in the projection booth, the low-quality image resolution that plagued Digital Pictures work was nowhere to be seen. *I'm Your Man* was a movie first, a videogame second. Audiences weren't quite sure what to make of it. The no-budget production design didn't help matters but nor did the silliness of the story itself. It was meant to be played for laughs - the whole idea of pressing colour-coded buttons on remote controls too ludicrous in itself for the filmmakers to aspire to being Bergman. But even having lowered the bar in anticipation, it was incredible how dorkish the humour was. Think Mad Magazine with a frontal lobotomy. Bob Gale, the screenwriter on *Back to the Future* who'd later make his own Interfilm, *Mr. Payback*, saw it in New York just after it opened. "I thought the technology was really cool and the movie was really terrible," he remembers. "Bejan wasn't a filmmaker he didn't know how to tell a story. He was a brilliant guy but he wasn't a filmmaker."

Whatever *I'm Your Man*'s shortcomings, the 20-minute film attracted plenty of attention. "We made the front page of the New York Times and the LA Times," recalls Bejan. "It was like the world paid attention to us. We caught lightning in a bottle and lucked out." Almost immediately, Sony offered Interfilm a three-picture deal and agreed to retrofit 10 more Leows cinemas around the United States at a cost of $70,000 a pop. Two more exhibitor deals brought the number of cinemas fitted with laserdisc players and voting buttons to 50. When Interfilm went public in the autumn of 1992, it raised $20 million. It also began to attract the interest of Hollywood directors. Both Steven Spielberg and Robert Zemeckis were among those filmmakers who flew up to New York to see *I'm Your Man* for themselves. Videogame designers like David Riordan came to play with the pistol grips. Tom Zito and Bejan compared notes.

Among those in Hollywood who believed it had potential was Gale, who signed on to make *Mr. Payback* as part of the Sony/Interfilm deal. "It was a breath of fresh air for Bob Bejan to have someone who had real credit in Hollywood come in and say, 'I get this'," remembers Gale. "He was like, 'Oh my God, finally!'" The filmmaker's involvement helped raise Interfilm's profile even further. "To me that was the height of the Hollywood zeitgeist," comments *RoboCop* screenwriter Ed Neumeier, "because Bob Gale was a pretty respected guy."

Mr. Payback had a $1 million budget and starred Billy Warlock as a futuristic cyborg, essentially a Terminator with an ethics chip upgrade. His programming is simple: help those in trouble, chastise able-bodied pricks who park in handicapped spaces; and punish the film's villain Christopher Lloyd. Like *I'm Your Man*, the humour is largely puerile - fart jokes, S&M and the odd poisonous dart fired out of a robotic fingertip. Meanwhile, audience interaction revolves around choosing which storyline to follow or punishment to mete out. In a nod to the granddaddy of branching narrative fiction - Edward Packard's *Choose Your Own Adventure* books - Gale liked to describe the film as "Choose Your Own Revenge".

For Bejan, what mattered more than Sony's money was the access they offered him. It took him all the way to Hollywood and Columbia, Sony's recently acquired movie studio. "The Sony deal was unbelievable, it was like they waved a fairy wand," he says. "They gave us offices and we were the digital kids on the lot. They let us meet everyone and it was great fun. But half those meetings - I'd say probably even three quarters of them - got adversarial."

Bejan experienced the Siliwood culture clash close up. "It was a very controversial lunch to have with people in Hollywood. They were affronted by what we were doing. Any director you'd talk to would go, 'This isn't making movies! The whole point of me as a director is I want absolute control.' My argument was always that you're only giving the audience the illusion of control, it's really a much bigger canvas for you to be egomaniacal on. But I didn't win the argument very often..."

When he wasn't fighting his corner in meetings, Bejan liked to check on the audience reaction at his local Loews theatre. In between screenings of *I'm Your Man*, he'd watch Richard Attenborough's *Chaplin* biopic on the screen next-door. The scene where Chaplin rails against the new-fangled "talkies" struck him with a certain degree of irony. It was exactly like the refuse-nik mentality he was confronting in meetings.

For Bejan the problem was that the studios - and the filmmakers who worked for them - simply couldn't see the potential of interactive. What Interfilm was offering was too new, too raw. "The truth is that period was very Flintstonian. It was very unsophisticated and it was really as though we were holding down the blades of grass on something that would become a trail one day," he says.

For many, Siliwood was a state of mind rather than an actual, mappable place or even a bona fide business model. It was characterised by a hunger for innovation, a willingness to grope blindly in the dark in an attempt to make cinematic interactivity possible. During this period the majority of the videogames industry went blithely about its usual business. Titles like EA Sport's *Madden NFL* series, Nintendo's *Super Mario Kart* and Capcom's *Street Fighter II* had no interest in Hollywood. But there was a core of companies like Digital Pictures, Hyperbole Studios, Philips POV, Interfilm and others who tried to forge a different path. Innovation often ended in failure, yet the learning curve of trial and error in itself was immensely valuable.

The rules of interactive movies had to be written from the ground up - and so did the software tools to cope with them. Ian Kelly, *Mr. Payback*'s editor, grappled with an eight-foot long flow chart of potential scene combinations. Interfilm put together a loose-leaf notebook of best practice and stuck the title "Authoring" on the cover. Meanwhile Tracy Fullerton, the company's creative director used database software FileMaker Pro straight out of the box as the first version of the company's authoring system. Later, the team would write their own software and ship it. It was exactly the same sort of seats-of-the-pants approach to the structural challenges of interactive narrative that staff at Digital Pictures and elsewhere had become familiar with.

Like anxious farmers, most of the major entertainment and technology companies were watching to see which seeds would germinate during this fecund period. However, the company with the biggest stake in a decent crop was Sony. "They drove about 90% of the investment in interactive in that period," says Bejan. The Japanese corporation's fingerprints are all over the most exciting developments during these years. Digital Pictures' games were published on the Sony Imagesoft label; Interfilm had a development deal with them; and Sony's own Interactive Entertainment division was pushing the boundaries of licensed movie games in titles like *Cliffhanger*, *Bram Stoker's Dracula*, *Mary Shelley's Frankenstein* and *Johnny Mnemonic*.

Forcing an interplay between the movie and game divisions was one of the company's key aims. Paul Franklin, then an employee at British software house Psygnosis, and today the Oscar-winning visual effects supervisor of movies like *The Dark Knight* and *Inception*, remembers convergence being paramount: "We had quite a few Sony people over [at Psygnosis] and we made a videogame of Francis Ford Coppola's movie *Dracula*. As far as I could see it was a political, negotiation thing. It was the company trying to demonstrate that it could take this imagery and achieve this level of integration with the filmmaking arm of Sony. It didn't really matter, in a way, whether the game was any good or not. It was about setting up this working relationship." Whatever its importance to Sony, the *Dracula* game made little impact at retail.

Such peaks and troughs of expectation and disappointment were typical of the times. The interactive revolution of the early '90s was a vibrant but largely frustrating period dominated by scattershot development and exuberant marketing. Ideas and products were tossed around with wild abandon, yet few stuck. Not even Interfilm had staying power, the initial interest quickly fizzling out.

Initially, Sony was keen on championing the Interfilm development alongside their interest in IMAX projection. "They were really interested in revolutionising the theatre experience," says Interfilm's former creative director Tracy Fullerton, now an associate professor in USC's Interactive Media Division. "They were looking for the next big attractor, the big audience draw." The company also had plans to move into the videogame console business: the Sony PlayStation was released in Japan in December 1994 and in the US the following autumn.

When Sony took a $3.2 billion write down in 1994, however, blood flowed in the corporation's corridors. Their disastrous acquisition of Columbia and a string of movie flops including Schwarzenegger summer blockbuster *The Last Action Hero* hurt them badly. It was one of the biggest write offs ever experienced by a Japanese corporation and the effects reverberated throughout the industry. Among the casualties was *Mr. Payback*, which was due to premiere in February 1995. "The dictum came down: cut all unnecessary expense," recalls Gale. "And *Mr Payback*'s promotion was considered unnecessary." With little fanfare, the film limped in - and quickly out of - around 40 cinemas.

It didn't help that it was savaged by critics. Roger Ebert, who has since become one of the most vociferous naysayers over the artistic merits of videogames as a medium, was particularly scathing. "It was clear after two viewings that most of the movie remains essentially the same every time, and that the 'choices' provide brief detours that loop back to the main storyline," the cantankerous critic wrote in his Chicago Sun-Times review. "Choose a different villain, and he or she still gets gassed in the back seat of the limousine. It's said that two hours of material are shot for every 20-minute movie. Nothing on Earth could induce me to sit through every permutation of *Mr. Payback*. Is there a future for 'interfilms?' Maybe. Someday they may grow clever or witty. Not all of them will be as moronic and offensive as *Mr. Payback*. What they do technically, they do pretty well. It is just that this is not a movie. It is mass psychology run wild, with the mob zealously pummelling their buttons, careening downhill toward the sleaziest common denominator."

After *Mr. Payback* vanished from cinemas, it was followed by the company's third film *Ride for Your Life* in 1995, a quirky story about an alien invasion that hinged on a bicycle race between two Manhattan couriers. It starred Adam 'Batman' West. Unlike previous Interfilms, this was much more like a game and it tracked and collated audience data during the first reel so that at the end of it the most influential voter got to solely decide what would happen next. It was a true moment of live theatre among the audience themselves but it couldn't stop Sony calling Game Over on the Interfilm experiment.

The company's failure didn't come as a surprise to many. David Riordan, who was experimenting with a different version of interactive narrative in *Voyeur*, was aware that *I'm Your Man* was a tough pitch. "Bob Bejan basically took on the hardest thing, which was trying to do this kind of interactive storytelling in a movie theatre," he says. "I think a lot of people walked into the theatre and saw Bob's thing and said, 'If this is interactive, I'm not interested.'"

With hindsight, Gale believes that they misjudged the exhibition mode. "If I was doing it again, I'd say let's not do this in a movie theatre, let's put this in a special venue in Times Square or at Universal tour, or in Disneyworld, or in Dave & Buster's videogame emporiums. Put it in places where people go to have a different kind of experience. We messed around with people's expectations of what was supposed to happen in a movie theatre and they weren't comfortable with that."

The resistance that Interfilm met with, however, was actually endemic within Hollywood. Interactivity was scary to many since it suggested a brave new world where the storyteller was no longer a God-like figure who could decree an absolute story. Rather, they had to begin second-guessing themselves for the sake of the new medium. Those who misunderstood interactive believed that it was even worse than that: they thought that the filmmaker's control over the finished product was being eroded and that audiences themselves were taking control. Since any interactive branching narrative could only go down paths the storytellers had already written, such fears were nonsense. But they were prevalent.

Mostly, though, the problem was a generational one. Nobody in power wanted the tried and tested methods of storytelling to be shaken up by anyone whether it was Bob Bejan or Tom Zito. While the traditional cinema experience was a passive, "sit back" one, interactivity was a "lean forward" experience that invited the viewer to become an active participant. The problem was, nobody could quite figure out how to make that interactivity work within the constraints of film, nor how to make products that could be financially profitable over the long term. Tellingly, both Bejan and Zito would graduate from their work with film to the growing online world: Bejan joined MSN and Zito set up online indie record label garageband.com and internet marketing resource IMMI. The internet was a medium in which interactivity was already built into the technology and the model itself.

As Bejan argues: "If you look at the people who were populating [Digital Pictures and Interfilm] and then where they went, all of us basically went into the interactive content programs of the world's biggest portals as they start to launch in 1994, 1995 and 1996. We take all that production learning and all that production methodology that we worked out at the studios and apply it to the jobs we get next. That's exactly what I did at MSN."

Yet the real issue remained: did consumers even want their linear media to become more interactive? Did they really want to control a story? Neumeier, who worked for Digital Pictures on *Ground Zero Texas*, wasn't convinced. "Ultimately I don't think there's a threat to dramatic movies or TV," he told the New York Times. "People still want to be taken away by a story and a character, and the average individual doesn't have the ability to create that himself. If we could all make up our own stories, we wouldn't go out and see Shakespeare or Steven Spielberg - we'd sit at home and listen to Sid from next door."

Another person not afraid to call the emperor out on his new clothes was Strauss Zelnick, who resigned as president of Twentieth Century Fox to head up Palo Alto videogame company Crystal Dynamics in 1993. His departure from Fox to become chief executive of - gulp - a videogame studio sent a shockwave through the movie business. Here was a highly respected, senior executive at a major motion picture company abandoning cinema for Silicon Valley, the "New Hollywood". To many it seemed like a sign of the times: Old Hollywood was losing its lustre.

For Zelnick, though, the decision was purely strategic. He wanted to run his own studio and capitalise on the entrepreneurial advantages of the growing videogame business. Using his entertainment industry experience he hoped to help forge ties between Hollywood and Silicon Valley while leading Crystal Dynamics to develop games for the much-hyped 3DO console. In the eyes of many commentators, Zelnick's career shift was illustrative of the flow of talent out of Los Angeles and into the Bay Area that began in the '90s. As one executive head-hunter put it at the time, "It's deadly to be a so-called motion picture executive [in the '90s]. In the long run, it's much better to be an entertainment executive. Zelnick is a fantastic example of that. He's like a modem that allows one industry to communicate with another."

For all his passion for interactive entertainment, Zelnick was no cheerleader for the more literal convergence that companies like Digital Pictures and Interfilm were trying to forge. He was convinced interactive media should be limited to games, not narratives. "If you take live-action footage, add branching stories and call that an interactive movie, it's not commercial, except as a short-term novelty," he said in 1993. "A game is about mastering and winning. Movies are stories. Once you make the story interactive, it isn't a story anymore. A game, but not a story."

It's a belief that he still holds today and one which gives him a contrarian perspective on the past history of companies like Interfilm and Digital Pictures. "Bob Bejan failed egregiously in the business. He had zero credibility and zero success. He's a very nice man but he knows nothing about interactive entertainment," says Zelnick, currently chief executive of Take-Two Interactive which publishes franchises like *Grand Theft Auto* and *BioShock*.

"This isn't 20:20 hindsight. I was on a panel with him [in the early '90s] and I said 'What you are doing is crazy, it's going to fail.' It was obvious. It was obvious to anyone with a brain about the entertainment business," he says. "The Zitos and the Bejans of the world had it wrong. Their view was we take movies and make them interactive and that's a videogame. That's wrong, it failed and it will always fail. Because movies are linear in their storytelling; we want a story to be told to us. Interactive entertainment lets us drive the action and we want to drive the action and then a story can be superimposed upon that to the extent that it adds value to the gameplay. The necessary factor for success is gameplay."

If one thing was certain, it was that the future of storytelling was unclear. For every prophet predicting the creation of a new form of entertainment, there was a doom-monger calling them out on their stupidity. Many came to the conclusion that videogames didn't need narrative, any more than movies needed interactivity. But history has proved them wrong. The very nature of entertainment began to change in the early 1990s.

While the Zitos and Bejans were indeed mistaken in many of their assumptions, they realised that videogame technology was going to explode the dominance of linear entertainment. Today everything from audience participation on *The X-Factor* to the moral choices of *BioShock* proves that there is an appetite for stories in which the viewer/player has some control. Ironically though, at the end of 1993 something unexpected happened. Tom Zito was no longer just telling stories. Suddenly, he was about to become the story himself.

* * *

Senator Joe Lieberman had never played *Night Trap*. But he knew he didn't like it. Women were murdered. Vampires sucked blood. And decent, God-fearing Americans' kids could buy a copy in Toys R Us. What was this great nation coming to, he wondered? And what political mileage was there to be had in making a stand against such depraved filth?

In the early 1980s, Britain had been engulfed in hysteria over so-called 'video nasties' - violent horror films like *The Evil Dead*, *Zombie Flesh-Eaters* and *The Exorcist* that were available on VHS tape. The crusade against them was a grubby, sordid campaign stirred up by moral watchdogs, opportunistic politicians and baying tabloid editors. In the early 1990s, Lieberman and a coterie of do-gooders gave the American videogame industry its own version of the phenomenon with a trumped-up campaign against violent games that would see Digital Pictures dragged before the Senate.

Night Trap became public enemy number one. The scene in the game that Lieberman particularly took issue with was the one where actress Debra Parks stands in the bathroom in a lace teddy and is attacked by the black-clad vampires in boiler suits. Here, argued the incensed moral guardians, was everything that was wrong with videogames: titillation, exploitation, and women-hating violence. They were also aghast at Midway/Acclaim's gory fighting game *Mortal Kombat* where digitised versions of real actors fought each other in brutal battles. The selling point of the game was its "finishing moves", violent death strokes that saw characters ripping out their opponents' spinal cords. The third target in the senators' sights was Konami's *Lethal Enforcers* coin-op. Reputedly based on a real-life police marksman simulator, it let you shoot realistic-looking bad guys with a light gun. What linked all three games was their use of digitised footage. It seemed that the more real these games looked, the more trouble they stirred up. Zito's comment that real people could evoke real emotions in players had come back to haunt him.

Although the Senate hearings were undeniably serious - and led to the game industry's ESRB age-rating system - they were also rather comic in that clumsy slapstick manner that often happens when moral campaigners try to ban things they know very little about. Among the highlights during the hearings was the bizarre spectacle of Captain Kangaroo, aka Bob Keeshan, railing against violence in games on network TV. But the main event was the head-to-head battle between Nintendo of America's chairman Howard Lincoln and Sega of America vice-president Bill White.

It was a particularly undignified slanging match that quickly descended into farce. Both tried to score points by painting the other as morally bankrupt. When Lincoln asserted that Nintendo was family friendly and didn't do violent games - unlike its rival - White coolly pulled out a massive plastic bazooka from under his desk and showed it to the court. The deadly-looking Super Scope was, of course, a piece of Nintendo kit.

A further piece of comedy came when Zito arrived to defend Digital Pictures from the accusations. Consigned to the public gallery, he was allowed no right of reply. "I flew to Washington to go to these hearings," he recalls.

"On the morning of the hearings they said 'Gee, thanks so much for coming. We're really sorry but we decided that there isn't any time to hear your testimony'. And then at some point in the hearings [Senator Byron] Dorgan says: 'It's a shame Mr Zito couldn't be here to defend this horrible filth that this company is putting out'. I said: 'Senator, I am here and I'd be happy to talk about it'. He said: 'You're out of order! Be quiet back there!'"

Zito knew how to turn an apparent PR disaster to his advantage. After Toys R Us felt compelled to ban *Night Trap*, sales went through the roof. The game was on the news every night for weeks. It was incredible, free publicity and *Night Trap* went on to sell 800,000 units bringing in $32 million from its estimated $1.5 million cost. Everyone who bought it expecting an R-rated, *Texas Chainsaw Massacre*-style bloodbath was disappointed. In contrast to what the Senators seemed to believe, *Night Trap* was totally tame: *Family Ties* with vampires, as the actors had joked while shooting it.

During the height of the controversy, Zito scored himself an editorial slot in the Washington Post. As the hearings raged the prodigal son briefly returned to the pages of his former paper to pen a robust rebuttal of Lieberman's agenda. The article, "Senate Demagoguery: Leave My Company's Video Game Alone", served as a brilliant mission statement for Digital Pictures and succinctly summed up the chief executive's obsession with movies. Zito's argument was convincing: the senators and their allies hadn't played *Night Trap* and they'd taken one scene out of context. Worse still, they had completely misinterpreted the gameplay. You weren't trying to kill these pretty co-eds but rescue them. After spelling all that out in black and white, Zito pushed onto the real meat of his argument: videogames weren't just for kids. The Atari generation had come of age and wanted material that didn't simply involve cartoon characters jumping from block to block. They wanted technology to push the boundaries of the medium itself and to aspire to tell stories.

"We don't even consider Digital Pictures to be a videogame company; we make films that are interactive," he wrote. "[If] my name were Steven Spielberg or Francis Coppola, they wouldn't be criticising me [...] Much of the reaction to *Night Trap* is the shock of the new. When Thomas Edison started making short films around the turn of the century, patrons ran from theatres in horror when they saw a steam engine barrelling directly toward the front-row seats. If you're unfamiliar with technology, the realization that you can press a button - and I don't mean the remote control - and affect what happens on your TV screen is overwhelmingly profound. It has resounding implications for education, entertainment, advertising and even politics. Perhaps it would have been better if the senators' introduction had been something other than a flimsy nightgown and a trio of low-budget vampires. But maybe not. The shock of the new can force us to face issues. Interactive TV is here, and like rock-and-roll it's here to stay. We can stick our heads in the sand, or face the music."

There was no doubting Zito's talent for self-promotion. The accuracy of his predictions were rather less impressive, though. Far from being the future, FMV proved to be a cul-de-sac. Its direct influence on the wider videogame industry was limited. For a while it briefly served as a convenient shorthand for the convergence between the two industries that began in the early '90s. Ultimately, though, it proved a failed experiment. "I think that the idea that you could take existing properties and then create interactive entertainment out of them is a misguided, misunderstood notion," Zito says today. "In a funny way, Don Simpson was right. Sticking the name *Top Gun* on some videogame may or may not be a good product, but I don't know that you can take the footage from the movie *Top Gun* and make a good immersive experience from that. I think that we were misguided. We thought we could take existing material and repurpose it."

By 1994, Digital Pictures was beginning to unravel. It didn't help that the company was burning through money at an incredible rate. Noah Falstein, who spent a year as a game designer at Digital Pictures as it began to collapse, recalls being alarmed by the cavalier attitude towards budgets during the production of *Corpse Killer*. "It was set in the Caribbean and we assumed it would be shot in South California where there are plenty of palm trees. Instead it was shot in Jamaica and had something like a $3 million budget, which was outrageous at the time. It could have been easily done for less than half that if it had stayed in the US. But it was more exotic to be going off to Jamaica. My sense was that Zito wanted to have an opportunity to fly back and forth to the Caribbean to see how his production was going. In that sense, I think there was a kind of Hollywood envy at work."

Zito disagrees: "I don't think I was a frustrated filmmaker. I realised after a semester in film school that I didn't want to be a filmmaker. The irony of Digital Pictures was - what's the great line in *The Godfather*? - 'Just when I thought I was out, they pulled me back in.' Making films was just a necessary evil involved on the road to interactive television, which was what really interested me. If I had to make products in order to seed the process, so be it. But I didn't want to be the guy who was signing checks for movie productions. Every time we went into production it would drive me crazy. I don't think I had the right psychological makeup for it. Being in a business where some crazy actor could completely screw up what you were trying to do is not something that was appealing to me. To some people it is."

Digital Pictures was also struggling because the videogame market was shifting under its feet. 3D graphics technology was the big worry. Showcased in id Software's revolutionary first person shooter *Doom*, 3D graphics offered a very different - and much cheaper - way of creating a realistic world for a gamer to enjoy. Far removed from the use of live action footage, it was a tech-driven means of keeping the means of production firmly within the world of the computer programmer.

In many respects, 3D began to solve the problem that FMV had posed: how do you make videogames into photorealistic, immersive experiences? Digital Pictures had tried to do it by using real actors and film. The new 3D engines could approximate it in purely virtual terms. "In some ways I think 3D saved the industry from being the perennial little brother of Hollywood," suggests Falstein. A company like id Software didn't need film crews and they didn't need Hollywood talent. They arguably didn't even need narrative. *Doom*, released in December 1993, was proof of what was possible when programmers wrote their own solutions. It was an action-packed rollercoaster that eschewed the problems of how to tell a non-linear narrative in an interactive environment by offering a realistic but graphical 3D world and reducing narrative mechanics to fundamentals: have shotgun, blast slobbering demons from hell.

It was a triumph of atmosphere, generating tension thanks to the sense it gave players of moving through virtual rooms and corridors where demons were all around - and even behind - you. The sound effects, the lighting, the graphics all combined to provide a sense of immersion, something that ironically felt more organic and immediate than the real-life footage of FMV. Where FMV had tried to create a virtual world using real-life assets, 3D turned that on its head. It was a truly virtual virtual world. True something was lost in the process, a dumbing down of videogames' potential as a narrative medium. But much was to be gained: immersion, agency and, perhaps most of all, sensation. Although it was nothing more real than bits and bytes, you only had to play it to sense its power to excite and terrify. Its immediacy more than compensated for the lack of photorealism.

There's no doubt that 3D killed Digital Pictures, FMV and the interactive movie. In the final days of the company, the staff weren't blind to what was happening. Being an interactive film studio in the new era of 3D graphics was a hard sell. Everybody realised that a momentous change was coming.

"By the end of '93 into '94 at Digital Pictures, Noah Falstein, Ken Soohoo, Mark Klein and myself (the very few people at Digital Pictures with any actual game design background) could clearly see that 3D was the future and we had better get with it, immediately," recalls Melville. "But Zito adamantly refused to hear any of it. Simply because it would mean an end to his gigantic expense accounts playing the mogul-poseur in La-La Land."

The desperation of the situation was so obvious that Digital Pictures programmer Ken Soohoo, who had a background in 3D, started giving lunchtime lectures to his colleagues. He talked to them about the new technological shift that was rapidly approaching them in their rear-view mirrors. There were discussions about streaming live action footage onto 3D surfaces and plans were drawn up to make Digital Pictures less reliant on FMV technology. But Zito remained, as journalist J.C. Herz described him in a piece for Wired in 1996, a "rendering refusenik". Deep down, though, even he knew it was over.

By 1994, Digital Pictures' story was coming to an end and the credits were about to roll. In the aftermath, Zito would retire from videogames and - like so many of the people involved in that era - segued into internet start-ups. Today he has little interest in Digital Pictures' legacy. "You could certainly call us pioneers. And one of the definitions of pioneers are people who have arrows in their asses," he says. "In the bigger scheme of life, I think videogames play a very minor role. I concede we did some very interesting things, we created some interesting products. We certainly were on the forefront of technology and art but at the end of the day, so what?"

Twenty-odd years later, Digital Pictures' reputation rests on shaky ground. FMV is considered something of a joke among gamers, the poor interactivity of the products that shipped roundly mocked by most. Yet its experiment in creating non-linear game-stories using filmed footage marked the first true convergence between movie and videogame industry talent and the birth of today's digital Hollywood. The trail it blazed may have been a dead end - FMV is virtually extinct today other than as a historical curio - but it was a cul-de-sac videogames needed to experience in order to learn where the line was drawn between lean forward and lean back entertainment.

The lessons learned were harsh but incredibly valuable in terms of the evolution of interactive storytelling. If videogames' evolution were compared to the Cold War space race, then FMV would be the hapless dogs and the chimps blasted into orbit. What happened next - Neil Armstrong's giant leap, the arrival of immersive 3D game engines - wouldn't have been the same without them.

Digital Pictures gave videogames the ambition to not just imitate but actually outdo Hollywood cinema. Although FMV died, the dream of offering cinematic, immersive experiences lived on and continues today. You can trace a line from *Night Trap*'s branching storytelling and use of live actors to the cinematic, interactive plot structure of *Heavy Rain* or the use of facial capture technology in *L.A. Noire*. That evolution would be a lengthy, winding road. But then, as William Blake once said, the paths of genius are often crooked not straight.

CHAPTER 5

It's A-Me, Mario

"In the first script meeting [New Line CEO] Bob Shaye walked into the room threw the screenplay on the table and said 'I hate this fucking thing'. That's how we started Mortal Kombat. No one thought it was going to be a hit, least of all New Line."

Larry Kasanoff, producer of the Mortal Kombat movie

Mojo Nixon isn't the kind of man who shocks easily. The "psychobilly" musician has led a wild life. He was once knocked unconscious by legendary saxophonist Clarence Clemons after invading the stage during a Bruce Springsteen concert. He later fielded threats from Eagles fans after releasing a single entitled "Don Henley Must Die". Like the late Hunter S. Thompson, he's a guy who believes that when the going gets weird, the weird turn pro. But not even Mojo was ready for the *Super Mario Bros.* movie.

Arriving in Wilmington, North Carolina in summer 1992, the musician found himself standing in the shadow of a cement factory's cooling tower. The converted industrial estate was the headquarters of the production, as well as its main soundstage. It was there that Nixon caught his first glimpse of Rocky Morton, the 37-year-old British director famous for co-creating TV personality *Max Headroom*. Morton was sitting on his own at a table with his head in his hands and Nixon, no stranger to the deleterious pleasures of Mad Dog 20/20 himself, assumed he was hungover. At least he did until Morton started sobbing. He wasn't nursing a sore head but crying big, meaty man tears of rage, frustration and despair.

"I'd been in a couple of other movies, so I knew what to expect," Nixon drawls when asked about his arrival on set. "But what I didn't expect was to see the director sitting at a picnic table crying. I knew right then that things weren't going too well." The actor's suspicions were only confirmed when he reached the wardrobe trailer. As the crew kitted him out for his first day of shooting as Mario's buddy Toad - complete with a bizarre quiff and cornrow hairdo - Nixon started hearing horror stories. It was like joining the passengers of the Titanic in the sea, treading water as they watched their mighty ship sink.

"The crew started telling me how they'd just fired the director of photography the night before," Nixon remembers. "They'd been trying to do some real complicated shot and it had gone wrong. Everything was behind schedule, nobody knew what the fuck was going on and everyone was hoping that Max Headroom was going to come and save them. It was all fucked up."

Hired as a cheap substitute for Tom Waits ("a second-rate Tom Waits at a third of the price," he jokes), Nixon was only supposed to be on set for four days. He ended up staying for four weeks as delays on the special effects shots, shooting problems and general production chaos kicked in. He was bored but happy since they were paying him by the day, and he watched with wry amusement as the shoot went bad from worse. Right before his very eyes *Super Mario Bros.*, the bestselling game series that propelled Nintendo into the hearts of America's gamers, was turning into the *Heaven's Gate* of videogame adaptations.

Mario was Nintendo's mascot and its cash cow. Founded in Japan in 1889, Nintendo had been in games long before they added the "video" bit. It built its fortune selling traditional hanafuda playing cards and as it grew, the company dabbled in everything from love hotels to instant rice and taxi firms. By the 1970s, its president Hiroshi Yamauchi, a straight-laced millionaire with a lifestyle so frugal he owned neither house nor car, began to think about branching into electronic entertainment. Yamauchi's idea of a game was the ancient, Chess-like Go, rather than anything that came with a fire button. But he could see the writing on the wall. When Taito's *Space Invaders* coin-op caused a shortage of 100-yen coins in Japan in 1978, it was obvious that the old ways were dying. So Nintendo branched out into videogames.

Mario the Italian plumber was the star of Nintendo's first big international hit, the 1981 coin-op game *Donkey Kong* - although back in the beginning he was known simply as Jumpman and he preferred carpentry to plumbing. Shigeru Miyamoto, a shy and lowly staff artist at the company, was given the task of designing a game that would appeal to the American arcade audience. He initially wanted to license an established cartoon hero, someone like Popeye the Sailor Man. With his bulging biceps, corn pipe and white cap, Popeye would be instantly recognisable even when rendered in crude, pixelated graphics.

When King Features Syndicate, who owned the character's copyright, turned down Nintendo's offer, Miyamoto pulled out his sketchbook and started doodling. What he came up with was Jumpman, the red overall clad hero of *Donkey Kong.* The idea was simple: players had to guide their portly avatar along the girders of a half-finished skyscraper dodging barrels thrown by runaway gorilla, Donkey Kong, who has kidnapped Jumpman's girlfriend. The coin-op proved an instant, unexpected hit and by the end of its second year Nintendo of America had generated $100 million worth of sales.

In time, Jumpman would become Mario and upgrade from carpenter to plumber while keeping his by now iconic moustache, overalls and cap. When Nintendo released the NES console in the US in 1985, it was the *Super Mario Bros.* cartridge bundled with the machine that turned it into a smash hit. This side-scrolling platform game led you jumping, running and dodging through a surreal world called the Mushroom Kingdom which was being menaced by King Koopa, a fire-breathing turtle. In search of the kidnapped Princess Toadstool, Mario and his brother Luigi had to negotiate piranha plants, green pipes and villainous fungi called Goombas. Despite its mushroom-munching, hallucinogenic trappings it was designed as a cute, family-friendly game.

Super Mario Bros. turned Nintendo into the videogame industry's leading company. The Japanese firm's arrival in the US helped the market bounce back from the Atari-led crash. Sales of the NES console were awesome: by 1989 a quarter of American homes had one of the grey shoeboxes underneath their TVs. A year later the NES was in a third of all US homes. Mario became a pop culture icon. In 1990 a Q Scores consumer survey suggested he was more recognisable to American children than Mickey Mouse. Meanwhile, Nintendo were pocketing more gold coins than the virtual ones Mario collected. They enjoyed an 85 to 90% share of the global videogame market.

In the early '90s, while companies like Digital Pictures were trying to make videogames seem dangerous and cool, Nintendo were happy to be wholesome. "Game industry experts - some of them Nintendo addicts - believe the company could be the next Disney," claimed Fortune magazine in 1990. "Just as Mickey Mouse helped pioneer the animated picture in the 1930s, so might Mario help establish a new medium called interactive entertainment."

Like Disney, Nintendo were no strangers to merchandising. They milked every cent out of Mario's success. While the company's name, which translates as "leave it to heaven", hints at a Zen-like Eastern spirituality, its business sense was hard-nosed. Nintendo of America hired Al Kahn, then head of TV production and licensing company Leisure Concepts in New York, to handle the development of its characters as financial properties. Mario soon became a juggernaut of a brand: there were cereals, wallpaper, bedspreads,

TV cartoon shows running on NBC's Saturday morning line-up, and action figures. You name it, they flogged it.

Since it was such a popular console, it wasn't long until the developers making games for the NES started looking at movie licenses and striking deal with the Hollywood studios. In 1989 LJN Toys published a NES *Who Framed Roger Rabbit* videogame; Sunsoft released a NES *Batman* game based on the movie; and Capcom released *DuckTales* based on the Disney TV series. In fact, Disney shows and movies proved perfect for Nintendo's family remit. The movie-to-game licensing business – which had started with Atari and had never gone away – remained strong during the Nintendo years. There was little creative partnership between the movie studios and game developers. Both sides treated such games as nothing more than a merchandising arrangement.

The major studios couldn't help but be interested in Nintendo's success. It was Universal, so intrigued by the marketing potential of videogames in the early '80s, who first approached Nintendo. Tom Pollack, president of Universal Pictures, and his deputy Casey Silver wanted to make a film that would tie-in with the upcoming release of *Super Mario Bros. 3* by using the game in a kids' movie. Nintendo, who had already set up marketing promotions for the game with Pepsi and McDonalds, were amenable to the idea.

The Wizard was a $7 million Saturday matinee movie about an autistic kid who's a wiz at playing videogames. It was a blatant piece of marketing, essentially a feature length advert for Nintendo products that gave screen time to everything from the NES console itself, to its various peripherals and games. Far from being seduced by Hollywood, Nintendo apparently treated it as nothing more than another promo to be filed alongside Happy Meals and Pepsi cans.

According to Howard Lincoln, then chairman of Nintendo of America, licensing their properties to be made into movies was seen as something of a distraction. The limited financial rewards of such a strategy largely weren't worth the trouble. "I don't think there was much interest in making deals with the studios," he says. "You have to understand the way Nintendo thinks. They're very, very focused. With the kind of money we were making - and still are making - we could easily have diversified and acquired movie studios just like Sony did. But working for a guy like Yamauchi [Nintendo's president], his point was 'No, no, no we're not going to take our eye off the ball, we're going to focus on what we do well. I don't want to hear about investing in movie studios.'"

Certainly Nintendo didn't need Hollywood's cash. By the early '90s, the entertainment industry landscape had shifted irrevocably. Things were no longer the same as they were in the '70s, when Warner Communications bought out Atari. By 1992, Nintendo were profiting more than all of the Hollywood studios and the three main US televisions combined. They were an entertainment industry giant and the dominant partner in any deal with the studios. "The licensing of these characters, whether for T-shirts or movies, was a business but not our primary business," says Lincoln. "That's one of the reasons why we used Al Kahn at Leisure Concepts; we just didn't want to screw around with it."

This refusal to bow in wonder at the Hollywood altar was something the major motion picture studios found hard to swallow. When Universal's team flew up to Washington State to discuss *The Wizard* with Nintendo, they were surprised by the lack of enthusiasm the proposal was met with. "Nintendo had no need, no desire, no want to make this movie," says producer Ken Topolsky, who enjoyed great success with ABC TV series *The Wonder Years* starring *The Wizard*'s lead Fred Savage. "In Hollywood we think that everybody wants to be synergistic with us. We don't understand that we really need to be synergistic with them in order to be successful. [...] I have worked on the Sony lot doing *Party of Five* and things and everyone there thinks they're at ground zero in the cultural capital of the world. It's all, 'We're making movies.' Then you realise that less than 2% of Sony's business is making films. They're making components for spacecraft and God knows what else. They don't sit around in Tokyo going 'What about the movie business?'."

There was some irony that it was Universal that would be interested in brokering a deal with Nintendo. Seven years earlier, the Japanese company had been dragged into an acrimonious litigation with Universal over its bestselling *Donkey Kong* coin-op. Universal had claimed the machine infringed their *King Kong* copyright. Considering it featured a giant ape, a kidnapped girl, a skyscraper location and the use of the name Kong in the title, many thought the studio had a point. Sid Sheinberg, the man who helped launch Spielberg's career and a studio executive renowned for his love of litigation, spearheaded the attack on Nintendo. The case would become known, as the judge dubbed it, "a dispute over two gorillas".

Thanks to Lincoln, then Nintendo of America's legal counsel and later its chairman, the legal battle wasn't the disaster many suspected. Sensing that Universal were pursuing litigation purely for profit, and taking umbrage at the studio's strong arm tactics (which involved bullying Nintendo's business partners), Lincoln confronted the studio's legal team. It was a classic piece of stonewalling: "If you own *King Kong* and it is infringed by *Donkey Kong*, then we'll settle," he told them. "But I'm not going to buy the goddamn Brooklyn Bridge. First you'll have to prove to me that you own *King Kong.*"

His instincts were proved right. Far from owning the *King Kong* copyright, Universal had settled a previous litigation over their 1976 remake by proving that it was actually in the public domain. Nintendo waltzed out of court without a care.

By 1989, such events were ancient history and Universal received a suitably cordial welcome at Nintendo of America's headquarters. "We took a chartered jet, a Gulfstream, up to [Redmond], Washington and they threw a lovely lunch for us," recalls *The Wizard*'s producer Topolsky. "They were mostly interested in showing us their Game Boys and gave us one or two of them to play *Tetris* on [...] My sense when we went up there was that we were movie people and I don't think that Nintendo cared that much about movies." The negotiations were pleasant but difficult. "We were told it was a very aggressive negotiation on Nintendo's part [...]This was a real leap of faith by Universal to go up there, take all of us up there, and say 'We really believe in what you're doing and we want to make this movie, let us do this...'"

Given such a genesis between these two media giants, it was hardly surprisingly that the finished movie had a hardnosed commercialism to it that was quite at odds with its sweet storyline. *The Wizard* plays like a kiddie version of The Who's pinball ace rock opera *Tommy* crossed with *Rain Man.* But it contains more product placement than a weekend of back-to-back QVC broadcasts. The story follows three kids - one of them a withdrawn nine-year-old coin-op wiz traumatised by the death of his twin sister - on a road trip across the Nevada Desert. They're heading for Video Armageddon, a $50,000 videogame contest in LA. Every other scene plugs Nintendo clobber: Christian Slater carries a NES around with him; the family's dad, Beau Bridges, stays up all night addicted to playing *Teenage Mutant Ninja Turtles*, and there's a hilariously cheesy moment when a cool but villainous kid unveils a snazzy new Nintendo peripheral ("I love the Power Glove, it's so bad..."). The climax is the tournament itself where the child contestants battle it out for glory by playing the about-to-be released game *Super Mario Bros. 3.*

For kids in the audience of *The Wizard*, this was their first sneak preview of Mario's latest adventure. To cement the anticipation, cinemas handed out free copies of Nintendo's Pocket Power magazine after screenings. Meanwhile, Universal also got in on the act by showcasing the Universal Studios Hollywood theme park in the film during a lengthy chase sequence on and over its rides.

Made for a "tween" audience years before Hollywood demographics analysts even knew there was such a thing, *The Wizard* didn't embarrass Universal (it took around $20 million on a $7 million budget) although many expected it to perform much better. In comparison, *Super Mario Bros. 3* grossed over $500 million and set new records for videogames sales. Still, the movie was proof of concept for the studio. "It showed that this is a demographic merchandise works for," says Topolosky. "If *The Wizard* is historically important, it's because of this: it proved you could reverse engineer a film from an existing property. *Pirates of the Caribbean* is just another form of *The Wizard*."

After *The Wizard* hit cinemas, the natural progression was to make a movie that featured Mario himself. After all he was already in Saturday morning kids cartoons. How much of a leap was it to think about a live-action movie? There were several concerns, though. "I believe that Japan resisted the idea because of concern with 'bringing Mario to life' in this form," recalls Peter Main, former head of sales and marketing at Nintendo of America (NOA). "Mario in animation left much to the player's imagination, whereas a live-action actor/movie could pop the fantasy. [But] NOA/marketing prevailed."

Hollywood couldn't help but be interested in Nintendo and in *Super Mario Bros.* in particular. Yet, although several studios had already begun to make overtures to the Japanese company about the possibility of a movie based on Mario, they faced unlikely competition. A pair of independent filmmakers - Roland Joffé, the British director of heavy-hitting dramas like *The Killing Fields* and *The Mission*, and Jake Eberts, producer of the Oscar-winning *Dances with Wolves* - were way ahead of them.

Joffé first visited Nintendo of America in 1991 after the idea of a *Super Mario* movie was mooted during a script meeting at his production company. He met NOA's then president Minoru Arakawa, Yamauchi's son-in-law. The filmmaker presented a pitch for the *Super Mario Bros.* movie with illustrations and a rough storyline. "Arakawa was getting lots of suitors," recalls Joffé. "But something tickled him about the personal presentation I made. We weren't a studio and, at one point, he said to me: 'You know we've had people offering us $5, $10 million to buy the rights'. With a gulp I said, 'We could probably run to $500,000'. He just smiled a rather monkish sort of smile: amused and rather touched."

By all accounts, Nintendo should have kicked him out of the office for offering such a laughable sum. But they didn't. A month later, Joffé flew out to Nintendo's corporate headquarters in Kyoto. "I was told [Yamauchi, head of Nintendo] would see me but I had to go through a process which involved a number of visits to his secretary, really. Each time I brought a different kind of tea which I bought in a tea shop in Kyoto. I'd keep hearing little vibrations that said Paramount is putting up so much money, Disney is putting up so much."

The producer spent 10 lonely days in Japan, sleeping on tatami mats and waiting for an audience, never knowing when the phone would ring. In between visits to Yamauchi's secretary, he'd return to the Kyoto tea shop and asked them to pick out the finest teas they had for Nintendo's president. "It was an expensive process," he recalls, "although not as expensive as being Paramount, or Disney, or whoever it was, wanting to spend $5 million on the rights."

Finally Joffé received a phone call summoning him to Yamauchi's office. He pitched Nintendo's boss a storyline involving Mario, Luigi and a host of dinosaurs. Yamauchi listened quietly to the presentation. The producer, who describes the *Super Mario Bros.* game as "a food chain game - it tells us we're all just somebody else's dinner", was determined not to do a simple kid's fantasy. "One of the things I said [to Yamauchi] was, 'Look we're not going to do a sweet little lovey-dovey sort of story. It's got to have an edge to it'."

Nintendo's president was intrigued. "I think he just kind of really liked it," recalls Joffé. "I think he really liked the tea too." When Yamauchi quizzed him why Nintendo would want to sell the rights to a boutique producer instead of a major studio, Joffé argued that Nintendo would have more control over the finished product - although it turned out that the company actually had little interest in a creative partnership. For Nintendo the whole thing was an experiment and they believed the Mario brand was strong enough not to be derailed by a movie. "I think they looked at the movie as some sort of strange creature that was kind of rather intriguing to see if we could walk or not."

After Nintendo sold Joffé and Eberts the rights for a song - around $2 million - Hollywood was uproar. No one could quite believe that these two filmmakers had bagged the most sought after brand name of the new decade. "There was a general sort of looking around among the studios saying, 'Why didn't we buy this?'" recalls Joffé. Little did the studios realise that they had had a narrow escape.

* * *

The Ideal Cement factory in the town of Castle Hayne in Wilmington, North Carolina, looked like a film set even before it came one. Poised somewhere between a Cold War nuclear silo and the setting of a post-apocalyptic sci-fi thriller, it was decommissioned in 1981. As soon as the power was switched off it became the backdrop for a couple of movies. Arnold Schwarzenegger spat out one-liners between its cooling towers in *Raw Deal* and the *Teenage Mutant Ninja Turtles* span on their half-shells in the abandoned cement dust while shooting their first cinematic outing.

Wilmington was no stranger to the movie biz, which is why the locals refer to it as "Wilmywood". North Carolina's clement weather and the city's sprawling, 32-acre Screen Gems Studio complex had attracted dozens of productions from LA. But *Super Mario Bros.* was the first to use the abandoned cement factory as more than just a backdrop. At a cost of several million dollars, the production team spent two months gutting the interior, cleaning out the cement dust and wiring up the five storey mill building for power. A prop shop and machine shop were set up, areas were prepped for the visual effects team to work in and the whole facility was turned into a mini-studio.

It was hot that summer with temperatures hitting 100°F inside the cement bunker that housed the sets. Yet the heat was nothing compared to the conflagration that raged on-set as the production fell apart. Tempers frayed, nerves were shot and the family-friendly world of Mario was filled with expletives, sex and violence as the shoot turned into chaos.

Some movies can be hell to make but heaven to watch. *Super Mario Bros.* wasn't one of those. It was an abject box office bomb, a Hiroshima that completely nuked Hollywood's nascent enthusiasm for turning videogames into movies. Certainly it was a catastrophe on a scale that Nintendo had little experience of. Mario, their signature property, emerged relatively unscathed. However, the company felt so badly burned it turned its back on Hollywood. In years to come it restricted its movie output to the licensing juggernaut of *Pokémon* with its Japanese-made animated feature films.

Like *Heaven's Gate*, it wasn't just the movie's box office ($20.9 million in the US on a production budget of $48 million) that proved devastatingly toxic. It was the negative publicity surrounding its release. True, Hollywood Pictures weren't bankrupted by *Super Mario Bros.* as United Artists had been by Michael Cimino's epic Western, but the fallout was deadly: Disney's new brand was dented by its association with such a universally panned movie (*"Super Mario Bros.* is 1993's answer to *Howard the Duck*," sniffed Variety); and the directors' Hollywood careers ground to a complete halt. What's more, the curse of *Super Mario Bros.* cast a radioactive mushroom cloud over every videogame-to-movie adaptation that followed. "This ain't no game," the original marketing for the movie claimed. They were right. It was more like game over.

Getting *Super Mario Bros.* onto the screen certainly wasn't easy. Indeed the production could be taken as a blueprint of how not to adapt a videogame. Budgeted at around $40 million, the project had a torturous pre-production process. Director Greg Beeman, who made the little-seen film *Mom and Dad Save the World*, was initially hired to handle the shoot, but no studio would buy the project and Joffé decided Beeman "didn't have the stretch for it". Meanwhile, there were multiple screenplay drafts by Barry Morrow, co-screenwriter of *Rain Man*, and Parker Bennett and Terry Runte (*Mystery Date*). Beginning with just a concept and a name, it was hard to hammer out a story for the videogames' paper-thin characters.

After Beeman's departure, Joffé turned to British directors Rocky Morton and Annabel Jankel. The husband and wife team were the co-creators of *The Max Headroom Show* which ran in the mid-1980s on Channel 4 in the UK. An MTV-style selection of music videos strung together, its main draw was Max, a fake artificial intelligence with a distinctive, looping stutter, who served as the programme's presenter. After its success, the directors broke into Hollywood with their 1988 remake of classic film noir *D.O.A.*, starring Dennis Quaid and Meg Ryan. But it was *Max Headroom* that was their calling card. The TV show - along with their coffee table book on computer graphics - made them an obvious shoe-in for a videogame-to-movie adaptation.

From the producers' perspective they were just the kind of hip, young, visionary directors the project needed. "I thought they were very exciting. They loved the project, were extraordinarily enthusiastic, keen and interested" says Joffé. The movie's CGI visual effects - including the transformation of Mojo Nixon's character Toad into a humanoid dinosaur - made their involvement seem a smart choice.

Although both directors knew *Super Mario Bros.* - as everyone did in 1992 - neither were particularly immersed in videogame culture. "We weren't wildly enthusiastic gamers," says Jankel. "I don't think either of us had ever fully involved ourselves in the game at all, which might have had something to do with the end result. We played it for research. It's a bit like if you're doing an adaptation of something, you do your due diligence. But it's not like we were up all through the night playing it." What they did have, though, was a vision. Morton was determined not to make a kids movie. Like Joffé, he thought *Super Mario Bros.* should be dark and edgy. "That's where the conflict happened," the co-director says. "I knew *Super Mario Bros.* looked visually like a kids' videogame but I also knew it was played by people of all ages, including adults."

Morton and Jankel took the screenplay through several revisions, the best of which was written by veteran British comedy writers Dick Clement and Ian La Frenais (famous for their work on British TV comedies *The Likely Lads* and *Porridge*) in early 1992. It was weirdly adult, full of street walkers and drug references and *Mad Max*-style desert death races. Unlike Miyamoto's colourful games, it was set in a drab, parallel universe New York that was ruled by dinosaurs who'd evolved into humanoids. It was strong enough to attract a cast: Bob Hoskins and John Leguizamo signed on as the Brooklyn plumbers who stumble into this other world; Samantha Mathis was Daisy, the cute palaeontologist who're they trying to save. Dennis Hopper played the villainous King Koopa, changed from the fire-breathing turtle of the games into a dinosaur man with an eight-inch tongue. Despite nodding to some of the *Super Mario Bros.* franchise's most memorable features and characters - including the sewer pipes, Mario's dinosaur helper Yoshi, and baddies Iggy and Spike - the screenplay had little to do with the games it was based on.

Depending on who you listen to, what happened next was possibly the moment that everything started to go wrong. Late in pre-production, just before shooting began, several big-hitting executives from the major studios flew down to visit the sprawling sets that were being built in the abandoned cement factory. What they saw surprised them. Production designer David L. Snyder's sets looked post-apocalyptic, full of battered New York taxis, flashing neon and a sprawling mass of metal walkways that looked as if they were leftover from his work on *Blade Runner.* They had little to do with the primary coloured backdrops familiar from the games. Clearly, this wasn't going to be the kids' movie everyone was expecting.

Among the executives who visited was Disney's chief executive Jeffrey Katzenberg, who personally flew out to North Carolina apparently convinced that *Super Mario Bros.* was a good fit for the Mouse House. He eventually bought the US distribution rights to the movie in a negative pickup, although it would be the company's subsidiary, Hollywood Pictures who ultimately distributed the film theatrically. The new label, set up to handle teen-orientated movies like creepy-crawly horror-comedy *Arachnophobia*, was better suited to darker, less traditional Disney fare.

Joffé was adamant that *Super Mario Bros.* wouldn't be for kids. His production company's research suggested that Mario's appeal stretched beyond just the under 12s. It included teenagers and adults too. The screenplay called for scenes with strippers, hookers and much raunchiness. "This wasn't Snow White and the Seven Dinosaurs," says the producer. "The dinosaur world was dark and we didn't want to hold back." Mojo Nixon described it as "a cross between *Peewee's Big Adventure* and *RoboCop 2*".

Morton believes that the movie studios executives who visited the cement factory weren't happy with the tone set by the screenplay. Audiences would expect Mario to be a cute, family movie. The problem was that it was too late in the day to repurpose the whole project. Instead, the production became caught between its original vision and a lot of last-minute tinkering. "The producers decided to take onboard the comments of the studio and change the material to accommodate the comments that were coming back from the studios: which was, this was supposed to be a kids' movie," says the co-director. "They panicked". A week before principal photography, with the cast about to arrive and the sets built, a new screenplay was commissioned from Ed Solomon, who co-wrote *Bill & Ted's Excellent Adventure*. When Morton called the writer to discuss the new draft he was reprimanded. "The producers found out I'd made this call and they forbade me to speak to the writer - the writer who was going to write the script I had to direct."

Joffé, in contrast, says that the studio's involvement came too late to have much impact. "They left us alone," he says. "They couldn't come into it at a very early stage and say we want it to be this or that." Either way, when the cast arrived they weren't happy. The screenplay they had signed up to had been replaced by a hasty revision, written in just 10 days according to Morton, that everyone considered inferior. There were continuity issues, there were tonal issues. The bottom line was, says Morton, "it made no sense".

The directors faced a tough choice: should they walk, or stick it out? "For Annabel and me it was an absolute nightmare," says Morton. "We thought about walking away from it, but how could we? We'd cast it, we'd built these sets, all this incredible effort had gone into it. It just didn't seem right. We thought, maybe as we're shooting we can steer it and make it into the film that we wanted. We made the wrong decision: we were unable to do that and it became this huge mess." To add insult to injury, the directors found themselves championing the new screenplay, even though they hated it, in order not to lose the actors.

When shooting started, Morton and Jankel tried to salvage what they could of the story. Pages were rewritten on a daily basis. It got to the point where the actors didn't bother reading the new pages, knowing full well that more would likely follow before the clapperboard clapped. The general atmosphere on set was totally anarchic. Actors Fisher Stevens and Richard Edson, who played Iggy and Spike, improvised their own rap routine (it never made it into the finished film); original director of photography Peter Levy was fired in the first couple of weeks.

It didn't help that the whole production was diverging so drastically from the source material. Nintendo were nowhere to be seen. Morton and Jankel met the games' shy and retiring co-designer Shigeru Miyamoto during pre-production. "I don't remember much communication going on," says Jankel. The games company's only input was the gift of a beautiful poster containing all the characters from the various games and a consignment of Super Scope light guns that were retooled by the prop department to serve as the villains' "Devolution" weapons. Nintendo didn't even have a representative present during the shoot. Connections to the videogame were tenuous at best. The creature design teams abandoned the game's Goomba villains - walking shitake mushrooms - and replaced them with an army of surreal dino-humanoids with oversized bodies and pinheads. They looked like something out of Tod Browning's horror film *Freaks*. Meanwhile the costume department threw together rubber, PVC and leather outfits like something out of a Skin Two catalogue. For an outing that was inevitably always going to be seen as a kids' movie, given the franchise it was based on, it was wildly inappropriate. If you'd never played the games, the production made no sense. If you had played the games, it still made no sense.

According to many accounts, Jankel and Morton were out of their depth, pulled between the demands of the producers, their attempts to rewrite on-the-hoof and the logistical enormity of the production. "I think they were largely overwhelmed by the whole thing," says Nixon. "I could just tell that the whole thing was eating them away. They were being pulled in five or six directions at once. They didn't have as much control as they wanted."

Used to shooting commercials and TV, the scale of the film was a shock. They became obsessed with minutiae. Joffé recalls finding the directors and cast locked in a script meeting in the middle of shooting over a scene that was just 11 lines long. "I had to jolly everyone back on set. It was like being a schoolmaster," he says. Morton remembers himself and Jankel being hauled into the producers trailer on a nightly basis. "We were told we were going to be fired, we were doing a terrible job. Every night we were told this. We were [told we were] behind, spending too much money, the budget was haemorrhaging, and the whole thing was a disaster."

At a more basic level it was a clash of personalities. "The arrogance of Rocky and Annabel was a real problem," recalls make-up artist Jeff Goodwin, who watched the saga unfold close up. "Everybody was shocked by these people and their behaviour." The directors, nicknamed Rock-a-bell and Rocky and Bullwinkle, became the focus of the increasingly demoralised crew's anger. As decisions were delayed or revised, the production schedule began to flounder. "It was like being directed by Chip & Dale," claimed Leguizamo. "That's why a ship only has one captain."

For the producers, the decision to hire two directors was one they soon regretted. "I think Rocky and Annabel began to interpret the characters differently and they never resolved that between them," Joffé says. "Rocky would be rather expansive and optimistic and Annabel would be darker and more twisted. I think the actors got very confused. The production got away from the two of them, but one has to be careful. It was a big thing, which is why I haven't criticised them very much. They generally did the best they could, but it was just too big and I think their ambitions were enormous, honourably so."

Hoskins - gruff, cockney and never one to suffer fools gladly - was particularly aggrieved by the directors' behaviour. "The worst thing I ever did? *Super Mario Bros.*," he claimed years later. "It was a fuckin' nightmare. The whole experience was a nightmare. It had a husband-and-wife team directing, whose arrogance had been mistaken for talent. After so many weeks, their own agent told them to get off the set! Fuckin' nightmare. Fuckin' idiots."

To keep himself sane during filming, Hoskins apparently ordered a crate of Scotch, the contents of which he worked his way through with the help of Leguizamo. Needless to say, the cockney star clashed with the directors relentlessly. "Bob's got an edge," says Joffé. "I think he felt a bit lost. He probably felt he could have directed the movie in many ways, certainly as far as the actors were concerned."

One problem came when Hoskins was shooting a chase sequence in which the brothers escape from Dinohattan's Boom Boom Bar by jumping off a bridge onto a passing dumpster truck. Hoskins, who once described himself as "five-foot-six and cubic", gamely agreed to make the jump without a stunt double. As makeup artist Jeff Goodwin recalls, after several takes of the star crashing onto the safety mats below had been shot, Jankel approached him with a suggestion.

"Bob, next time just try to linger in the air a little longer."

Hoskins was lost for words. "Lady," he snapped back, "I'm doing the best I can."

"Maybe we should get Wile E. Coyote to do it," joked Goodwin, who was on hand to touch up the actor's makeup between takes. It was a reference to Hoskins's animated co-stars in *Who Framed Roger Rabbit* and he began chatting to Goodwin about what a great actor Wile E. Coyote was. Jankel looked at them like they'd lost their minds and wandered off.

"Kid, this is great," Hoskins told Goodwin. "Whenever she comes over, start talking about these kooky characters from *Roger Rabbit* like they're real and maybe she'll leave us alone..."

It became a running gag between the star and the makeup artist, although Jankel says has no memory of the incident: "A lot of these things are urban legends. I don't remember falling out with Bob Hoskins. He was really accommodating. It wasn't the actors who were the problem. It was the script and the production." The motivations for Hoskins' vociferous denouncement of both the film and its directors over the years are, she says, a mystery to her.

Morton's attitude didn't endear him to the crew either. According to several sources, the crew was left shocked when he took his frustrations out on an extra. The victim was one of the Mushroom Kingdom's garbage truck operators who were dressed in head-to-toe rubber suits and gasmasks. While prepping the brief sequence featuring them Morton said he wasn't happy with the way the suits looked. As production supervisor Moe Lospinoso recalls, he wanted the rubber to look wet.

"I want it wetter."

The wardrobe assistant sprayed it down.

"No, wetter".

She sprayed it again.

"No, wetter!"

She sprayed it again.

"No wetter, you bitch, wetter you fucking bitch! Wetter!"

Lospinoso says Morton then emptied the cup of hot coffee he was holding over the extra's head. The mask and body suit offered little protection and the actor suffered second-degree burns ("Oh well, he's just an extra," was Morton's take on it, according to Leguizamo). "We had to deal with it. That was the kind of stuff they'd pull off and just think they were able to do," says the production supervisor grimly, who remembers the on-set medic being called over. "I think it was frustration. This was a big production [of the kind] that they weren't used to."

Joffé says has no memory of the incident: "I think if I'd seen coffee being poured on someone's head I would have remembered that. It must have happened when I wasn't there." Meanwhile, Morton himself disputes the incident's retelling. According to the co-director, the coffee was lukewarm, there were no burns and his aim was simply to wet down the costume in a bid to stop the light from glinting off it. The extra's surprised reaction at having a cup of coffee poured over him simply convinced onlookers that he'd been hurt - when he hadn't. "People love to read about directors who are out of control and arrogant," Morton says, and accuses Leguizamo of exaggerating the incident in order to drum up sales of his autobiography.

Whatever the truth, it was apparent that there were enormous tensions on the set. After principal photography wrapped, the directors returned to LA to discover that various cast members had spoken to the LA Times. The story ran on the front page of the paper's Calendar section and contained a lurid catalogue of complaints about the directors and accusations that the movie was a total car wreck. When Morton arrived at the editing suite he found he'd been locked out, but there was worse to come.

"CAA [one of Hollywood's leading talent agencies] dumped us immediately," he remembers. "We couldn't get an agent. No scripts would come. We couldn't get meetings. Literally, the phones stopped ringing. It all was because of that front page article. Everyone reads Calendar in LA. Nobody wanted to touch us. We were like lepers in Hollywood. Still to this day I have projects and I call up the managers and agents to try and represent it and they say 'You did *Super Mario Bros.*? Oh God...' It was like 20 years ago, but it's still there. What can you do?"

When the film had its red carpet premiere at Disney World in Florida in 1993, it was apparent to everyone that it captured none of the magic of the games. Miyamoto, *Super Mario Bros.* co-designer Takashi Tezuka and various

Nintendo employees flew in from Japan to see how their bestselling franchise looked the big screen.

Polite to a fault Miyamoto has yet to comment candidly on Hollywood's bastardisation of his most iconic creation. In an interview with Edge magazine in 2007 he noted: "I wasn't terribly involved because my feeling was that I make videogames. I wanted someone who makes movies to create the *Mario Bros.* movie and that would be the best way for it to be an entertaining movie." Joffé recalls Miyamoto being "lovely and quite ethereal [...] he had no interest in the movie at all. [For him] it was all about the game and all these things bouncing about from one to another. It was as much mathematics as anything else."

Nintendo and its employees certainly weren't seduced by movie glamour. They were already undisputed leaders in the entertainment field and their attitude towards the process spoke volumes about the changing power dynamic between the two industries. "I think they were amused by the whole thing and wanted to see what would happen," says Joffé, who compares the movie to the Wright Brothers' airplane ("It got up in the air but one would have liked it to have gone further"). He also believes that Nintendo felt totally protected: "They didn't think it was going to damage their franchise in any way whatsoever."

They were right. There was no immediate fallout from the *Super Mario Bros.* movie and certainly no executive heads rolled at Nintendo. "The movie tended towards the darker side and bombed [but] no lasting harm was realised," says Main, Nintendo of America's former head of sales and marketing. After the film's release, Japan called a moratorium on further dalliances with Hollywood studios. The decision came right from the top. "Yamauchi correctly saw that we had a tiger by the tail and was very adamant that we stay tightly focused on videogames in the purest sense, without being distracted with other 'leverage opportunities'," Main continues. "In the end, the company felt there was more potential down-side risk to the core business with these kinds of short-term, loosely-controlled licensing opportunities than were warranted." In short, Hollywood needed Nintendo, but Nintendo had no use for Hollywood.

Despite its box office failure and troubled production, Joffé remains proud of *Super Mario Bros.* "It's not that I defend the movie, it's just that, in its own extraordinary way, it was an interesting and rich artefact and has earned its place. It has strange cult status." The producer never heard what Yamauchi thought of the finished movie that he pitched to him in Japan in '91. "They never phoned up to complain," he says. "They were very polite, Nintendo. I'm sure they had their own feelings, but they never sent the tea back..."

* * *

When Paul W. S. Anderson was in his 20s, geography was a bitch. The Warwick University graduate knew he wanted to make movies. The problem was that Soho, the hub of the UK film industry, was 300 miles away from his hometown of Newcastle Upon Tyne by Intercity train. While trying to break into television, eventually writing for ITV's Costa Del Crime cop show *El C.I.D.*, Anderson got used to making the trip to London's King's Cross station then hopping on the tube to Wardour Street. In between taking meetings, he'd hang out in Soho's arcades.

Ever since he'd been a kid, Anderson understood the allure of games. "I think I was definitely one of the first generation of filmmakers who grew up with an appreciation of videogames," he says. In his youth, he'd spent summer holidays in Scarborough playing pinball on the pier and vividly recalls seeing the first *Space Invaders* machine. "It was like the monolith from *2001* had suddenly appeared. It had all these kids clustered around it. It really had a magnetic pull."

By 1993, there was a new coin-op in his life: *Mortal Kombat*. While he was drumming up finance for his debut feature *Shopping*, a nihilistic, ram-raiding thriller starring Jude Law and Sadie Frost, it was *Mortal Kombat* that kept luring him back into the arcades. Unlike Capcom's *Street Fighter II*, another fighting game coin-op that had taken arcades by storm in the early 1990s, *Mortal Kombat* had a hard edge. Its creators, two American 20-somethings Ed Boon and John Tobias, decided to counter Capcom's manga-influenced animation style by using real martial artists as the basis for their characters. Shooting the fighters on Hi8 videotape, the designers digitised the footage and created realistic-looking sprites. It gave the action a vicious, visceral quality as blood spurted in garish hues and spinal cords were ripped out.

While the characters looked convincing, the story was flat-out demented. The fighters in *Mortal Kombat*, performing in an inter-dimensional martial arts tournament to decide the Earth's fate, were an outré bunch. There was Johnny Cage, a Jean-Claude Van Damme-alike movie star who wore sunglasses to each bout; Sub Zero, a magical ninja with the power to deliver icy knockout blows; and Raiden, a supernatural being whose body crackled with elemental lightning. Whenever the coin-op wasn't being played the attract mode cycled through the characters offering snippets of their biographies.

It proved a tantalising hook. The allure of *Mortal Kombat* was its mystery. Each fighter had signature moves and combat styles that relied on players discovering which button and joystick combinations unleashed what attack. There were also teasing glimpses of its star villain Goro, a half-human dragon with four arms and a couple of millennia of ass-kicking experience. You had to be good to face in him battle; even luckier to unlock some of the secret characters like Reptile, a hidden green ninja the existence of whom was whispered about by veteran players in hushed tones.

Sneaking in as many games as he could, Anderson loved the coin-op's mix of mythic characters and martial arts. "*Mortal Kombat* reminded me of movies I loved as a kid, like epic quest movies made by Ray Harryhausen." As he climbed his way up the game's high-score table, though, he never guessed it would take him to Hollywood and into the office of producer Larry Kasanoff.

Fighting games are all about the death match. The rules are primal, a survival of the fittest that requires you to batter or splatter your opponent into a bloody pulp. Last man standing wins and only in death is there dishonour. Kasanoff knew that well, which is why when he heard that Midway/Williams had a game coming out that looked like it was going to be bigger than their earlier hit *Terminator 2: Judgement Day* his feathers were ruffled. This was a fight he couldn't pass up. The *T2* coin-op was Kasanoff's baby, one of the fruits of a groundbreaking series of merchandising deals brokered by Lightstorm, the production company that he and director James Cameron had founded together. When Cameron made his $100 million sequel to *The Terminator* in 1991, Kasanoff was in charge of production, marketing, publicity and merchandising. The truth was *Terminator 2: Judgement Day* the movie was so costly they had to merchandise it to death: "At the time it was the most expensive movie in history and, honestly, out of fear we tried to wring every drop of blood out of the stone we could. I got very involved in making sure it became a franchise - although we didn't use that term in those days."

It was during a visit to Midway's offices in Chicago, that Kasanoff saw the company's new hot property, the *Mortal Kombat* coin-op. They took the movie producer down to a local arcade where it was testing off the scale. As kids crowded around the machine, Kasanoff realised they had a hit on their hands. That wasn't news to Midway. But the producer was also convinced it had potential as a movie. Their response? "Bullshit! There's no way you can do that. This is an arcade game, there's no way you can turn it into a movie." Kasanoff told them, "I don't just want to just make a movie. I want to make a franchise."

The producer spent the summer of 1993 convincing Midway of its big screen potential. When he finally won their approval, he set up Threshold Entertainment and sat on the movie rights while *Mortal Kombat* did a victory lap of the arcades. It wasn't long before the machine pummelled every coin-op out there including the top-earning *T2* machine. After Acclaim released their home console versions of the game in the US that autumn - on "Mortal Monday", 13 September 1993 - the title broke sales records. A little later, Kasanoff announced his deal with Midway in the Hollywood trade press.

Despite the huge interest in *Mortal Kombat*'s success, the reaction was largely one of derision or outright bewilderment. Hollywood, always risk averse, was convinced that videogame movies were the kiss of death after the corrosive impact of *Super Mario Bros.* "Everyone was calling me up saying, 'What are you doing? This is going to ruin your career. This is a videogame, this can't happen'."

Videogames were still considered a new phenomenon. The older generation of studio executives simply didn't get it. "My best story of what it was like back then was the meeting I had after I announced I had the rights to *Mortal Kombat*," says the producer. "[One of the studios] said, 'This is great, come right up'. When I got there, I'm in a boardroom with millions of people and they're going: 'This is fantastic, this is great, you've got *Mortal Kombat*, this is wonderful...er, what is it exactly?' I tried to explain to them but nobody even had a Nintendo console to play the game on. So we got a golf cart to drive around the lot until they found the merchandising guy. He had a console. We plug it in, I show them *Mortal Kombat* on Nintendo [the sanitised, bloodless version]. They looked at it for about 30 seconds, turned to me, stuck out their hands and say: 'Well, thanks for coming.'"

Despite the knock back, Kasanoff continued to push on with development. Ed Boon and John Tobias put together an extended *Mortal Kombat* "Bible", fleshing out the arcade game's storyline and characters. Getting the creators involved made sense, especially since Midway had already published a comic book, based on the game, which was written and illustrated by Tobias. The original coin-op machine even hawked it in the attract mode, asking players to send $3 to Midway for a mail order copy. The cross-marketing potential of the game was apparent right from the beginning.

"My philosophy always was: the reason why people fail making movies from videogames is because they try to make movies from videogames,"

Kasanoff explains, somewhat gnomically. "I thought: we're not making a movie based on a videogame, we're making a movie based on the story that the videogame is based on. The story is the centre of the wheel and the videogame is the extension of one of the spokes." With a screenplay ready, Kasanoff began to look for a studio.

In the end it was New Line that would make *Mortal Kombat*. The maverick studio was run like a family business by Bob Shaye, a self-made mogul who was notoriously blunt when it came to voicing his opinions. But it was also a company that understood the value of a franchise. They'd made a bundle on the *Teenage Mutant Ninja Turtles* phenomenon and the long-running *Nightmare on Elm Street* series had been so lucrative for them that industry insiders dubbed New Line "The House That Freddy Built".

The thing was, New Line didn't think *Mortal Kombat* was another Freddy. In fact, they thought it was a piece of shit. The screenplay was penned by Kevin Droney, a TV veteran of *The Equalizer* and *Hunter* who'd go on to write the *Wing Commander* movie a few years later. In the first script meeting, Shaye burst into the room and threw a copy of the screenplay onto the table in a fury: "I hate this fucking thing."

Kasanoff, who knew New Line didn't have much else to fill their summer slate with, cut a deal: "They needed a hit for the summer and because of my track record, they thought, 'What the hell maybe this is it'." Kasanoff agreed to halve his fee but in return he'd keep sequel, merchandising and TV rights. It was a bold move, reminiscent of George Lucas's deal with Fox on *Star Wars*. After *Mortal Kombat* became the franchise that Kasanoff believed it could, he cleaned up. "Once the movie became a hit, and those rights became enormously valuable, [New Line] were constantly trying to get those rights back from me. I think they were somewhat resentful." As the screenwriter William Goldman once said, in the movie biz "nobody knows anything". In the grey zone where videogames and movies met, that statement was doubly true.

New Line, at least, had a passing understanding of videogames. They were a hip, young studio after all that prided themselves on their work hard, play harder ethic. Head of production Mike De Luca, the boyish, good-looking exec styled by many as the son Shaye never had, built a reputation in Hollywood circles as a man who liked to party. He became infamous in 1998 when he attended a pre-Oscars bash at the home of William Morris Agency exec Arnold Rifkin and received a very public blowjob from a young actress.

His host had him forcibly ejected by security and the story entered Hollywood lore. If De Luca was anything to go by, New Line, much like Atari years before, understood the value of play.

Videogames slotted pretty nicely into that mindset. This was a company that prided itself on understanding what its core, youthful audience wanted: *House Party, Teenage Ninja Mutant Turtles, Dumb & Dumber, Deep Cover, Menace II Society*, and *King of New York* to name but a few. If it was hip and cool, it probably had New Line's film strip logo stamped on the front of it. For *Mortal Kombat* to be a success, it needed a hip, young director too - someone who understood videogames. As the net was cast, Kasanoff began to receive call after call from one particular director's manager: "She was unbelievably aggressive. She kept calling me saying 'You've got to meet this guy, you've got to meet this guy'. He'd directed some unsuccessful art film in London. I ignored her like 25 times [but] finally agreed to meet him."

The guy in question was Paul W. S. Anderson. He'd been taking meetings in Los Angeles after his debut *Shopping* - hardly an art movie - stirred up tabloid controversy in the UK. Unlike some of the other directors touting for *Mortal Kombat*, Anderson could actually claim truthfully to have played the game in question. At New Line, he met De Luca and instantly realised he'd found a kindred spirit. They were both young, both gamers.

"Mike didn't look anything like a studio executive," recalls Anderson. "He had torn jeans, a Black Sabbath T-shirt and you know he just looked like a skater kid. He was the first person I saw in Hollywood who had game consoles in his office. Nowadays you go into any young executive's office in Holly-wood and they have toys, game systems. It's almost de rigueur - like an interior designer puts all these things there when they do the office. Mike really was the first person I'd met working in Hollywood who had an appreciation of this aspect of youth culture."

In hiring Anderson, Kasanoff and New Line were taking a big risk. But the feeling was that the project needed someone who could connect the dots to the fan audience. "There was this belief that videogame movies just didn't work, the idea of adapting videogames into movies was a flawed one," the director says. "My feeling was, it wasn't a bad idea. They really were a justifiable intellectual property to adapt into movies. It was just that no one had made a very good movie out of one yet that reflected the game correctly and that was also a movie-going experience that pleased fans as well as non-gamers. *Mortal Kombat* was probably the first movie to deliver that."

It didn't hurt that the coin-op came with a built in notoriety. Just as the Senate hearings had helped Digital Pictures ship a truckload of *Night Trap* inventory in the Christmas of 1993, the hope was that *Mortal Kombat*'s brand awareness would pull gamers, martial arts fans and moviegoers looking for a fast-paced popcorn flick into cinemas on the strength of its name alone.

Throughout 1993, the *Mortal Kombat* phenomenon had been mentioned in nearly every newspaper in America - even before it joined *Night Trap* in the dock at the Senate hearings. It was synonymous with everything that was cool, edgy and violent about videogames. Parents and politicians hated it, moral crusaders denounced it. You couldn't buy publicity like that and the kids quickly claimed it as their own. Even though the movie wouldn't arrive until 1995, the brand's cultural half-life was still strong enough to make most young moviegoers' Geiger counters click like crickets on speed.

Mortal Kombat cost around $20 million to make. It had no stars to speak of, unless you count Christopher Lambert, who played Thunder God Raiden. What it had instead was a colourful location shoot in Thailand, a clutch of martial artists flown in from the Far East, and Alison Savitch, the visual effects supervisor on *Terminator 2*. Goro, the four-armed Shokan Prince, was created by visual effects firm Amalgamated Dynamics (who had worked on *Alien 3*). Unknown actors Robin Shou, Linden Ashby and Bridgette Wilson brought Liu Kang, Johnny Cage and Sonya Blade to life. Kevin Droney's screenplay was strictly B-movie but it had a certain zing, cheesy dialogue raising smiles rather than groans. No one was under the impression that they were making great art. Rather the aim was to offer a movie that would have street cred appeal, a mix of what Kasanoff describes as *"Star Wars* meets *Enter the Dragon"*.

During production, as a courtesy more than anything, Tobias and Boon were flown out to visit the set. Kasanoff was keen to get them involved, though he was concerned about the impending culture clash as these Chicago videogame engineers found themselves dazzled by the bright lights of the movie biz. "There's always a tendency for people to show up in LA, get an Armani suit, a convertible and a bimbo and boom! they've gone Hollywood. There's always a risk that you're going to lose a percentage of people in doing that," he says. "But the thing with John and Ed was that they didn't believe in it. Nobody believed in this movie."

Tobias begs to differ: "I don't ever remember thinking it was going to be a complete bomb. I was kind of hopeful [...] But I was scared given previous videogame adaptations like *Super Mario Bros.* and *Street Fighter*." Certainly the designers didn't have time to experience any showbiz hedonism. "We were working 12-, 14- hour days on *Mortal Kombat 3*," Tobias remembers. "There were a lot of stories about what New Line was at the time. I don't know what their partying issues were or whatever but we were totally not exposed to that. Either we were shielded from it by Larry [Kasanoff] or the Midway higher ups [...] We visited the set, had real meaningful conversations about the direction of the film, the story and characters. There were no Ferraris or bimbos."

What did surprise the designers was the deference they were shown. Hollywood has always been good at playing to talents' egos and when Tobias and Boon arrived on-set they got the red carpet treatment. "Everybody was very gracious. Even the stuntmen would come up and shake our hands and thank us. What they were thanking us for was us creating the game which ultimately led to them having a job. I wasn't expecting that at all and I got a real sense of what we had created and what it had snowballed into."

While the collaboration with Midway was smooth sailing, New Line was a different story. "The reality was that the studio in those days was such a mess," says Kasanoff. "You couldn't find anyone. During one of the *Mortal Kombat* movies I'm sitting in a teak long boat in the South China Seas [on location] and I get a phone call from the New Line office saying, 'You know, you're not greenlit yet...' I just hang up the phone and say, 'Action' and nobody bothers to call back until after we've finished the movie."

The studio's haphazard management style was a headache. Executives would disappear for weeks at a time and Kasanoff occasionally had to fight to get his requests met. "You'd tell them: 'I have to fly this guy in from Xianju, China because he's the best wushu kicker in the world' and they'd look at you like you're fucking crazy: 'Who cares? Just kick somebody'. But that's not what you do. We took extraordinary care with the martial arts. The biggest tenet of *Mortal Kombat* is the martial arts."

The first test screenings confirmed that. Audience feedback suggested there was too much talking, not enough punching. New Line ponied up more money and additional fight scenes were shot. When they ran it again, the reaction tested off the scale. "The audience couldn't sit still," remembers Kasanoff. "It was like they were at a Black Eyed Peas concert. Kids were getting up and fake punching each other in the aisles. That's when I realised it was a hit."

Even still, Kasanoff claims no one had faith in it, neither at New Line or Midway. Or even in Hollywood generally. "After the test screening an executive at New Line said the movie was a piece of shit," says Kasanoff in his inimitable style. "When I finished the movie I took it to Chicago to show Neil Nicastro, who was chief executive of Midway. I said, 'You see, you said I wouldn't do it but here it is.' He sits and watches it. When it's over, he looks at me and says: 'Three out of 10. Piece of shit.'"

Even during the opening weekend, the producer fielded calls from acquaintances telling him his career was over. "But this is Hollywood, so when it turned out it was a hit, the same people called me up and said 'I knew it, I was behind you all the way!'"

When *Mortal Kombat* was released in August 1995, videogame movies had already suffered three strikes. *Super Mario Bros.* had flopped. So too had *Double Dragon*, a silly, low-budget quickie based on the beat-'em-up arcade game that played on-screen like *Bill & Ted* with martial arts. Then there was *Street Fighter* starring Jean-Claude Van Damme and Kylie Minogue, a spin off from *Mortal Kombat*'s main arcade rival. It was candy-coloured, frenetic and largely ludicrous - and didn't quite break even at the US box office (although foreign earnings helped its total gross climb to three times its $33.5 million production budget).

Watching all these movies as a group, you're struck by how distinctly unambitious they are. It's as if their producers looked at the lacklustre storytelling ability of the videogame world and said to each other: "Holy crap, is that all gamers expect? We can commission shit like that in our lunch breaks and still have time to get *Judge Dredd* and *The Island of Doctor Moreau* greenlit before pre-steak cocktails at Morton's..." Indeed, Edward R. Pressman, producer on *Street Fighter, Dredd* and *Moreau*, pretty much did exactly that.

What the *Street Fighter* movie suggested - and *Mortal Kombat* would prove for certain - was that videogames had their own built-in brand name recognition. When it was turned into a movie, Capcom's *Street Fighter* kick-started a franchise: D.C. Comics published a tie-in comic book, rapper Ice Cube wrote and performed a tie-in single, Invision Entertainment produced a cartoon for US TV, and Capcom released a coin-op using digitised footage from the film entitled *Street Fighter: The Movie*. In 1999 there was a feature-length anime, *Street Fighter: Alpha*. As late as 2009, there was another, poorly-received, live-action outing, *Street Fighter: The Legend of Chun Li*. Here was a franchise with legs as strong as Chun Li's famous, muscular pins.

Franchising the hell out of these properties became the standard approach. If nothing else, *The Wizard* had been prescient about the way videogame movies would become an issue of commerce over art. Kasanoff, who had the confidence to secure the *Mortal Kombat* rights early on, reaped the benefits of this approach. *Mortal Kombat* cost $20 million to produce and took over $23 million in just its opening weekend in the States. By the end of its theatrical run, *Mortal Kombat* had grossed $70 million in the US alone and $122 million worldwide.

That was just the tip of the iceberg of what would become a $3 billion cross-media franchise. "It's a lot more than a movie," Kasanoff told Cinefantastique magazine in 1995. "It's an animated video special, a live-action tour that we're doing, a series of toys and merchandise licenses, a making-of-the-movie book, a novelization of both the movie and, separately, the underlying story. It will one day be a live-action TV show, and an animated series. All that stuff is in the works or has already happened. *Mortal Kombat* is more than a videogame we turned into a movie. It's a phenomenal story we are cross-publishing in every medium that exists. That's what I formed the company [Threshold] to do. It's not just a movie, it's a way of life."

Despite the movie's success, Anderson boldly passed on the chance to direct the sequel - although he'd soon return to the videogame movie world with the even more successful *Resident Evil* movie in 2002. Despite a critical mauling it kickstarted an on-going, billion dollar movie series for Sony Screen Gems, making it Sony's most profitable movie franchise after *Spider-Man*.

Significantly, it was Kasanoff's career that was most transformed by the lucre *Mortal Kombat* generated. The producer had spotted and exploited a hugely successful property, spinning it into a franchise. Yet there was something dispiriting about this blatant milking of a brand. The interplay of videogame/movie/comics/Radio City stage show looked less like artistic innovation than a sure sign of the snake eating its own tail. This was the pop culture ouroboros in action, the fruition of the seeds that George Lucas's merchandising empire had sown back in the late-1970s.

Taken individually the *Mortal Kombat* products, with the exception of the original videogame, were largely uninspired. Cumulatively, they were unstoppable. Each property fed off the others, generating heat from its cousins' exposure. As a business model it was brilliant. From a fan's perspective it was like being spoon-fed one pureed Big Mac after another. The success of *Mortal Kombat* - undeniably a phenomenon - told every Hollywood producer with their eye on a videogame property that the bar didn't have to be set that high. New Line and Midway's executives were right: *Mortal Kombat* the movie was a piece of shit. But with the right Midas Touch even turds could be gold-plated.

* * *

A long time ago, in a galaxy not that far away lived a young boy called Chris Roberts. Chris wasn't just a *Star Wars* fan. He was the kind of Jedi geek who could tell you the difference between a tauntaun and a bantha in torturous detail. Born in California in 1968, he grew up in Manchester, England in the 1970s. When he was eight-years-old, he went to the cinema to see George Lucas's space opera. It changed his life. The moment he got back home he started building X-Wing fighters and Tie-fighters out of his Lego set. "That whole sense of being transported to another world had a big impact on me," he says. "Everything I've done has been about creating worlds that you can escape into."

When he wasn't talking about Tie-Fighters, Roberts was busy tapping away at the red and black keys of his school's BBC Micro computers. He dreamed of making games that could capture the magic of Lucas's universe. If you'd told his younger self that one day he'd be living in California, running his own software company and directing Luke Skywalker - destroyer of the Death Star and the last of the illustrious Jedi Knights, aka actor Mark Hamill - he probably would have shat his pants.

Fast forward to 1990 and Roberts was already achieving all his dreams. He'd been making games since he was 11-years-old but it was only after moving to the US to join Origin Systems that he began work on what would be his magnum opus, the *Wing Commander* series. A futuristic universe populated by hot stuff fighter pilots, space freighters and feline aliens called the Kilrathi, the *Wing Commander* games were phenomenally successful. Each box was emblazoned with the legend "A Chris Roberts game" and the programmer/designer auteur quickly attracted a huge following.

PC gamers were seduced by his space opera franchise and its ambition to tell a story as well as let you dogfight in outer space. Each new instalment raised the narrative stakes, following pilot Christopher Blair as he became a decorated veteran of the Terran-Kilrathi conflict. The universe the games opened up was as intricate as anything Lucas created. It was filled with Arrow fighters, Temblor Bombs, and a weary hero who'd had a bellyful of war.

The *Wing Commander* world was shaken up in 1994 when *Wing Commander III: Heart of the Tiger* made the jump to full motion video. No longer would Blair and his fellow pilots be animated sprites. Now they were live actors whose stories played out in cinematic cut-scenes (the dramatic, non-playable sections between game levels). Hamill starred as Blair. John Rhys-Davies and Malcolm McDowell lent thespian weight as Terran Confederation officers. Shoots against green screen allowed the game designers to flesh out a digital sci-fi world around their characters. Roberts suddenly found himself morphing into a filmmaker. Understandably he was terrified, since he'd never even been to film school. "I'd learned everything I knew from watching movies," he says. "But in terms of knowing how to do a master shot, two shot and singles and all the different things you need to know on a technical basis about how to shoot something and put it together to make the scenes flow, that was pretty intimidating."

Wing Commander III had a $3 million budget for its video shoot. *Wing Commander IV: The Price of Freedom*, shot on 35mm, had an $8 million budget. Those were not figures to be sniffed at and nor were the sales figures. *Wing Commander* marked out its turf as one of the bastions of PC gaming in the '90s. While other FMV titles were largely derided, the *Wing Commander* series managed to create a balance between its live action narrative scenes and the comparatively lo-fi, animated game sequences that let you fly through space. The franchise's loyal fans didn't seem to mind the jarring shift from passively watching FMV to actively shooting sprites. The tremulous FMV drama, where Hamill deals with romances and fallen comrades, gave a much-needed emotional dimension to what was essentially a spaceship cockpit simulator.

For Roberts as a creator, though, the game portions were losing their appeal. *Wing Commander* had grown into a huge pulp sci-fi saga and it was outgrowing its videogame format. After EA bought Origin Systems, he started writing a spec screenplay for a movie and put out feelers in Hollywood, uncertain about what would happen but hoping all the same: "It was my passion project, my baby."

When the movie finally happened it was all about the deal. Of course, all movies are essentially all about the deal, but *Wing Commander* was in a class of its own. Producer Todd Moyer put together a financing package so complex it made Maxwell's partial differential equations look like something a toddler might chalk up on their PlaySkool blackboard during the ad breaks in *Bear in the Big Blue House*.

To be fair, it was a stunning deal - or rather series of deals - that jigsawed together money from all over. It began with a small domestic minimum guarantee from Fox and was followed by a Luxembourg tax incentive, some French investment, an Australian tax shelter, UK financing and foreign sales. In all, the independent production secured a $30 million budget. "At the time it was a tonne of money," says Moyer.

Moyer knew all about exploiting intellectual property across mediums. He'd been an executive vice president at Dark Horse Comics and had arranged a lot of the big movie licensing agreements - comic books like *Aliens*, *Predator* and their eventual crossover *Aliens Vs. Predator*, which would become both a movie and a videogame. He'd headed up Steven Seagal's production company. Plus he'd worked with Van Damme on *Time Cop*, Pamela Anderson on *Barbed Wire* and Jamie Lee Curtis on *Virus*. Like Larry Kasanoff, Moyer had an eye for a potential franchise. Games, he believed, were much like the comic book properties he'd dealt with: they were the foundations on which you could build a movie, using the original intellectual property to show potential investors that there was both a market and a vision capable of sustaining a feature film. Much as with *Mortal Kombat*, the deal was the bottom line: how much leverage could you get from a property to spin it off into profitable properties in other mediums?

This was the McDonaldization of entertainment at its most naked and it said a lot about the movie industry's approach to adapting games for the big screen. While novels and plays could claim cultural legitimacy, videogames were largely seen as toy-like systems rather than art. In the eyes of Svengali producers like Moyer they were simply brands waiting to be exploited. "I'm not very reverential towards videogame creators," he admits. "Games just don't get me excited." Instead, their value was as intellectual property. "Once you own IP you can carve out very different deals for the creators with that and for a lot of people."

When Moyer heard about Roberts and the *Wing Commander* series' dominance in the PC market from an agent friend of his, he set up a meeting. "Chris had a pretty bad script, that unfortunately only got a little bit better," the producer remembers. "Basically it was a C-rate *Star Wars* rip off." Things might have ended there if it weren't for two plusses. It helped, naturally, that the *Wing Commander* franchise had made millions of dollars. More importantly, Roberts was putting a chunk of equity on the table. He was essentially buying himself a shot at feature film directing. Nothing wrong with that in the movie biz, of course; yet this was the first time a videogame creator had made the leap into making studio distributed movies.

You might think Fox were taking a huge gamble. Here was a young, novice filmmaker stepping up to direct his first movie, an epic space opera with a $30 million price tag. The studio suits must have been worried, right? Wrong. Well then, they must have been swayed by the videogame designer's showreel with all the FMV footage he'd shot on video and 35mm film for the games? Wrong again. Surely when they saw him directing Mark Hamill and Malcolm McDowell they felt reassured? Not at all. In fact, they barely glanced at it.

"No one gave a shit about Chris Roberts as a director or not a director," says Moyer. "All they cared was that the videogame had huge sales, there was a built-in audience, and they could crunch the numbers. Like many of these movies, at the right price, nobody cares who directs them." With a minimum domestic guarantee from Fox, the filmmakers could basically go off and make whatever movie they wanted. Fox's exposure was so low, they had no interest in keeping tabs. It was a disinterest that would both make and break the *Wing Commander* movie's fortunes.

For Roberts, stepping into the director's chair was something of a poisoned chalice. The young Brit, on the cusp of his 30th birthday, was about to get a firsthand lesson in how the moviemaking machinery could chew you up and spit you out. At Origin Systems, Roberts had become used to flexing his creative muscles: "In videogame terms I was like a very big film director. I got what I wanted and didn't have to compromise. Then I stepped into the film business and, all of a sudden, I wasn't." On the set of the *Wing Commander* movie, which was shot in Luxembourg, the big fish from a small pond suddenly found himself in the deep blue sea surrounded by sharks. Unlike *Mortal Kombat's* John Tobias - who recalled being lauded by cast and crew during a brief visit to the production - Roberts wasn't just passing through. He was now part of the food chain.

It was a tough gig, not least of all because the game designer's creative instincts as a director were constantly overruled by the economic necessities of the deal. Like *Super Mario Bros.*, *Wing Commander* was being made as an indie movie. "In my opinion, independent movies that are produced from franchises like this tend not to be very good. The reason why is because you have to satisfy too many different cooks," says Moyer. "There were all kinds of concessions made in that movie that you wouldn't do if you were making it as a studio movie."

As part of the deal, Fox wanted Freddie Prinze Jr. and Matthew Lillard, who were hot, in the cast. Sales to the UK, Germany and France were threatened because those markets had never heard of either actor. So, Moyer added Saffron Burrows and David Suchet for the UK, Jürgen Prochnow for Germany and Tchéky Karyo for France. "You would never do that on a big studio movie. It was all about trying to get a bigger number from those territories," he says.

Wing Commander had one advantage over previous videogame movies: it had a detailed, rich mythology which its director knew intimately, since he'd designed it himself. Serving as a prequel to the games, the movie follows a young Christopher Blair (played by pretty vacant Prinze Jr.) on his first combat mission against the Kilrathi. It's like a war movie in space: the pilots are like World War I aerial aces, deadly in the cockpit but struggling with human dramas on the ground; the hulking space vessels are like aircraft carriers or the submarine from *Das Boot*, metal canisters its troops are locked inside while war wages around them. It's no surprise to lean that Roberts referred his crew to *Tora! Tora! Tora!* and *The Battle of Midway* for inspiration.

Visually, the film did a little with a lot. Its CGI team beta-tested Maya, a 3D animation and modelling tool now used extensively in both the movie and game industries, and used it to create quite spectacular space battles. Less convincing were the Kilrathi, cat-like aliens whose design resulted in a blazing row between Roberts and his producer over whether or not they should be CGI. "When you're working with a creator, you can try to be as persuasive as you want," Moyer explains. "Try telling Frank Miller what should be in or out of a property, good fucking luck. It's hard to tell Chris Roberts, who made a tonne of money off *Wing Commander*, what he has to do with certain characters. You're always going to lose because he can say, 'This is important to the core audience, we have to do this to satisfy them'. I was like: 'Dude, people barely remember the videogame it was [so long] ago.'"

Roberts, who'd used animatronics while shooting the cat-like Kilrathi on the *Wing Commander* games' FMV sequences, was adamant he wanted the same old school approach. When Moyer refused on the basis that it was "a complete waste of time and would look like shit," Roberts used his own money to pay for the extra work. But the problem was that the Kilrathi - puppeteers in eight-foot suits too tall for the sets that had by now been built - looked ridiculous. "It was laughable and it sucked," says Moyer, "You had a villain that was funny." In the end, the Kilrathi all but vanished from the finished cut of the movie. Roberts asked Fox for more time and money to fix the problem but the studio refused.

What finally killed *Wing Commander*'s box office chances, however, was its chief inspiration: *Star Wars*. Arriving in cinemas in March 1999 just a couple of months before the long-awaited prequel *Star Wars: Episode I - The Phantom Menace*, *Wing Commander* inevitably suffered. The movie's core demographic were eager for Lucas, not Roberts. No sci-fi outing could compete against such fevered expectation not even, it turned out, *The Phantom Menace* itself. "Everyone had this belief that *The Phantom Menace* was going to be like the Second Coming of Jesus Christ," says Roberts philosophically. "Then after it came out they said, 'It's got Jar-Jar Binks in it, it isn't that good'."

Yet the real damage to *Wing Commander* was actually done in the meeting rooms at the studio that distributed it. Again, it was all down to the deal. Fox, who were releasing *The Phantom Menace* and *Wing Commander*, were obviously going to put all their bets on just one of those two horses. "Fox was not very supportive of the movie," recalls Moyer. "We talked about P&A [prints and advertising] and the screen commitment and they basically wouldn't come up with a satisfactory plan."

Convinced *Wing Commander* could make money if handled properly, Moyer made a deal where he could sell the movie to another studio as long as Fox got a $2 million profit on their initial investment. Much to Fox's surprise, the producer secured an agreement from Sony who were willing to put the film out on 2,500 screens with a big P&A commitment. They were also willing to invest in the movie and push back its release date, giving Roberts the chance to fix the Kilrathi. Everybody, even Fox with a guaranteed $2 million profit, would be happy. But then all hell broke loose. While Moyer was in the middle of finishing off negotiations with Sony, his cell-phone rang. It was Tom Sherack, then head of distribution for Fox. He had bad news.

"Todd, I'm not giving you the picture."

"But we had a deal. I'm here closing the sale."

"Good fucking luck, I'll never sign the papers. I don't give a shit, I'm not doing it. If you want to have a huge lawsuit, go ahead."

"Tom, I've got to tell you..."

"No, it's coming out in six weeks and it's going to have the *Star Wars: The Phantom Menace* trailer on it."

He hung up.

Six weeks was barely enough time to market *Wing Commander* properly even if Fox had wanted to. But apparently they didn't. There was no theatrical trailer, no press build up, no TV campaign. The movie was dumped in cinemas in mid-March, an expensive hook to hang the second trailer for *Star Wars: The Phantom Menace* on.

Moyer, convinced that *Wing Commander* could easily have done $10 to $15 million on its opening weekend, was furious. The film took around $5 million, putting it fourth out of the five movies that opened that weekend. It was also a critical flop. "Star Bores," joked Entertainment Weekly. In retrospect, Moyer is sanguine about the movie's release. "That's the way the business works," he reflects. "Really, it's pretty funny: the fact that it was a C-rate *Star Wars* was actually our undoing." Although *Wing Commander*'s release was far from triumphant, the deal was strong enough to bear it. "I don't think anyone lost money on that movie," he says. "When you run it through the cycles [theatrical, DVD, TV] *Wing Commander* did just fine. The only people who didn't make money on it were Chris Roberts and me."

For Roberts, who'd been attracting a lot of industry heat as a young director before the film's release (Fox offered him a mooted *Silver Surfer* project), the movie was a mixed blessing. Despite the compromises, he'd directed a feature before turning 30 and taken his baby onto the big screen. "It was like a very expensive film school for me," he says. After a brief return to videogames he started out as a Hollywood producer, making films like *Lord of War* (2005) starring Nicolas Cage and *Lucky Number Slevin* (2006) with Josh Hartnett and Bruce Willis. No videogame designer had ever made such a jump into producing Hollywood movies before.

Wing Commander's genesis, production and release say a lot about the state of things in 1999. Here were the realities behind videogame movies laid bare: the original videogame properties guaranteed brand recognition with a built-in audience; the funding was drummed up in piecemeal fashion; big studios were willing to distribute without committing themselves to developing the projects in-house. These projects were, in short, a way of milking a franchise from another medium. Hardly surprising, then, that videogame movies would be plagued by mediocrity.

* * *

In the history of videogame to movie crossovers, one name stands out: Lara Croft. Back in 1996 the buxom British adventurer, with her impossible 34-

24-34 curves, emerged as the star of the bestselling series of videogames developed by Core Design and published by Eidos. No shrinking violet, she was a cultural phenomenon whose reach was as global as Mario's and as sexy as Madonna's.

In the summer of 2001 she broke out onto movie screens in a tent-pole summer blockbuster, *Lara Croft: Tomb Raider*, financed and distributed by Paramount. It was the first time a videogame had ever been given the full Hollywood treatment but jumping from the PC and PlayStation to the big screen meant crossing a chasm wider than anything Lara had encountered in the game itself.

Lara began life in the offices of English videogame developer Core Design back in the early '90s. Setting out to create a game with the look of a movie, designer Toby Gard took the basic Indiana Jones premise - a rugged archaeological adventurer venturing into far-flung locales - but changed the protagonist's sex. Lara was an English aristocrat who could climb, shimmy and clamber through abandoned ruins and mysterious temples in an action-orientated, third-person puzzle game. On its release in November 1996, *Tomb Raider* became an unstoppable success for both Core Design and its parent company Eidos. By 2010 the multi-platform videogame franchise had sold over 35 million units worldwide.

The real story wasn't the *Tomb Raider* games, though. It was much bigger than that. Eidos soon realised that Lara was a brand in herself. She was a female action heroine who had the potential to become a "transmedia" icon. The term, first coined by Marsha Kinder in her 1991 book *Playing with Power in Movies, Television and Video Games: from Muppet Babies to Teenage Ninja Mutant Turtles*, defined a new kind of branded storytelling that could take a single intellectual property across media from comics to movies to games.

Lara was arguably the first female transmedia star of the internet era. Her success was strengthened by the burgeoning power of the web as a promotional tool - more than 2,000 fan websites sprung up seemingly overnight - but also by the chord she struck with her audience. Here was a strong female character, in the era of the Spice Girls and Britney Spears, who was sexy, sassy and totally without precedent in videogames.

Her ascent was as unstoppable as it was carefully orchestrated. Keith Boesky, an American attorney who specialised in the protection and exploitation of franchise properties, became president of Eidos Interactive in 1997. He could instantly see the power of this virtual celebrity. As Lara's fame grew, there was inevitably talk of a movie. But the Hollywood studios were largely agnostic. *Super Mario Bros.* and the lacklustre box office returns of *Mortal Kombat II: Annihilation* had poisoned the well. "Nobody wanted to do another videogame movie," says Boesky, "especially not one led by a female action hero". The executive pushed instead for a live-action, syndicated TV show, inspired by the success of series like *Xena: Warrior Princess*, *Hercules* and the ratings smash *Baywatch*. With Eidos making around $16 every time a game sold, it made sense to license Lara for a TV series that would ensure faster, wider and longer exposure than a one-shot movie. Boesky's boss Charles Cornwell, the chief executive of Eidos, disagreed. He wanted the perceived prestige of a movie launch.

Hiring a PR company to manage Lara's growing celebrity, Eidos pursued her branding with single-minded determination. It was a marketing juggernaut: there were Lara action figures (the first ever action-figure line led by a female videogame character); a bestselling comic; a spot on the video wall on U2's international Zoo TV tour; and adverts for Lucozade, Fiat and Toys R Us.

Eidos's strategy was to put Lara out into the mainstream as a real person, all the while covertly targeting their marketing towards the movie industry. There was a bestselling book co-written by Douglas Coupland; a Lara album; a photo spread of her modelling a black digital bikini by Gucci in The Face magazine; models hired as Lara lookalikes; and her picture on the covers of Entertainment Weekly and Time magazines. Finally, and most symbolically, there was a two-page, self-congratulatory advert in Variety - the first for a videogame - in which Eidos announced Tomb Raider's then $458 million takings at retail. The message to Hollywood was simple: sit up and pay attention.

They did.

"In Hollywood at the time there was no *Harry Potter*," says Boesky. "*Titanic* was just coming out and there was no film for 14-year-old girls coming after that. There was no teen film and the studios were desperate for something that would appeal to a teen audience." A bidding war for the movie rights broke out as MGM, Warner Bros., Paramount, Sony and Fox all vied for the opportunity to take Lara onto the big screen. Paramount ultimately won the battle, but they were confused about the next move. "They bought it because everybody else wanted it, but they didn't know what to do with it," Boesky says. A few weeks after Paramount optioned the movie rights, Boesky met the studio's presidents of production, marketing and consumer products and showed them the global appeal the brand had: how many units it had shipped, all the different sponsorships Lara had done and photos of the crowds in London who appeared whenever Lara made a "live" appearance courtesy of a stand-in actress. Paramount's marketing execs were amazed.

Excited, they quickly set up an emergency photo shoot and mocked up a poster of Lara enveloped in shadow with the question "Who is Lara Croft?" A week later, at the 1998 Licensing International Expo in New York, they gave Lara Croft equal stature with *Star Trek* at their booth. Clearly what interested Paramount wasn't the videogame's story or characters per se, but the brand recognition it possessed. Lara's reach - among the core demographic of 13- to 34-year-old males - was enormous and exactly what Hollywood needed to be tapping into. What they weren't prepared for was the fervour that Lara would generate.

"All of a sudden they got trampled by people who wanted a Lara license," remembers Boesky. "This was the first presence of *Tomb Raider*, a worldwide phenomenon that no one knew how to get to, at the licensing show. Paramount called me up that morning urgently and said, 'We've got a problem, everyone wants a license for *Tomb Raider*.' I replied, 'That's wonderful.' They said, 'We don't have the rights!'" Paramount, it turned out, only had the property under option and when they were under option they couldn't enter into any agreements over the licenses. "They didn't know what they had," says Boesky, "They didn't know what the potential was." Eidos, on the other hand, knew exactly the potential of their D-cupped cash cow and they were much savvier about their side of the movie deal. When Paramount optioned the property, the videogame publisher hammered out a watertight contract and sought the involvement of two powerful, veteran producers: Larry Gordon (*Predator, Die Hard, Field of Dreams*) and Lloyd Levin (*Event Horizon, Boogie Nights*). They were similarly savvy and aggressive in their deal-making.

While later game-movie deals like *Doom* were based on a cast-iron production deadline - a date at which point the studio would either have to greenlight the movie or write off the development costs and let the rights revert back to the owners - *Tomb Raider* was different. Eidos had a unique provision in the contract that meant the property would revert to them if Paramount stopped work on the movie for more than 45 days. But they didn't set an absolute deadline for production. It gave the producers and the games company leverage to ensure that the movie would be made - but not before a decent screenplay was ready. As a result *Tomb Raider's* release was pushed back from 1999 to 2001.

Producers Gordon and Levin were also valuable partners. Gordon was powerful enough to have final cut and casting approval, and neither producer needed convincing that videogames had the potential to become lucrative movie franchises. Before *Tomb Raider*, they had tried to take Activision's tank game *Battlezone* to the big screen.

When writers John Zinman and Patrick Massett were called in for a meeting about *Battlezone*, they saw a life-sized cut out of Lara behind Levin's desk and instantly knew that they wanted to adapt it even though they'd never played *Tomb Raider*. Levin himself was already a big fan of Lara. "I warmed to Lloyd instantly the first time we met because he kept asking for tips about the game he was stuck on," later said Core Design's operations director Adrian Smith. With its cinematic camera angles and fleshed out heroine (in every sense), *Tomb Raider* was ripe for a movie simply because it was so influenced by movies itself.

"We pursued the movie rights because it had a real character at its centre and the game storylines were very cinematic in approach," Levin said. "We told Eidos and the Core Design team what they didn't want to hear. Other studios seemed to be offering them everything in the world to secure the rights: yes, we will put the movie into production immediately; yes, it will be out this time next year. Well, we went in and said we wanted to take it very slowly and assured them we wouldn't disrupt the mythology they had worked so hard to build up."

At Paramount, videogames were less of a known quantity. The project's champion was Alex Young, a fresh-faced junior executive who was a long-time gamer. To him, *Tomb Raider* represented a generation shift. "You had a lot of people running things in Hollywood who had no idea about videogames; had never played videogames, had never spent their entire allowance in an arcade pumping in coins playing *Mortal Kombat* or *Zaxxon*; and who didn't know what an Amiga was. It just wasn't part of their DNA. What you saw in the mid-90s was the tip of the spear of people who were coming up in the movie business who had grown up with this stuff. We were born in the early '70s and videogames were part of our upbringing much like comic books were part of the upbringing of people who grew up in the 60s."

Few executives at Paramount - or in Hollywood generally - shared Young's passion for games. "My sense is, of all the people I met with only one of the core group of producers and executives had played [*Tomb Raider*]," said Brent Friedman, the first screenwriter who worked on the project (his past credits included *Mortal Kombat II: Annihilation*). They were jumping on a bandwagon that they didn't even understand.

Certainly the studio's approach to the material often seemed clueless. Steven De Souza, director of the *Street Fighter* movie, was one of the army of screenwriters brought in to work on the *Tomb Raider* movie. He recalls a meeting with an unnamed Paramount exec who suggested that Lara should pick up health and ammo packs in each new area in the movie. "Larry [Gordon] and I were dumbfounded by his literal interpretation, so we told him we'd make sure to write in Lara bandaging herself and reloading her weapons. He was pleased with that."

What Paramount did understand was that this movie had the potential to be a summer blockbuster. This wasn't a negative pickup like *Super Mario Bros.*, a B-movie like *Mortal Kombat* or a semi-indie outing like *Wing Commander*. *Lara Croft: Tomb Raider*, as the project became known to cash in on Lara's growing personal fame, was a summer tentpole movie with a $100 million budget.

The production was suitably epic. The screenplay called for a globetrotting location shoot that took in Iceland, England and Cambodia. It saw off one director during pre-production (his replacement was former BBC man Simon West, who'd made two $100 million-grossing Hollywood movies: *Con Air* and *The General's Daughter*). It chewed up and spat out 11 screenwriters and forced its star Angelina Jolie into a punishing regimen of kickboxing, canoeing, yoga, and total abstinence from alcohol or cigarettes - quite a radical lifestyle change for Hollywood's then most infamous wild child. She was also forced to squeeze into Lara's trademark hot pants ("Those fucking shorts," she called them) and a cleavage-enhancing bra.

Jolie had never played the game but had watched her first husband, actor Jonny Lee Miller, guiding Lara through caverns. "Like every woman, I'd go 'Ugh, her! Oh boy, there's a woman who makes me look average and feel inferior.' I hated her." Although she had initially had doubts about playing the role, she eventually made it her own. "I see Lara as like a creature, an insane wild animal firing on every cylinder all of the time," she declared. It was the first time an actor in a videogame movie could actually talk about their character with a straight face: Lara was more than just a bunch of pixels, she was a celebrity.

Not surprisingly, Lara was considered a plum role among Hollywood's young actresses. Young says both Catherine Zeta Jones and Nicole Kidman were originally considered for the part. But Jolie, who was about to win an Oscar for her role in *Girl, Interrupted*, was undoubtedly the only star to get Lara's mix of sex and sass just right. The movie's seminal teaser poster - showing Jolie as Lara, with her hands on hips looking back at the camera as if daring you to follow her - was eye-catching. "If you had never even heard of the game before [the poster] looked so cool, provocative and awesome," reckons Young. "She embodied the spirit not just of the character, but of this new generation."

Director Simon West agreed. "It's just like finding Sean Connery in 1962 for James Bond," he told the Los Angeles Times in 2001. "The actor and character became so close you know you've hit gold. Once I had Angelina and saw her the first couple of times in the role, I felt it almost doesn't matter what I do. As long as I keep on pointing the camera at her, the film can't fail. I now can't see how I'd have done the film without her."

When *Tomb Raider* finally arrived in cinemas on 15 June 2001, it proved a smash hit. Its worldwide gross of just under $275 million, set a new record for a movie based on a videogame and spawned a sequel, *Lara Croft Tomb Raider: The Cradle of Life*, in 2003. For Eidos, the movie cemented Lara Croft's status as an international brand. Although few critics lauded the movie, it wasn't exactly excoriated either. "*Tomb Raider* will go down in history, as the first movie that was based on a videogame but wasn't unwatchable garbage," claimed the New York Times in a textbook-worthy definition of faint praise.

Yet in Hollywood's eyes, *Lara Croft: Tomb Raider* was part of a much bigger shift. It was the coming of age of a new audience: the fanboys (and girls) born in the 1970s and 1980s and weaned on comics, videogames and cartoon characters. Arriving during a period that included *Men in Black*, *Blade*, *X-Men* and *Spider-Man*, *Lara Croft: Tomb Raider* helped change attitudes in the movie industry. It legitimised interactive entertainment as potential movie franchise material - much as those other movies did for comic books - and it showed studio executives that they needed to start taking the videogame sector seriously.

"Before *Tomb Raider*, videogames had been dismissed as a category," says Young. "For the first time you had a big budget mainstream Hollywood movie with a true movie star being made the right way. I think it largely changed people's perception. [It made the studios realise that] there are people who not only play these games, but will show up on a Friday night to see these movies. We have to take this audience more seriously. It created a critical mass.

Comic-Con became taken more seriously. The audience was more carefully catered to."

The key to blockbuster success in today's Hollywood has begun to revolve around a now familiar pattern: identify a pre-existing property with brand name recognition (a comic, a videogame or even an '80s toy) that the fan audience identifies with and build that franchise into a movie. Lara Croft was the first videogame character to prove that games could be as valuable as comics to producers hungry for IP to adapt. After the deaths of *Super Mario* and *Wing Commander*, it was Lara who gave videogame movies a much-needed extra life.

CHAPTER 6

A Tale of Two Empires

"Steven [Spielberg] would always beat the hell out of us when we played 8-player Tank together. Whereas I don't think George ever played a videogame. It just wasn't something he did."

Hal Barwood, former LucasArts games designer

The press called them "The Dream Team" and for a while, it looked as if it were true. On 12 October 1994, at a press conference at The Peninsula Hotel in Beverly Hills, three men stepped into the Verandah Room where rows of eager journalists waited for them.

Each was a leader in his field: Steven Spielberg, film director, producer and Hollywood powerhouse smirked behind a greying beard; Jeffrey Katzenberg, a buttoned down former Disney executive, who'd left the Mouse House under a cloud of negativity, was dressed as always in a shirt and tie. David Geffen, the media giant who created Asylum and Geffen Records, brought up the rear. He was last but by no means least. His $1 billion personal fortune dwarfed that of his millionaire colleagues.

Their announcement that day sent a shockwave through Hollywood although, in truth, the secret was already an open one. These three giants of the media industry were coming together to create a new studio, DreamWorks SKG. The aim was to create a 21st century powerhouse, a multimedia studio that would span live-action, animation and interactive entertainment.

As its name hinted, DreamWorks was not short on ambition. Over the coming weeks and months, grand plans were unveiled. There was talk of creating two studios, one live-action, the other feature animation; a record label; and a television division. There was also a dream of constructing a state-of-the-art studio facility on a thousand acres of marshland just north of Los Angeles International Airport at Playa Vista, the site where Howard Hughes once built his famous Spruce Goose seaplane. In retrospect, it would become a painfully apt metaphor. Like Hughes's oversized aircraft, the ambitious DreamWorks project would fail to soar.

In 1995, though, the sky seemed to be the limit. Spielberg, the wunderkind, appeared to be on the verge of finally growing up: becoming a mogul as well as the industry's most profitable filmmaker. For some, his investment in DreamWorks seemed to speak of a restless desire to build an empire, something similar to what his friend George Lucas had created years before on Skywalker Ranch in Marin County, California.

True, Spielberg had Amblin, his $4 million facility housed on the Universal lot with its offices, cutting rooms, gym and wishing well with its own miniature shark (a nod to the director's breakout hit). Amblin, though, was strictly a movie production company. DreamWorks had the potential to be something more, a fully-fledged multimedia studio that would operate in all fields of popular entertainment. And that included videogames.

Back in 1995, most of Hollywood was still in thrall to the buzzwords of "multimedia", "interactivity" and "electronic entertainment". The fact that few actually understood the reality behind those tags didn't stem the tide of enthusiasm. Digital was the future and as multimedia titles like *Myst* - a beautiful, first-person puzzle videogame - captured the public's imagination, the studios began to clamber onto the multimedia bandwagon. The interactive mania that had begun in the early '90s with the first Siliwood mash-ups, Digital Pictures' FMV and the entry of Sony into the movie industry, were reaching critical mass.

Every major motion picture studio wanted in on the action and began setting up their own interactive divisions. They were all playing catch-up with the speed at which technology was evolving. Even a senior studio executive like Jeffrey Katzenberg was struggling to grapple with the rapid shift in communication that the internet's explosion was forcing on the entertainment industry. In the mid-90s he reputedly still faxed back replies to emails; and ordered his assistants to search the web on his behalf. They videotaped the results for him to peruse offline.

While it was sometimes painful to watch, there was no doubting the commitment of the studios in investing in this new arena, particular in videogames. At the Los Angeles Times, where journalist Amy Harmon kept a close eye on the rise of digital Hollywood during the '90s, the movie industry's sudden return to the games sphere was pithily summed up in a single headline: "Move Over Sega - Here Come the Conglomerates".

Over on the Universal lot Sid Sheinberg, the president and chief operating officer of MCA, tasked two executives - Skip Paul, the former Atari lawyer whose mind had been boggled by Spielberg's deal on *E.T.* and Rob Biniaz, senior vice-president of business development in the MCA Music Entertainment Group - to set up Universal Interactive. The aim was to add videogames to Universal's media interests. Sheinberg, who years before had tried to sue Nintendo over *Donkey Kong*, knew that the growing industry could no longer be ignored.

Paul hired former Atari games designer Mark Cerny to head up the boutique studio in 1994. At its peak Universal Interactive had around nine employees but it built up strong relationships with two external developers: Insomniac Games, who created *Spyro the Dragon*; and Naughty Dog who developed *Crash Bandicoot*.

"What we did had much more to do with games than Hollywood," says Cerny. "*Crash* and *Spyro* are not everybody's image of what Hollywood does when it creates games. Most people would expect a movie studio to be doing the best possible *Transformers* videogame as an ancillary product or teaming up with someone like Guillermo Del Toro. What we did was work with two really talented teams - Insomniac and Naughty Dog - and give them the opportunity to work with some of the best professionals in the movie business."

While Universal Studios was largely uninterested in the interactive division, at least until it started making huge profits, they were helpful when it came to giving the newcomers access. "The other groups at Universal Studios opened up all of their contacts to us," remembers Cerny. "For example, they gave me the home phone numbers and biographies for 50 of the top industry production designers and said, 'Just tell them you're calling from Universal'. And I did. I was 29 and very nervous about calling these people up. I ended up working with Catherine Hardwicke [who'd later direct hit vampire movie *Twilight*]. She did the production design on Insomniac's maiden project [sci-fi shooter *Disruptor*]. We were able to work with Hollywood talent: animators, production designers, set designers."

On *Spyro* and *Crash Bandicoot*, Cerny brought in Stewart Copeland (drummer with The Police) and Devo singer Mark Mothersbaugh to compose the background music. "Being located in Hollywood certainly did make it easier to meet people," he says. It was indicative of how videogames were evolving. Unlike in the '70s and early '80s, they were now technologically advanced enough to support the creative input of artists from other mediums. That technological leap - the same leap that fuelled the multimedia-mania of the '90s - was what legitimised the studio's interest in these products.

With their high-spec production values, *Crash* and *Spyro* both became huge hits and launched two bestselling series. The franchises sold around 40 million units combined and brought in a couple of hundred million in profit. Indeed, *Crash Bandicoot 2* was Universal's fourth most profitable entertainment property across all media in 1997.

Clearly the studios could see that there was money to be made in videogames. By 1998, Forbes magazine was writing the movie industry's obituary again: "Guess it's time to say good-bye to Hollywood." Just as in 1982 it was pure hyperbole, but the sentiment was bolstered by figures from American videogame trade group the Interactive Digital Software Association (IDSA) showing that the interactive entertainment industry generated $16 billion in software sales in 1997. It was, claimed Forbes, "equal to the amount of economic activity generated by Hollywood".

Suddenly the videogame industry was no longer the invader. It was being invaded itself. Hollywood suits were everywhere, eager to get a slice of the digital action. Videogame industry veterans were largely unimpressed by the new arrivals. As Activision's chairman Bobby Kotick bitched: "Every failed talent in Hollywood, everyone that hasn't been successful in linear media, sees this as a second chance."

It was a sentiment that was shared elsewhere too. Patrick Gilmore, who began his career as a young producer at Walt Disney Computer Software in the early '90s and would later work at DreamWorks Interactive and co-direct the DreamWorks animated feature *Sinbad: Legend of the Seven Seas* in 2003, recalls the feeling well. "The attitude on the games side was that a lot of marginal studio people, who had either dropped out of the film industry or had trouble getting work in it, were bringing their credibility from their past and landing jobs in interactive," he says. "At that time in the industry there was a palpable sense of everyone you met: do they game or not game? If you were in a meeting and you were looking at a build and someone handed you the controller, did you say 'No thanks' or did you take the controller, jump on it and go?" A worrying proportion of executives in meetings were so "Hollywood" that would refuse the controller out of either fear or distaste.

When the movie studios descended on the Consumer Electronics Show (CES) in Chicago in June 1994, the battle lines were drawn. "Just because a bunch of Hollywood guys show up with 'interactive' on their business cards doesn't mean they're going to be successful," sniffed Bing Gordon, executive vice-president at Electronic Arts. "Next year the show is in Philadelphia.

It will be interesting to see how far the glamorous and exciting people in Hollywood are willing to travel to make a show of participation in the interactive business."

A year - like Philly - was a long way away, though. In Chicago, Hollywood's interactive emissaries were feeling bullish. "You take the property content owners, like Fox or MGM or Sony or any of the others, and we can now step into this industry and provide the consumer with great games and video clips from our libraries," said Ted Hoff, chief of Fox's new interactive division who clearly hadn't got the memo about the death of full motion video.

Every major entertainment corporation was rallying around the new flag, even the diehard conservatives at the Walt Disney Company. Six months earlier, at the "Superhighway Summit" held at UCLA's Royce Hall in January 1994, Disney's chairman Michael Eisner had made no secret of his scepticism about the "multimedia craze". Although he was rubbing shoulders with Rupert Murdoch of NewsCorp, Robert Iger of ABC Television, Barry Diller of QVC, and then US Vice President Al Gore as they discussed the implications of the World Wide Web, Eisner believed multimedia had little to offer Disney. "[We're] not a technology company," he famously claimed. By the end of the year, though, Disney launched its new interactive division, the last of the major US entertainment conglomerates to do so.

Gilmore was among those who watched as Disney's attitude towards interactive evolved at a breakneck pace. The modest early titles he produced at the company's software division, like *World of Illusion starring Mickey Mouse and Donald Duck* (1992), were soon dwarfed by *Aladdin* (1993), a Sega Mega Drive/ Genesis hit that sold over two million copies. Developed by Virgin Interactive in collaboration with Disney, the *Aladdin* videogame set a new benchmark. It used the venerable movie studio's own feature animators to bring its graphics to life. At E3 the game's visual beauty amazed onlookers, many of whom were convinced that the developers were hoodwinking them by using a super big memory card or an accelerator chip inside the console. Instead it was simply a belated *Dragon's Lair* moment: Disney finally realised that its animators' skills were transferable across the two mediums. Don Bluth had just got there a decade earlier.

Like the movie it was based on, the *Aladdin* game was a sign of changing times at Disney. Under the watchful eye of studio head Jeffrey Katzenberg, Disney's struggling feature animation department was being turned around. Hit movies like *The Little Mermaid*, *Beauty and the Beast* and *The Lion King* were re-establishing the brand's pre-eminence with family audiences; Hollywood Pictures was taking a punt on the *Super Mario Bros.* movie. Videogames were just part of a bigger strategy.

Released in time for Christmas 1994, *The Lion King* game was another landmark outing that also used Disney's features animators. Tied into a movie that was even bigger than *Aladdin*, the game's importance to the company couldn't be underestimated. That spring, Katzenberg and Eisner appeared - along with Gilmore, the title's senior producer at Disney Software - on stage at CES cuddling a 50-pound lion cub. No one was quite sure whether the muscular little furball would freak out when the dancers came out of the wings.

"It was a symbolic moment for Disney Interactive," says Gilmore. "We'd proven what we could do with *Aladdin* and *The Lion King*. The joint production with Disney animators participating in games was the wave of the future: how do you take Disney-level production values, Disney level-character development and storytelling and bring that to videogames? In the same way that the company had successfully launched a consumer products division which revolutionised retail for Disney properties through the Disney Stores, it was clear internally that there was the same potential for games and interactive."

For Disney, videogames were becoming increasingly important. Not just as merchandising products but as entertainment vehicles in themselves. For the first time ever the studios were beginning to recognise the value not just of making games but of making good games. The growth of the interactive market and the power of the technology driving it meant that it was becoming increasingly unwise to simply farm out videogame licensing.

What executives like Katzenberg were also slowly beginning to understand was that games were beginning to pull their weight as a place in which stories could be told. As games' sophistication increased, it behoved companies like Disney and Universal to throw resources at them. As Rob Biniaz, chief operating officer of Universal Interactive put it, "The whole thing is the game. We've seen from the marketplace that it doesn't matter how popular the movie was - the game has to be good. Not everyone in Hollywood recognises that." Twelve long years after Atari's *E.T.*, lessons were finally being learned.

With every major studio now invested in interactive, it was inevitable that DreamWorks would announce its own games division sooner or later. Like everything at the glitzy new studio it was no disappointment. Not content with simply announcing a publishing partnership with Sega or throwing together a new media team, DreamWorks teamed up with software giant

Microsoft. The deal would create what BusinessWeek dubbed "Hollywood's Digital Godzilla".

In industry terms, the deal was enormous. Few could argue with the symbolic partnership of Bill Gates and Spielberg, two giants of their respective fields. The money also told its own story. Paul Allen, one of Gates's closest allies and the co-founder of Microsoft, sank $500 million into DreamWorks in March 1995 in exchange for an 18% stake in the new studio. Meanwhile, Microsoft invested $15 million in a 50-50 partnership with the studio's interactive division named - what else? - DreamWorks Interactive (DWI).

Without Paul Allen's whopping personal investment in the parent company, DreamWorks SKG itself might never have got off the launch pad. For Microsoft, the deals offered exposure to two areas that they had little experience of: videogames and, perhaps even more importantly, Hollywood. For DreamWorks, Microsoft's 50-50 investment made DWI a reality. What united both companies was their desire to push the burgeoning convergence that was happening around them. Hooking up programming talent with storytelling talent would, the blue sky thinking went, usher in a new era in entertainment.

"It really will be the meeting of two different worlds," Gates said at the news conference announcing the partnership. Spielberg gave it a different spin: "The wide line dividing this technology from the kind of technology that I've been working in, which is basically the art of storytelling, is disappearing every year." There were enough hopeful dreamers in both industries willing to bet on DWI and Microsoft being able to narrow the gap into non-existence.

For Spielberg, DWI was more than just another string to the company's multimedia empire. It was a fantastic opportunity for him to dip into an arena that he'd been obsessed with for years. On a hiatus from filmmaking, he wasn't about to slide into the director's chair straight away - no matter how much it would have helped DreamWorks' fortunes.

What he was happy to do, though, was pursue his hobby. A deal was struck between DreamWorks, Sega and Universal to build futuristic video arcades and themed rides with Spielberg playing an active design role. Meanwhile, Spielberg invested in internet start-ups, and pursued plans for DreamWorks' Playa Vista complex. He also dabbled at DWI, where he acted like an informal, excitable creative consultant pitching in on anything and everything that the company was working on without actually taking on a dedicated role.

Compared to other movie studio interactive divisions, DWI was an anomaly. It was largely staffed by Microsoft employees, who had been lured away from lucrative stock options by the glitzy dream that DreamWorks represented. It was also built around a unique vision. While Spielberg left the corporate side of the division in other hands, he was vocal about his desire to turn DWI into something progressive. It wouldn't just churn out licensed titles. It would be a hothouse from which, the director hoped, something better and bigger would flourish. Not content with merely making games, Spielberg wanted to make games that mattered; games that could have the high-impact force of a blockbuster movie.

Nobody was under any illusions about how difficult that was. But Spielberg relished the challenge. This would be his moment to prove that all those years playing videogames had been more than just a childish diversion. He wanted to put his stamp on this virgin medium. He, Steven Spielberg, the movie industry's chief games master and a veteran cheerleader for all things interactive (or, as Newsweek put it, Hollywood's "ultimate Gameboy"), was promising to unite Hollywood and videogames in happy harmony.

The expectant faces waiting at Oakwood Apartments, where DWI had an early office, had faith in him. Those who said it couldn't be done were wrong. Spielberg knew that in his heart of hearts. How? Because he'd already seen it was possible. Not in his dreams. Not in Hollywood. But in Marin County.

* * *

In the beginning there was *Star Wars* and *Star Wars* was the Word. The 1977 movie didn't just make George Lucas, it minted him. He earned just $150,000 to write and direct the movie for Fox. But his percentage of the profits brought in big bucks.

For Lucas, who had negotiated an incredibly bold deal with Fox in which he gambled on the movie's success, it was his entry into the rarefied universe of multi-millionaires. What made him a billionaire, though, was his savvy decision to keep the merchandising rights under his control. Fox, who foresaw little profit in selling toys, acquiesced. It stands as one of the most incredible missteps ever made by a major motion picture studio. After *Star Wars* came out, Lucasfilm was earning $10 million a year from the sale of action figures alone. In its first 30 years, the *Star Wars* franchise as a whole would generate in excess of $22 billion.

Lucas had never planned to reinvent movie merchandising. "I had visions of R2-D2 mugs and little wind-up robots, but I thought that would be the end of it," he later said. Instead, *Star Wars* become a movie merchandising juggernaut. As the revenues streamed in, Lucasfilm and its founder were in an enviable position. Lucas had more money than God.

A true geek, the filmmaker wasn't much interested in Hollywood's more hackneyed measures of success: red Ferraris, mid-morning blow jobs and a $500-a-day coke habit. Instead, he put the profits into Lucasfilm and, in particular, his vision of an entertainment empire - writing off the investments against tax as business expenses. "It was really an extraordinary dream," remarked *The Empire Strikes Back* director Irvin Kershner. "All the billions of dollars ever made in the film business, and no one has ever plowed it back into a library, research, bringing directors together, creating an environment where the love of films could create new dimensions."

The lynchpin of Lucas's dream was Skywalker Ranch, a 2,600-acre facility that would house the filmmaker's production company. Located in Marin County, 350 miles from Hollywood's tainted heart, Skywalker Ranch was designed as a state-of-the-art facility that would allow Lucas to make the films he wanted to make with the new technology his employees were about to create. Convinced that the world of analogue film was in its last years, Lucas saw the future as digital and invested his own money into giving birth to it.

Lucasfilm's offshoots led several fields: there was research into editing tools, cinema sound, visual effects and a computer division dedicated to using processing power to create cinema quality CG images that would eventually evolve into the computer animation house Pixar. The reach of Lucas's empire was impressive, but technology was seen as a means to an end. Lucas, who famously still eschews computers in favour of writing his scripts in longhand, was less interested in the tools than the end results.

In the early 1980s, as Atari helped invent the home videogame industry, Lucas saw the potential. Although he had the bad gene that meant he wasn't a committed gamer, the filmmaker could see the cultural relevance that videogames might one day attain. He could also see their potential profits. Lucasfilm's empire prided itself on pushing the envelope of entertainment technology. Videogames were just another string to the bow.

In 1982, Lucas set up his games division. It was headed by Peter Langston, a UNIX programming guru and sometime folk musician. He had made a name for himself in the computing world after programming groundbreaking real-time, multiplayer political/military/economic simulation *Empire* in the 1970s. "In terms of the Lucasfilm empire, we were something new," he remembers. "We were the first non-cinema part of Lucasfilm, and I guess I was the first non-movie-related employee of Lucasfilm."

Langston's brief was simple. Lucasfilm wanted to expand into other areas of the entertainment industry beyond film. "When *Return of the Jedi* was nearing completion and a tsunami of money was seen approaching, George wanted to continue investing in high-tech support for the movie industry, but the Computer Division already had projects going to innovate in all the interesting areas of movie-making that they could handle. So the suggestion was made that maybe similar high-tech innovation could benefit other, non-cinema areas of the entertainment industry." For Langston there was only one obvious contender: videogames.

A deal was quickly inked in with Atari, then in rude health, who Lucasfilm had already licensed *Raiders of the Lost Ark* game to. Atari gave Lucasfilm Games a $1 million development pot with the remit to "See what you can make." What they didn't make, surprisingly, was a game that featured Luke Skywalker.

The Force has always been strong in videogames. In part that's because Lucas's mythic story played like a giant videogame right from the very start, constructed around a series of challenges that were akin to videogame levels: shoot the Stormtroopers; rescue the princess; fly your spaceship; destroy the Death Star. Despite not being a gamer, Lucas pre-empted the objective-progression-new objective flow of this fledgling medium even before it had established its internal logic itself. It helped too that his sci-fi universe was packed with the kind of imagery videogames would thrive on: Star Destroyers, laser beams and droids. Indeed, if Lucas hadn't created *Star Wars* the videogame industry might have had to do it for him.

When Atari's 1983 *Star Wars* coin-op became an instant classic and Parker Brothers' *The Empire Strikes Back* VCS cartridge sold over a million units, it was clear that Lucasfilm was sitting on another potential goldmine. Videogames were seen as another merchandising revenue stream to file alongside *Star Wars* figures, lunch boxes and duvet covers. Ironically, though, the newly-created Lucasfilm Games was told to stay away from Lucasfilm's sacred cows *Star Wars* and *Indiana Jones*. With videogame companies willing to pay huge licensing fees for the rights to make products based on the franchises, Lucasfilm Games was instructed to develop original titles instead.

There were quality issues to consider too. "Games were so primitive in the beginning that the idea of a crossover seemed laughable," explains screenwriter-turned-games designer Hal Barwood, who joined Lucasfilm Games in 1990. "George was very reluctant to allow a licensed movie tie-in until *Indiana Jones and The Last Crusade*, for fear the primitive look of games would sully his movies." Up until that 1989 game, Lucas merely tolerated videogames based on his intellectual property. The money they generated was enough to help him swallow his pride.

Lucas had little personal interest in the work Lucasfilm Games was doing, although he was intrigued by the idea of telling stories in games. Mostly, though, he left them to their own devices treating the team, as Barwood put it, like a rich uncle who "paid the tuition fees to get you through college but never knew what your major was."

Within Lucasfilm itself, the games division was treated with a mixture of deference and irreverence. "To the magicians in the computer division obsessed with perfect graphics and sound we were the embarrassing black sheep of the family," recalls Langston. "To the public relations part of Lucasfilm and to the videogame industry we were the guys who could make an Atari produce movie-quality graphics. To the accountants at Lucasfilm Ltd. we were the only part of the computer division that actually made a profit in our first year!"

During one of his rare visits to the division, the boss of Lucasfilm offered them a simple piece of advice: "Stay small, be the best, and don't lose any money". It was a mantra that Lucasfilm Games would stick to over the next few years as they worked on a series of critically-acclaimed titles like *Ballblazer* (1984), *Rescue on Fractalus!* (1984), *The Eidolon* (1985) and *Koronis Rift* (1985) that helped established the Lucasfilm Games brand among consumers.

In many respects, the team was actually relieved not to be forced into working on *Star Wars* titles. "We weren't all that eager," remembers Noah Falstein, who joined Lucasfilm Games in 1984 after beginning his career at Milton Bradley and Williams Electronics. "We were working in the shadow of Industrial Light & Magic and we were a bit intimidated," he recalls. "They were leaders in their field and there wasn't a lot of eagerness on our part to jump into making games based on the movies they'd worked on." The general feeling among the games division was that they were "the little kid brother trying hard to live up to a much older and more ambitious tradition."

Branching out into military simulations like *PHM Pegasus* (1986) and adventure titles like *Maniac Mansion* (1987), Lucasfilm Games quickly showed it could turn a profit independent of the brand-recognition that the company's big franchises traded on. It proved to be a unique division within the company. While their peers were experimenting with computerised tools that could help filmmakers like Lucas make movies and drag cinema into the coming digital age, designers like Falstein were building a totally independent medium: the videogame. As Lucasfilm Games honed their programming skill, they began to ponder the issue of actually employing narrative in videogames. After all, they were all big cinema fans. "You didn't come to work at Lucasfilm unless you were a big movie fan," says Falstein. According to Steve Arnold, director of Lucasfilm Games in the early years, the team spent time considering the possibility of narrative: "How can we invent new storytelling that makes it more fun to play these games, without really inventing new technology?"

In the very early days, moments of cross-pollination between games and the other divisions were rare but not unheard of. Computer division whiz Loren Carpenter used fractal technology to create an impressive 60-second, on-screen special effect in *Star Trek II: The Wrath of Khan* in 1982, the moment when a barren planet is terraformed into lush life. It won plaudits and in the wake of its success the games division "borrowed" Carpenter to design a simplified version of the same fractal technology that could run on the Atari 800. *Rescue on Fractalus!* used Carpenter's code to generate jagged mountainous terrain that player pilots had fly to their spaceships over in search of downed comrades in need of rescue. It was one of the first intersections between Hollywood visual effects and videogame technology.

Around the same time, publicity shoots for the *Rescue on Fractalus!* packaging - which featured a downed space fighter and Lucasfilm Games employees dressed in pilot outfits - were put together by model builders and wardrobe assistants from Lucasfilm. True, such bold instances of convergence were the exception rather than the rule yet they highlighted what was unique about Lucasfilm Games. Unlike Atari, which was simply a game company owned by an entertainment conglomerate, the games division was part of a more inclusive, even collegiate, multimedia empire. The team were encouraged to think about interactive entertainment and about what the division's manager Steve Arnold cryptically described to Atari-focused Antic Magazine as "significant new kinds of experiences available for bringing together computer and film."

Among the ideas they looked into was doing something like Don Bluth's laserdisc arcade cabinet *Dragon's Lair.* Production issues prevented them from jumping in. "At that point no one was making a convenient one-off videodisc production tool," says Langston. "We spent some time trying to convince manufacturers of videodisc players that they also needed to mass produce videodisc recorders. They didn't get it."

Storytelling was becoming increasingly important to the games division's thinking. Graphic adventure titles like *Maniac Mansion* (1987) and *Zak McKracken and the Alien Mindbenders* (1989) used Ron Gilbert and Aric Wilmunder's SCUMM engine, which allowed players to interact by pointing and clicking with a computer mouse. It helped marry the strong storytelling of traditional text-heavy adventure games with games that had a graphical focus. The games, developed by a small core team, were instantly recognisable: funny, irreverent and fiendishly difficult. "Back then we thought games and movies would merge," says Gilbert, although he himself no longer believes that today.

Over the coming years, during what many regard as Lucasfilm Games' golden age, graphic adventures like *The Secret of Monkey Island* (1990) and *Day of the Tentacle* (1993) raised the bar on narrative in games and established the Lucasfilm Games brand through distinctive IP. Around the same time, the company moved into releasing incredibly realistic simulators like *Battlehawks 1942* (1988) and *Secret Weapons of the Luftwaffe* (1991), created by Larry Holland. These games brought a stunning new authenticity to the flight simulator genre.

It was inevitable that Lucasfilm Games would eventually start making games based on movies. They began in 1986 with *Labyrinth: The Computer Game* based on Jim Henson's film starring David Bowie and a variety of puppets. Three years later, Lucasfilm Games renounced the first commandment and made a title based on the company's own IP: *Indiana Jones and the Last Crusade: The Graphic Adventure*, which Falstein oversaw as project leader. Using the SCUMM engine, *The Last Crusade* was a brilliant example of how games based on movies could work. The movie's screenplay was retooled into an adventure that put players in control of Indiana Jones as he globe trots solving puzzles, fighting Nazis and trying to rescue his father. Compared to other *Indiana Jones* games, it was streets ahead with a subtle appreciation of character, plot and emotional connection. "We did take a very strong pride in trying to make the games as good as the films they were inspired by," says Falstein modestly.

It didn't go unnoticed, not least of all among Hollywood filmmakers. The original aim of Lucasfilm Games was to provide George Lucas himself with opportunities for telling stories in games. Ironically, it was Lucas's friends who benefited more from his investment in the division then he did, at least in artistic terms.

Spielberg could see the potential of Lucasfilm's foray into the medium right from the beginning. He frequented the games division in much the same way as he had dropped in on the Atari campus at Sunnyvale earlier in the 1980s. When he visited Skywalker Ranch in 1989, while the team were working on *Indiana Jones and the Last Crusade*, he was instantly impressed by the progress they were making in the field of interactive entertainment. "Unlike George, Steven is a huge game-player," says Falstein. "When he was editing the movie *Always* he was coming in and doing some of the sound editing at Skywalker Ranch. I think we were working on *The Last Crusade* at that point. He asked George if he could stop by and see what we were doing. You can imagine how excited we were at Steven Spielberg coming by and George Lucas being the one to show us off! Steven wanted to see what we were doing, play the games. George was never so interested in getting his hands on a keyboard."

When the game was released, Falstein and his colleagues Gilbert and David Fox sent the director a pre-release copy along with their direct phone numbers in case he had any questions. He did. Within a day or two their phones were constantly engaged as Spielberg quizzed them about how to solve the game's various puzzles. "He'd basically sit down and play the game while on the phone and ask one of us to steer him through it rather than solving the puzzles himself," Falstein chuckles. "I guess if you're Spielberg, you might as well go straight to the top like that."

Having just come through a costly $100 million divorce from his first wife Amy Irving, Spielberg had time to play. A well-known war buff he reportedly "went nuts" over the team's World War II flight simulators, *Battlehawks 1942* and *Secret Weapons of the Luftwaffe*. He was playing, Falstein estimates, about five or six hours a day. The team tracked his progress informally: every time he'd drop in or call, he'd talk about whatever new level he'd reached.

No doubt Spielberg was ever so slightly envious of Lucasfilm's foray into videogames, especially since Lucas himself was so disinterested in playing. Why wasn't he pushing this medium forwards himself? After the fiasco that was Atari's *E.T.*, Spielberg had stayed away from the business side of games. But at the close of the 1980s, almost a decade after the bulldozers had buried that embarrassment in the desert, he must have wondered if it wasn't time to jump back in. Lucasfilm Games looked like the perfect opportunity. During one of his marathon walkthrough phone calls to Gilbert, the director dropped a hint: would you be interested in hearing some ideas for games? How could the games designer refuse? "I told Ron he had the chance of a lifetime there," jokes Falstein. "If he'd only said 'Yeah, I have this screenplay Steven, so if you'd be willing to look at that...'"

Spielberg wasn't the only filmmaker enticed by Lucasfilm Games. His old friend and collaborator Hal Barwood, who co-wrote the director's early movie *The Sugarland Express*, made a permanent jump into interactive entertainment. A filmmaker with the demeanour and smarts of a Harvard professor, Barwood had already proved himself in Hollywood: his credits included writing duties on *MacArthur* and a writer/producer credit on *Dragonslayer*. Yet he was increasingly seduced by videogames.

In 1981, while overseeing a sprawling set-piece on a farm in England for *Dragonslayer* with over 200 extras, pyrotechnics and a set of 10K arc lights, Barwood suddenly realised he was less interested in the thrill of Hollywood moviemaking than in spending time in his trailer. The lure was his new HP-41C calculator and a homemade version of the early computer game *Hunt the Wumpus*. He began to wonder if he was in the wrong industry.

By 1990 Barwood had put aside his Hollywood career and joined Lucasfilm Games with the blessing of his old friend and former USC classmate George. Naturally, the games division was thrilled. For a filmmaker of Barwood's calibre to be enticed into interactive entertainment was a coup. "We were amazed he was leaving a successful career as a filmmaker to work in games," remembers Falstein. "We were just jumping at the chance to collaborate and share what we knew about videogames with what he knew about film."

Working at Skywalker Ranch, Barwood wasn't immune to the idyllic beauty of a setting where eagles soared overhead and bobcats would sometimes saunter nonchalantly across the grass. But if he spent his first few weeks staring out his office window it wasn't because of the wildlife. It was because he was stumped by a puzzle as fiendish as anything in Lucasfilm Games' adventure titles.

On arriving at Lucasfilm he had been given the task of project leading a sequel to the *Indiana Jones and the Last Crusade* game. Management handed him a Hollywood screenplay called "Indiana Jones and the Garden of Life". They hoped it would be the basis for the game. Penned by Chris Columbus, the screenwriter behind *Gremlins* and *The Goonies*, it was originally earmarked as the fourth movie in the franchise. George Lucas had rejected it; yet, in his infinite wisdom, he suggested it might make a decent adventure game. It was a kind of snobbery: the script wasn't good enough for a movie but it would surely be good enough for a mere videogame. Barwood wanted nothing to do with it. "It really wasn't a very good script," he explains, "and certainly not Chris Columbus's best. It was rooted in an Afro-Chinese mythology that I don't think anyone in the West has any idea about. It was too obscure and it had Jones running around in Africa, old equatorial Africa, where nothing much was going on. I thought it was troubled from that point of view, and dragging the Nazis along on this adventure seemed preposterous."

For everyone at Lucasfilm, the project was a puzzle. It wasn't a licensed movie game in the traditional sense, since there wasn't a movie to base it on. That terrified management. Unable, or too intimidated, to commission a story that would have to stand beside the movies *Raiders of the Lost Ark*, *Temple of Doom* or *The Last Crusade*, the Columbus script was all they had. Other men might have baulked about going against Lucas's wishes. But Barwood, who'd sat in classes at USC with Lucas before the director knew the difference between a Wookie and a Jawa, wasn't afraid to stand his ground. Like all the best puzzles, the answer was staring him in the face. What should a screenwriter turned games designer do with a shoddy script? Why, rewrite it, of course...

When he pitched his treatment for what would become *Indiana Jones and the Fate of Atlantis*, the games division's management breathed a huge sigh of relief. "They'd been clinging to the Chris Columbus script because it was all they had. But when they heard my idea, they let go of the life-raft and jumped into the boat."

Collaborating with Falstein on the project, Barwood thrashed out a treatment for the game that would become one of the company's best-loved adventures. Gone was the quest for eternal life. Instead, Barwood and Falstein raided Skywalker Ranch's library, stocked with visual-heavy books for the tech heads at Lucas's special effects house Industrial Light and Magic, and found a picture of the sunken city of Atlantis showing it as three concentric circles. "It looked just like a game in waiting," he says. From there he fleshed out the back-story, drawing on Plato's discussion of Atlantis in *Timaeus and Critias* and creating the character of Sophia Hapgood, Indy's ex-girlfriend who's abandoned archaeology in favour of a rather dodgy career as a psychic. The Nazis were thrown in for good measure - seeking out the city's magical orichalcum for their own nefarious purposes.

What made *Fate of Atlantis* so unique, though, was its decision to take an iconic movie character and create a new story for him that was - for fans at least - part of the *Indiana Jones* canon. Although no one guessed at the time, it would be almost 20 years before the fourth movie arrived in cinemas. In the intervening period, it was the graphic adventures, novels and comics that kept the Jones story ticking over and by that yardstick, *Fate of Atlantis* was an early and incredibly polished example of transmedia storytelling that crossed over from movies to games. Coming from a screenwriting background, Barwood had no qualms over prioritising storytelling, transmedia or otherwise. Perhaps that explains why *Fate of Atlantis* retains its brilliant charm even today. It's a game that pivots on character and dialogue, the banter between Jones and Sophia as snappy as that in any summer blockbuster.

It wasn't just the dialogue that was aping cinema. Using 8mm cameras and tracing paper, the team experimented with basic rotoscoping techniques for the character animations. Combined with the mouse-drawn, 256 colour backgrounds and Barwood's knowledge of camera angles, it helped give the game an unexpected emotional depth.

Falstein recalls being surprised when Barwood explained how they would track Indy and Sophia walking on-screen having a conversation. Instead of simply following them from left to right, he wanted them walking towards the camera. Technically, it was much harder to achieve than simply scrolling the background behind them but the effect - seeing these two characters literally walking into the player's lap as they chatted - made you sit up and pay attention.

"It was a very basic thing for him as a filmmaker," recalls Falstein, "but I had never heard any game developer talk about camera angles or think about them in terms of their emotional impact." Working with the SCUMM engine, which privileged storytelling over fast-moving graphics or the caffeine rush of twitch gaming, *Fate of Atlantis* fell somewhere between a novel and a movie, an interactive narrative experience.

For sure, no one would ever mistake a game screen for a movie still. Yet the title's storytelling managed to compete with the film franchise that spawned it. The chutzpah peaked when artist Bill Eaken designed movie-style poster as the cover art, with Harrison Ford's likeness front and centre. Falstein still has one of the original posters hanging in his office. "You get funny reactions from people who see it like, 'Hey I never saw that movie, what was that one?' Once someone said 'That was such a great movie...' It turned out they'd played the game years earlier and in their minds it had been so vivid they had forgotten it wasn't actually a movie. That was very flattering."

Fate of Atlantis was a huge success and is widely considered the best adventure game ever made. In terms of living up to the expectations of the Lucasfilm brand, Barwood had achieved everything his old friend would have wanted...and more. Here was proof that games based on movie licences could be artistically valid, that cinematic techniques could be used to engage audiences and that interactive storytelling could expand and enrich movie IP in much the same way that novelisations and comic books could.

For Lucasfilm Games, it was apparent that their movie properties had an entertainment value that stretched far beyond the multiplex. Instead of milking a movie license dry, the company focused on building on its silver screen properties by continuing their stories over multiple platforms. Transmedia storytelling was clearly something that was of great use to an entertainment media company like Lucasfilm. Not just in terms of revenue streams but also for keeping audiences engaged with characters between movies.

Lucasfilm inevitably carried the strategy over to its *Star Wars* properties too. As the company grew, and its corporate arm set up new distribution deals to give it greater independence when it came to publishing its titles, the value of keeping the *Star Wars* games in house became apparent. In 1991 Lucasfilm Games released their first *Star Wars* title through publisher JVC on the NES. The game, simply titled *Star Wars*, was the beginning of a shift that brought the license back to Lucasfilm where internal teams would design and develop games based on it. Since the Lucasfilm Games group had proved its ability to handle the company's movie IP with immense polish, Lucas's concerns over tainting the brand were shelved.

After a corporate restructure in 1993, the games division became LucasArts Entertainment. The same year, two new games proved the viability of the *Star Wars* license. The first was *Star Wars: Rebel Assault*, a PC CD-ROM title that capitalised on the full motion video craze by shooting the first new footage set inside the *Star Wars* universe since the movie *Return of the Jedi* back in 1983. Lucas watched nervously as the gap between cinema and games narrowed even further. He had serious concerns that shooting video might disrupt the canon of the movies. For the sequel, released in 1995, Barwood was brought onboard and gave the shoot the benefit of his Hollywood expertise.

At the same time, the company's flight simulation expert Larry Holland applied his own unique talents to the *Star Wars* universe with *Star Wars: X-Wing*, which put players in the pilot's seat of the movie's iconic fighter ships. It became the year's biggest-selling PC title; meanwhile, *Rebel Assault* broke sales records for a CD-ROM game. Arriving at the same time as Lucasfilm were experimenting with other transmedia avenues, including Timothy Zahn's *Heir to the Empire* series of novels, these titles proved the value of expanding and consolidating the *Star Wars* universe across a variety of platforms.

The *Star Wars* franchise has since proved itself a perfect fit for videogames from first-person shooters, to combat and flight sims, to arcade games and even massively multiplayer online worlds. Titles developed in-house or in conjunction with third parties - like *Star Wars: Dark Forces* (1995), *Star Wars: Rogue Squadron* (1998), *Star Wars: Battlefront* (2004) - have proved the immense value of the brand and its connection to the core audience of gamers keen to play interactive experiences set within the universe that the movies helped create.

Star Wars has become so embedded in popular culture that it's easy to forget how groundbreaking it was and still is. Not just as a movie but as a cultural and business phenomenon. The Lucasfilm empire has created a benchmark in transmedia storytelling, a universe that has unfolded across books, games, comics and movies. Anyone who wants to understand the way in which today's cross-platform media franchises work - in particular the relationship between games and movies - need look no further. "*Star Wars* is an IP that has affected the world so dramatically," says Peter Hirschmann, who joined LucasArts in 2002 and became vice-president of product development in 2004. "It's a rich, deep legacy spanning over thirty years that you can make compelling interactive experiences out of."

Certainly, LucasArts sometimes fumbled. A slew of lesser *Star Wars* titles hurt the brand in the late 1990s and early 2000s, many of which were based on the movie prequels *The Phantom Menace* and its successors. As LucasArts grew, the innovation that characterised its work in the 1980s and 1990s - where small development teams led by passionate designers like Falstein, Barwood, Gilbert, David Fox and others – gave way to a corporate structure which was happy to lazily fall back on unimaginative rehashes of the *Star Wars* license.

It led to a corporate "reboot" in 2004 with Jim Ward brought in as LucasArts's president and quickly turned things around by publishing the hugely successful *LEGO: Star Wars* series. Yet whatever the company's ups and downs, it remains ironic that it was Lucasfilm - that most un-Hollywood of entertainment giants - that would show the major motion picture studios the value of making critically-acclaimed, profitable games based on movies.

For Spielberg, LucasArts served as a useful arena to experiment with interactive. Coming into the office as an unofficial consultant, the director enjoyed several benefits: he got firsthand experience of how interactive experiences were created from the ground up; he got to talk about games with industry leaders in the field; and he could try his hand at creating a game without having to jump through the hoops of creating his own interactive company. His passion project was *The Dig*, a graphical adventure game about a group of astronauts sent to destroy an asteroid heading towards Earth. Originally the concept, a cross between *Forbidden Planet* and *The Treasure of Sierra Madre*, was conceived as an episode of TV show *Amazing Stories*. It was shelved after the producers decided its sci-fi vision was too expensive to bring to the screen in the late 1980s when CGI was still in its infancy.

Videogames had no such budgetary restrictions when it came to bringing interplanetary settings to life and Spielberg transposed his idea into the interactive arena. *The Dig* would prove to be a frustrating experience for the filmmaker, though. Plagued by development woes it went through four project leaders beginning with Falstein, who sat in on brainstorming sessions with Lucas and Spielberg at Skywalker Ranch.

Gilbert, who was also present in the early stages of the game's development, says Spielberg's approach was different from Barwood's. While the former screenwriter got his fingers dirty - literally coding and creating games from scratch - Spielberg's approach was more that of a hobbyist with a remarkable, intuitive sense of games design. "I have a lot of respect for Spielberg, I think he's one of the greatest directors to live and he's very creative. I've always respected the fact that he really plays games, he doesn't just tinker with them, he plays them and loves to play them," Gilbert says. "He wanted to make them - as seen in *The Dig* - but it was just a 'hobby'. I never got the impression that Spielberg wanted to make games like he wanted to make movies."

Having someone as famous as Spielberg involved certainly gave the designers insight into a very different world, one dominated by celebrity and deference. During one early brainstorming session at Amblin with some of the director's associates, Gilbert recalls Spielberg throwing out a rather unworkable idea. "Noah says, 'I don't think that will work'. There was this collective gasp from everyone else in the room. I could hear everyone thinking: 'Oh my God, he just told Spielberg his idea wasn't any good!' Then Spielberg says 'Yeah, that was kind of stupid' and everyone lets out their breath. I found it amusing. I wondered if all brainstorming with Spielberg was like this."

The Dig would turn out to be a far from smooth production. The design team first met on the day of the 1989 San Francisco earthquake. It was an ominous sign of what was to come as the project took six years to complete and went through four project leads. It has since become a cult game - not least of all because of fan interest in its convoluted production history - but it never achieved the hopes LucasArts had for it. A suggested movie tie-in for the game never came to fruition and despite the project's commitment to getting a filmmaker to tell a story in the interactive sphere, it fell rather flat. Clearly, telling stories in games was no easier than making movies.

For Spielberg, who still remembered the disaster of *E.T.* on the Atari VCS 2600, *The Dig* wasn't the success he hoped for. Interactive entertainment was still waiting to feel the benefit of his famed Midas Touch. He'd suffered two strikes. One more and he was, arguably, out... In keeping with his status as the world's most famous filmmaker, Spielberg decided to think big. His next interactive project wouldn't just be another videogame. It would be a videogame company. DreamWorks Interactive would prove he could do more than just play great games. He could develop them too.

* * *

Ask former DreamWorks Interactive (DWI) employees how they ended up working for Steven Spielberg and you get a sense of just how glitzy the company seemed to most games designers. When Daniel Kaufman, a Silicon Valley veteran who became DWI's co-chief operating officer, was offered the job, his wife's reluctance to move out to Hollywood made him falter. DWI responded by flying her and her husband out to LA, putting them up in a suite in the five-star Peninsula Hotel and wining and dining them into submission. "She decided Hollywood wasn't such a terrible place after all," remembers Kaufman.

When Matt Hall, an artist with hopes of breaking into feature animation, received a cold call from a DWI recruiter, he hung up thinking it was a joke. After the recruiter rang back, Hall soon found himself watching Spielberg shoot dinosaurs among giant redwood trees in a California forest as he prepared to work on the DWI PlayStation game *Jurassic Park: The Lost World*. "I was pinching myself, thinking 'How in the world did a kid from the Midwest get a job like this?'"

At DWI, Hollywood glitz wasn't in short supply. With offices first on the Universal lot, then in Oakwood Apartments, a favoured temporary residence of child stars and their families, the early days of the company made it seem like part of Hollywood. Later, when the company moved into a former strip mall in a U-shaped building in Brentwood set over two floors (which had the disastrous effect of keeping the development teams isolated from each other), they found themselves miles from DreamWorks' home base. Yet, Hollywood glitz came to them: Spielberg popped in and out of the offices taking meetings, offering feedback, play-testing and chatting.

In its first few years, DWI achieved only modest results. With former Microsoft talent involved in much of the programming - and Patty Stonesifer, the former vice-president of Microsoft's Interactive Media Division onboard as a consultant - the emphasis was largely on PC CD-ROM titles rather than console games. Having made itself to some extent in Disney's image, perhaps inevitably in light of Katzenberg's history with the company, DWI initially focused on children's multimedia titles.

"There was an interesting tension about who we would be and what we would do," says Kaufman. "There was also this notion that we were going to make new products, the next generation of products - things that were worthy of a Spielberg or a Katzenberg rather than just making another game. In hindsight, I think one of the mistakes we made was not doing a good enough job of defining the criteria of success. Was it the most profit, the most revenue, the best reviews, or pushing the envelope of what should be in games? Any of those is valid. Chasing all of them was probably a mistake."

Spielberg's influence was apparent in many of DWI's early titles. He secured Jeff Goldblum to shoot the live-action video for kids' game *Goosebumps: Escape from Horrorland*, released in 1996 to fairly solid sales. He came up with the concept and helped cast the voice talent for *Someone's in the Kitchen*, a PC recipe game designed to encourage kids to cook. "It went nowhere," says Kaufman of the $2 million game's lack of retail success.

Elsewhere Spielberg's filmography was the basis of some of DWI's biggest, licensed titles: *Jurassic Park: The Lost World* on the PlayStation and *Jurassic Park: Trespasser* on the PC. Annoyingly, even though Spielberg directed the *Jurassic Park* movie, the IP belonged to Universal. That meant DWI had to licence the title for a princely sum to make the games and pay extra if they wanted add-ons like permission to use movie composer John Williams' score.

It was an example of how convoluted the film-to-game transition could be when the thinking behind the production process wasn't joined up. While *The Lost World* sold well on the PlayStation, *Trespasser* proved a terrible flop. Billed as "the digital sequel" to Spielberg's movie, it reportedly cost anywhere from

$8 to $11 million to develop at a time when most games were made for around a quarter of that. Many at DWI expected it to be the company's flagship title. They were wrong. Despite the wild claims about its physics and dinosaur AI, it was a broken game. "They were trying so hard to simulate everything that they forgot it needed to be entertaining," says Hall, who'd worked on the company's other *Jurassic Park* game, *The Lost World*. *Trespasser* reputedly took around a $1 million in sales, a fraction of its budget. One former DWI employee called it the company's Vietnam.

Despite Hollywood's misconceptions, making games was hard work. For the non-gamers in DreamWorks's corporate hierarchy the mechanics of development remained a mystery. As Nicole LaPorte recounts in her DreamWorks history *The Men Who Would Be King*, Katzenberg was particularly troubled by delays to DWI's slate. Accustomed to the exactness of movie scheduling, he was aghast when DWI's teams explained that software wasn't like movies. Hollywood production methodologies struggled to get to grips with such cultural differences. Meanwhile, although some DWI employees hoped to use their tenure at the company as a stepping stone into the movie biz, most of the games developers were simply non-plussed by the Hollywood connection.

"On *Trespasser* we were games people through and through, and were mostly just bemused by the Hollywood side of things," remembers designer Richard Wyckoff. He recalls being summoned to present *Trespasser* to Katzenberg one Sunday morning at 8am - "A time and day I've never done games business before, or since" - and sitting in a level design meeting with Spielberg and his teenage son Max on a Saturday: "He brainstormed for a short while with myself and lead designer Austin Grossman, and then turned Max over to us while he proceeded to do a lot of important-sounding Hollywood business on his cellphone in the back of the room."

If Katzenberg was focused on the business side of the enterprise, Spielberg saw DWI as an opportunity to experiment with videogames as a storytelling medium. Although DWI made its share of lucrative, movie-licensed games, it wasn't the company's primary aim. Spielberg hoped to do something much bigger. "I think he was inspired by the invention and toy-like sense of creation and engagement that overtook people in the games business," explains Patrick Gilmore, the ex-Disney Interactive employee who launched DWI's console development team with the million-selling *Lost World* videogame. "He thought games could unlock new ways to tell stories."

The ambition in the company trickled down from the top. Could DWI make the videogame equivalent of a smash-hit movie like *Indiana Jones* or *Star Wars*? Was it possible to even achieve that level of audience connection and storytelling prowess in a videogame? "The question really was, 'Can you make videogames into an art form?'" says Kaufman. "Spielberg would come in and say, 'Games are all about adrenalin, they're one-trick ponies. But in a movie theatre you don't see just one type of movie, you see rom-coms, horror movies.... Games need to be able to add that level into them.' He challenged the team to make him a game that wasn't just about adrenalin and said, 'Let's do a rom-com'."

No one in the team knew how it could be done. Excited to be thinking outside the box, Spielberg dialled Nora Ephron, queen of the Hollywood romantic comedy from *When Harry Met Sally* to *Sleepless in Seattle*. Before she knew what was happening, Ephron was signed up for her first foray into the interactive sphere. The game, tentatively titled *That's Life* was supposed to follow its protagonist over the course of an ordinary day, letting players take God-like control over an individual's life as they made dinner, cleaned the house and worked on their personal relationships.

Spielberg thought it was dynamite. The rest of DWI were less enthusiastic and they weren't alone. Over the course of several meetings with Ephron it became apparent that the screenwriter was only involved as a personal favour to Spielberg. "She was great but I don't think she understood it either," says Kaufman. "We were both looking to each other. We couldn't articulate to her how to make this interesting. The easiest thing was to do a branching story game but that was tired. What I also think surprised her was the amount of work that would go into doing something like that. It far exceeded the work of a screenplay. To make a deep, interactive story you're writing much more. At some point she, or her agent, went 'So I'm going to write six times as much for a fiftieth of the audience...?' It's a fairly difficult argument to make. We couldn't pay her squat, we didn't have any money."

Ephron got as far as producing a script for the game. It was immediately obvious that project was a blowout. Spielberg may well have been presciently reaching for something akin to bestselling future PC title *The Sims* with its day-in-the-life gameplay. In 1996, though, *The Sims* was just a vague flicker in designer Will Wright's eye; the technology simply wasn't ready to support such a game. Instead, *That's Life* became yet another marker on the bumpy road of convergence, an unreleased project that proved how hard it was for linear filmmakers to enter the alien world of interactive entertainment - even if they were as successful as Spielberg and Ephron.

Although *That's Life* was a failed experiment, it taught the company a lot about how to tackle their next projects. Spielberg's desire to create interactive entertainment remained strong. It was only a matter of time until it found a proper outlet: ever since the birth of the company, he had been talking about making a World War II game called *Normandy Beach* (or "Beach Ball" as it was affectionately known by DWI's staff). The director, who was already planning his 1998 movie *Saving Private Ryan*, handpicked designer Noah Falstein to lead the *Normandy Beach* project in 1995. Falstein, DWI's third employee, had bonded with Spielberg during his visits to LucasArts where they had long chats about the *Indiana Jones* games and *Secret Weapons of the Luftwaffe*.

"I spent my first six months at DWI developing this idea for a squad-based game," Falstein says. "My concept was that you would follow two brothers - one assaulting the beach and another who was a paratrooper who came in the night before and landed behind German lines. You'd go back and forth flipping between missions as a paratrooper and an army guy assaulting the beach. They worked their way in and twelve days after D-Day they would meet at some critical point in a small town in Normandy. We had quite a sophisticated storyline." It was an interactive precursor to Spielberg's *Saving Private Ryan* and TV series *Band of Brothers*. Cinematic sweep was a big part of the planned game's remit. Falstein had already proved his storytelling chops on LucasArts' *Indiana Jones* games and Spielberg was fascinated about immersing players in a scripted narrative that was also interactive. "A core of us believed that the age of story in videogames had come," recalls Kaufman. "Spielberg would say: 'Tell me a story that I'll really care about.'"

In an early DWI meeting that included Spielberg, his long-time collaborator Walter Parkes (the producer and screenwriter who'd written Atari-era thriller *WarGames* in the 1980s) and Kaufman, the director asked for ideas on how to inject emotion into games. There was talk about scripted set pieces in games, moments where the games designers would funnel the player's experience of the narrative.

Discussing the *Normandy Beach* game, Spielberg threw out an idea for an interactive plot twist: imagine if the player was moving through the hedgerows in occupied Europe as a US soldier. He sees a glint of light, hears a shot and realises there's a sniper nearby. Over time, the game trains the player to associate the glint of light from a gun sight with a sniper. Every time you see a glint, you fire back and kill a Nazi sharpshooter. "Eventually, you see a glint up in a high church tower and you shoot that one too," explains Kaufman, recalling the pitch. "Now you fight your way up the tower - the church steeple where you saw the glint. You're killing Nazis and doing all that good stuff. You go all the way up to the top and there you find a girl in a little white communion dress with a silver cross around her neck and a bullet hole right in her forehead. You realise that was the glint. You took the shot... What would that moment be like? When Spielberg was telling us this, we got goosebumps. We were like 'Oh my God, people would drop the controller! You can't do that!' But that is the next level of interactive entertainment; and, in a way, it's more powerful than seeing it as a movie. In a movie you see that and feel a little manipulated, you're invested in the character and think: 'I wouldn't do that.' In a game, you pulled the trigger. You made the call."

Back in 1995, this was explosive stuff. Few games designers were thinking about the moral implications that interactive could force players to engage with. Today videogames - from *BioShock*'s moral dilemmas over killing child-like "Little Sisters" to *Call of Duty: Modern Warfare 2*'s controversial, civilian-shooting "No Russian" level - are still grappling with the thorny issue of choice and consequence. In the end, however, the idea of innocent casualties never gained traction. "We thought people would get upset," says Kaufman, when asked why it didn't come to fruition. "The sense was you couldn't shoot little kids in a game."

Normandy Beach eventually stalled. After DreamWorks got a new chief executive, Glenn Entis, the project was shut down and resources were focused on *Jurassic Park: Trespasser*. The general feeling among DWI's corporate management was that World War II was too niche a subject for games. After Falstein left the company, the project was officially declared dead. For Spielberg, though, the idea of making a videogame set in World War II remained a keen ambition. After he signalled that his next film would be *Saving Private Ryan*, it wasn't long before the *Normandy Beach* idea was resurrected, this time under different leadership and with a different agenda.

The game that would become *Medal of Honor* began, appropriately enough, on the 11th day of the 11th month of 1997. Spielberg, who was then in post-production on *Saving Private Ryan*, came into the DWI offices and outlined his idea. He saw *Saving Private Ryan* as an educational experience as much as an entertainment property and was frustrated that the movie was too violent for kids. He'd watched his teenage son Max and his friends playing *GoldenEye* on the Nintendo 64 console. Could DWI build a World War II shooter, he wondered, that would let them learn about the conflict through playing?

Addressing the team, Spielberg sketched out an ambitious concept: a first-person shooter on the PlayStation set in the European theatre of war and named after America's highest military award, the Medal of Honor. It would be fun to play, historically accurate, and a tribute to the fallen. Orders given, Spielberg closed the meeting with that smirk of his and a parting shot: "I'll be back in a week..."

At the time, there was little enthusiasm among DWI's corporate management for the project. Console games weren't the company's main focus and the PlayStation wasn't an obvious platform for a first person shooter. Plus, hard as it is to believe today, World War II was considered passé. "People were really dubious," recalls producer Peter Hirschmann. "They said: 'World War II is old, it's got cobwebs on it. People want ray guns, hell-spawn and laser rifles'. The idea of doing something with historical relevance set in a low-tech game environment was a challenging sell."

But this was Spielberg who was asking, and at DWI what Spielberg wanted, Spielberg got. While almost everyone at DWI thought *Small Soldiers*, a game based on the animated movie, would put the company on the map, Hirschmann's team - "a ragtag group of misfits, very much the underdog institutionally" – took on the new project with little fanfare. No one expected much from it. Over the next seven days they put together a demo using the engine from their previous project, the PlayStation game *Jurassic Park: The Lost World*. Hirschmann, a former Amblin intern who had worked with the director on his 1996 FMV project *Steven Spielberg: Director's Chair* before coming onboard at DWI, felt the pressure. "It was a crazy week. We took *Jurassic Park*'s renderer and put together a demo with bailing wire and chewing gum." Spielberg had set in motion a white-knuckle ride. When the director returned a week later, the finished, rough-and-ready demo proved the concept: shooting Nazis was extremely satisfying.

Medal of Honor was Spielberg's great passion project and the game that would become DWI's greatest legacy. It was no ordinary licensed movie title and it shared none of *Saving Private Ryan*'s plot. Instead it was designed as a companion piece that would possess the same reverential feel.

Working for a Hollywood videogame company had its advantages when it came to accessing resources and opening doors. Hirschmann spent time doing research at the Imperial War Museum in London and when art director Matt Hall needed to photograph World War II-era weaponry he was made welcome over at Hollywood armourers Stembridge Guns.

Early in development, Spielberg told Hirschmann to call up Captain Dale Dye, the retired USMC officer turned Hollywood military advisor who'd worked with him on *Saving Private Ryan*. "I was like 'Oh no, he's gonna think we're a bunch of pencil-necked geeks who don't know what the hell is going on'," recalls Hirschmann. "It turns out he thought we were a bunch of pencil-necked geeks who didn't know what the hell was going on. The last thing he wanted to do was babysit us. It was like 'Oh shit' on both sides."

Dye arrived at DWI's offices in intimidating drill instructor mode, convinced they were making what the producer calls "an exploitative, tone-deaf, irresponsible thing". Once he saw their intentions were honourable, however, his mood softened. He became a valuable ally of the team, running them through an impromptu boot camp in the desert and calling them out on their military and historical goofs. He also harangued them about making their level design more realistic. "Captain Dye helped us with mission structure, particularly the idea of infiltration and then exfiltration," says Hirschmann. "Once you do the thing you've been sent to do - blow up the bridge, steal the map - then you have to get out. It became a fantastic structure for every mission in that first game, giving each a three act structure." Dye also lent his distinctive, authoritative voice to the game's epic opening narration. The use of such Hollywood production values certainly wasn't cheap but it gave the proceedings considerable polish.

As a game, *Medal of Honor* remains a fantastic achievement. Playing O.S.S. operative Jimmy Patterson, you're parachuted behind enemy lines and forced to wage a one-man assault against the Nazi war machine. Its storyline has none of the emotional sweep or D-Day landings carnage of *Saving Private Ryan*. What it offers instead is a sense of breathtaking immersion and reverential historical authenticity. Mini-history lessons give background on everything from the O.S.S. to the Gestapo and V-2 rockets, while nostalgic art and video clips capture a sense of the period. Not just an adrenalin rush, it's arguably the most educational first person shooter ever made.

With the game in development before Sony's twin-stick DualShock controller even arrived, the PlayStation's technical limitations were a challenge: "We couldn't even show day," laughs art director Hall, "so every level is a night mission!" The programming team did their best with what they had. "Enemies had 250 polygons max, it's laughable today" says Hirschmann. "We had a hierarchical animation system that we thought was pretty cutting edge. We blew our memory budget running that on a 2Mb console."

The attention to character animation and AI gave the combat a raft of emergent possibilities: throw a grenade and a Nazi soldier would try and kick it back at you or dive on it to protect his comrades; wing an enemy and they'd drop their weapon; score a headshot and a helmet would fly off. "To be crass about it," Hirschmann says, "whenever you shot a bad guy, something cool happened." Even the German Shepherd dogs could be made to play "grenade fetch", carrying a tossed explosive to their unlucky owner.

One of the delights of working on *Medal of Honor* was the scope to innovate. Max Spielberg, the 14-year-old son of the director who'd later become a videogame designer at EALA, remembers being thrilled by the DWI offices when he spent a fortnight doing quality assurance work on the game. "I'd grown up around movie sets and studios, but I'd never felt more excited than walking around DWI," he recalls. "This was a place where they'd use building blocks and green army men to map out the next level. I mean, it was basically taking all my tangible childhood toys and bringing them to life. I thought it was so cool they had arcade machines and a kitchen with larger soda cups than any man should ever drink from. It was that initial excitement around the work environment that made me realise I needed to become a part of that world."

As a creator, Spielberg Senior was open to ideas and suggestions from all quarters, including his son. "My dad always had this yellow pad in which he kept all of his notes for *Medal of Honor*. We would listen to movie scores in the car while going to school and at stoplights he'd write our ideas down. I do recall one idea he had where if you shot a Nazi while he stood on a balcony, he would flip over the railing and hang on for a second before either climbing back up or falling off to his death. I added the part where you could shoot his hands off while he held on for dear life."

The director was particularly interested in seeing how far interactive entertainment could be pushed. Ideas like the "show me your papers" scenes - where the player brandishes fake ID papers instead of a gun to bypass Nazi guards - were pioneering attempts to expand the scope of the first person shooter beyond simply shooting. Together with Valve's *Half-Life*, released a year earlier in 1998, *Medal of Honor* redefined the genre. "Suddenly our interaction with the AI has changed," argues Max Spielberg. "We no longer need to use cover to hide from them. And now we are unsure of how long the disguise will hold, eliciting a state of nervousness and perhaps fear. These changes are mainly cosmetic but by doing so the *Medal of Honor* team was able to alter the behaviour of the player. This was way back in 1999."

Such innovation, when combined with the game's fantastic audio design - the ping of an M1 Garand rifle as it runs out of ammo; shouted German phrases; ambient sounds of planes flying overhead; and Michael Giacchino's sweeping score - made it a game destined for greatness. When Electronic Arts received a demo disc in Easter 1998, staff traded it around the office all weekend. EA immediately signed DWI up to their Partners Program, agreeing to publish and distribute *Medal of Honor* internationally.

Then the Columbine High School massacre happened. Two high school kids, Eric Harris and Dylan Klebold, went on a shooting spree in April 1999 killing their fellow students and teachers. The tragedy was hastily blamed in part on the killers' love of videogame *Doom*. Rightly or wrongly, that belief turned videogames into public enemy number one. For DreamWorks, a company that had modelled itself in part on Disney's wholesome image, the potential bad publicity was troubling.

"DWI was working on this game at the same time as they were forming their brand and identity in the minds of the consumer," explains Gilmore, a producer on *Medal of Honor*. "A lot of soul searching went on at DWI. I think it would warm people's hearts to know how much thought went into crafting an appropriate experience in the context of something that was as controversial as a first person shooter."

It didn't help that at least one early build of the game had been incredibly gory. "I recall shooting a Panzerschrek rocket directly into a Nazi and as the smoke cleared, all that was left was half his upper torso down to his feet," says Max Spielberg. "He would dance around for a little bit, blood particles squirting from his wounds, and then finally collapse. It was more fitting for an *Evil Dead* movie than *Medal of Honor*."

After Columbine, the team pulled all the blood from the game. It was a decision that, regardless of issues of sensitivity, helped give *Medal of Honor* a more impressive, grown-up tone. Imagine, in the aftermath of Columbine, if the game had included that little girl in her white communion dress...

Controversy has a habit of rolling downhill. A few months later, Paul Bucha, the Congressional Medal of Honor Society's president, heard about the game before its release and wrote an angry letter to Spielberg. As Hirschmann recalls, "Bucha said: 'What you are doing is terrible. You are dishonouring the *Medal of Honor*. Please change the name of the game.'"

In an attempt to limit the damage, Bucha was invited to Amblin on the Universal lot for a meeting with Spielberg, DWI's chief executive Glenn Entis and Hirschmann as well as Spielberg's personal publicist Marvin Levy. The former soldier, a Vietnam veteran who was awarded the Medal of Honor for his courage under fire, stated his case against videogames. Strongly.

Spielberg was absolutely gutted. *Medal of Honor* was his passion project, a game that was supposed to give kids a genuine insight into the history behind World War II. A proud American, the filmmaker was heartbroken by Bucha's verbal tirade. "It was an intense meeting," recalls Hirschmann. "Paul came in and laid it out on the table. We just sat there and let him speak. He didn't know anything about the game but laid out a case: 'When it comes to the Medal of Honor, it's a serious and sacred thing. You don't turn it into a videogame. It's an awful thing to do.' He made a really compelling case we shouldn't be doing this." The director knew he was facing a debacle even bigger than *E.T.* on the Atari VCS 2600.

At the end of the meeting, it looked as if *Medal of Honor* was done for. Even though it had just reached "Release To Manufacturing" stage - and millions had been spent on its development and production - Spielberg was seriously thinking about abandoning it. "He was willing at that point to cut his losses and just pull it from the shelves," believes Hall. Bucha's blitzkrieg assault seemed to have ended in victory. It was only Hirschmann's intervention that saved it. "Peter is a really humble guy, he never toots his own horn" continues Hall. "But he saved that franchise. I would wager that well over half the people at DWI didn't know that story." As the meeting wound down and papers were shuffled, Hirschmann respectfully asked the war veteran a question: would he like to play it?

Setting up an impromptu demo and explaining in detail the team's passion about honouring American servicemen, Hirschmann convinced the Vietnam veteran of the project's weight. Not only did the society drop their objections to the game, they decided to endorse it too. "I give all credit to Paul Bucha in the world," says Hirschmann. "He had won the conversation, but he was willing to listen."

Released in November 1999 and distributed by EA, *Medal of Honor* was DWI's most successful title. It was something of a pyrrhic victory: DreamWorks' bosses, hit hard by the interactive division's losses, had already put in motion the sale of the company to EA. The *Medal of Honor* franchise would make north of $1 billion in its lifetime, yet DWI's owners and Spielberg cashed out before the profits rolled in. "EA got an incredible deal," reckons Gilmore. "It was the Louisiana Purchase of game company acquisitions." Kaufman, who by that point had long abandoned ship, agrees: "DWI didn't get a lot; EA got a tonne. I think DWI was worth more and they should have got more. From EA's perspective they wanted to finish *Medal of Honor* and get a hook-up with Spielberg. If I were their shareholders I would have been very happy."

Spielberg later described the sale as both the "smartest and dumbest" thing he ever did (financial details of the deal have never been released). On one hand, the director stepped away from what would become a lucrative franchise. On the other, he recognised that EA had the expertise to grow *Medal of Honor.*

John Batter, who had been chief finance officer at DWI since its beginning before moving across to EA prior to the sale, believes that EA took the series to the next level. EA brought in a new chief technical officer, offered greater engineering support and gave the franchise the benefit of its vast product knowledge.

"Without the infusion of talent from EA and the much deeper understanding of the videogame consumer that EA had, I simply don't believe that *Medal of Honor* would have reached the heights that it reached," he says, noting EA's talent for identifying potential franchises. "I think it was a great start by DreamWorks Interactive [but] it took EA to move it from a niche title to mass market premier franchise. I really think it took the best of both companies."

Despite Spielberg's regrets, he personally handed out a bonus cheque to the original DWI team. Hirschmann, who'd gone far beyond the call of duty, got something even better: a letter of recommendation to Spielberg's friend George Lucas. After working on several *Medal of Honor* sequels at EA, the producer moved over to LucasArts.

From EA's perspective, the acquisition of DWI did more than just give them the rights to a lucrative videogame property. It would also become the kernel of EALA, the flagship Los Angeles studio based at Spielberg's beloved Playa Vista that would cement EA's growing status in the wider entertainment industry and help them build ties with movie studios like Warner Bros.

More specifically, the acquisition also cemented EA's growing friendship with Spielberg himself. What videogame company wouldn't want to have the entertainment industry's biggest player in their corner, legitimising them? "EA loves Steven Spielberg," says Bing Gordon, the company's executive vice-president at the time. "As we got more involved with DreamWorks Interactive, he thought we should just own it. That led to opening EALA. Tactics, not strategy."

The sale of DWI marked the end of Spielberg's dream of having his own videogame empire like LucasArts. There was no missing the irony that it was Lucas, the non-gamer, who stuck it out in the industry while Spielberg folded his hand early. Over at LucasArts, Barwood, who had been close friends with both men since their first forays into filmmaking, watched events unfold with interest. "I think George has as much business sense as he does creativity, and also a fierce pride of independence," he concludes. "Steven has always been much more inclined to leverage his contacts with Hollywood to his own advantage, and is maybe less interested in actually running a company."

What he was interested in, though, was the medium of videogames. Even after the sale Spielberg remained a passionate supporter of the *Medal of Honor* franchise. Hall, who later worked on several of the sequels, remembers Spielberg taking Lucas to see *Medal of Honor: Allied Assault* at EA's E3 booth in 2001. Spielberg proudly showed his friend the game's outstanding Omaha Beach assault. It was an intense interactive sequence that captured the nerve-jangling horror of the D-Day landings much as *Saving Private Ryan*'s famous battlefield sequence had done. "It was a big deal for Steven to show his buddy what he had put together," says Hall.

In Hollywood terms, Spielberg was the first major director to see the interactive sphere as a worthwhile medium for expression. The directors who followed him into the industry - filmmakers like Peter Jackson, John Woo and Guillermo Del Toro - all took inspiration from his experience at DWI and later EA. In comparison, Lucas never personally made games - although he did use game technology to further his interest in pre-visualisation for his movies.

Spielberg's continuing relationship with EA after DWI's sale would yield fruit, in particular the critically-acclaimed family puzzle title *Boom Blox* (2008) and its sequel. They were fun, throwaway outings - hardly what one expected from the director. Meanwhile a stalled project, codenamed *LMNO* promised much, with the player helping an alien called Eve break out of an Area 51 style military base. Focusing on letting the computer-controlled Eve assist the player as they escape from the FBI and military, *LMNO* had Spielberg's stamp all over it: aliens, a blockbuster chase plot and an ambitious attempt to redefine the possibilities of interactive entertainment. "*E.T.* meets *North By Northwest*," was how Newsweek described it.

No mere AI character, Eve was supposed to respond to how you treated her, potentially changing the course of the game's narrative. "The challenge is, can the game have an emotional impact on players while they are actively manipulating the world?" Spielberg asked. The director consulted with the team during development - EA even videotaped his brainstorming meetings with lead designer Doug Church to be shown to the rest of the staff - but the project never got beyond the prototype phase and was shut down in 2009.

One wonders what might have been. Perhaps more pertinently, one also wonders what still might happen if Spielberg actually takes time out of his schedule to devote his total attention to a videogame, much as he would a movie. His approach to videogames has always been that of the hobbyist rather than the full-time professional. It's a pity because Spielberg is a rare example of a movie director who can move between both mediums with ease - and success.

The continuing problem for the games industry is that while every filmmaker thinks they can build a game, very few understand the unique challenges of games design. The Hollywood trade press regularly announces new collaborations between filmmakers and videogame studios - from John Woo's *Stranglehold* released by Midway Games in 2007, to Zack Snyder's unfruitful three-game deal struck with EA in 2008. Little of lasting impact has ever come from such outings.

To date, the *Medal of Honor* series remains Spielberg's greatest contribution to interactive entertainment. In retrospect, its legacy isn't the mammoth sales of the franchise it launched. According to producer Patrick Gilmore, *Medal of Honor* was a landmark because it represented "the public acceptance of videogames", particularly in the aftermath of Columbine. Hirschmann, who attended several Congressional Medal of Honor Society meetings, recalls recipients telling him how much it meant to their families. "They all had grandkids who were experiencing their stories through the game. That was a wonderful payoff to the whole thing. All that work we put into the gameplay, the historical movies that played at the end of every level - that shit was hard, it took a long time. It was great it had an impact."

More than just legitimising games in the public's imagination, *Medal of Honor* also had an impact in Hollywood. For those in the entertainment industry who had been watching the growth of videogames closely, this

World War II shooter represented something else: the first sign that this new medium could conceivably support the unique vision of a storyteller like Steven Spielberg. "*Medal of Honor* is one of the few great marriages of game and film," says the director's son. "It was that first rickety bridge built between the silver screen and the home console."

CHAPTER 7

Generation Xbox

"Both the videogame and the movie industry thought that they had the bigger dick. But the reality was they both had big dicks."

Larry Shapiro, founder of CAA's Games Division

In the autumn of 2001, Larry Shapiro had fifty Xboxes stacked against the wall of his office at Creative Artists Agency (CAA) in Beverly Hills. He was the envy of every agent in the building. The Xbox, dubbed "Microsoft's secret weapon" by Wired magazine, was the hottest item on the planet. Everyone in Hollywood wanted one and Shapiro, co-head of CAA's Games Division who counted Xbox among his clients, was responsible for seeding the movie industry's top tier of talent with them.

He drew up a list of the movie biz's prime movers and shakers. There were high-powered executives, A-list directors and, of course, stars. Nicolas Cage, Will Smith, Tom Hanks, Tobey Maguire and even Julia Roberts - a huge, if unlikely, fan of the Xbox's first-person shooter launch title *Halo: Combat Evolved* - all received a complimentary console and games from the Aladdin's cave in Shapiro's office.

Microsoft wasn't just launching a new game platform: it wanted to change the entire entertainment business overnight. Although few in Hollywood realised it, what Shapiro calls "the battle for the living room" had just begun. "It was the tipping point," says the former agent. "The Xbox and the PlayStation 2 had movie-quality graphics and they were about to start telling movie-quality stories." The moment was crystallised when Shapiro took one of his Xboxes over to Chris Albrecht, then head of cable broadcaster HBO. In Albrecht's office, he unpacked the chunky black and green box and plugged it into the back of the TV. First, though, he had to unplug the cable signal.

"Albrecht wasn't a gamer," Shapiro remembers, "but he right then realised, 'Oh my God, you've just unplugged my cable channels!' If these gamers, who are 18- to 35-year-old males, are playing these games 10 hours a week, how many hours a week are they watching HBO? What the networks and the cable companies realised was that they had to get involved in this because it was game over otherwise."

Albrecht was right to be concerned: the new generation of games consoles were a huge threat. Over the following few years, the Xbox and PlayStation 2 would evolve from mere games machines into multimedia centres. The next generation of consoles - the Xbox 360 and PlayStation 3, would not only be capable of playing DVDs and CDs but also Blu-ray discs as well as downloading and streaming TV and film content (including HBO programmes). In that moment in 2001, Hollywood was witnessing the coming of age of Generation Xbox and the beginning of a new chapter in the story of convergence.

It was a moment Shapiro had been waiting for a long time. He'd begun his career working as a producer at Propaganda Films. In the '90s, the production company was the epicentre of Hollywood's next generation of talent and Shapiro watched the MTV auteurs - young, hip music video directors like David Fincher, Michael Bay and Antoine Fuqua - charge to the forefront of popular culture. He also saw how these creative talents, who worked into a medium that spoke directly to the kids, could use that power base to leverage huge careers in motion pictures.

Later, while working at Propaganda offshoot Palomar Pictures, Shapiro came across two videogames: Valve's first-person shooter *Half-Life* (1998) and *Oddworld: Abe's Oddysee* (1997). They changed his career path forever. "When I played them, I realised that the next generation of talent was going to come out of the games industry," he says. MTV had been successful because it allowed people to connect to music through their televisions. But for the next generation, the platform wasn't the TV but the videogame box sat beneath it. Videogames were the new MTV.

Half-Life broke new ground for cinematic storytelling in videogames. Its plot about creatures from another dimension invading a scientific research base in the New Mexico desert could have come from any mediocre sci-fi thriller. As an interactive, first person experience though, it was utterly thrilling. Players guided crowbar-wielding physicist Dr Gordon Freeman through a story that was told entirely via supporting characters' dialogue and scripted set-pieces. No longer was story consigned to non-interactive cut-scenes that robbed you of control. Story instead unfolded in-game. It was incredibly immersive.

Oddworld's cinematic credentials were even more apparent. Its creator Lorne Lanning had come from the movie business doing visual effects work at Rhythm and Hues Studios - which won an Oscar for its work on the talking pig movie *Babe* in 1995. *Oddworld* was a freaky, subversively funny platform game set in a rich alternate universe with a memorable central character. Looking at the quality of both the animation and the storytelling, Shapiro could see that the crossover between the two industries was already happening in earnest. He realised the potential revenues were huge.

At Palomar, Shapiro worked with Electronic Arts (EA) and used his producing skills to bring Hollywood polish to the cut-scene sections for *Nuclear Strike*, *Soviet Strike*, *Road Rash 3-D* and *Jane's Combat Simulations: Fleet Command*. A little later he became vice-president of EA affiliate Stromlo Entertainment. Along the way, he started to think about how you could transfer the skill-sets of filmmaking and videogame production from one industry to another.

In 2000 it led him to the doors of powerhouse Hollywood talent agency CAA, where he joined their new media division. It was the height of the tech boom. "Everyone and their mother was coming up with ideas for dotcoms," he remembers. "There were nannies of actors who we represented who had ideas for dotcoms and we had to sit with them and listen to these pitches. We were clawing our eyes out." When the bubble burst, Shapiro founded CAA's standalone Games Division, concentrating on creating intersections between the videogame market and Hollywood.

Agents are natural bridge builders. They know that a stuffed Rolodex is only as valuable as the person who can connect up the names it contains. Find the right spark between your clients, hook them up in the right way, know their foibles and exploit their egos and you will make money. Shapiro became a pioneer: the first agent to truly appreciate the way that the videogame and movie industries could cross-fertilise. As Alex Young, the movie executive who had championed *Tomb Raider* and later became co-president of production at Twentieth Century Fox, puts it: "Larry Shapiro was absolutely ahead of the curve."

CAA was Hollywood's leading agency when it came to putting together packages and that approach extended into videogames too. Shapiro's interests were wide and varied: he took movie actors and screenwriters and put them into games; he coaxed game creators to sell movie rights to the studios; he helped Hollywood studios find developers who were willing to license their movies to make games; and he also kept an eye on game engines - the software that lets games designers create their virtual worlds.

His clients included Valve, the creators of *Half-Life*, whose Source engine impressed him. He also represented id, the creators of the *Doom* franchise and the Quake engine; and then Epic, whose Unreal engine set a new benchmark in 3D graphics. Along the way he set up potentially lucrative movie deals for all his videogame clients. Valve met DreamWorks and later Sony for a potential *Half-Life* movie. "When Steven Spielberg walked into the room, you saw the Valve kids' jaws drop," Shapiro recalls. But the deals weren't rich enough for them and negotiations stuck over the progress to production agreement, as well as the deal points Valve wanted on any potential sequels. Shapiro helped id get a *Doom* movie made at Universal and led Epic's *Gears of War* game to New Line, where it was optioned for a movie adaptation. "I made good on all my campaign promises," he says.

The CAA agent was particularly interested in game engines since he was convinced that they had potential as creative tools for Hollywood. He'd witnessed how expensive visual effects were while producing music videos. "When I saw these videogame engines I was like 'Wow! If I could have used this to make music videos or commercials I could have saved hundreds of thousands of dollars using this technology. This technology needs to be in Hollywood'."

Realising that the quality wasn't yet ready for the big screen, Shapiro instead concentrated on television. "Here you had game engines that were rendering graphics in real time. It was unbelievable. How do you take that technology and intersect it with a Hollywood creative to make a TV show?" His thinking proved correct. As an example, today Epic's Unreal engine not only brings the steroid-pumped space marines of *Gears of War* to life but also - somewhat improbably - powers the virtual sets used on kids' TV show *Lazy Town*.

Shapiro could see that Hollywood and the videogame industry had much to learn from one another. Yet he was also aware of the huge gulf that separated them. "It was almost like two big kids from two different towns," he remembers. "They're the big shots in their own town and so they don't want to go to another town and try to be the big shot there because they have to prove their cred. It was really hard to get both sides to talk to each other."

Coming together meant both sides had to leave their comfort zones. "The core business of videogames companies was making videogames," he explains. "It was all about the technology, they wrapped a little bit of story around it and - at the time in the late 1990s and early 2000s - they sold to a niche audience. The movie studios were like 'Yeah, yeah, yeah we see these games, they're making money, but we're pulling in $20 to $30 million in a weekend from movie openings and that's our business, we're not technologists.' So it was very difficult to merge the two and to get the two sides to talk."

What was needed was something that could shake both sides out of their complacency. In the autumn of 2001, looking at the Xboxes stacked against his office wall, Shapiro realised he'd found it. The sixth generation of videogame consoles had the power to run games that didn't just look like movies but could tell movie-quality stories too. It was perfect timing. Earlier that summer, the *Tomb Raider* movie had secured the number one spot at the US box office with a $48.2 million opening. "It showed the studios in their own metrics that the game industry was now a source for new movie and franchise material," says Shapiro. "It basically said to them 'there is gold in those hills.'"

Games like *Halo* were no longer just games; they were becoming bona fide entertainment properties. A shift was happening in Hollywood. "The studios noticed that videogames had made a great evolutionary leap forwards with the Xbox," says *Doom* producer Lorenzo Di Bonaventura. "They recognised that convergence was inevitable. It was the sense of inevitability more than the actuality at that moment that made people at the studios pay attention."

What Shapiro brought to the table was an understanding of both sides: he'd worked in both film and videogames and he was able to build bridges between the two. "Often when you're trying to do convergence, one side talks at the other," says Di Bonaventura, former president of worldwide production at Warner Bros. where he played a pivotal role in getting *The Matrix* into production. "They sit, they're very cordial and they're going on and on and on but it doesn't work. My memory of Larry was that he was able to understand both mediums. Why was a he a good bridge builder? Because he was able to talk to both sides in way that both understood and didn't feel threatened by."

The testament of Shapiro's skill lay in the deals he set up. Among the many firsts he brokered were lucrative agreements between Activision and Columbia/Sony over the licensed *Spider-Man* games; and packaging Will Wright, creator of *The Sims* franchise, for a television development deal with ABC. The deals that didn't stick told their own story about the gulf that still existed between the two industries. CAA brokered a movie outing for Microsoft's *Age of Empires* franchise: a trilogy of films, based on the strategy games, that would go straight-to-DVD. Sam Raimi was lined up to produce. "The games publishers never understood the value of true talent," says Shapiro. "I was telling Xbox: 'Hey, it's Sam Raimi, he did *The Evil Dead* and he's a big fan of *Age of Empires*.' I put this deal together and Microsoft walked away from it. They said: 'Yeah, Sam does those movies and he did *Evil Dead* and he's cool, but we'll pass.' I told them he was doing *Spider-Man* and their response was 'Comic book movies always suck'. They didn't get it. Six months later *Spider-Man* comes out and makes almost a billion at the box office and the rest is history."

Despite the setbacks, it was apparent that a revolution was happening. The studios couldn't ignore the fact that games were no longer just niche, ancillary products. The best videogames were now comparable to movies in that they had talented creators behind them, photorealistic graphics and truly involving narratives. On the other side of the fence, videogame giants like EA and Activision were making considerable profits from licensed games based on popular movies; Hollywood talent was being lured into voice work for games; and developers were being approached by producers looking for new material to option. Clearly, neither industry had the luxury of ignoring the other.

While Shapiro and his team at CAA were the bridges between these two industries in the 2000s, many actors felt they were being squeezed by the two sides. Their Screen Actors Guild (SAG) contracts weren't much use to them and the union was slow in understanding the different dynamics that powered the videogame industry. It made for some awkward interactions between Hollywood talent and game developers: as late as 2005, SAG was battling to get its members residuals for videogame work, staging a protest at annual videogame conference E3 in Los Angeles for good measure - and to little avail. Although videogames had been using Hollywood voice talent since the '90s, the power of the new generation of consoles and the mainstream penetration that they were enjoying meant that actors could no longer afford to be condescending about the medium. Voice and, as time went by, motion capture work meant that Generation Xbox was dragging actors into videogames whether they liked it or not. It was a shock to many.

Lev Chapelsky, general manager of Blindlight, a company which works with the videogames industry to secure Hollywood talent for games, told Edge magazine about the sea change that occurred among Hollywood's stars in the mid-2000s. "I remember the day when most of them just thought, 'Videogame? No. I'm a professional actor, this is not something I would do any more than I would do an endorsement for snake oil'. [Then] it kind of eclipsed into, 'Wow, these guys are making a lot of money on videogames'. And when the hype came out [in 2004] about gross revenues of videogames exceeding film, that one statistic had impact here like a nuclear bomb. Nothing has affected the film industries more than that."

Although the revenue comparison was far from accurate - videogames revenues include expensive hardware sales as well as game titles; meanwhile, movie revenues exclude DVD, pay-per-view and other post-theatrical run outings - the statistic filtered through the movie industry. "It's a ridiculous comparison but, typical Hollywood, they look at the five-word nugget and it just melted down their grey matter," continued Chapelsky. "When that happened, instead of saying, 'This is an important medium artistically, creatively, we should get involved in it as artists,' they said, 'Holy shit, there's money out there, we've gotta get a piece of that'. So then they started demanding ridiculous money. It made things uncomfortable for a while."

The problem was that the videogame companies realised they weren't in a position to pay what artists and their agents were demanding. The bottom line was that Hollywood talent was a luxury rather than a necessity. Paying exorbitant amounts of money - like the rumoured $1 million that Bruce Willis pocketed to lend his voice and likeness to PlayStation flop *Apocalypse* back in 1998 - made no sense because gamers weren't interested in marquee names in the same way as moviegoers.

"Celebrity involvement with videogames generally comes with more costs than it comes with benefits," says Chapelsky. "There's a huge misunderstanding of the value equation. In any other medium you can think of - commercials, TV, movies - the actor drives the entertainment experience and they are massively important in terms of moving revenue. But the Hollywood guys don't understand that actors don't drive videogame sales. Actors aren't instrumental to the experience of a videogame. They can't get their head around that."

Dealing with star egos was something that few videogames companies had time for. By the early 2000s, Keith Boesky had left Eidos, where he was president, to set up the videogame division at CAA's competitor ICM, where he represented the likes of John Woo and Clive Barker. For him, dealing with celebrity talent in the videogame arena was often a nightmare. "I've had actors and actresses who did voice work on games who required hair and makeup at reception," he says, without joking.

That culture clash between the Hollywood star system and videogames turned into a bloody battle throughout the 2000s. It culminated in the threatened SAG strike of 2005. The SAG negotiators, who were demanding that all actors involved in games be paid residuals for their involvement, tried to play hardball. "What we told SAG was that they didn't have the videogame industry by the balls, they couldn't cut us off or shut us down," says Chapelsky who attended many of the meetings. "Hollywood studios can't do that with the talent community. They really are in bed with them and have to get along with them."

What actors slowly came to understand during this period was that although they weren't important enough to a videogame's success to be able to demand huge pay cheques or backend deals, there were ancillary benefits to working in the medium since the core demographic of videogame players (13- to 34-year-old males) was much the same as that of moviegoers. On one level they had no choice since, as studios began to realise the value of tie-in videogames, many actors were increasingly contractually obliged to be involved in game productions or be denied certain royalties under their merchandising contracts.

For the biggest stars, contractual disputes weren't such an issue. Shapiro secured a royalty for Sean Connery in EA's *From Russia With Love* Bond game in 2005. It was one of several retro-licensed titles that emerged in the mid-2000s including *The Warriors*, *The Godfather*, *Scarface: The World Is Yours* and a cancelled *Dirty Harry* game. Connery, who knew nothing about videogames until he was offered the job, took a PlayStation 2 out to his house in the Bahamas to get a feel for the medium. He found the experience an awkward one. "It was a little frustrating for Sean because the amount of data you were dealing with meant he couldn't take his time with the lines," recalls Shapiro. "They had to be done quicker to make them smaller files. But he did it, he was a trooper."

The agent had brokered a similar deal for another Bond, Pierce Brosnan, when he lent his voice and likeness to *James Bond 007: Everything or Nothing* in 2004. Securing royalties for both actors was no easy matter. "It was a tough one to negotiate, but we got it because of EA's willingness to get involved in Hollywood. Also, I had a really good relationship with EA by the time of those deals. That's where doing the lunches and all those things pays off. That's what it's about, you build those relationships."

Catering to the gaming demographic of Generation Xbox also helped stars maintain their core audience: the kids who could make or break a summer blockbuster movie. What stars began to appreciate was that appearing in videogames had a certain non-monetary value that more than compensated for the comparatively smaller pay-check that a few hours of voice recording for a game production might deliver. One actor who realised this early on was Vin Diesel, who set up Tigon Studios in 2002. The company, named after a tiger-lioness crossbreed, brokered a deal with Universal to import Diesel's Riddick character from the movies *Pitch Black* (2000) and its sequel *The Chronicles of Riddick* (2004) into the videogame arena. Its first title *Escape from Butcher Bay* (2004) proved a grandslam hit and helped maintain interest not only in Diesel but in the movie franchise too. It was a lesson that many actors who were lending their voices and likenesses to games were beginning to appreciate. In videogames, the wisdom went, the money was rubbish but the core audience penetration was impressive. Hollywood actors realised what talent agents already knew: there was now a new screen to consider.

* * *

At the same time as videogames were invading Hollywood during the early to mid-2000s, the Hollywood-isation of the games industry was also happening. EA was one of the leading examples of how videogames companies had evolved since the Atari days. Long gone was the era when individual coders created unique, original games. EA was more like a movie studio where sprawling teams of animators, programmers, designers and producers were mere cogs in enormous production pipelines. Fittingly, EA was also one of the first companies to see the real financial and creative benefit of building close ties with the major motion picture studios.

Buying out DreamWorks Interactive (DWI) in 2000 was only the first step in a much wider strategic move. DWI's development studio became the kernel of EALA, the original staff of 80 ballooning to 1,000. In October 2003, EA announced that it was building a new 250,000-square-foot studio in the Playa Vista neighbourhood in Los Angeles, about twenty miles down the road from Warner Bros. Studios. While its headquarters would remain, as ever, in Redwood Shores, California, the move seemed highly symbolic. EA wasn't just cementing its presence in Los Angeles. It was, in some senses, picking up the real estate pieces of DreamWorks' broken dream at Playa Vista.

Most of all it was cosying up to the movie industry. "EALA was a commitment on EA's part to have a centre of excellence in Los Angeles and near to Hollywood," says John Batter who, after moving from DWI to EA, managed EALA along with the Redwood Shores studio. Why did EA need a Hollywood connection? Partly because the convergence that had been promised in the 1990s was now happening in a very unexpected way.

"People in the videogame industry thought [convergence] was going to be about making interactive movies or making games with more stories, but it was really about movies and games at a business level," says Batter. "We realised that we needed Hollywood talent to take games to the next generation - by talent I mean we needed the digital artists, the CG animators, the effects artists, people who were working on the big VFX movies in LA."

As the technological gulf between videogames and movies slowly closed during the digital age, Los Angeles became premier place to access that kind of talent. EA spearheaded this crossover of talent between the two industries at EALA, and also at the Redwood Shores studio, which was in the same neighbourhood as Pixar and DreamWorks Animations' Northern California campuses. These movie studios, devoted to CG animation, were ripe places to poach artists and animators from.

"It was a revolution in the videogame industry," says Batter. "Previously videogame artists had to be extremely technical. The tools were very crude and the artists were half-engineer, half-artists. They tended to be generalists. They did their own textures, their own lighting, they maybe even animated. The idea of specialisation - where you'd bring in people who only did lighting, textures, character rigging or the character animation - was an entirely new working method for the videogame industry at the time and it was a fairly rough transition."

Suddenly the teams making games ballooned - from a core of 20 to 30 people in the late-90s to around 200 in the mid-2000s. As a result, EA started looking to Hollywood production managers for help. Making videogames was becoming comparable to making movies, especially CG animated movies or VFX-heavy live action films.

Founded in 1982, EA was ancient enough to remember the days when games were made by auteurs, but it had always been forward looking when it came to business strategies. It built its fortune by releasing long-running, influential sports titles like *John Madden Football*, a franchise that has sold around 85 million copies since it was first released in the 1980s and earned more than $3 billion in revenue.

Along with Activision, another industry giant that had begun back in the early 80s, EA had grown into one of the companies that the major motion picture studios regarded as a safe pair of hands. It was big, corporate and dependable. It had the distribution model to get games onto shelves worldwide. It was, in short, the videogame equivalent of a movie studio.

Along the way EA earned an unenviable reputation among some industry watchers. It was infamous, unfairly or otherwise, for its takeovers of smaller, financially vulnerable videogame developers. It also took flak over its bland cubicle corporatism; its cynical exploitation of its key brands; and its rumoured sweatshop treatment of staff that, according to the New York Times, was so bad "Charles Dickens himself would shudder".

More than any other videogame company, though, EA understood the value of the franchise model. Its successful exploitation of sports brands like Madden, FIFA and NASCAR had made billions. Making games out of movies, the thinking among EA's senior executives went, couldn't be much different from making games out of sports. "In the early 2000s," says Shapiro, "EA looked at their stock, they looked at their company and they looked at the studios and said 'Who are we most like? Well, we're most like Warner Bros. We're the biggest publisher out there; Warner Bros. is the biggest movie studio out there. Let's make a relationship with them.'" It was a profitable move, not least of all when it came to the task of licensing the multimillion dollar *Harry Potter* franchise for videogames.

This was a very different world to the '70s when Warner Communications bought out Atari. Videogames were no longer an upstart business that the giant entertainment corporations eyed suspiciously. They now had legitimacy and were slowly moving themselves into a position to dominate the mass market. Indeed, the companies behind them were becoming giant entertainment corporations themselves: EA launched its Next Level Music label with Cherry Lane Music Publishing in 2004; in 2005 it dabbled in television while planning an interactive TV show based on *The Sims*. Being the world's largest videogames publisher gave it incredible clout in the wider entertainment industry.

"EA resisted working with the studios for a long time due to a mix of envy and competitive spirits," recalls Bing Gordon, who was EA's chief creative officer during the period. "We wanted to be the 'New Hollywood'". In time, though, EA realised that there was more to be gained in partnership than competition. By the mid-2000s, EA had climbed into bed with the movie business and was eager to impress. "Right now, videogames [are] as much a part of entertainment as movies and music are," John Mass of William Morris Consulting told the Los Angeles Times in 2003. "This is a creative community, and games is another medium where it will be able to express its ideas."

How much were things changing? Well, when EA made its first tie-in for the Potter series - *Harry Potter: The Sorcerer's Stone* - it was released day and date with the movie in 57 countries around the world. That was more than just a marketing move. For many observers it spoke volumes about how far the videogame industry had come.

There was no doubting EA's dominance in the videogame industry in the 2000s. If you wanted to make games that were guaranteed to reach a mass audience EA was the place to be. It was a beacon for programmers, artists and animators. Among them was Jason Vandenberghe, who'd cut his teeth in the industry as a coder on FMV outing *The X-Files: The Game*. With his thick black beard and silver jewellery, Vandenberghe looks like a modern day Mephistopheles - appropriate, perhaps, for a man who was willing to make a Faustian pact by working on some of the company's biggest movie games. Moving between titles like *007: Agent Under Fire* and *The Lord of the Rings: The Third Age*, he was one of the pioneers trying to triangulate good games out of Hollywood IP. On titles like *James Bond 007: Everything or Nothing*, where he was the lead designer, he succeeded.

When Vandenberghe first joined EA one thing that struck him was the psychological fallout from the videogame industry's rapid evolution. In the beginning, videogames had been made by individuals, visionary coders and garage auteurs. As corporate giants like EA began to dominate the landscape many from that older generation struggled to get to grips with the realities of working in what was now a corporate, global industry. "In the 1990s and early 2000s, everyone who got into the games industry ended up there by mistake," Vandenberghe says. "We didn't have a sense of what it should be like. We projected our artistic desires and then when someone came along and said actually what you're going to be making is *Harry Potter* or *Barbie's Wonderland*, it felt like a missed opportunity."

For many videogames industry veterans, cosying up with Hollywood was difficult. Back in the 1930s, the movie business had chewed up and spat out many of the great literary talents it had lured to Los Angeles. F. Scott Fitzgerald, purveyor of one rejected screenplay after another, turned to booze. Hemingway sniped that Spencer Tracy in *The Old Man and The Sea* looked like a fat, rich actor pretending to be a fisherman. Nathanael West dreamed of angry mobs rioting outside Hollywood premieres in his novel *The Day of the Locust*. For the videogames industry in the 2000s, the situation was similar. Here they were, giants in their field, being forced to work on titles that had "soulless cash-in" stamped all over them.

"What I saw again and again when I came into EA," recalls Vandenberghe, "was people who wanted to be game artists and who wanted to make the cool game that was in their brain... and they were being hired to work on James Bond. They wanted to make *Quake* but instead they were making Bond. It created this incredible tension dynamic where people were deeply frustrated."

In response, Vandenberghe developed a talk he'd give recruits to explain the dynamics of working with movie studio IP. Its bullet points where simple: embrace your constraints; understand the limitations of the franchise; satisfy the expectations of your audience. "If you're going to be working with Hollywood, you need to put your ego aside and say 'Why do people love this brand?' and then construct your gameplay around that."

In such discussions it was possible to see how videogame design was becoming caught between its commercial, technological underpinning and its awareness of its own ability to reach for something bigger - a medium that was capable of visual and storytelling art. That schizophrenic tug was also being played out at a much bigger level too. Rubbing shoulders with the studios, videogames companies like EA were starting to demand that they be taken seriously on an artistic level as well as a commercial one. Games, they felt, were beginning to take on cultural significance. They deserved to be treated with more respect than lunch boxes. It sometimes led to an incredible amount of antagonism between the movie studios and the games companies.

One memorable instance of that came as EA tackled the Bond franchise. The character's copyright on-screen was held by Danjaq, co-founded by Albert R. Broccoli after the release of *Dr. No* back in 1962. While working on *GoldenEye: Rogue Agent*, EA found itself completely out-scaled by Danjaq and its vice-president Barbara Broccoli. "This one organisation was the size of all of Electronic Arts," recalls Vandenberghe, "so they really considered us an extension of their marketing arm. We were in there with the backpacks and the comic books. We were calling up saying, 'Hey we want to be taken seriously. We want to make these changes to your IP, push it in this way, and be artistic with it'. The response was, 'No, no, and NO, friend. You're not going to do that.'"

The relationship between EA and Danjaq became increasingly fraught, particularly as EA tried to push itself as a creative, artistic force. They weren't content to be seen as a mere toy company. They knew that videogames, as a medium, had the power to be much more - to engage with the Bond character just like a movie could.

"It took a while for the Bond franchise to work out how to benefit from the movie," says designer Phil Campbell who worked on three of EA's Bond games. "At first it seemed like the games were a totally separate entity. But then we started using the real Bond. When Pierce Brosnan became the character, and the games went third person, that totally changed everything."

The closer videogames moved towards the photorealism of movies, the more pressure there was on the relationship between the two industries. "There was a moment on *GoldenEye: Rogue Agent* where they wanted to have Bond go bad," recalls Vandenberghe. "They pushed Danjaq on this but they said no. So one of the directors on the project [at EA] picked up the phone and called Barbara Broccoli directly and said: 'Hey, you're not getting this information. Your monkeys underneath you are not passing this information through'. And the story goes that her response was: 'This question has already been answered. I don't have time to be worried about your little game.' And CLICK, she hung up." Vandenberghe and his colleagues at EA were shocked. The corporate directors - who the design teams always thought of as the "macho, business guys" - had been totally emasculated.

The Danjaq story was typical of how EA found it necessary to raise its game in its dealings with Hollywood. It wasn't enough to merely be a successful videogame publisher or to hire Hollywood artists and animators. They needed corporate talent that could hold its own in the air-conditioned boardrooms of Los Angeles. What was slowly happening was the coming of age of the videogames industry in corporate terms.

Despite the profits that industry giants like EA and Activision were making, licensed movie games cultivated a bad reputation among gamers - and often quite rightly so. Born out of a sometimes fractious, sometimes careless, relationship between the two industries, the games themselves were frequently stunted things that satisfied neither side. Comprise was endemic: deadlines were rushed to meet movie tie-in dates; resources weren't always freely shared; and movie studios often failed to understand the demands of the interactive medium they were asking their products to be ported over to. EA's Gordon notes that one of the problems was that movie studios had licensing departments that got paid on cash advances, which "undermined the motivation to partner for quality". Once you stripped away the marketing hype and Hollywood glamour surrounding these titles, it was obvious that they were largely shovelware: low-quality games churned out quickly and cheaply. Squint and you could be back in 1982, just with better graphics.

According to Neil Young, who headed up EALA from 2004 to 2007, the problem with licensed games is the economics of the model. "Let's say you've got a finite amount of cash, call it $10 million. The license costs $6 million. Now you've only got $4 million for development. By default, you're trading out dollars you would have been investing in making the game better, for having a game that's immediately recognisable. That's why many games based on movies aren't good."

Factor in the secondary issues - the problems of collaborating with movie production companies over sharing assets; the tight turnaround schedule needed to meet a movie release date; and the fact that you're more likely to be dealing with the studios' marketing departments rather than creatives on the film side - and it's obvious why licensed games are a difficult balancing act. "It turns out that movie games are riskier than games or movies separately," explains Gordon.

When they were successful, though, they were golden. Both *The Lord of the Rings* and *Harry Potter* franchises were huge hits for EA. "Those games sold tens of millions of copies and generated somewhere close to a billion dollars of revenue over the course of their life at a relatively low royalty rate," says Young of *The Lord of the Rings* games. EA struck lucky with the deal. Because *The Lord of the Rings* rights weren't consolidated, the royalty rates were reduced. Thus the licensing fee wasn't as high as it might normally have been. "It was an important driver of our business both at the top line level but also at a margin level," says Young. "*Harry Potter* was a much more expensive franchise but clearly touched tens of millions of people and generated many hundreds of millions if not billions of dollars in revenue for the company."

The advantage of the *Harry Potter* games was that, unlike Danjaq with Bond, Warner Bros. were a receptive collaborative partner. "Warner Bros., and J.K. Rowling in particular, embraced videogames as a way of extending the world of *Harry Potter*," says Batter. "It was very fruitful from that perspective. There was a great deal of creative collaboration as well."

EA's strategy went far beyond the individual titles themselves. Although it was chiefly focused on its relationship with Warner Bros, EA was also building ties with individual Hollywood directors from Spielberg to Peter Jackson to Zack Snyder. EA's multi-million dollar donation to the USC School of Cinema-Television in 2004 was a good example of this kind of thinking. Not only did the donation prove invaluable in training the next generation of students interested in interactive media but it also cemented relationships with the movie business. EA executive Don Mattrick joined the board of councillors alongside the likes of Jeffrey Katzenberg, George Lucas, Spielberg, John Wells, and Robert Zemeckis. It was prestigious but also smart - legitimising the company while also giving it access to some of the movie business's most powerful creators.

Not every videogame company was willing to build bridges with Hollywood during the 2000s, however. Others were happier telling the studios where to stick it by refusing to be seduced by star power and performing a smash 'n' grab raid on Hollywood profits. The leader of that pack was Rockstar Games.

* * *

Anyone who's ever been to Vice City always returns with a story to tell. Most involve the kind of psycopathy that, in the real world, would get you locked up in a straitjacket and muzzle combo like Hannibal Lecter's. When players tell you what they've been up to, you'll hear about the time someone stole a Rhino tank and crushed a row of police vans. Or when they picked up a virtual hooker and parked in some bushes to watch the car shake and shudder while the occupants got down to business. Or how someone jammed an intersection in Little Haiti, rolled a grenade under a car and set off a domino cascade of explosions that char-grilled passing pedestrians. Inevitably, most stories end with SWAT teams, helicopters and the Feds arriving to take the narrator down with extreme prejudice.

Occasionally anecdotes from Vice City involve less havoc and more nostalgia: memories of early-evening drives along the beachfront on a PCG 600 bike, the setting sun glinting off the water as Michael Jackson's "Billie Jean" plays in the background. Moments like that, when the emergent chaos and player-inspired havoc abated and you simply soaked up the sun-kissed beauty of '80s Miami's alter ego, made visiting Vice City into a kind of virtual tourism. It lasted until you veered onto the pavement and ran over a Hispanic gang member, triggering another impromptu gun battle.

If you were one of the production team at Rockstar Games, though, the stories that *Grand Theft Auto: Vice City* generated were very different. For Sam and Dan Houser, the creative geniuses behind the *Grand Theft Auto* franchise, the game was the validation of a career path that had taken them from the London offices of music label BMG to the mean streets of New York City. For the developers at the company, led by Leslie Benzies at Rockstar North, who worked for years to create the engine that drove *Vice City's* predecessor *Grand Theft Auto III*, the game was a showpiece of technology that let players explore the open, sandbox world without hideous, finger-tapping load screens. For the artists and animators who perfected its gorgeous take on '80s Miami - all art deco facades, suntanned pedestrians and garish pastel fashions - it set a new benchmark for immersive, realistic environments.

But the best stories belonged to the team who ran the vocal recordings. Headed up by the game's cinematics director Navid Khonsari, they witnessed Rockstar's seduction of - and eventual disgust with - Hollywood at first hand. The call sheet for *Grand Theft Auto: Vice City* was impressive. Ray Liotta spent weeks in the recording booth. At other times the production team had to make an early morning Starbucks run for Dennis Hopper, Debbie Harry, Burt Reynolds and '80s star Philip Michael Thomas. Then there was the day when Jenna Jameson - diminutive, pneumatic breasted orgasm queen of a zillion porn flicks - arrived. Her script pages as Candy Suxxx, a hooker turned adult actress, arguably contained more lines of husky dialogue than any skin movie she'd ever starred in. If you were a fly on the wall in the Los Angeles or New York recording studios used during the production of Rockstar's flagship title in 2001, you couldn't help but be impressed by the line-up of A-list (and XXX) talent who'd been lured into the game. It didn't matter that the stars were only there to use their voices - the game's motion capture team used barely known actors to give bodies to the voices in the narrative-heavy, cut scenes. The big names were simply the icing on top of what was a fantastic game.

For the Houser brothers, getting the star names was both a coup and, it turned out, a curse. No other *Grand Theft Auto* game would ever again be so willing to rely on Hollywood talent agents for its hires. Indeed, the real chutzpah of *Vice City* lay in sticking it - culturally at least - to Hollywood. It wasn't just a game but a sneering "Fuck You" to the movie industry. It was the first time games had dared to crow about their achievements and boast that they could be more daring, more exciting and more hip than movies.

Such gall wasn't accidental. Taking their cues from rap, hip hop and mob movies, Rockstar created a melting pot of references any street savvy kid could get. The *Grand Theft Auto* series tapped into an adolescent, male fantasy of violence and aching coolness that most Hollywood studios had fumbled long ago. "You see, we're not competing with Konami, Hasbro, or Mattel," explained Rockstar's chief operating officer Terry Donovan in 2001. "We're competing with Def Jam, Adidas, and New Line Cinema."

Sam and Dan Houser were born into a family that combined showbiz with silver spoon privilege and great connections. Their mother, Geraldine Moffat, acted opposite Michael Caine in the classic British gangster movie *Get Carter*. Their father, Wally, was a jazz musician and director at Ronnie Scott's famous

Soho club who sometimes picked up his sons from their exclusive London fee-paying school St Paul's in his Rolls-Royce. Among Sam's classmates was the UK's future Conservative Party Chancellor George Osborne.

Obsessed with American pop culture - from rappers Run DMC to Walter Hill's cult B-movie *The Warriors* - the pair befriended fellow St Paul's student Terry Donovan. He was another kid with a hip father: Terence Donovan, the Swinging '60s fashion photographer and the director of Robert Palmer's *Addicted to Love* video with its iconic, lip-glossed human mannequins. When Terry finished his homework, he spent his weekends as a techno DJ. All three were desperate to be the cool kids on the block. They all dreamed of being rock stars. Thing was, rock 'n' roll stardom was so last century. After getting jobs at record label BMG in London's Soho, the Housers started plotting their next move. The music business was all very well but they wanted to push the envelope. Games were up and coming. Technological advances in the '90s were making them look bigger, badder and bolder. You didn't need a crystal ball to see the transfer of power that was going on.

The Housers saw the opportunity and made the most of it. Moving over to BMG's new interactive division in 1993 they began to dip their toes into the medium. None of them had any great experience of working with interactive entertainment, yet they had the means and the wherewithal to make it work for them. The arrival of the Sony PlayStation in 1994 was a game changer - even though it would be some time before any of them would exploit its potential. Released with real verve and a sense of its own adultness, particularly in the UK, the PlayStation reclaimed videogames for clubbers and cool kids from the dorks and orcs brigade. Games were morphing into a credible mass market entertainment medium, a viable pop culture force to ranked alongside movies, books, comics and music. "We believed that the business was changing more rapidly than [the major players] or anyone else appreciated," Dan Houser reflected in 2003. While most software developers saw their market either as hardcore PC gamers, sports fans or kids, the Housers were convinced the medium could appeal to a bigger audience: "People with an interest in film, music, books and a broader sense of popular culture."

As Donovan would cockily put it after the release of *Grand Theft Auto III* in 2001: "I think the videogame industry was actually crying out for us. We don't make games about Puff-the-fucking-Magic Dragon [...] If you've got 30 million households with PlayStations, you aren't just dealing with kids anymore - you aren't just dealing with people who don't smoke weed."

The *Grand Theft Auto* series began life as a prototype called *Race and Chase*, a top-down urban mayhem generator that retooled cops 'n' robbers for PC gamers. It was created by DMA Design a developer in Dundee, Scotland that would later become Rockstar North. Looking for a publisher, the developers pitched the concept at BMG Interactive where Sam Houser championed it. He instantly saw the appeal: it was violent, chaotic and controversial. It was videogames' answer to gangsta rap. BMG Interactive snapped up *Race and Chase* and re-titled it *Grand Theft Auto*.

Looking down over the city from the skies - like a police helicopter pursuit - players controlled a low-level hood as he worked his way up through the mob by running errands, performing hits and jacking cars. What made the game feel so different was its amoral sense of humour and, best of all, the sheer anarchy it let you unleash. The digital city, full of pedestrians, vehicles and roaming cops was your playground. Jack a car and you could listen to music on the radio. Shoot a policeman and the cops would put an APB out on you. Shoot another and they'd set out roadblocks. Continue your rampage and every law enforcement officer in the city will converge on you. Naturally the first thing everyone did when playing the game was go postal. *Grand Theft Auto (GTA)* was a hit and over the next few years Rockstar Games would be born under the banner of publisher Take-Two. Sam and Dan Houser decamped across the Atlantic along with colleagues Terry Donovan and Jamie King. By 1999, *Grand Theft Auto 2* was on shelves and selling fast. Virtual crime, it seemed, did pay.

What separated *GTA* from its peers was its aching sense of cool. Everything in the game was tooled to appeal to its core demographic of young adults. The games had style, a strong sense of personality and branding. Rockstar was like the Def Jam or Death Row Records of the games world. You saw the distinctive R* logo and you knew you'd be getting a game full of sex, drugs and rap music. "We always wanted to be more like a good quality record label," said Dan Houser. "If you bought one Rockstar game and you liked it, you could buy another one and you might like it - even if it was a genre you might not normally like. We want people to think: 'Well Rockstar made it, they do interesting stuff, so we might give it a go.'"

Grand Theft Auto III was released in 2001 and was a landmark. Gone was the top-down bird's eye viewpoint. The series shifted into a 3D world. The streets of Liberty City were yours to run through, the game camera positioned behind your silent mobster's back as he explored this open world. Where most games drew defensive rings around where you could go and what you could do, *GTA III* prided itself in letting you do as much as was technically possible. It was a virtual world you could inhabit. In between missions, cut-scenes using animated sequences based on motion-captured actors fleshed out a story of mafia allegiances and betrayals, romances and power struggles that nodded heavily to the likes of *Goodfellas* and *The Sopranos*. It was less a mere videogame than a complete entertainment experience that combined music tracks with movie references, a dramatic storyline and an interactive game. In tone, nothing had altered. But in terms of immersion, this was something totally new. Rockstar had finally achieved the dream set out by Dan Houser when he spoke of "a product which was three things at the same time: a game, a movie, and a chance to explore and to be amused by a strange place".

GTA III wasn't alone in its attempt to create this kind of sandbox world. Back in 1999 Yu Suzuki's *Shenmue* series had tried something similar, even replicating the rhythms of working life by asking players to get jobs driving forklift trucks; so too had David Cage's urban sci-fi epic *Omikron: The Nomad Soul*. But *GTA III* was easily the most cinematic. It also became the bestselling videogame of 2001 in the US. More than that, it was a broadside to Hollywood. Rockstar had the ambition not just of a record label but of a major motion picture studio. All that was stopping them were the limits of the technology available. But if the *GTA* series could transform itself in four short years from a fun little top-down game into an immersive world, it seemed only a matter of time before Rockstar achieved a game that could compete with movies.

If you were to pinpoint the moment when Rockstar made something more than just a videogame, you'd have to go back to 2002 and the release of *Grand Theft Auto: Vice City*. Building on the success of *GTA III*, *Vice City* offered players a world replete with cultural references, a narrative and an immersive interactive entertainment experience. It was bold in its conception: a period videogame set in the 1980s. Creating a virtual Miami of neon signs and pastel suits, *Vice City* had incredible self-confidence. You only had to play it for five minutes to realise that it had ambitions to be a playable movie - not only in its delirious violence, but in its attempts to say something about American culture. Few videogames had ever had the vision or ambition to tackle the recent past or make any pretence at sociological commentary.

"To me, [the '80s is] still hands-down the grooviest era of crime because it didn't even feel like it was crime," Sam Houser, the publicity-wary president of Rockstar, told Edge magazine in a rare interview years later. "You had Cuban hitmen coming across and gunning people down in the street, but it was still celebrated in a sort of haze of cocaine and excess and Ferraris and Testarossas, and it was a totally topsy-turvy back-to-front period of time. It was everything that was crazy about the '80s, and it was in America so it was crazier."

Satire, a mode rarely used by videogames, was the order of the day. Set in the decade when greed was good, *Vice City* became a meditation on the American culture of excess: cocaine, fast cars and silicone babes. There were porn stars and drug dealers. Cops and mafiosos. It was a game that demanded to be taken seriously - even while pandering to the adolescent joys of blowing shit up.

None of that would have mattered so much if it wasn't for the cut-scenes. Controlling mobster Tommy Vercetti as he gets out of prison and falls into bad company again, players found themselves embroiled in a gangster narrative that was familiar from a dozen movies: *Scarface, Goodfellas, Carlito's Way* and TV show *Miami Vice*. With motion captured performers acting in the cut-scenes and Hollywood celebs providing the vocal talent, *Vice City* sat somewhere between game and movie. Ray Liotta, star of *Goodfellas*, was Vercetti (in voice, but not body) and *Vice City* played like an interactive pastiche of director Brian De Palma's greatest hits. "Controlling a character in a world made you feel like the star of your own movie or TV show," explained Dan Houser in an interview with Variety.

Rockstar's achievement lay in creating one of the first true aesthetic crossovers between games and movies. The FMV experiments of the '90s had been too literal in its use of 35mm film and studio shoots. What Rockstar's use of voice talent and motion capture showcased was the middle ground that lay between live action and animation. It was a CG hybrid that gave its sandbox world a narrative backbone. You didn't have to go through Tommy's story. Ignore it and the game could be played as a simple mayhem generator, or a toolbox to create your own (albeit limited) stories. But if you did play along the path the designers gave you, it added real drama and a sense of character to this open-world version of '80s Miami. In fact, it allowed you to feel as though you were inside a film. Playing *Vice City* was like watching a gangster movie where you took control over the protagonist for the action set pieces. True you were spoon-fed the narrative's dramatic sequences. But the shootouts and car chases were yours to play out however you wanted. This wasn't an interactive movie. It was completely the opposite: a cinematic game.

Vice City's production underscored the point brilliantly - although, tellingly, Rockstar would never again show such deference to Hollywood's star system. In keeping with its theme and setting, *Vice City* was seduced by glamour, glitz and talent in creating its cut-scenes. The roster of Hollywood stars was enormous from Liotta's leading man to character actors like Luis Guzmán and '80s stars Lee Majors and Philip Michael Thomas. Topping it all was Dennis Hopper as Steve Scott, a porn director locked in "a struggle between artistic integrity and the humping, pumping action" who churns out Spielberg pastiche skin flicks called Bite and Closer Encounters. Such casting choices were brilliantly judged for maximum coolness, the Rockstar trademark.

Vice City's performance capture shoots were undertaken at Perspective Studios in Brooklyn. Non-celebrity actors like Jonathan Sale dressed in Spandex bodysuits dotted with reflective markers - used as reference points to allow the computers to record movements - and shot for a week in front of a grid of 14 cameras. It was gruelling work.

Khonsari, who directed the cinematics, motion capture and audio sessions that drove the game's cut-scenes, treated the motion-capture shoots as if they were film shoots. He deliberately ignored the technology to concentrate instead on the quality of the performances. The actors found themselves in a world of complete make-believe. When they were supposed to be in a car - during an early scene in *Vice City* where Tommy escapes from a coke deal gone wrong - the vehicle was represented on the motion-capture stage as just four metal folding chairs and a plastic toy steering wheel made by Fisher-Price.

None of the Hollywood talent donned the motion-capture suits. Instead, they recorded their voice work several weeks later at studios in LA, New York and in Scotland while watching video feeds of the computer graphics cut-scenes. "We certainly had the option of trying to bring celebrities in to do motion capture," says Khonsari. "But we thought that was going to be an absolute disaster. Putting anyone in Spandex tights is asking for trouble let alone people who've been coddled and have a certain amount of ego based on their celebrity status. We decided that it wasn't going to work and the best thing to do was to do separate performances. To be quite realistic, we were also looking at the finances. We were looking at paying a lot of money to get these celebrities in and would have paid five or six times more if they'd been involved in the performance capture."

Even still, the celebrity involvement wasn't without its difficulties, not least of all because few of them appreciated quite how the playing field had shifted. Most of them were from an older generation - Liotta said his previous exposure to videogames had stopped with *Pong* in the

1970s - and they struggled to get their heads around the concept of *Vice City* as a breathing living world. Khonsari had to get them up to speed. "We had to educate them about the game, about the technology," he remembers of his first meetings with the likes of Liotta, Hopper and Reynolds. "Then I'd have to strip it all away: 'Forget everything I just told you, it has no bearing on the performance that we require'. I think it was crucial. When actors hear the word 'animation' they think they have to take their energy through the roof and be almost cartoon-like. We had to make sure we got proper performances from them otherwise the player would wince and hit the X button to skip the cut scene."

Several weeks of vocal recording followed. Khonsari treated the process much like an ADR session - something common enough on most movies. Yet it was soon apparent that there were problems with courting Hollywood talent. Not least of all the amount of cosseting that was required. "We went in there with the attitude of 'Let's do whatever we can to make sure the talent is taken care of and they're comfortable. Let's give them everything they're used to in their LA/Hollywood lifestyle,'" says Khonsari. "Aside from the standard requirements - first-class air tickets, five-star hotels and meals - we always went the extra mile. A happy actor will give you a performance of a lifetime if they feel they are in trusted hands - and with *Vice City* on at the forefront of merging Hollywood and games we had to go the extra mile to make our talent feel comfortable performing in a media that they were not so familiar with."

Egos needed to be stroked, performances needed to be coaxed. When Burt Reynolds sweated through his shirt during his three-hour recording session in the booth, the team ordered him a new shirt from his New York tailor and had it delivered to the studio "to make sure he was able to leave the studio in a manner that he was comfortable in. It meant the world to him." For a videogames company this was a new aspect to the business of development - something more volatile and indeterminate than dealing with lines of code.

While it shouldn't come as any surprise that a company called Rockstar would understand the mechanics of stardom, the reaction of the actors themselves was often odd. Back in 2002, voice acting in videogames was still seen as somehow second-rate by Hollywood actors. "Most of them were great to work with. A few kicked up a stink and felt that they had to educate us about the art of acting," Khonsari recalls. "Their unfamiliarity with the gaming process gave us an ace in the hole. We could say: 'Listen, what you're saying is absolutely right but I need you to do it this way because of this.'"

Ultimately, though, Rockstar's management found the whole attitude of some of the stars they'd hired condescending and demeaning. "I'll be honest," Sam Houser told Edge. "It's easier to work with someone who's keen and enthusiastic, and not been in hundreds of films. Sometimes you get a famous person in and they literally just read off the script, they want the cheque, and they want to go. I find that insulting and depressing."

However, it was only after the game was released in 2002 that the real problems emerged. Liotta was reportedly unhappy with the game's smash hit success - ironic since neither he nor any of the other celebrities involved had been willing to help market the title when it was released. "Liotta was a very interesting guy to work with because we had to have him in for quite a long time," Sam Houser told Edge. "In some sessions he was so fired up and he was so into it, but then sometimes it'd be like he was in some kind of a hole, and he was very dark and couldn't work. He's a pretty amazing guy, kind of an amazing actor."

Rockstar's president had little time for Liotta's post-release attitude. "He made some comments later on through his agent, something like, 'Hey, that game was so big I should have charged them more money', and I hate that kind of chat. It's so cheesy. Like he's saying: 'Next time I'm really going to pin it to them'. Well, how about we just killed off your character? There is no next time. That's how we handle that." Liotta, tellingly, wouldn't be invited to return for the sequels.

Then again, neither would any other major Hollywood talent. Although follow-up game *Grand Theft Auto: San Andreas* roped in a few gangster rappers and Samuel L. Jackson to flesh out its '90s LA setting, the writing was on the wall as far as Rockstar were concerned. For Sam Houser, a huge film nut, the *Grand Theft Auto* series' evolution represented a radical break with his own, personal, past tastes. "There was something about *GTA III* that just drew a line in the sand between games and movies, and it felt like: this is us taking over now," he told Edge in 2008. "And it may be another 10 years or 20 years until that really happens, but to me, I'm never going to be able to go back to, say, an action movie and watch it in the same way, because with *GTA III*, I'm in it - a movie just isn't relevant in the same way anymore. Now, that's a slightly extremist approach, a slightly hardcore approach, but that's how it made me feel. For someone who loves movies, suddenly I could not sit still and take in a movie in the same way; it wasn't speaking to me in the same way. It's depressing because a large part of my leisure time suddenly took a knock because I couldn't take it seriously any longer. This is also connected with celebrity culture and how this stuff has rolled out. Now, when I watch a movie, I see the actors. I see a guy - whoever the actor is; let's not pick on any one person - who's getting paid $20 million: he's playing dress-up, he's reading out some lines. By definition he is acting, and there's something fundamentally unbelievable about that if you push it too much in your own head. Something just changed almost overnight."

It was an attitude that could be seen in Rockstar's business relationships too. Unwilling to kowtow to the demands of celebrity culture, they simply refused to play the game. One infamous story, circa 2005, sums up the company's "fuck you" approach to the Hollywood star system quite literally. Eager to book a certain celebrity for a vocal recording, Rockstar called up the actor's agent and enquired how much it would cost to hire them - admittedly a rather naïve question since any agent is always going to quote an astronomical figure in such circumstances. The price, the agent explained, would be a cool $1 million. As the story goes, Rockstar's emissary pulled the phone receiver away from their head, stared at it in disbelief and said 'Fuck you!' before hanging up. The next day an internal memo was circulated warning staff never to deal with that agency ever again. What that story illustrates isn't just the antagonism that existed between the two sides, but the realisation among developers that they had the freedom to walk away from exorbitantly priced actors - a freedom that movie and TV producers simply didn't have. Rockstar had learned that celebs were more of a pain in the ass than they were actually worth and, despite its name, the company became leery of pursuing star talent.

Ultimately, games sales didn't require celebrity involvement. *Halo* was starless, so were *Half-Life*, *Tomb Raider* and *The Sims* to name but a few. In fact, videogames were emerging as the only mass market entertainment medium that didn't need to be structured around the Hollywood star system. Even the Housers, legends in the videogame business, retreated into a cloak of anonymity and refused to give many interviews about themselves. "When we finished *Vice City*, the *Grand Theft Auto* brand was bigger than any of the celebrities we had brought on board," reckons Khonsari. "Rockstar don't need the celebrity status or a good chunk of the fluff that comes with Hollywood. They've got a great writer in Dan Houser and a producer in Sam Houser who's got with a definitive vision and won't sway from it. Sam Houser is the Stanley Kubrick of videogames."

While EA was a games company trying to operate like a movie studio, it was arguably Rockstar who had real ambition. They didn't want to conquer

Hollywood. They wanted to be bigger than Hollywood. It's telling, then, that when the studios tried to set up a *Grand Theft Auto* movie, Rockstar would have no part of it. "Everybody in Hollywood wanted *Grand Theft Auto*," remembers CAA's Larry Shapiro, who was trying to broker a movie deal for the anime-influenced *Oni* game in the early 2000s that Rockstar collaborated on with *Halo* creators Bungie. As he pushed the property, his phone was ringing off the hook with people who assumed that the *Grand Theft Auto* rights would be up for auction next.

When Rockstar walked away from a movie deal for *Oni* with Paramount and writer/producer Dean Devlin (*Independence Day*), Shapiro tried his luck. Would the company consider selling the movie rights to *Grand Theft Auto*? "There's no way I'm doing it," was Sam Houser's response. Much as he would have liked the kudos of securing the deal, Shapiro maintains Rockstar's decision was the right choice. "GTA is one of the major [properties] and sometimes a movie can deter from a game franchise." Anyone who's seen the movies based on *Hitman*, *Tekken* or *DOA: Dead or Alive* would be hard pressed to argue with such logic. When you already have a billion-dollar IP why risk its reputation by selling the movie rights?

Frustrated, Shapiro tried to convince CAA client Imagine Entertainment, who owned the rights to the 1977 car chase movie *Grand Theft Auto* starring Ron Howard, to do a remake that could cash in on the name. "I was saying 'Guys, remake the movie. It doesn't matter. Make it bloody, make it violent, it doesn't have to follow anything. You have the movie!' They couldn't wrap their heads around it because they just didn't understand the [videogame] franchise."

Rockstar's off-hand attitude towards the studios was a breath of fresh air in an industry that was often only too happy to let itself be positioned as Hollywood's little brother. "Basically they're saying 'We're not here to tell you that we're the new kids on the block and are here to stay,'" explains Khonsari. "It's more like, 'We've got just as big of a house as you and we don't need to be your neighbours. We'll create our own neighbourhood, thank you very much'. I think the problem is that there aren't enough people in the gaming industry who have that attitude. The majority of publishers still go to Hollywood talent for answers. That's a broken system. We're making games not movies."

Since Rockstar stepped away from using marquee names, some of the biggest games using performance capture - including Naughty Dog's bestselling *Uncharted* franchise - have similarly turned their back on stars. In *Uncharted* the actors are performers who are willing to commit a year plus to the production schedule and have no qualms about treating the product with the seriousness and rigour of a movie shoot. Performance capture is creating its own stars: not least of all actor Nolan North, who plays the voice and body of Nathan Drake in the *Uncharted* games. Moving between film, TV and games, actors like North are in the vanguard of a much greater shift in the performing arts as the digital, 3D worlds become a legitimate - if intangible - stage.

Today, *Grand Theft Auto* is one of the most valuable entertainment franchises in any medium. The ramifications of that - for the both the movie and games businesses is enormous. By 2008, when *GTA IV* was released, the movie studios were already on the run from Rockstar's share of the entertainment market. The game's release in the same week as *Iron Man* gave Paramount the jitters. According to EA's chief executive John Riccitiello, who was watching events from the sidelines, the buzz among movie executives was "that *Iron Man* the movie is going to get killed by *Grand Theft Auto* the game. I don't think I've ever heard of that before."

Iron Man's breathtaking $100 million opening weekend was just third of *GTA IV*'s $310 million first day sales. *Iron Man* was no dud - it entered the record books as the second-highest, non-sequel superhero movie opening ever behind 2002's *Spider-Man*. Depending on how you stacked the figures, though, *GTA* arguably outclassed it. "Videogame makers," Dan Houser claimed, "are challenging the Hollywood hegemony." It was hard to disagree.

* * *

The Master Chiefs left the offices of CAA around midday on 6 June 2005 in a fleet of limo vans. In their green, red and blue Spartan armour the cybernetically-enhanced super soldiers made quite a spectacle. Each stood six-foot-three tall, visored helmets obscuring their faces. Each carried a red bound document folder stamped with the CAA logo that contained two things: a copy of the *Halo* screenplay commissioned by Microsoft and written by Alex Garland and a terms sheet. None of them spoke a word.

The security guards on the gates of the major motion picture studios are used to seeing many things. Still, a hulking soldier from the future striding towards them and demanding access to the studio's top brass was inevitably going to end in some kind of shooting incident - whether involving a United Nations Space Command BR55 Battle Rifle or a security guard's arguably more deadly .38 revolver.

Fortunately Larry Shapiro's team at CAA had called ahead and warned the studios' security heads what was going on. The Master Chiefs were allowed onto the lots at Universal, Fox, New Line, DreamWorks and others without firing a single shot. If this was the videogame industry literally invading Hollywood, it was remarkably bloodless. They delivered their scripts and waited outside the meetings rooms in silent character, flicking through the pages of Variety. Everyone knew the clock was ticking: studio executives only had a couple of hours to read the *Halo* screenplay and decide whether or not to make an offer before the Master Chiefs returned to CAA with the screenplay. It was the deal of the century, and a fantastic piece of showmanship.

The Master Chief suits were Shapiro's idea and they ensured that the *Halo* deal made headlines even before the trade papers learned how rich the demands were. It was a spectacular attempt to turn Microsoft's first foray into Hollywood filmmaking into a theatrical event and it very almost worked. Master Chief, the hero of Microsoft and Bungie's bestselling *Halo* games, made his debut in Hollywood. Sadly, though, his Tinsel Town ascension was short-lived.

While Rockstar told Hollywood to stick it, Microsoft was aggressive in pursuing the idea of taking *Halo* to the big screen. It's easy to understand why. The games, developed by Bungie Studios, were perfect blockbuster material: high-octane, intense sci-fi shoot 'em ups with a dense mythology and storyline and a dedicated fan-base of millions. Combined sales of the first two *Halo* games grossed in excess of $600 million over four years, selling north of 13 million units. The movie biz looked on in envy.

When Microsoft approached CAA about their movie ambitions, Shapiro told them about *The Day After Tomorrow* auction set up by CAA agent Michael Wimer and director Roland Emmerich. With a script for the apocalyptic eco-movie in hand, Wimer called the major studios and invited them to bid for it. The process was unusual: every studio would send a messenger to CAA at an allotted time, pick up the script and then have 24 hours to read it and make an offer. Each script was despatched with a terms sheet: here's how much we want; here's how much we want for the director; and it has to be a "go" movie (in other words, a picture with a guaranteed start date for production). Each studio responded by trying to negotiate terms. The only exception was Fox, who simply wrote on the term sheet: "Yes".

Microsoft, unaccustomed to Hollywood's culture, was impressed by that story. It wanted to be able to dictate the terms even though it was a newcomer in the movie biz. *Halo* was its prize property and they wanted to protect it.

Microsoft also wanted to make a bundle of money from its sale. For Shapiro, it was typical of the gulf between the two industries. Games creators are, by their nature, engineers who deal in absolutes. For them the subtleties of Hollywood production, with its ebb-and-flow of egos and power plays, were often alien. "To sell a movie into a studio and actually get it made is a lot of work," he says. "It takes a lot of conversations and a lot of pixie dust being thrown about while you're getting the deals done. In the games industry, they're technologists and they're data driven. They're looking at data points and saying: 'We need the movie to be made, it's got to be this, this and this. If you get A, B and C to be part of the movie, then great we'll sell you the rights.' You can't do that." But, if that's what Microsoft wanted, CAA was willing to try.

To set up that kind of deal, Microsoft needed to be ready. Most importantly it needed to have a screenplay so it paid Alex Garland (*28 Days Later, The Beach*) $1 million to pen a spec script. The screenplay was supervised by Microsoft, which meant it was - for good or ill - heavily steeped in the games' mythology. Still, the project now had a blockbuster screenwriter and was based on a high-profile videogame franchise.

Next, it was a case of setting up the auction. Peter Schlessel, the former president of production at Columbia Pictures, was one of the main negotiators in the *Halo* movie deal and served as Microsoft's Hollywood liaison. Together with Microsoft and its lawyers, Schlessel and the CAA team hammered out a term sheet. "We were literally setting out to be the richest, most lucrative rights deal in history in Hollywood," says Shapiro. "You have to remember that no property, not even *Harry Potter*, was getting [what we were asking for]." Microsoft, a global software giant used to getting its own way, wasn't about to kowtow to Hollywood. It knew *Halo* was the jewel of videogame movies, the one that could be a true blockbuster hit. According to Variety, Microsoft wanted $10 million against 15% of the box office gross, in addition to a $75 million "below-the-line" budget and fast-tracked production.

Those were big demands. Not least of all since, at the time, videogame movies were still floundering on the edge of respectability. *Tomb Raider* had made a pot of money and pushed towards the mainstream but its 2003 sequel, *Lara Croft: Tomb Raider - The Cradle of Life*, suffered a disappointing opening weekend at the US box office and limped by on its foreign grosses. The Lara Croft franchise was running out of steam early. And most other videogame movie outings weren't even in the same neighbourhood as Lara. Paul W. S. Anderson, the director of *Mortal Kombat*, parlayed his success into the zombie-themed

Resident Evil franchise distributed by Sony Screen Gems. The first movie based on Capcom's survival horror game series took $102 million worldwide and did gangbuster business on DVD selling over a million units. But it lacked the prestige and mainstream crossover potential of *Tomb Raider.*

The *Resident Evil* sequels followed a similar pattern - strong DVD numbers buoying up the theatrical releases - and remained largely impervious to critics' carping. While the films were largely dross, the statistics told a different story. There was an audience for this material, an audience of gamers - and, judging by the numbers, non-gamers - who enjoyed Anderson's throwaway blend of eye-candy actresses, zombies and non-stop action. As its star Milla Jovovich put it: "You have to think like a 15-year-old. Wet dress. Zombies. Guns. Cool!" That thinking was enough to get the films to match the long-running game franchise's $1 billion turnover.

From a business perspective, with their relatively small outlays for big profits, the *Resident Evil* movies were successful on their own terms. They also illustrated the power of synergy: "The games and the movies pretty much go hand in hand and support each other," says Anderson, "When the first *Resident Evil* movie came out, the *Resident Evil* franchise had peaked and was declining in terms of sales. The movie revived the fortunes of the videogame franchise." But they were hardly Hollywood blockbusters. Far from proving, as *Tomb Raider* had done, that videogames could produce movies that reached beyond a niche audience, the *Resident Evil* movies seemed determined to stick them back in the ghetto.

Other game movies - like *Silent Hill* (2006), *Hitman* (2007) and *Max Payne* (2008) - didn't do much to help the cause. Further down the scale, filmmaker Uwe Böll used German tax shelter money to secure the licenses to game franchises like *House of the Dead* and *Alone in the Dark*. His indisputably atrocious movies earned him an unenviable reputation as the Ed Wood Jr. of Generation Xbox. Yet the funding method meant he could afford to hire household names like Jason Statham, Ben Kingsley and Christian Slater.

As with *Resident Evil*, Böll's DVD sales buoyed up the theatrical grosses and often far outstripped them. *House of the Dead* was made for $12 million and only grossed $13.8 million worldwide theatrically. Yet on DVD it shipped 1.48 million rental units and sold around 253,000 DVD retail units in the US. According to Home Media Magazine, those rental numbers were what one would normally expect from a $50 million budgeted movie. When asked if he deliberately filled a gap created by the studios' failure to cater to gamers, Böll says proudly: "I think I was the first strategic 'game filmer' who bought and made a full line of game movies."

Böll's movies are infamously awful, yet he has a good eye for publicity stunts. Indeed, his career has often been more colourful than his films: he took on critics in a Las Vegas boxing bout; he called filmmaker Michael Bay "a fucking retard"; and he announced that if an online petition calling for him to put down his camera got a million signatures, he'd comply. He also has a masterful way of whipping up controversy. "*House of the Dead* is a brainless shooter, where you shoot zombies into pieces," was one of his typically candid statements. "So what are you expecting from the movie, *Schindler's List?*"

Despite the free publicity, Böll's output did little to help the cause of game properties among the major studios. However, his canon of clag proved two things: that there was a keen market who would willingly buy tickets for or DVDs of any movie that had a videogame brand name slapped on it; and that game companies were willing to use such movies as marketing extensions. "The reality is that a lot of the videogame companies are quite sloppy," Böll claimed in 2006. "They are happy to sell the licence, but then they don't give a shit about it, and this is not the right approach [...] Sega did nothing for [the movie of] *House of the Dead*, and Atari did nothing to support [the movie of] *Alone in the Dark*. They developed *Alone in the Dark Part 5*, parallel to my movie, and then they closed the LA facility and never finished the game. And I was standing there alone in the rain with my movie."

It was a typical complaint from the filmmaker. Of his experience working on *Far Cry*, which was released in 2008, Böll says: "Crytek [the game's developer] were very good co-workers on that movie but Ubisoft [the publisher] sucked. They didn't even have any interest in working on the [movie's] CGI."

It begged a question: why would videogames companies sell movie rights to a filmmaker with such an appalling track record? According to Peter Moore, president and chief operating officer of Sega of America at the time of the *House of the Dead* movie (and who would later join Microsoft, where he was involved in the *Halo* movie negotiations), it was a marketing play. The rights sale generated only a couple of million dollars, a drop in the ocean given that the *House of the Dead* franchise's lifetime grosses run into the hundreds of millions. It was the publicity - and the perceived aura of legitimacy - that mattered. "We saw it as a tremendous way to promote the game as a piece of mainstream entertainment," he says. "Back in the '90s, videogame companies still had an inferiority complex. The idea of your game being turned into a movie was seen as validation of the intellectual property itself into the big, bad world of movies. We saw it as an extension of the platform, almost as free marketing. It was primarily an extension of the marketing to a similar consumer base: males aged 18 to 34."

In fact, Sega's executives were so enthusiastic about the idea of seeing their game became a movie - even an Uwe Böll movie - that Moore made a marathon, overnight trip to the location shoot. He flew up from San Francisco to the woods outside Vancouver, then stayed up all night to film a cameo as a zombie in the pouring rain alongside game creator Rikiya Nakagawa. He returned to work the next morning on the first flight back, still pulling latex off his face. Adding to the excitement was the awareness that actually getting a movie made out of a videogame property was quite something. Sega did sell movie rights to other titles like *Crazy Taxi* around the same time but, says Moore, they never went anywhere. "Most of these things were optioned out and held and never, ever used. You almost thought sometimes producers were just being defensive and making sure nobody else did it."

In 2005, Microsoft were aiming higher - much, much higher - than Böll's brand of videogame movie schlock. CAA's deal-making matched the software giant's aspirations. According to the New York Times, Microsoft were demanding creative approval over director and cast, plus 60 first-class plane tickets for Microsoft personnel and their guests to attend the premiere. It wouldn't be putting any money into the production itself beyond the fee paid to Garland, nor was it willing to sign over the merchandising rights. To add insult to injury, Microsoft wanted the winning studio to pay to fly one of its representatives from Seattle to LA. They would watch every cut of the movie during post-production. Clearly, Microsoft was entering into negotiations brandishing a very big stick.

With the screenplay written and the ink still drying on the terms sheet, the agents called up the major studios and advised them to be prepared. It was a bold, some might say arrogant, show of power. As Shapiro remembers it, "We told them: 'You need to have all your decision makers in a room because we're going to deliver the script for you to read together with a terms sheet. But there's a fuse on it. You'll only have a certain amount of time to make a deal.'"

Because Hollywood is a town built on relationships, CAA's agents made sure they called all the major players. Even then there were some who felt snubbed; Miramax head honcho Harvey Weinstein called up to shout about being left off the list. Everyone had assumed Miramax wouldn't be interested in the property. Truth was they probably weren't, but there was prestige to be had in being invited to the *Halo* party. The only major studio Microsoft refused to approach was Columbia, which was owned by Sony, its chief rival in the console war.

With his production background, Shapiro decided to add a little razzle dazzle to the proceedings. Remembering the Master Chief costumes he'd seen at Comic-Con, he tracked down the one person in the US who was fabricating the game's official Spartan UNSC battle armour and hired seven suits: a Red, a Blue and several in Master Chief green. "I had them shipped out to CAA," recalls Shapiro, "they came in crates and had instructions about how to put them on. I hired character actors to wear the suits because, you know, you don't just put anyone in these suits. They had to feel like Master Chief."

For a few hours on 6 June 2005, Hollywood became Halowood. Everyone was buzzing about the Master Chiefs spotted walking through the studio lots and - more importantly - about the richness of the deal Microsoft was demanding. No one had ever seen anything like it before. Microsoft, the global corporation whose products sat on every desktop, had come to Hollywood and wasn't afraid of throwing its weight around. "If showmanship and arrogance and Hollywood don't go together, I don't know what does," says Moore who was Microsoft's go-between with Universal during the negotiations, reporting to the software company's point man Steve Schreck.

Not everyone was impressed. Movie executive Alex Young, who by the time of *Halo* had moved from Paramount to Fox, recalls reading the screenplay under Master Chief's watchful eye. "It was one of those gimmicky Hollywood things: hey, force everybody to be in a room, make it feel urgent, have a guy show up in costume and 'Oh my God! This feels like a big deal'. It probably served Microsoft and CAA well at the time, but ultimately it seemed like a bit of manufactured theatre to me."

Another problem was that the *Halo* property was so well-known by that point that everyone knew what to expect. "You either loved the idea of making a *Halo* movie or you did not," suggests Young. Having a guy in costume deliver the screenplay wasn't going to convince you one way or the other.

In the end, though, it wasn't the Master Chiefs' fault that the deal stumbled. Nor was it CAA's. The failure of the *Halo* movie remains a potent illustration of the gulf that still lies between Hollywood and the videogame business. It should have been the tent-pole movie to die for, instead it became the one that got away. Millions of *Halo* fans around the world wanted a movie, yet it failed to launch. Partly, it stemmed from the on-going inability of both sides of the deal to understand each other's culture, needs and language.

Most of the studios who read the *Halo* screenplay passed immediately. Microsoft's terms were simply too demanding. By the end of Master Chief Monday there were only two horses in the race: Fox and Universal. Microsoft hoped to use each to leverage off the other but hadn't banked on the studios' very different approach to doing business. "What the games industry doesn't understand is that this town is all about lunch," explains Shapiro. "It doesn't happen like that in the games industry. If there was a movie studio going out to the games publishers to license *Avatar* or something like that, they'd say 'Ok we're licensing *Avatar*, send us your best deal. But none of the games publishers would talk to each other and say 'Hey, what are you going to offer them?'"

The studios weren't so reticent in sounding each other out. "What happened was Universal called Fox and asked them what they were going to offer," continues Shapiro, who watched events unfold close-up. "They decided to partner on it. 'Let's offer the same deal and offer to partner'. So now we lost our leverage." Universal agreed to take US domestic, Fox would take foreign. In the blink of an eye Microsoft's bargaining position had been pole-axed.

The immensely powerful Microsoft had wandered into the deal naïvely expecting everyone to play by its rules and the resulting culture shock put immense strain on the *Halo* deal. For Moore, then corporate vice-president of the Interactive Entertainment Business division at Microsoft, there was clearly culture clash during the negotiations: "You work for a company like Microsoft, where you do what you say, you say what you do; you think you have an agreement, you're ready to go, and then...[the deal falls apart.]"

It was something that talent agents working at the intersection between the two industries have experienced many times. "When the videogame industry talks to people they do it open-kimono and they expect the same transparency back," says Blindlight's Lev Chapelsky. "Hollywood doesn't function that way, they dance and they sing and they play games and go through their ritual haggling. To somebody who's not accustomed to that, it can be insulting."

Microsoft clearly weren't accustomed to it. They were used to being the strongest contender in any negotiation they entered into. But this time they were far out of their comfort zone. "We don't understand Hollywood," Microsoft Games Studios general manager Stuart Mulder confessed to the trade papers in 2002 as the company inked in its deal with Shapiro at CAA. It was a throwaway comment that would turn out to be disturbingly prophetic.

What was apparent during the *Halo* deal-making was that Microsoft was far from home, perhaps even surrounded in enemy territory. In the middle of the *Halo* negotiations, as all parties sat around the table, Shapiro recalls the discussion between Microsoft's Hollywood liaison Peter Schlessel and Jimmy Horowitz, Universal's co-president of production, taking an aggressive turn. "Schlessel was getting really tough on some of the terms with Horowitz: 'Come on, don't be a jerk, blah, blah, blah...'. It was getting really heated. The guy from Microsoft [Steve Schrek] was like, 'Wow, this is really good.' Then we took a break and Schlessel goes to Horowitz, 'Are you coming over for Passover?' Because they know each other. You don't have those kinds of relationships in videogames. In Hollywood you can be getting at each other but then you're playing golf together the next day."

Even after the deal was struck, the misunderstanding over how the movie business operated continued to be a problem. Microsoft wanted a big-name director, but Peter Jackson, helmer on *The Lord of the Rings* trilogy, decided to sign on as a co-producer alongside Peter Schlessel, Mary Parent and Scott Stuber. Jackson wanted his new protégé, an up-and-coming commercials whiz kid called Neill Blomkamp, to direct. With Jackson's fee running to several million dollars the studios knew there was an advantage in hiring a cheaper, less well-known talent to sit in the director's chair. Microsoft was reputedly not happy with the decision.

Blomkamp, a South African director who had made his mark with commercials for Nike and had shot an intriguing short about alien apartheid called *Alive in Joburg*, was concerned about getting chewed up and spat out while making his first feature with these three enormous corporations and a budget north of $100 million. "My instinct was that if I crawled into that hornet's nest it would be not good, and it was a clusterfuck from day one," he admits. "There's no question that there was a clash of worlds, for sure. The two sides weren't seeing eye-to-eye."

What lured him in, beyond the obvious kudos, was his love for the property: "I told Tom Rothman [co-Chairman of Fox Filmed Entertainment] that I was genetically created to direct *Halo*." However, Blomkamp quickly realised that the studio didn't share his artistic vision and was uncomfortable at the prospect of his gritty, post-cyberpunk aesthetic - all blurry video feeds and radio chatter - dominating a summer blockbuster. "Rothman hated me, I think he would have gotten rid of me if he could have," says the director. "The suits weren't happy with the direction I was going. Thing was, though, I'd played

Halo and I play videogames. I'm that generation more than they are and I know that my version of *Halo* would have been insanely cool. It was more fresh and potentially could have made more money than just a generic, boring film - something like *G.I. Joe* or some crap like that, that Hollywood produces."

Blomkamp's relationship with Fox was particularly fraught. The way the deal was split between three major corporations and a handful of Hollywood producers caused several unusual imbalances in terms of power. "The way Fox dealt with me was not cool. Right from the beginning, when Mary [Parent, Universal's former president of production turned *Halo* producer] hired me up until the end when it collapsed, they treated me like shit; they were just a crappy studio. I'll never ever work with Fox ever again because of what happened to *Halo* - unless they pay me some ungodly amount of money and I have absolute fucking control."

He was also being pressured by Microsoft's demands too. One of the biggest issues was creative control. Microsoft had paid Garland to pen the screenplay to their specifications in order to retain control over what was clearly a very valuable property to them. *Halo* was an Xbox exclusive title, a billion-dollar franchise, and its chief weapon in the console war against Sony. The problem was, though, that filmmaking was a collaborative exercise and total control simply wasn't possible.

"If you're dealing with a company that doesn't understand the film industry, its sense of assurance comes with glossy names that have done a lot of big projects that have made a lot of money," says Blomkamp. "I think the guys at Bungie liked what I was doing. I'm fairly confident in saying they liked where I was going. It's highly possible that that artwork was getting back to Microsoft and Microsoft itself, the corporate entity, was not happy with it because it was too unconventional. I don't know if that's true or not, but it was entirely possible." Shapiro notes Microsoft's displeasure over Blomkamp's lack of previous credits and draws a comparison with the company's reaction to Sam Raimi over the mooted *Age of Empires* movies: "The games publishers are name snobs. They don't understand the up-and-comers."

Against this fraught background, Universal funded $12 million of preliminary development on the movie. Some of the money was spent before Blomkamp came on-board by director Guillermo Del Toro, who was initially attached before going off to make *Hellboy II: The Golden Army* instead. The rest was spent on Blomkamp's watch and included paying various screenwriters - Scott Frank, D.B. Weiss, Josh Olson - to redraft the original screenplay.

Meanwhile, Weta Workshop, the New Zealand physical effects company co-founded by Jackson, was fabricating real-life versions of the weapons, power armour and the Warthog assault vehicle from the game. Blomkamp would eventually use them to shoot a series of thrilling test shorts. "The legacy of a movie never made," is how Moore describes the collected footage, which was later cut together under the title *Halo: Landfall* and used to promote the *Halo 3* videogame release in 2007.

With development proving slow, Fox and Universal were beginning to get impatient. The gross heavy deal and costs increased the growing sense of unease. In October 2006, right before a payment was due to be made to the filmmakers and Microsoft, Universal demanded that the producers' deals be cut. Jackson consulted with his co-producers and Blomkamp, as well as with Microsoft and Bungie, and refused. In a stroke, the *Halo* movie was pronounced dead in the water.

What ultimately killed the *Halo* movie was money. "Microsoft's unwillingness to reduce their deal killed the deal," says Shapiro. "Their unwillingness to reduce their gross in the deal meant it got too top-heavy. That movie could have been *Avatar.*" Blomkamp agrees: "One of the complicating factors with *Halo* was that Microsoft wasn't the normal party that you'd go off and option the IP from and make your product. Because Microsoft is such an omnipresent, powerful corporation, they weren't just going to sit back and not take a massive cut of the profits. When you have a corporation that potent and that large taking a percentage of the profits, then you've got Peter Jackson taking a percentage of the profits and you start adding all of that stuff up, mixed with the fact that you have two studios sharing the profits, suddenly the return on the investment starts to decline so that it becomes not worth making. Ultimately, that's essentially what killed the film."

Beyond the movie itself, Halo's collapse also threw light on the culture clash between the two industries. Garland suggests that the company's showy, take no prisoners stampede into Hollywood was antagonistic: "Being candid about it, I think they pissed people off," he says. "You're talking about Universal and Twentieth Century Fox, they're not shrinking violets." From his perspective, Microsoft should have been less combative. "I think they did it wrong. I think you can accept that within the film world you will be involved in combat [but] partly what you should be trying to do is also find allies. I think the way to have done it was not to go in there saying, 'We're going to stick it to the studios' but to choose which studio to work with."

The screenwriter also blames himself - a little harshly it must be said - for not penning a screenplay that would have been strong enough to build bridges between the two industries. As a committed gamer, he remains deeply upset that the project never made it to the screen. "If I had written a slamdunk script that when everyone read it they said 'Fuck we've got to make this,' then it would have been made. Whatever obstacles existed en-route to do with Jackson, Schlessel, Fox and Universal and all those big, big important and powerful people and corporations that were in the mix - if the script had made the point in a compelling enough way, I think it would have got made."

Frustrated by Microsoft's domineering stance, the gross heavy deal and the internecine warfare between the parties involved, the studios began to look for an exit. Blomkamp was savvy enough to see where things might lead: "I have a feeling that Fox didn't really know with how to deal with basically collapsing the entire film, and I think that some blame was placed on me for the budget spiralling out of control. I remember reading about that and I got a bunch of emails from people in Hollywood going 'Dude, how high was the budget?' All of that was fabricated, none of that was real. I remember before the film collapsed having inklings that, if this whole thing collapses, it's very easy to place it on a first time director. I was in a writing meeting and I remember thinking that in the back of my head, and going: 'This is just an absolute fuck up.'"

Even for some of Microsoft's key executives involved in the negotiations, the deal's collapse in October 2006 was a complete surprise. Moore - who'd flown up and down between Los Angeles and Seattle, had met with Universal and producer Mary Parent, and had helped set up a merchandising deal with Mattel for toys based on the movie - remembers being stunned by the news. "It was all a mystery to me," he says. "The deal was done. Then one dramatically eventful day we got a call saying: 'Oh, we've changed our mind, all done. Off.'"

Infuriated by the deal's collapse and how badly things had been handled, Jackson and Blomkamp went off to make sci-fi movie *District 9*, a $30 million sci-fi movie set in South Africa and based on the director's *Alive in Joburg* short. Its computer-generated aliens clearly owed an artistic debt to the *Halo* development and to videogames generally, although its masterful apartheid subtext was all its own. Distributed by Tristar, the film became a sleeper hit in 2009. It grossed $211 million worldwide, won a stream of critical plaudits and picked up four Academy Awards nominations. To many it looked as if Blomkamp was flipping the studios the finger. "That's probably true," he laughs.

Although the project in its current form remains stalled, Microsoft knows the value of *Halo* as a transmedia franchise. The *Halo: Legends* anime series, a Japanese-animated anthology released on DVD by Warner Bros. in 2010, sold 168,000 units (equating to around $2.56 million) in its opening week. Similarly, *Halo* novels and comics are big business: the total franchise's worth was estimated at $2 billion by September 2010. Master Chief is for Generation Xbox what *Superman* was for comic fans in 1978; and *Halo* is Microsoft's *Star Wars*. "We have a lot in common with *Star Wars* when it comes to having a big universe, recognizable characters and fundamentally really cool stuff," Frank O'Connor, the former Bungie employee who now oversees the *Halo* franchise for Microsoft, told Variety in 2010. "A lot of studios and film companies and game companies have tried to create [their own *Star Wars*]. But you can't set out to make a successful franchise on purpose. It has to be something that fans are attracted to and love. There's only so much you can do to achieve that deliberately. But it always comes down to a great story and characters."

A live-action *Halo* movie is inevitable eventually. DreamWorks was rumoured to be interested in the property and reputedly looked at adapting the tie-in novels as a way of sidestepping any potential claims from Universal and Fox over the money they previously spent on the aborted movie. Meanwhile, Microsoft and Bungie's marketing campaign for the games has relied on live-action commercials set in the *Halo* universe. Each new trailer - like "The Life" released in 2009 to promote *Halo 3: ODST* and that boasted outfits by Oscar-winning costume designers plus a cast of ex-special forces soldiers - prompts paroxysms of excitement online. There is undoubtedly a huge and hungry audience who want to see a movie set in the universe of the games.

Obviously the biggest question is: does Microsoft even need Hollywood? Certainly, there's no doubt that making software is the company's core competency. But it has the financial clout to bankroll a movie if it wanted to. Reflecting on the aborted *Halo* movie in 2009, Jackson claimed: "They are just trying to figure out what their relationship with Hollywood is. If any company can make a film independently without the need of a Hollywood studio, it would be Microsoft." No doubt Microsoft have noted the success that Marvel Studios - the Hollywood production arm of the comics publisher - has enjoyed during the 2000s.

It seems clear that videogames and Hollywood are on the cusp of creating something entirely new: a synergy between movies and games that will enthral like nothing before. If it ever happens, *Halo* would be a true blockbuster moment. Or, if not Microsoft's space-marine-combat property, one of *World of Warcraft*, *Gears of War*, *Uncharted* or *Mass Effect* is destined to do for videogame movies what *X-Men* and *Spider-Man* did for comic book films. When A-list talent begin adapting videogames into successful movies and the two industries finally overcome their long-standing rivalry and fulfil the potential of game/movie convergence, Generation Xbox's invasion of Hollywood will have entered a new phase. There's still everything to play for.

CHAPTER 8

Emotion In Motion

"I think the real indicator [that videogames are a storytelling art form] will be when somebody confesses that they cried at level 17."

Steven Spielberg, speaking at USC in 2004

There's no rain in Paris on the evening of 16 February 2010. It's not often that the organisers of a red carpet premiere would pray for a downpour, but on this particular evening it would have been appropriate. Outside the Gaumont Cinema on the Champs-Élysées, photographers line up behind the red, velour ropes with their cameras at the ready. Publicists armed with clipboards and burly security guards in regulation black form an impenetrable phalanx around the entrance. Among the big names on the guest list are Terry Gilliam, the former Python turned filmmaker and Hollywood director Neil LaBute.

If you were a Parisian passing the event, you'd no doubt think it was just another film premiere. On the evening of 16 February, though, the title being launched wasn't a movie. Nor was it quite a game. It was called *Heavy Rain* and it was an interactive thriller with a plot as tightly coiled as a Hollywood movie, a cast of live actors made into CG avatars and a branching storyline that reacted to players' choices.

After the assembled audience of cast, crew, guests and journalists settled into their seats at the Gaumont, they watched an hour of gameplay footage that had been edited into a movie. Appetites whetted, they then watched an eight-minute movie shot by Neil LaBute with talking heads including Samuel L. Jackson, Nicolas Roeg and Peter Bogdanovich talking about how far they'd go for love, the game's big theme. In the lobby there were drinks and hors d'oeuvres and a giant ice sculpture in the shape of an origami bird.

The evening was capped off by an on-stage panel discussion between the game's writer/director David Cage, Gilliam and others. Finally the game's actors, performance captured thespians who lend their bodies and voices to each of the on-screen characters, were invited on-stage. The audience gasped as they saw the striking similarities between the real-life actors and their digital avatars.

In videogame terms, this was a premiere like no other. It had a dash of Hollywood glitz, an unusual intellectual and emotional heft and incredible self-confidence. It was, in other words, the perfect premiere for *Heavy Rain*, a game that took the convergence of interactive entertainment and cinema to a completely new level.

Playing the game, a downbeat story of a father's quest for his missing kid, is unlike any kind of virtual experience most gamers have ever had before. Kicking off with the disappearance of Ethan Mars's son Jason from a crowded shopping mall, it's less interested in the usual videogame mechanics than the emotional peaks and troughs of a drama. Domestic scenes of play sword-fighting with your kids in the garden or laying the dining table are set-up to be interactive. The right button presses will amuse your kids or keep the best china from being smashed. Later, after your son has been kidnapped by a serial killer who insists on seeing how far you'll be willing to go to save him, those same button presses and shakes of the PlayStation 3's Sixaxis controller will be used to slice off one of your own fingers in a burned out apartment building.

Like *Crash* or *Amores Perros*, the multi-strand plot of *Heavy Rain* follows several protagonists: an asthmatic private detective, a drug-addicted cop and an insomniac photojournalist. But its Ethan's story that's the core. At the opening of the game, Ethan is a successful architect blessed with a pretty wife and two cute kids. Before the prologue's out, he loses his first son in a shopping mall and watches in horror as he's killed in a traffic accident on the road outside the mall. Videogames have always asked you to kill, but rarely asked you to battle with the aftermath of bereavement. It was a watershed moment. In the aftermath of the accident, Ethan's life falls apart. His wife abandons him, his surviving son Shaun hates him and he ends up living in a crummy terraced house in a blue-collar Philadelphia slum. Gone are the sunlit, suburban environments that opened the game. From this point on everything takes place in downbeat rooms full of peeling wallpaper and rain-swept city streets.

The aim of Quantic Dream, the development team, is to hit the emotional high notes. "We believe that games can be more than just toys and we are convinced that the media is mature enough to be able to express emotions and offer experiences that are deep in terms of meaning," says Quantic Dream's co-chief executive, and Cage's right-hand man, Guillaume de Fondaumière. "Our work is like movies because movies to a certain extent depend very much on character and ultimately emotion. If you watch someone playing *Heavy Rain* you could think that it's a movie. It feels like a movie, you can watch it like you'd watch a movie. On the other hand, when you're holding the controller you're really playing a game, and you feel like this isn't a movie because I'm the actor, I'm the director, I'm everything I can't be in a movie. I'm really in control of the actions, of the destiny of my characters."

In one of the game's most affecting sequences, you guide a bereaved Ethan through an after-school evening with Shaun as he makes sure his son does his homework and microwaves him a crappy pizza for his tea. Outside, the rain falls. Upstairs, a hastily assembled kid's bedroom captures the awkward attempt of a broken man to reconnect with his sullen offspring. Not long afterwards Shaun goes missing. He's been abducted, we later learn, by serial murderer The Origami Killer.

Cage based the opening shopping mall sequence on his own experience of losing his son Quentin on a Saturday afternoon in Paris. "My son was five years old. I thought he was with my wife, my wife thought he was with me, and when we met again we realised he wasn't with either of us. For the next 10 minutes, it was a total state of panic and fear - it's impossible to describe what goes through your mind in this situation." After what seemed like an eternity, the tannoy system announced that Quentin had been found. He'd wandered off to look - ironically enough - at videogames in a nearby shop. Following Quentin's disappearance, Cage was left with a spark of inspiration. He wanted to make a game that could recreate the terror and relief he had felt in the shopping mall. A novel could do it, a movie could too, but could an interactive title convey to an audience what it means to love one's son? Instead of run, shoot, kill could a game get players to sympathise, emote and empathise?

Heavy Rain was a project that Cage, a scruffy, tubby French musician turned videogame designer, had been working towards for 13 years. He began his company, Quantic Dream, as a start-up in Paris in 1997 after putting together a 200-page design proposal for a game called *Omikron* that was, by his own admission, too ambitious to succeed. "I was dreaming of a game with an open world city where I could go wherever I wanted, meet anybody, use vehicles, fight and transfer my soul into another body," he says. "When my friends read it they said, 'David, this is impossible. It's not technically feasible, don't even think about it.'"

Visionaries don't have time for the impossible. Cage ignored the advice and used the money he'd made from scoring commercials to hire a team of six friends with development experience. They started production on *Omikron* in a sound-proofed studio that once belonged to poetic Belgian pop singer Jacques

Brel. There were thick doors, no windows and just 161 square foot of floor space. Trapped in a shoebox, they were trying to make a game without limits.

Cage insisted on paying the team, not for altruistic reasons, but so that he could be the boss. After all, it's hard to be an auteur when everyone's an equal. "I wanted to be able to demand something of them, ask them to be there on time in the morning and work long days," he recalls. The team went into instant crunch mode: they had just six months to make the impossible demo. After that, Cage would be broke and Quantic Dream's dream would be over.

In the penultimate week of development, Cage got on the phone and spoke to game publishers in the UK in his heavily-accented English: "'ello, my name iz Dav-eed. I 'ave nice demo in real-time 3D, do you want to see eet?" Eidos said yes and when John Kavanagh, the vice-president of product development, saw the impossible demo with its dynamic city environment and motion-captured, canoodling pedestrians he signed Quantic Dream immediately. It was just three days before Cage's start-up money ran out.

The demo turned into *Omikron: The Nomad Soul*, a sci-fi adventure game set in an open world city. Its dense storyline featured demons, the transmigration of souls and a contribution from David Bowie who wrote the game's sweeping soundtrack. Bowie also agreed to spend a month in Paris where Quantic Dream filmed him with the help of a French motion-capture (mo-cap) studio. He played two parts - the youthful lead singer of The Dreamers, an underground band who held furtive concerts in the city's clubs; and the older Boz, a blue-skinned, digital entity who leads the resistance fighters.

"We wanted to capture Bowie doing his 'signature' moves," recalls Phil Campbell, then a senior designer at Eidos who'd later jump ship to join Quantic Dream. "But Bowie didn't think he really had any signature moves so he gave us his choreographer Édouard Locke and we captured him doing 'Bowie' routines." They also captured Bowie's guitarist Reeves Gabrels. Cage then spent 30 hours on each concert, filming the mo-capped avatars within the game engine using a virtual camera.

It was the first time a real-life performer had gigged inside a videogame, nearly a decade before *Grand Theft Auto IV*'s comedy clubs would showcase the likes of Ricky Gervais. Bowie's dual role also tied into Cage's obsession with schizophrenic identities, something that was only underscored by the game's fluid shifting between avatars. Cage particularly liked the early moment when the player, occupying the body of policeman Kay'l, beds the cop's wife. "The idea of being in the body of a guy and making love to his wife - when she believes you're her husband, even though you're not - was a very strange position to be in. That's exactly the kind of thing that I try to explore in all my games today. How can we put you in the shoes of someone else?"

Bowie, a legendary chameleon, totally understood the pleasures of the virtual realm and its Dorian Gray potential. He even roped in his wife Iman, who appears in the game as a sultry bodyguard. "He sometimes joked about leaving his Bowie character in *Omikron* forever," says Campbell. "He would have totally transcended to the digital side - and 'come out the other side' as just David Jones again."

Movies were Cage's chief inspiration. Beginning with *Omikron* he started to create immersive experiences in real-time 3D, "emotional rides" that blended cinema with interactivity. His vision, much like that of Rockstar Games, was to provide gamers with an experience that was just like a movie. Yet while Rockstar offered players the keys to a gangster movie kingdom - tool up, shoot 'em up, steal cars - Cage was fixated on something more resonant. He wanted to let them interact within an all-encompassing cinematic story that would bend and change based on their decisions to provide an emotional payoff.

"The problem with games is that they are completely empty in matters of meaning," Cage explains. "You blow things up, you don't know why, you don't know who you are or what you're doing there. Maybe when I was 15 I could find that kind of thing exciting. Today, I do this for 20 minutes and I say 'OK what else?' I have no interest in blowing things up just for the sake of it. I need to understand, I need to feel something. It's all about meanings and emotions. I think these are the two main parameters that are really neglected by most games today. What do games have to say? The most interesting movies are the ones that convey something - an idea, a vision, a feeling. But when they don't convey anything, they are usually just boring. This is what most videogames do today. They are totally empty."

After leaving Eidos, Campbell became chief creative officer at Quantic Dream. He helped set up its San Francisco office before moving to EA to work as a designer, including a stint on retro-licensed title *The Godfather.* He sees Cage as videogames' answer to the movie auteur: "I think he is very much aware he's setting himself up in that way. We had endless chats about Truffaut and Hitchcock. He has a very strong vision, it's been there from day one."

Pascal Langdale, the actor who'd play Ethan Mars for Cage in *Heavy Rain,* agrees. "An auteur is like a warship. They need to know about every department and have absolute control over the project. That would be a fair description of David. He was the guy who had the entire script in his head. He was the guy who wrote and directed it. He was *Heavy Rain*. There was a real feeling of 'This is the boss' whenever he walked into a room. He had that aura about him. People didn't want to cross him, that's for sure. He was a nice guy but absolutely obsessed with *Heavy Rain*."

For a game with such ambition, *Omikron*'s commercial fate was painful. "The titles I create seem to be too weird for the American marketing guys," says Cage. "In the US, Eidos didn't support the game at all, which was really disappointing. The big sales were mainly in Europe, where we sold between 400,000 and 500,000. It was too arty, too French, too something for the American marketing department."

In 2005, Quantic Dream tried again with its second game *Fahrenheit* (re-titled *Indigo Prophecy* for its US release). It fulfilled Cage's promise. Here was a game in which the player could literally play with a linear story itself, turning it into a kind of rubber band that could be bent and stretched and twisted by their in-game actions and decisions.

Set in a wintry Manhattan, *Fahrenheit* opens with you as Lucas Kane, a nerdy IT technician, who has just involuntarily stabbed a man to death in a grubby diner bathroom. Aware that Lucas has been possessed by some strange, supernatural power, you're forced to start making decisions. Since you know Lucas is innocent, you face a choice: do you hide the body or flee the crime scene? As you're wondering what to do, the game suddenly switches into split-screen so you can see the beat cop in the diner preparing to come into the bathroom. The clock is ticking.

It's a moment familiar from a dozen "Wrong Man" movie thrillers. The difference is that here it's you, the player, who's literally having to make decisions and carry them out as the seconds tick away. Whatever actions you take will mould the story's direction in small but subtle ways. For instance, when Lucas's ex-girlfriend comes to his rundown apartment to pick up her stuff, your responses will decide whether she will leave with a tear in her eye or offer her ex a desultory, farewell fuck.

Fahrenheit feels like a TV soap opera, its cast of characters working through personal issues, relationship problems and even pouring their hearts out to their neighbours over a bottle of wine. Playing as multiple characters, you are part of an ensemble, multi-thread drama: *The Wire* of videogames. True the game's story eventually goes off the rails, descending into a bizarre third act that throws everything and the kitchen sink into the mix - voodoo, Mayan prophecies, angels and sentient internet beings included. But for all its flaws, *Fahrenheit* was an ambitious attempt to redefine what games were about.

Fahrenheit featured cinematic visuals and a soaring score, penned by David Lynch's favourite composer Angelo Badalementi. But it was the motion capture work that really elevated its narrative ambition. Using a system designed by motion-capture experts VICON, Quantic Dream spent 40 days shooting live actors dressed in spandex suits fitted with sensors. Their motions then became the raw data for each character model's animation. It helped make the game's avatars into more than just CG puppets. Their movements were real, guided by a human intelligence that no animator could ever hope to mimic. Getting emotional realism into games meant getting real human actors to do the emoting. Cage knew that the line between videogames and movies was blurring. He'd even flown out to Burbank, California to pitch his vision for *Fahrenheit* to Warner Bros. Studios. "It was just after *Omikron*," he recalls. "I wanted to illustrate that it was possible to tell a story through interactivity and that it would be very interesting and meaningful and could open up new horizons."

At Warner Bros. Studios, the Frenchman and his team laid out the brave new world they were part of: videogames were becoming increasingly cinematic; they could tell stories as big and bold as any blockbuster; they were using human actors. What if Warner Bros. hooked up with Quantic Dream? Perhaps they could collaborate on a new kind of drama, an interactive one that could be released episodically via broadband much like a playable, online TV show. Looking around the room, Cage saw little but bafflement. He was prepared for that and had brought a demo with him. The executives watched as the team fired up a prototype for this new kind of interactive drama. The point, Cage told them, is that the two industries were now at a point where they could complement each other brilliantly. Imagine if Warner Bros. released a movie and Quantic Dream simultaneously released an interactive experience that was part of its universe.

When they saw the prototype, the faces of the Warner Bros. suits fell. The demo was something they instantly recognised: a scene from *The Matrix*. Quantic Dream had mocked up a model of the room in the movie where Morpheus offers Neo a choice between the red and blue pills. The idea was to demonstrate how the player could interact with a scene that they couldn't do in the passivity of the movie theatre. "The idea was that within a very strong story you could choose your path and see what happens depending on your choice," says Cage. "That was really the basis of *Fahrenheit* and *Heavy Rain*."

The Matrix, a movie that was hugely influenced by the virtual realities of videogames, was the perfect choice. Or at least, that's what you might have thought. The problem was Quantic Dream didn't own the copyright for *The Matrix* franchise. Nor did they have permission to build a demo out of it. After telling Cage off for his imposition, the executives began to discuss the merits of the demo itself. Cage, who was effectively trying to bypass videogame publishers and put interactive drama directly in the sphere of influence of the Hollywood studios, was attempting something really innovative. Here he was, an artist, offering Warner Bros access not only to his unique vision but to a different distribution pipe: games, downloadable episodic content, interactivity. Surely they'd bite his arm off, right? Wrong...

"They just didn't get it," recalls one former Quantic Dream staffer. "It was weird. They were saying things like 'But if you take the other pill, nothing happens, the movie's over, right?'" For Cage, who often speaks with the grumpy impatience of a man who's already seen the future and is waiting for everyone else to catch up, the experience was disappointing. "At the time, absolutely nobody in Hollywood had a clue what we were talking about," he complains. By now, it was a depressingly familiar story: the gatekeepers of linear media encountering interactive entertainment and recoiling from it as if it were an alien language. First contact protocols had improved in the years since Hasbro's NEMO courted Hollywood in the 1980s, but not by much.

Meetings with other Hollywood contacts, including visual effects house Digital Domain, were equally fruitless. "We were quite surprised by the conservatism we faced," admits de Fondaumière. There were some suggestions that the company's real-time 3D technology could be used to run pre-visualisation sequences for filmmakers planning their movies. It was something that, as we'll see, had been gaining traction in Hollywood's visual effects houses during the 2000s. For Cage and his team, though, that was akin to using a Ferrari to pull a caravan. "It was really a conceptual misunderstanding to a certain degree of what we were doing and how this could be used potentially in making a movie," says de Fondaumière. "And so we stopped going there and showing our technology and thought maybe one day those guys are going to come to us and ask for it and we'll talk again."

What Quantic Dream was really interested in was creating a cross-platform title: a transmedia story rather than a licensed tie-in. "We always thought it would be possible to develop a movie and a game at the same time," says Cage, "that didn't tell the same story but were complimentary. The game would allow you to see what the movie didn't show you, what would have happened if this character made a different choice at this point." For Cage, Hollywood were the big boys and he wanted to run with them. It was a desire driven by Quantic Dream's basic starting point: that videogames were on the verge of becoming the artistic equal of movies, rather than a merchandising tool. Unfortunately Cage believes that, even today, "very few people in the movie industry think games are a valid creative medium that could be complimentary with what they're doing."

For the French director, motion capture was the key to creating emotionally resonant stories. He wondered if it might also be a way of making the studios realise the value of what he was doing: using actors, scripts and digital film shoots was already blurring the line between Cage as a game-maker and as a movie director, at least in technical terms. Surely the studios couldn't ignore that? In the hope of gaining traction in the industry, Quantic Dream also held a meeting with Leonardo DiCaprio, superstar of *Titanic* and *The Beach*. They spent a whole afternoon with him and his manager talking about the possibility of collaborating on something like *Fahrenheit*.

Despite the fact that Robert Zemeckis had already tempted Tom Hanks into the motion capture suit by this point (more on that in a moment), DiCaprio was agnostic. "He told us clearly, 'It's too early for this'. He wasn't sure that it would fit his image as an actor, as a performer," says de Fondaumière. "Although we could clearly feel he was tempted by it, it never really happened. It was sad but we could understand it, to an extent, because the tech simply wasn't there. At the time we were still on the PlayStation 2 or Xbox. What was the point in having DiCaprio if you weren't going to be able to capture his performance in all its depth?"

Ultimately, *Fahrenheit* didn't have a Hollywood connection other than the sheer cinematic sweep of its thriller narrative. On seeing the game there were those who became convinced that Cage was nothing more than a frustrated filmmaker, a man trying to sneak into film through the backdoor of videogames. He has always vehemently denied such assertions and has been keen to stress instead that his true ambition lies somewhere between games and movies, a grey zone that he is exploring almost singlehandedly.

In many respects, Cage stands on the cutting edge of the ongoing evolution in interactive storytelling that began with *Dragon's Lair* and continued through the FMV fad of the '90s right up to the likes of *Grand Theft Auto IV*, *L.A. Noire* and the *Mass Effect* franchise today. Cage's desire to invent games with malleable, rubber-band like narratives owes a discernable debt to the past.

Cage's third game, *Heavy Rain* is the closest the Frenchman has come to making a movie so far. In fact, his downbeat serial killer thriller was signed as a movie first. A traditional screenplay based on the game's concept attracted the interest of New Line Cinema and Mark Ordesky, one of the producers on *The Lord of the Rings* trilogy, in late 2005. It was in development for 18 months and Cage hope it might be possible to release the game and movie simultaneously. "Both experiences would be complimentary to the point where we thought, 'Maybe we don't tell players who's the killer in the game and they have to watch the movie to find out,'" explains de Fondaumière. Quantic Dream's hopes were dashed when Warner Bros. bought out New Line and the project stalled. Frustrated, Cage concentrated on the videogame side of the equation. Sony agreed to publish *Heavy Rain* as a PlayStation 3 exclusive. With its cinematic style, photorealistic graphics and use of motion capture, *Heavy Rain* promised to showcase the console's abilities brilliantly.

Performance capture was the driving force behind Cage's vision for the game. Much as Tom Zito and Digital Pictures had responded to the rebuffs from Hollywood by simply moving into film production themselves in the '90s, Cage had set up his own motion capture studio at Quantic Dream's Paris office. If you wanted to create an interactive movie, he decided, you had to be able to actually shoot movies independently. It turned out to be a sound investment. Across the industry, performance capture was becoming one of the standard tools for blockbuster games. "It's much more powerful when you can build characterisations through game play rather than cut scenes," Cage explains. "Mo-cap is absolutely key to achieving that."

Hiring a group of actors to play each of *Heavy Rain*'s four protagonists, Quantic Dream prepped an extensive shoot: the cast was dressed in Lycra suits fitted with light sensors and their movement was recorded on the VICON motion capture system. Facial animations and voice work were captured separately later and the whole performance was assembled by Quantic Dream's animators.

On a technological level alone games and movies were clearly colliding: VICON's system was simultaneously being used on blockbuster movies like *Tron: Legacy* while the company's House of Moves studio in Los Angeles is now used to working on everything from the *G.I. Joe* and *Spider-Man* movies to the *Call of Duty* and *God of War* game franchises. Motion, or performance, capture was building a new bridge between the two mediums and industries.

For videogames creators, motion capture has become a pivotal tool in telling stories that had depth and breadth. "Motion capture is important in finding the emotional dimension to the story," says de Fondaumière. "The tools we use to capture the performance of actors help create an emotional response in the player. We are trying to capture reality and turn it into pixels - using technology to mimic life."

For the actors involved, *Heavy Rain* offered them a glimpse of how the acting profession was evolving alongside entertainment technology. Langdale literally felt as if he was creating a new style of acting - not linear but expansive. "Within the first month of performance capture work, I realised that we were doing things that no one had ever done before," he explains. "You can reinterpret *Hamlet* a million times but the videogame medium is the first time anyone will have attempted to put a dramatic character into a game in that manner."

Faced with several thousand pages of screenplay - and with different variations on the same scene dependant on the players' actions and decisions - the actors were asked to embrace a schizophrenic style of performance. One in which multiple actions, reactions and emotions were constantly possible. "During the motion capture you are often in situations where the player has to make a choice what to do next: wash their hands, say something to someone, or express their anger," explains Langdale. "As an actor, the moment before the player makes a decision is a curious position to be in. You can't prefigure what's going to happen next because you don't know what it will be. You're caught in a holding pattern. You have to try and make it match what could be happening next. I've never had to do that in any other medium."

After Langdale spent a day cutting off one of his digits using a variety of imaginary implements, the crew began to fear for the actor's sanity. But he was actually exhilarated by the multi-faceted nature of performing for a non-linear game: "It's enjoyable. I'm not restricted to one possibility. I get to play all of them. It's like a workout for an actor: how does it feel to saw your finger off as opposed to snip it off with a pair of pliers?" It might not have been *Hamlet* but it was certainly a new kind of performing art.

Heavy Rain was also a new kind of videogame: revolutionary and bold in spite of its occasional missteps. It set a new standard for realism in games, its performance-captured characters and incredible lighting effects blurring the line between the real and the virtual. Meanwhile, its settings - down-at-heel locales based on real locations discovered by a movie scout in Philadelphia - captured some of the grub and grime of Hollywood serial killer movies from *Se7en* to *Saw*.

How it played was arguably more important than how it looked. "Interactivity, like literature or cinema, is a platform to trigger human emotions," says Cage and it was in *Heavy Rain*'s game mechanics that the truth of that - and the limits of it - emerged. The emotional potential of Cage's design was apparent: the father-son relationship of the opening act or the tragic sadness embodied in the face of Scott Shelby (Sam Douglas), a hulking private detective who the player controls in later sections as he trawls through sleazy motels investigating the Origami Killer were quite unlike anything to be found in other titles.

Videogames, it seemed, were reaching beyond their past towards an art form that had all the dramatic power of cinema. As EA's chief executive John Riccitiello put it in 2008 around the release of *Grand Theft Auto IV*, another dramatic, performance-capture heavy game: "It feels like what movie moguls might have seen in the 1920s and said: 'Hey, we've got talkies now, where is it going?' I feel like we've stepped through a time window where our games are so compelling and seem so real. Our industry is passing through a phase where I believe the greatest games will be viewed by almost everybody as being as important as Best Picture at the Academy Awards."

Heavy Rain proved that Riccitiello's vision was coming true. Released in 2010, the game was rapturously received by critics and sold around two million copies at retail. It was hardly a blockbuster title (in comparison, *Call of Duty: Black Ops* sold an estimated seven million copies in just its first 24 hours on sale that same year). But for a relatively experimental game it was impressive, particularly in terms of the coverage it received the mainstream media. Here was a game that asked us to reassess what games could do. It didn't win an Oscar for Best Picture, but it scooped three videogame BAFTAs at the 2011 awards.

Fittingly for a game about non-linear storytelling, no one was quite sure if *Heavy Rain* was the future of videogames. But it was certainly one possible future: proof of the dramatic and emotional potential that games using real, performance-captured actors could achieve. *Heavy Rain* was too keen to distance itself from the conventions of videogames to have anything as crass as a level 17. But if it had, we probably would have cried on it. After almost a decade of evolution in the movie and videogame industries, games finally had an emotional payoff. And it was all thanks to performance capture technology.

* * *

Human bodies move in unique ways. Right now you're sitting reading this book. Perhaps you're sitting on sofa, lying on a bed, or riding on a train. How are you holding your head as you read these words? When you turn a page, how does your arm bend? You probably don't know the answers to those questions because you take the movements for granted. It's so effortless, so instinctive that it doesn't need to be thought about.

For videogame artists and animators, that's a big problem. On a movie shoot, actors don't have to think about how to turn a page or open a door. They just do it. In videogames, every movement has to be plotted and created by the animators. Imagine you have a 3D character model that you want to bring to life. How do you make its complex movements look as natural as your own when you're doing simple everyday things? It can be laborious, pernickety work. Motion capture - or, as it later became known, performance capture - changed all of that. And in doing so, it narrowed the gap between film and games forever.

The coming together of these two mediums was beneficial for both industries: games became more photorealistic as 3D character models suddenly moved with the graceful ease of human actors. Meanwhile, films were given access to a new kind of digital fantastic as CG creations like Gollum in *The Lord of the Rings* were brought to life on screen with all the subtle nuances a human actor could provide. For both industries, motion capture promised a behind-the-scenes revolution that would totally change the way digital characters were animated. Neither film nor games would ever be the same again.

The history of motion capture begins in the 1990s. One of the leaders in the field back then was the game publisher Acclaim, a giant of the 16-bit era thanks to its close relationship with Nintendo and the lucrative approach it took to licensing movies for games. The company's real cash cow was its home console license for *Mortal Kombat*. Taking Midway's arcade game into the living room in the early '90s, Acclaim invested heavily in blue screen technology, shooting real-life martial artists and turning them into digitised 2D sprites. In return, *Mortal Kombat* helped make Acclaim very rich indeed.

Business was good but the party couldn't last forever. The world was changing: and fast. The new 3D game engines were on the verge of rendering the 2D digitised assets used in *Mortal Kombat* obsolete. Hoping to stay ahead of the pack, Acclaim's Advanced Technologies Group, headed by Wes Trager, began experimenting with 3D animation. The hope was to find a way of creating realistic 3D characters that not only looked real, as *Mortal Kombat*'s 2D digitised characters had, but that also moved in a believable fashion.

Among the staff at the company's Glen Cove, New York headquarters was Remington Scott. A softly-spoken, "crazy artist kid" with thick black specs, Scott was still in high school when he first realised that he wanted to make games more believable. One of his earliest jobs was working on 1987's *WWF Superstars of Wrestling*, an Atari ST computer title that broke new ground by using digitised likenesses of famous pro wrestlers. From that point on he was focused on using live performers to make videogame animation more realistic.

Arriving at Acclaim in the early 1990s, he became one of the company's three interactive directors who were responsible for handling actors during the mo-cap shoots. Little did he realise that it was the beginning of a career that would take him from games to films, working on Gollum in Peter Jackson's *The Lord of the Rings* trilogy and on Robert Zemeckis's *Beowulf*.

What Acclaim's Advanced Technologies Group quickly realised was that working with 3D models was a bitch. *Mortal Kombat*'s 2D sprites had wowed gamers because they were based on real-life martial artists. The best 3D models sucked in comparison: game engines simply couldn't support high-res polygons and texture memory was pitifully low. What they ended up with were blocky, low-res models with little detail. Sure they were in 3D but what a price to pay for an extra dimension. "We were really stuck in a rut," remembers Scott.

It wasn't until they started to look outside of the world of entertainment for inspiration that they struck gold. In hospitals, doctors were using digital scanners to analyse ball rotations for hip replacement surgery. Although the technology wasn't exactly fit for purpose - it didn't scan the full body of the patient, just a specific joint - it had incredible clarity. What would happen, wondered the Advanced Technologies Group, if they scanned humans and used the data to animate their 3D models?

"We knew if we made it full body and built a studio that could record this stuff we could drive these low-res, blocky characters with no texture," says Scott. "Even if they were stick figures it would convince you they were real because of how they moved."

In 1995, Acclaim decided to splash some cash. First the company went on a buying spree, snapping up developers and comic publishers, and consolidating its position as one of the games industry's powerhouses. It also spent $10 million building the world's first motion capture studio dedicated solely to entertainment rather than sports or medical analysis.

This was a new front in the battle for convergence. Back in the early '90s, companies like Digital Pictures had taken live actors, shot them on film and digitised the footage to make FMV games. When 3D game engines arrived, Digital Pictures' approach became outdated. Players wanted to enter immersive environments, not watch grainy, digitised movies. The new technology of motion capture offered the best of both worlds. It was an elegant solution to the problem that the full motion video of Digital Pictures had posed: how could you create more realistic-looking, digital experiences and avatars?

Thanks to motion capture, videogame developers could still work with live actors. Instead of shooting them on 35mm analogue film, though, the process was now completely digital. The motion capture teams would track the actors' movements on cameras that followed the optical sensors attached to their bodies, then upload the data to a computer. The computer would analyse the movement patterns and the data could be used to animate a 3D character model made out of polygons, computer-generated shapes that were put together to form surfaces. Instantly, videogame characters got a whole lot more real.

Acclaim's $10 million studio was state-of-the-art and used motion capture technology licensed from Biomechanics. Buried in the basement of Acclaim's new 70,000-square-foot headquarters in Glen Cove, Long Island, the motion capture studio served as a centralised asset production base for Acclaim's developers. Stunt performers were captured in full motion then shipped out to development teams working on the games at Acclaim's subsidiaries.

Shooting motion capture was weird, especially for the performers. Some of the earliest Acclaim titles to use the technology were sports games like 1995's *Frank Thomas "Big Hurt" Baseball*, which featured the Chicago White Sox's star batter swinging furiously. Invited into the motion capture studio, real-life athletes like Thomas were kitted out in black nylon-and-spandex outfits studded with 67 sensors about the size of a dime. The motion capture "stage" was a black-shrouded room as barebones minimalist as a Bertolt Brecht play. Each time the athletes moved, a transmitter emitted signals that reflected off the sensors on their suits. It let the computer track their movement in real-time. After some serious data crunching, the computer could render the data from the sensors into a crude animation on-screen as a digital stick-man replayed the performer's movements. Later the data could be transposed onto a polygonal 3D character model and used to animate it. Meanwhile, artists could "clothe" the model through a process known as texture mapping.

"We're going to get three sets of data coming from Frank [Thomas]'s femur," Trager, vice-president of engineering and advanced technologies told a New York Times reporter who was allowed to watch the baseball star's 12-hour session. "Without this system, you have to figure out how to animate certain body movements [but it] understands the connection between movements, muscles and bones."

At Acclaim, everything old was new again. Digital entertainment was having its Eadweard Muybridge moment. Like the work of the English photographer, whose stop-motion photography of a horse galloping had been one of the first seeds of early cinema in the 1870s, Acclaim's motion capture blended science, art and technology.

In the Advanced Technologies Group, pioneers like Trager and Mark Schafer, its director of R&D, pushed the process as far as they could. They began recognising the problems that the technique threw up: was it possible to record two bodies in motion simultaneously? What happened when two bodies covered in reflective markers became intertwined during an NFL football tackle? How would the computer keep track of which body was which?

Facing unexpected problems came with the territory. So did finding creative solutions. While working as interactive director on *Turok: Dinosaur Hunter*, a first-person shooter developed exclusively for the Nintendo 64 in 1996, Scott brought an emu onto the motion capture stage. "I really wanted to record the actions of a dinosaur, but seeing as they're extinct, that was a little challenging," he explains. Instead they needed to find another way to animate the game's dinosaurs. "We ended up doing some tests with large birds. The ostrich was too big and the trainer couldn't control it, but the emu was a better choice. We had problems adhering the markers to the animal and directing it, so we didn't end up with much usable data. But the reference material was valuable. I still come back to that on projects that come up, to this day, concerning dinosaurs."

When he wasn't chasing troublesome emus, Scott employed stuntman Brad Martin - later a Hollywood pro with credits on blockbusters like *Spider-Man 3* and *Salt* - to act out the motions of the human adversaries. Dressed in Lycra,

Martin gamely agreed to be launched off air ramps and trampolines to simulate enemies being blown up by grenades and rocket launchers. "We strung him up on a harness and flung him around like he was in the mouth of a dinosaur," Scott says.

Ultimately *Turok* would only use the motion capture data for the game's human adversaries, not its dinosaurs. But it was incredibly effective, in particular the death animations. Every time you killed a rival hunter they would stagger and choke or maybe clutch their throats as blood spurted out. Although the models were clunky, low-res figures made out of polygons - more like Lego puppets than human actors - their realistic movement was gobsmacking.

As *Turok* was prepped for release in 1997, Business Week asked: "Can dinosaurs save Acclaim?" It was a fair question. Acclaim was struggling financially, its share price had dipped an eye-watering 76% and Wall Street analysts were shouting sell, sell, sell. Then came 1997's E3 expo in Atlanta. Hidden away in a corner of the exhibition space, Iguana Entertainment, the small Texan developer that had built *Turok* for Acclaim, fired up a demo copy. Young project lead David Dienstbier began blasting away at raptors. No one had ever seen anything like it.

Turok was a first-person shooter set in a lushly vegetated outdoor world inhabited by motion-captured 3D humans, dinosaurs and the odd wild boar. Where *Doom* asked you to glide through high-tech corridors blasting hell demons, *Turok* was mapped out across fog-shrouded mesas. The mist helped limit draw distances but it also added an atmospheric feel, enhanced by brilliant audio design of monkey calls and jungle drums. An hour into the demo, Dienstbier had a gaggle of onlookers. By the end of the day, he had a crowd. "I pulled out a nuke and levelled half a dozen palm trees and they were like 'NO WAAAAY!'," he chuckles. "People had seen big guns on screen before but they'd never seen those sorts of effects. They just went ape-shit." In that instant, *Turok* became a sensation, especially among the corporate suits at Iguana's parent company Acclaim. "It was a very surreal moment because everyone at the company suddenly went, 'Oh *Turok* equals money... Dave, my boy! Have a Cuban cigar.'"

By the end of E3, Dienstbier had been slapped on the back so many times he was in danger of bruising. After it was released on 4 March - dubbed "*Turok* Tuesday"- the game went on to sell one-and-a-half million copies. Acclaim's stock price bounced back and the mayor of Glen Cove temporarily renamed one of the town's streets "*Turok* Boulevard" in its honour.

"*Turok* became a poster child for the kind of motion capture that was possible in 3D gaming," explains Dienstbier. "We wanted to make the game an event. We were saying: you may think you know everything about what first person shooters are. But we want to show you what they can be. We really wanted to fire up people's imaginations." It was, in large part, thanks to the power of motion capture.

Over time, Acclaim's experts began to recognise the different nuances that the technology offered them. Motion capture was, as Scott puts it, simply recording the movement of a ball across the studio. What they were doing, with actors if not emus at least, was capturing the natural animation of the human body. The technology allowed them to record the individual, unique characteristics of a person's movement. The possibilities for that in terms of giving animation the resonance of a human performance were huge. All the unconscious details of a human motion - from taking a breath to the tilt of a head in repose - could be captured effortlessly. *Turok* used the technology to give its human enemies realistic death throes but Scott began to wonder what a less violent game might be able to use it for. Could you give digital characters emotional depth? Aware that this was about more than just recording motion, he started talking not about motion but performance capture.

Meanwhile, the software needed to organise the motion capture data was being developed and tweaked. Editing tools were assembled and the asset management pipeline needed to process the raw data into workable animations was built from the ground up. "Everything you see going on in videogames today in terms of motion/performance capture, we were doing and defining back then - trying to figure out how to do it for the first time," Scott says. "I can't say that Acclaim made great games, but the technology and the group behind the studio were definitely ahead of its time."

Acclaim's motion capture facility was essentially a special effects studio. But unlike Industrial Light and Magic or Digital Domain, it was owned and controlled by an interactive entertainment company. Technological convergence between the mediums of games and films was just a whisper away. As filmmakers began to see the potential of motion capture, a process that was already being developed by VFX companies, Acclaim found itself gravitating towards film production.

In 1994, the motion capture stage was used to shoot odd scenes for the *Mighty Morphin Power Rangers* movie, where giant robots battled with Japanese katana swords. A little later John Dykstra, a legend in Hollywood's special effects community after his work on *Star Wars*, used Acclaim's studio to shoot a scene for *Batman Forever*. Collaborating with VFX house Pacific Data Images, Acclaim's technicians used motion capture to create a digital double for *Batman*. The aim was to seamlessly blend live action and computer-generated assets as the Caped Crusader plummeted from a window and fell to the ground. When Acclaim released the game of the movie under license from Warner Bros. Interactive, it contained its own motion captured assets too.

Acclaim realised that the technology it had been developing had huge relevance to the movie industry. "Everyone working for the company saw themselves as pioneers," recalls Chuck Mongelli, who joined Acclaim's motion capture division straight out of school and was one of their early hires. "Working on feature films like that out of a studio on Long Island was very cool."

It wasn't just action blockbusters, either. In 1996, Woody Allen's *Everyone Says I Love You* used the company's proprietary system in a funeral parlour sequence where a cadaver's ashes retake human form and dance to the song "Enjoy Yourself (It's Later Than You Think)". "There was a lot of excitement about movies," recalls Robert Davidsen, who joined Acclaim in 1994 and later took over from Schafer as director of R&D. "I don't think that was our original intention but, when the movie industry saw what we were capable of achieving, it was a logical progression. While movies only needed a minute or two of realistic animated movements, videogames needed hours of intricate motions. We just had so much experience in making it happen. It was also a big company morale booster. I remember when the *Batman Forever* movie came out, the whole company saw it together at the movie theatre and one of the highlights was seeing the credits roll after the movie ended. We all clapped and roared with excitement when the Acclaim names came up."

Acclaim closed its doors in 2004, a victim of its overreaching ambition and the changing fortunes of the videogame industry. As the company entered a terminal decline, its engineers were cut loose. Some had already left to found independent motion capture facility Auvis Studios in Long Island, New York in 2003. Others struggled to find jobs that could make the most of their unique skillset. Scott had seen the writing on the wall early on and headed out to Los Angeles in the late 1990s in the hope of finding movie work. "I was pounding the doors in Hollywood, going to visual effects studios and saying, 'Look at this great stuff we were doing at Acclaim.'" He found there was little enthusiasm.

In the late 1990s, Hollywood was still largely dominated by old school animators who were wary of the new-fangled digital technology coming out of the games sphere. "It was a very daunting time. I found that the Hollywood community simply wasn't interested. The technology was too ahead of its time, too advanced for them. The mindset was too old school. It was one that had been nurtured from the 1920s and they were still using the same technology: someone drawing with their hand. I had a real sense of, 'How am I going to find work?'"

Convergence works in both directions, though. If the movie industry wasn't ready to embrace motion capture, videogames were happy to force feed it to them. In Hawaii, strategically poised halfway between Japan's games and animation industries and the Hollywood studios, a new production was gearing up. It would take motion capture all the way to the multiplex.

* * *

In 1997 Scott received a call from a movie producer who said he was working with formidable Japanese videogame designer Hironobu Sakaguchi on a movie. The creator of the megahit *Final Fantasy* series wanted to create a tie-in film that would be the first theatrically-released feature film to use performance capture for its entire cast. Excited, Scott flew to Hawaii and became first the line producer and then the motion capture director on *Final Fantasy: The Spirits Within*.

The company behind the movie was Square Pictures, a subsidiary of Japanese videogame publisher Square. Bankrolled by the games' division's profits, Square Pictures was a bold attempt to move into film production. It set up brand new film studio in Hawaii, starting with 70 staff housed on two-floors of a skyscraper on Honolulu's waterfront. Four years later, it occupied five floors of the building and had 200 staff including artists and animators from both mediums. Among them was Andy Jones, future Oscar winner for his work on *Avatar*. He was about to take a job on the CG movie *Stuart Little* when the call from Square came in. "Do you want to animate a mouse or a real human being?'" they asked him. There was no contest.

Final Fantasy: The Spirits Within was a loose adaptation of the esoteric Japanese role-playing game series. Set in 2065 on a future earth ravaged by alien phantoms, it tells the story of Dr Aki Ross (voiced by Ming-Na), a scientist who is trying to learn more about the invaders. While humanity's few survivors crowd into bubble-like cities to protect themselves from the ghosts, Ross believes she's on the verge of discovering their purpose. But she'll need to act before the military, led by General Hein (irascibly voiced by James Woods), make the situation much worse. Story-wise the movie owed little to the games other than the creative vision of Sakaguchi. Where the similarities really began was in the use of computer-generated visuals. *Final Fantasy VIII*, which went into production in 1997 with Sakaguchi as executive producer, was the first game in the franchise to employ motion capture for its pre-rendered cut-scene animations. It wasn't much of a leap to envision using the same process to create a fully-fledged CG film in which the digital cast was animated via the power of motion capture.

Back around the turn of the millennium, though, such dreams were ambitious. Audiences had little experience of digital characters. The most famous was probably Jar Jar Binks, the much-hated, motion-captured digital alien with a lilting Caribbean accent who stirred up racial controversy in *Star Wars: The Phantom Menace* in 1999. But he was just a single character in an otherwise conventional human drama. What Sakaguchi envisaged was an entire digital cast in a completely digital movie.

That kind of dreaming came with a price tag. *Final Fantasy: The Spirits Within* needed a budget of $137 million, a large chunk of which was spent on setting up Square Pictures' studio. It also involved 18 months of motion capture work at the famous Hawaii Film Studio production facility where TV shows *Magnum P.I.* and *Baywatch Hawaii* were shot.

It was technologically revolutionary, a blend of acting and animation the like of which had never been seen before on this scale. The centrepiece was Dr Ross herself, whose animation was based on a physical performance by Tori Eldridge, a Broadway dancer and martial artist. Much as in the videogame sphere, in games like *Grand Theft Auto: Vice City*, it was cheaper and easier not to ask celebrity voice talent to don the Lycra suits dotted with ping-pong ball sensors. Instead, their voices were recorded after the motion had been captured using stunt players. It was an odd, if understandable, approach: a performance capture in which the actual performance of A-list stars was too tricky to bother with.

With the data from the shoots fed into the 3D animation software Maya, the team of animators used the movement to help bring Dr Ross to life, tweaking and perfecting her movements, smoothing her lip-synching, and working on her hair to make it flow realistically. Even when the team used hand-animation rather than the performance capture data to achieve some of the more subtle effects, they employed what they'd learned from watching the actors performing during the shoot. "The key to creating human beings was that we actually started with human beings," Scott told Cinefex magazine. It was a statement that would serve as a pointer towards the future of both games and movies.

While the animators had final control over the finished result, it was obvious that motion capture was adding a new dimension to digital characters. Acting was suddenly informing the animation. Motion capture allowed a performer to perform; animation only required an animator to copy. No previous computer-generated animation - from the high-tech work on *Toy Story* to the traditional, hand-drawn output of Disney - had ever been so rooted in such basic humanity.

It was no surprise that Sony, who had published the *Final Fantasy* game series on its Sony Computer Entertainment label in the West, wanted to distribute the movie via Columbia Pictures. Just as in the mid-'90s, the Japanese corporation remained committed to promoting close ties between its various entertainment concerns. "I think *Final Fantasy: The Spirits Within* was one of the ways that Sony was trying to realise that kind of synergy between the games and movie divisions," explains Chris Lee, a producer on the movie and a former executive at Sony subsidiary Columbia Pictures. This kind of crossover was exhilarating and new for most movie studios back in 2001. It was something Sony had been working towards for some time. While at Columbia, Lee was one of the first movie studio executives to be flown out to Japan to see the prototypes for the PlayStation 2. He'd also seen the development of Sony's other interest: the visual effects and character animation company Sony Pictures Imageworks, which had been set up in 1993.

Final Fantasy: The Spirits Within was more than just a movie based on a hit videogame franchise. It was the flagship for a very distinctive cross-pollination between games, movies and the visual effects industry. "I needed cutting edge computer graphic artists," Sakaguchi said at the time. "Back in Japan, I knew a lot of great digital artists who were making commercials, but couldn't fully utilise their knowledge and skills. And in Los Angeles, when I was out there working on *Parasite Eve*, I had a chance to work with the Hollywood digital artists. I realised that by putting these two talents together, it would be a great beginning in trying to overcome these technological hurdles. Building the studio in Honolulu was the best way to bring them all together." Square Pictures was, in other words, at the coal-face of game/movie convergence.

People certainly took notice: in 1999 UK trade paper Screen International ran a front page story under the headline "Synthespians to Invade Hollywood". The article quoted a Columbia Pictures spokesperson who claimed that the company was "ushering in a new form of entertainment". The story also made the potential marketing links between the film and Sony's upcoming PlayStation 2 and its "cinema-quality visuals" transparently clear.

Meanwhile, Square Pictures' Honolulu offices hosted visiting filmmakers. The Wachowski Brothers, then working on *The Matrix*, kept in touch with developments by phone. They would eventually hire Jones to direct the animated *Matrix* prequel *Final Flight of the Osiris* (2003), with Scott supervising the motion capture shoot. He used the same system as on *Final Fantasy: The Spirits Within*. Even more exciting for the production team was the arrival of James Cameron, who flew into Honolulu and watched 20 minutes of footage in a special screening.

Cameron had a vested interest in the movie's technological success. He was already planning his magnum opus *Avatar*. What he saw during his whistle-stop tour of the facility convinced him that performance capture was evolving to a point where it might be of use to him. "I talked to him about it when we were working on *Avatar*," says Jones, who the director knew from his work on *Titanic*'s digital extras. "He said that back then what we were doing on *Final Fantasy* was quite a good evolutionary step in terms of pushing the technology forwards. What I learned on *Final Fantasy* I was able to use on *Avatar*." Jones would win an Oscar for his work on Pandora's blue-skinned, 10-foot-tall Na'vi aliens.

It wasn't just Cameron who was impressed. *Final Fantasy: The Spirits Within*'s synthespians also snagged the imagination of the wider world. Dr Ross, a lithe digital beauty with Eurasian looks, appeared on the cover of US Maxim to launch a 100 Hottest Babes features. "It was their idea and we complied, though we refused to make her bust any bigger than it was," Lee told reporters after the event. "She's in a string bikini, and she looks kind of resentful of it, to be honest. She came in Number 87, and the magazine said to us: 'We feel sorry for the 13 who were beaten out by a cartoon.'"

For the animators, the biggest problem was negotiating the "uncanny valley". It was a term coined by scientists eager to explain people's psychological reactions to humanoid robotic design. In 1970 the Japanese scientist Masahiro Mori claimed that the closer robots come to looking human without quite fooling us, the more repulsive we find them. Something that is almost lifelike is more eerie than an obvious droid like *Star Wars*' R2-D2. The uncanny valley applied to games and films as well as robots. After all, if you're trying to create an immersive, photoreal world you don't want it populated with characters that look like lobotomised zombies.

Final Fantasy: The Spirits Within tried hard to claw its way out of the uncanny valley. The results weren't always perfect and the effort involved was huge. Dr Ross's chin-length hair was so time-consuming to render realistically - the flow of it; the way it bunched up; plus its shading and colour - that the animators decided to give every other character in the movie a short back and sides. Creating an entire universe from the ground up was as exhausting as playing God. If you begin with a void, every atom from the way light bounces off a surface, to the skin pores of your characters, has to be built from scratch. When it worked - as it often did with Dr Ross and her mentor, the aging bearded scientist Dr Sid (voiced by Donald Sutherland) - it was incredible. But just a single moment of awkward lip-syncing, or stilted movement could ruin the illusion. It was a 21st century version of the Freudian uncanny; E.T.A. Hoffman's automata updated for the age of interactive entertainment.

Across the ocean in Beverly Hills, A-list actors were beginning to feel jittery. "Movie Stars Fear Inroads By Upstart Digital Actors," was how the New York Times described the fast-moving situation. The newspaper quoted Tom Hanks worrying about what the future might hold for flesh and blood thespians. "I am very troubled by it," the star claimed. "But it's coming down, man. It's going to happen. And I'm not sure what actors can do about it."

From Square Pictures' perspective it was patently ridiculous. "It really is a silly idea," Jones told Cinefex magazine. "For every character in this movie, we had to use two actors - one for the motion capture sessions and one for the voice. And it is still animation. No matter how good it gets, it will always be animation." But according to others, there was a more political game happening behind the scenes of the movie industry. After all, Square wasn't the only company pursuing performance capture. Others, including Sony Pictures Imageworks, had also been developing a parallel interest in similar technology.

Far from running in tandem, the various research and development teams in the movie and games industries were competing with one another. It didn't help that Square Pictures was seen by some as an upstart new arrival in the movie industry. Ironically, though, this videogames company subsidiary, which had never made a movie before, was in pole position to deliver the first movie comprised entirely of performance captured CG characters. According to Scott, the problem was that Columbia Pictures, Square's distributors, wasn't sure what to do with Sakaguchi or his movie. "Columbia Pictures is owned by Sony and they were told by Sony to distribute this film because Sakaguchi-san was making games for them," he explains. "So the executives at Columbia at the time were like, 'Who is this guy? Why do we have to market this movie by this guy, what is this?' No one was really interested. Was it *Toy Story*? No. A furry animals film? No. They had no idea how to market it."

On its release, *Final Fantasy: The Spirits Within* was greeted with a combination of wonder and total indifference. Critics were united in their acknowledgement of the movie's technical triumph. But they were equally scathing about how spiritless it seemed. The uncanny valley had taken its toll. The sad truth was that, even if it had been shot with live actors, the confused and confusing storyline simply didn't have the necessary appeal to push a $137 million movie into profit. Gamers were left hanging since the film owed little to the role-playing franchise apart from its title and thematic concerns. Non-gamers were baffled by the abstruse script. Its worldwide theatrical gross of $85 million didn't bring the movie close to breaking even. In the aftermath, Square Pictures went out of business. Sakaguchi returned to videogames, his hopes of making a second movie dashed.

As *Final Fantasy: The Spirits Within* was nearing completion, though, some of Hollywood's biggest, most technologically-savvy directors were becoming increasingly interested in using performance capture. Among them was Robert Zemeckis, the filmmaker who had merged live action and animation to brilliant effect in *Who Framed Roger Rabbit* and who had used Sony Imageworks' digital expertise in movies like *Cast Away*. Having seen the potential of performance capture, Zemeckis was already beginning to consider the possibility of a feature film. That desire crystallised in 2001 when Tom Hanks sent him a copy of Chris Van Allsburg's children's book *The Polar Express*. With its story of a kid visiting the North Pole and meeting Santa, the book didn't seem suited to either live-action or animation. The solution? Performance capture. Sony Imageworks told Zemeckis that they could deliver him the next generation of performance capture, a system that could handle full body and facial capture simultaneously.

Opening in 2004, *The Polar Express* brought performance capture to a wide audience. Reading the excitable coverage surrounding its release, you'd be forgiven for thinking that Hollywood had invented this new technology itself. "When Bob Zemeckis started talking about mo-cap, and all of Hollywood was big on it," recalls former CAA agent Larry Shapiro, "me and my colleagues were like, 'Yeah, it's game technology. It started in the games industry five years ago, what's the big deal?'" Certainly few thought to mention the irony of Tom Hanks playing six digital characters in the movie given his earlier concerns over the impact of the "synthespian" revolution on human actors.

While *Final Fantasy: The Spirits Within* had bombed, it had been a fertile R&D lab. It had helped this new technology which evolved from the medical industry, through videogames and into film takes its first baby steps. For Scott it was a moment tinged with both sadness and excitement. Sakaguchi had failed to find the audience he needed, but out of the ashes of *Final Fantasy: The Spirits Within* had come an acceptance of motion capture as a filmmaking technique. A whole generation of artists, animators and technologists were now starting to work together to create photorealistic digital characters. Where would that take both movies and games?

* * *

Andy Serkis was originally supposed to play Gollum's voice. But when he stepped in front of the camera, he became the poster boy for a new kind of acting. Back in 2000, when Peter Jackson was shooting the second instalment of his *The Lord of the Rings* trilogy, the London thesp flew out to New Zealand to join the production. The brief was simple. Gollum, the schizophrenic hobbit of J.R.R. Tolkien's novels, would be created by a team of animators led by industry veteran Randy Cook. They were planning to bring him to life on-screen as a CG creation. Serkis would voice him, recording his dialogue in the vocal booth

Except, it didn't turn out like that.

One day, while Jackson was blocking out scenes on-set Serkis offered to stand in so that the actors had someone to react to. Slipping into character, the actor became Gollum, a misshapen hobbit whose pursuit of the One Ring has taken its toll on his mind and body. Jackson decided two things on the spot: he wanted Serkis to play Gollum in body as well as voice; and he wanted to be able to direct Gollum, not Serkis, in real-time. It was a decision that would illustrate the incredible potential of performance capture technology.

With Cook's plans for a key-frame animated Gollum shelved, a team of motion capture experts, facial animators, and prosthetics artists would instead bring the character to life. Among them was Scott, fresh from his work on *Final Fantasy: The Spirits Within*, who signed on as the film's motion capture supervisor. It was an incredibly daunting challenge: "This one lone character had the emotional, psychological and physical depth of one of the most complex personalities in literary history," the motion capture technician realised. But it was only going to be possible thanks to a new kind of convergence that was happening.

"Performance capture is the biggest example of videogame technology going into movies," Scott explains. "What Peter wanted to do was direct Gollum. He didn't want to direct Andy. This is the big difference. He wanted to look at a monitor and see Gollum on that monitor in real-time and be able to direct him. If Andy was scratching his head on stage, Peter could sit in his chair and see Gollum scratching his head on the monitor. That was the moment for Peter when he knew this was the way to do it. There's no interpretation here, I'm directing this guy and what I see is what I get. That was the game element coming through - the interactive technology from the videogames industry."

Gollum was a stunning, early crossover between these two mediums and his success showed just how important the flow between the two has become: not just in terms of technology but also in terms of artistry, acting and storytelling. Serkis was forging a new kind of acting, one where the actor donned the digital skin of a CG character via the performance capture process. It was part of a monumental shift in both mediums: cinema could finally create believable, emotionally resonant CG characters and videogames could too.

Scott knew they were making cinema history, using the same technology he'd seen grow out of Acclaim's work in the '90s. "I told Andy, 'This is acting for the 21st century. You have an opportunity here. This is the golden age all over again. You can be the Charlie Chaplin of this medium. You can be the one guy who in the future when we look back, will be seen as someone who defined this medium.' I think Andy really got that. He's a star who shines bright. The key is that he really embraces this new technology."

Serkis didn't need Scott's encouragement. He could instantly see how performance capture was going to change both industries. Not only did he return to the gimp suit again and again - including playing the eponymous giant ape in *King Kong*, runaway chimp Caesar in *Rise of the Planet of the Apes*, and Captain Haddock in *The Adventures of Tintin: The Secret of the Unicorn* - he also followed the technology back to its gaming roots.

In 2006 Serkis teamed up with Ninja Theory, a British developer based in Cambridge, to play the villain in the beat-'em-up game *Heavenly Sword*. He also introduced Ninja Theory's creative director Tameem Antoniades to the Weta Digital team. *Heavenly Sword* would utilise a new head-mounted rig that Weta had designed to capture actors' facial expressions. When Jackson showed the results to James Cameron, he decided the results were good enough to use in his upcoming *Avatar* project. Here was the flow of ideas between games to movies reaching its full potential.

On Ninja Theory's next game *Enslaved: Odyssey to the West* Serkis and Antoniades worked with screenwriter Alex Garland and actors Lindsey Shaw and Richard Ridings. They created an epic post-apocalyptic story that was cinematic not just in its (virtual) camera moves, but also in its attention to the nuances of character that a human actor could tease out of a videogame script's cut scenes. For Antoniades, it was the performance capture process itself that grounded the game's emotional content. "Ironically, performance capture is actually about stripping away the technology and bringing back the humanity," he suggests. "In creating any entertainment, the whole purpose is to give you a suspension of disbelief and transport you into another world. The things we respond to the most are people. We respond to the intonation of their voice, their movements, their body language. We understand people. In *Enslaved* we wanted to keep dialogue to an absolute minimum and understand the characters souls through their eyes, through their expressions, through their voice. It's one of those things gamers don't believe you need in a videogame until you actually see it."

What games like *Enslaved* and CG characters like Gollum show is that performance capture has already demolished the boundaries between both games and movies. Roles in both industries are now being reversed: games designers are increasingly finding themselves thinking about camera angles, actors' performances and story elements. Meanwhile, high-end film directors like Jackson, Cameron and Steven Spielberg are regularly using the tools of interactive entertainment to build fictional CG characters and virtual worlds. Performance capture is the crucible where both sides meet, a technology that takes the best of both industries and employs it in the service of giving the virtual a humanity it would otherwise lack.

What that means for gameplay as well as for filmic videogame cut scenes is huge, as both *Heavy Rain* and Rockstar's more recent *L.A. Noire* suggests. Casting players as a hardboiled '40s detective in the city of angels, *L.A. Noire* asks you to spend more time interrogating suspects than shooting bad guys as you try to solve homicide cases. Watching a suspect's performance-captured body language and facial animation is paramount if you're going to intuit when they're telling the truth and when they're withholding information. In its use of real actors - including *Mad Men*'s Aaron Staton and Greg Grunberg from *Heroes* - *L.A. Noire* doesn't just attempt to look photorealistic. It is also trying to redefine the dramatic scope of interactive entertainment too.

Ask gamers what's moved them recently and you'll hear tales of love triangles between characters in the *Mass Effect* games; the shockingly unexpected death of Eli Vance in *Half-Life 2*; *Heavy Rain*'s bleak nihilism; or *Red Dead Redemption*'s grandiose take on the death throes of the Old West. All share a common thread: performance capture's ability to give virtual characters the heft of a real-life actor's nuance. For videogames, the technology couldn't have come soon enough. Moving towards a greater maturity and aping the cinematic visuals the film industry, videogames began to rely upon performance capture to create believable characters with real humanity.

Despite how groundbreaking they were in their era, Mario had been little more than a mascot and Lara was just an over-inflated sex doll with a butter-wouldn't-melt English accent. The new avatars - from *Heavy Rain*'s Ethan Mars to the eponymous hero of *Alan Wake*, the survivors of the *Left 4 Dead* games, or the detectives and criminals of *L.A. Noire* - aren't mere ciphers. They're characters grounded in human performances with all the human subtlety and nuance that that suggests. Many of today's game developers don't just want us to play; they're asking us to feel something too.

"Performance capture is a necessary tool to reach a certain level of connection with the player," says former Acclaim employee Chuck Mongelli, who became head of motion capture production and operations at Rockstar Games. "It's not all about gameplay and what you can do. People want to step away from their lives and get absorbed in a different kind of world, establish relationships with the characters, know more about who they are, and where they came from. I think we are only scratching the surface of human interaction with virtual storytelling."

Performance capture is arguably just one aspect of a much wider revolution that's occurring in both industries through digital filmmaking, virtual production techniques and CG assets. Film, that old analogue medium, has been dragged into the 21st century kicking and screaming. As a result, the process of shooting blockbuster movies and making blockbuster games has never been closer. Forget Digital Pictures' attempt to digitise raw film footage. Today's convergence is one that's happening in the virtual realm and it's one that is redefining the limits of what is possible in both movies and games.

Increasingly, blockbuster movies look like games, just as videogames ape blockbuster movies. Ever since the mid-2000s - when films like *Sky Captain and the World of Tomorrow* (2004), *Sin City* (2005) and *300* (2006) - arrived, cinema has frequently used virtual sets and digital backdrops that make movies seem, aesthetically at least, much closer to videogames than ever before. What both mediums now share is a "virtuality" that advances in filmmaking and videogame technology have made possible.

"We don't call it convergence, we call it fusion," says Jim Riley, executive vice-president of development and a senior VFX supervisor at Stargate Studios in South Pasadena, California. Back in the 80s, Riley co-created, wrote and directed *Night Trap* with its groundbreaking use of full motion video. Today, Stargate Studios provides the VFX for, among other productions, the TV shows *The Walking Dead*, *24* and *Heroes*. Stargate's green screen Virtual Backlot technology - which allows their VFX technicians to create high-definition, 3D exteriors that filmmakers can use instead of travelling to distant locations - is illustrative of the kind of virtual production techniques that are now being used in the film industry. Rather than have the expense of flying a film crew from LA. to Times Square in New York for a sequence in the pilot episode of *Heroes*, the filmmakers simply shot Hiro (Masi Oka) against a green screen in LA. They then used real-life footage from Times Square, digitally manipulated, to put a background behind the actor.

Together with virtual production software like Orad: SmartSet - which allows VFX technicians to create 3D virtual sets - these techniques are revolutionising film production. Indeed, working in the VFX industry today can often feel a lot like making or even playing videogames, not least of all when interactive technology like game engines are used to light the virtual sets. "In a weird way, I'm in the ultimate real-image videogame in this digital VFX world," Riley explains. The groundwork that *Night Trap* and FMV represented has come to fruition in totally unexpected ways. "We're at a point now where we're working with videogame engines to manipulate real images to make movies. We're using the technology of the game world, a real time ability to manipulate the image. Because the power of that technology has gotten to the point where it can be applied to full resolution images, we're now mixing movies like you mix sound with the technology. The simple analogy is that it's like visual mixing. In a way the convergence of the videogame business with the TV business has come about from a technical standpoint."

In other areas of filmmaking, the rise of the virtual seems unstoppable. CG characters, pre-visualisation technology and virtual production tools are transforming filmmaking in ways that are still being defined. As Wired magazine put it in 2009: "High-end filmmakers aren't just making movies these days. They're building virtual worlds before shooting a single frame of film, using digital tools to blur the lines between animation and live-action, virtual sets and physical soundstage, photorealistic cartoon characters and motion-captured human beings."

Videogames can't help but benefit from this sudden shift of emphasis in the movie business. As the virtual becomes interchangeable with the real, the gaming industry has raised its sights. Film is no longer an alien, analogue medium as it was back in the days of FMV. Now it's digital too. The materiality of cinema itself has been exploded. No longer are filmmakers constrained by physical reality: digital CG offers them entry into a virtual sphere where anything is possible. Even actors - the last vestige of the world of flesh and physicality - can be transported into these binary universes of ones and zeroes thanks to performance capture. As movies begin to share the virtual virtuosity of games' visual imaginings, games are realising their potential for telling cinematic stories. EA and Spielberg's great challenge - a game that will make you cry on level 17 - has come to pass and it's clear that the emotional peaks of gaming over the last five or six years have largely been thanks to technology that has evolved out of both mediums. In 2009, we saw the first glimpse of what that could mean not just for games but for cinema too in a movie that was billed as a "game changer".

* * *

It took James Cameron 14 years to make *Avatar*. Quite a bit of that time was spent playing with videogames. Back in 1990, when Cameron and Larry Kasanoff first set up their production company Lightstorm, the two men had a smart understanding of how the game industry could benefit them. There was a lucrative *Terminator 2 - Judgement Day* coin-op game from Midway based on Cameron's hit blockbuster; and there was also a licensing deal with Acclaim. The Glen Cove publisher bought the rights to make games from the director's movies, beginning with the Arnold Schwarzenegger action comedy *True Lies* in 1994. "All the action of the movie megahit," promised the videogame's ads, "and none of the romance!"

When Kasanoff quit Lightstorm to build his *Mortal Kombat* empire, Cameron hooked up with Jon Landau, former executive vice-president of feature film production at Twentieth Century Fox. Together they'd break box office records with *Titanic* in 1997. It didn't get a videogame, although the director did collaborate with Fox Interactive on James Cameron's *Titanic Explorer*, a belated, three-CD virtual tour of the ill-fated ship using the sets created for the movie.

Cameron had a savvy sense of how the line between movies and interactive entertainment was blurring. His only disappointment was that CG imagery wasn't evolving fast enough for his purposes. When he took his treatment for sci-fi epic *Avatar* to the technicians at special effects house Digital Domain in 1995, they were blunt about its chances. "If we try to make this," they told him, "we're doomed. It can't be done. The technology doesn't exist." Like David Cage, Cameron found his creative vision running into the brick wall of the technologically impossible.

Still, Cameron knew that if he waited long enough, technology would catch up. So, between 1997 and 2005, the filmmaker took a hiatus from blockbusters. It wasn't so much a holiday as a sabbatical during which he was obsessed with one thing: his dream of an alien planet called Pandora. Everything he did - from diving to the bottom of the deep blue sea to film the Titanic wreck with a 3D camera for *Ghosts of the Abyss* (2003) or visiting Hawaii to see Sakaguchi's team working on *Final Fantasy: The Spirits Within* - was part of his obsession. Even when he was finally convinced that the technology was ready for him, *Avatar* proved so pioneering that it often felt like nothing was ready at all. "I liken the experience of making *Avatar* to jumping off a cliff and knitting the parachute on the way down," he joked.

Avatar stands as the greatest example of technological convergence between games and movies so far, a film enabled by digital technology and dedicated to the creation of a virtual world from the ground up. Lightstorm's business relationships on the movie illustrate just how involved the production was: they collaborated with Sony on a new 3D camera; they teamed up with Microsoft to build a digital asset management system; they worked with Ubisoft on a tie-in videogame; they utilised Weta Digital's performance capture expertise; and they set up a movie production deal with Twentieth Century Fox. More than just a movie, *Avatar* became the interface point between several different industries: movies, videogames, performance capture and CG visual effects.

For Cameron's backers at Fox, *Avatar* represented a slamdunk for digital filmmaking and IMAX 3D spectacle. The planet Pandora pushed the envelope of visual effects technology and invited audiences into a 3D realm inhabited by performance-captured CG aliens. It also offered non-gamers a taste of the kind of immersive virtual worlds familiar from the realm of interactive entertainment. According to a report by CNN, some cinemagoers were so overwhelmed by the experience that they didn't want to leave and started suffering from depression after the credits rolled.

The lush, 3D jungle of Pandora scooped most of the attention surrounding the movie. But the planet would have been nothing without its inhabitants, the blue-skinned, towering aliens known as the Na'vi. Led by actress Zoë Saldana, they were the centrepiece of the film's emotional heft since they were virtual characters who had the ability to convince us they were more than just a collection of bytes and bits. Using performance capture, Cameron finally delivered on the promise of CG characters. Here were virtual beings who had the presence and nuance of the actors who embodied them.

The key was Weta Digital's facial capture work, which shot the actors' performances with a single-camera facial-capture rig mounted on their skull caps. It was then finessed by a team of animators led by Andy Jones, who used the facial capture data to map expressions onto the faces of CG models. As with games, the aim in using performance capture technology was much the same: Cameron didn't want to capture his cast's movement as much as their humanity. "Actors," said the director, "don't do motion. They do emotion." Using CG characters to make us cry on level 17 was becoming a reality in the multiplex as well as on the Xbox and PlayStation.

Avatar was the moment that Hollywood and videogames finally reached the same page. Much of the technology that powered Cameron's movie had evolved in the movie and games industry in parallel. Interactive entertainment had indeed been a fecund R&D lab for the filmmaker's vision. Thanks to that, *Avatar* offered a tantalising glimpse of where convergence between the two industries might take us as storytellers in both mediums start to create immersive, virtual 3D worlds populated by performance-captured, CG avatars. "After all," said *Avatar* producer Jon Landau, "what do filmmakers do, if not create virtual worlds?"

Avatar proved to the Hollywood studios that the audience for live action blockbuster spectacles would happily sit through a movie that looked like an extended videogame cut scene where the environments and many of the characters were CG. In one stroke, *Avatar* narrowed the aesthetic gap between games and movies forever. The movies that follow it - from Cameron's planned sequels to big budget CG, performance capture studio projects like *The Adventures of Tintin: The Secret of the Unicorn* - are closing it even further.

Exposed to the world of videogames, even filmmaking itself is mutating. Cameron wasn't just using computers to create Pandora. He was also working with a virtual camera that let him film inside the non-existent world of Pandora. On the motion capture sound stage, he saw nothing of Pandora other than a few props and his cast standing around in their Lycra suits. When he looked through his virtual camera - an LCD monitor fitted with a bank of controls that acted like a window onto the virtual world stored inside the computer mainframe - the director could see something completely different. What were waiting for him were the actors' CG counterparts standing a low-res version of the alien planet rendered in real-time.

The director could guide his camera through Pandora's virtual world, filming performance-captured CG "actors" and setting up camera angles, lighting and shots at the touch of a button. Like a gamer moving through *Halo: Reach*'s corridors or the Cambodian jungles of *Call of Duty: Black Ops*, the director moved freely through this 3D space. Instead of a gun, he carried a camera and the only thing he was shooting was digital film. "If you came to our set," says *Avatar* producer Jon Landau, "Jim Cameron is out there with what we call a virtual camera and it looks like he's playing a giant videogame. And he's looking around that world and he's zooming in and the performances that we capture are playing back. That's really what it's like." On *Avatar,* the lines between the two mediums started blurring as never before. "We're building the same world that a videogame might build," says Landau, "but instead of playing it through a console, we're playing it through a projector in the movie theatre."

Orson Welles famously claimed that working on a film was like playing with the biggest electric train set a boy ever had. *Avatar* was like playing the most advanced first person shooter ever invented. At a flick of a switch Cameron's virtual camera could mimic a Steadicam, a dolly shot or a 100-foot crane move. Lenses and lighting could be adjusted instantly. No longer did the director need to wait for locations to be cleared or sets to be dressed. Once the virtual world was ready and the actors' performances were captured and applied to their CG alter egos, he could glide through his virtual set however he wanted. "In the past, filmmakers would hire a carpenter and go out and buy some lumber," says Landau. "Now we're hiring a CG artist and some computers. They're building our environments like that."

It wasn't the first time that Cameron had turned to videogames to push the envelope of filmmaking. As early as 1988, when he was making sci-fi thriller *The Abyss*, he'd hired David A. Smith, programmer of one of the first 3D games. Smith's 1988 Macintosh game *The Colony* was one of the first videogames to try and immerse a player in a 360 degree environment. Cameron used Smith's expert knowhow to build a primitive virtual camera that could let him pre-visualise scenes for *The Abyss*. Later, the game-maker would retool *The Colony*'s engine into Virtus Walkthrough Pro. That pre-visualisation (pre-viz) software became widely used in Hollywood and counted film director Brian De Palma, the director of *Mission: Impossible*, among its many fans.

While pre-viz used CG visuals to give filmmakers a preview of their movie before it was shot - a kind of moving storyboard of the action - *Avatar*'s virtual cameras were integral to its actual shooting. Using the technology, what Cameron saw wasn't pre-viz but a low-res post-viz: a real-time glimpse of how his CG assets, performance-captured CG characters and live actors would look together on-screen. His virtual camera system, known as Simulcam, let him see his physical actors and CG assets integrated together in the shot. It was the Hollywood director's answer to *Second Life*.

Gamers were already way ahead of Cameron in this regard. In many respects, *Avatar* played like a high-end, Hollywood version of the machinima ("machine cinema") that fans produced using assets from videogames. Many of these do-it-yourself movies - such as *Red Vs. Blue*, a series of shorts made using tools and assets from *Halo* - were shot inside the game worlds themselves. They were largely jokey novelties but *Red Vs. Blue* proved so popular that Microsoft struck a deal with the creators and let them produce a cottage industry of DVDs and merchandise. What they pointed towards, though, was the potential for creating CG movies using videogame engines.

Cameron and Landau weren't blind to the crossover that they were part of. Indeed, both men are on the advisory board of virtual world developer Multiverse. As Blizzard's multiplayer online role playing game *World of Warcraft* was making headlines by breaking through the 10 million subscribers mark, Landau gave a keynote speech at 2008's Virtual Worlds Expo in Los Angeles. "What we are doing, virtual production in a virtual world, right now it's at a business-to-business level," Landau told the Expo audience. "Ultimately, it's going to be at a consumer level. People [will] go in and record their stories and present their stories, just like they do [now] with YouTube. Virtual worlds are another avenue for people to be creative and tell stories."

Cameron could see the appeal of that. Virtual reality, that quaint '90s fad involving headsets and control gloves, had returned with a vengeance - updated for a new era. Consumers wanted immersive, 3D experiences and even the shock and awe of *Avatar* could only offer so much. It was linear and non-interactive, while anyone who visited Pandora wanted to stay and play in it. "When people see a movie that's really immersive, like *The Lord of the Rings*, for example, they don't want to stop living in that world," the director explained. "What if you could just go to your computer, then just click and stay in that world?"

When Lightstorm teamed up with French game publisher Ubisoft to create *Avatar: The Game*, they hoped to give viewers exactly that kind of on-going, immersive experience. It avoided the usual logistic pitfalls of licensed games: Ubisoft had access to Cameron himself, as well as the production's assets. The title was supposed to herald a revolution in the traditional relationship between developers and filmmakers.

"No longer does the videogame studio have to build the assets: because we already have them," says Landau of how *Avatar*'s digital pipeline could potentially change the development of licensed games from an afterthought to part of a bigger production canvas. "If the developers want a [Pandoran flower] we can give it to them. If they want a model of an avatar, we give it to them. They don't have to build it. Our process makes their process more efficient. Ubisoft came to us on the first *Avatar* game and said they wanted to have an ATV type vehicle that wasn't in the movie. We got our designers to design it and we put it in the background of the movie and Ubisoft put it into the game and then Mattel made a toy out of it!" Here was what was possible in a transmedia franchise where games, movies and toy designers all shared the same digital assets.

Yet *Avatar: The Game* was a huge disappointment. Dull gameplay and a lack of 3D-ready TVs that could take advantage of its optional 3D visuals meant it failed to make much of an impression. Even with so much momentum behind it, convergence was still liable to experience hiccups. "It was a disappointment from our standpoint too," admits Landau. "I think - and I'm not blaming Ubisoft in this in any way - we went after the technology and the idea that we could share all these things and we lost sight of the game's story until too late."

With its $2 billion gross, *Avatar* was described in Hollywood as a game changer. Certainly it proved to the studios that adult audiences were willing to embrace action movies that were predominantly CG animated, much as kids had responded to Pixar's CG cartoons. Films set in virtual worlds and populated by virtual characters could have the same thrill and emotional impact as a live action blockbuster. *Avatar* may yet change the face of videogames too. Two movie sequels are already in production and more videogames will inevitably follow. *Avatar* is a franchise that could run and run.

Meanwhile, both Cameron and Landau have frequently spoken about their desire to use *Avatar* as the basis of a massively multiplayer online (MMO) world, a virtual realm populated not by computer controlled AI characters but by the avatars of living, breathing players sharing the same virtual space. Like *Avatar*'s use of live actors to bring CG characters to life, an MMO would ensure that almost every character on Pandora had human agency behind them.

"What you want is for people to become immersed, to feel engaged," says Landau. "You want them to feel they have a stake in whatever you're doing and MMOs are a great way to do that [...] Technology is now unlocking the doors of people's imaginations. Everything is possible. You are no longer limited in what you can or can't imagine."

From that perspective, blockbuster directors like Cameron or Spielberg can no longer afford to simply see themselves as filmmakers. They're now franchise creators working in a digital age where their stories have the power to cross platforms and mediums and even become non-linear experiences. For Cameron, that potential is clearly exciting.

"Imagine a movie in which the viewer is swept along by a narrative, following the action from place to place, but without the intervention of a camera," he has suggested. "You can choose which character to watch in a scene, as if you're an invisible witness standing there while a real event plays out. This is still years away, at a level of realism people would consider cinematic, but certainly not decades away. I can imagine the dense fantasy worlds I like to create for movies having an equal or greater life in a world of interactive play, authored by others, in a partnership. Of course, add massive multiplayer capability to this, and people will never leave their homes."

Other filmmakers have tried such things before. In 2005 the Wachowskis collaborated with Warner Bros. Interactive and developer Monolith Productions on *The Matrix Online*, an MMO that continued the movie trilogy's storyline with episodic content. Although considered a flop, it ran for four years until 2009. An *Avatar* MMO, though, might have the jump even on *The Matrix*'s videogame-friendly universe thanks to its high quotient of digital assets, the movie's use of 3D and the fact that storylines wouldn't be hampered by quite as much mythology as *The Matrix* was saddled with.

Avatar's grosses certainly prove that tapping into the kind of virtual world familiar to Generation Xbox, the core movie-going constituency of 13- to 34-year-old males, is insanely lucrative. Gamers found in *Avatar* a blockbuster movie in 3D that felt like a game they wanted to play. Non-gamers saw in *Avatar* a sci-fi universe that seemed familiar and compelling because it had been percolated and matured via several decades of videogame aesthetics. Discovering crossover appeal, *Avatar* suggested that the movie industry can no longer ignore the predominance of videogames in pop culture, nor the convergence of mediums that their ascendancy points towards. *Avatar* is Fox's *Star Wars* for the 21st Century: a popular sci-fi franchise in an entertainment landscape where virtual worlds, MMOs, videogames, 3D movies and social networking are offering a new kind of digital immersion.

Games eclipsed movies as the biggest entertainment medium on the planet many years ago based on box office revenues. Now it's time for movies to catch up. *Avatar* changed Hollywood in many ways. Not least of all because it exposed everyone, even those in the audience who hadn't picked up a joypad since playing *Pong* in the mid-1970s, to the epic virtual worlds that are at the heart of today's interactive entertainment experiences. In Hollywood's eyes, we're all gamers now.

EPILOGUE

The Next Level

"For anyone in this business to not acknowledge the reality of the current forces at play would be doing the industry a disservice. All of us are looking for ways to make sure this isn't the time when theatrical movie-going really does go away."

Adam Fogelson, chairman of Universal Pictures, March 2011

Hollywood is in crisis. If this was a disaster movie, studio execs would be craning their necks skywards and dropping their iPhones as the meteor hurtled towards them. Or they might be cowering under the tables in the middle of their power lunches at The Grill on the Alley as UFOs reduce Beverly Hills to rubble. Except this is no Roland Emmerich movie. In fact, movies - of the disaster variety or otherwise - just ain't what they used to be... and that's the problem.

In 2010, US box office attendance sank 5% to its second-lowest level in more than a decade. Theatres sold a disappointing 1.34 billion tickets, although revenues remained around the same at $10.6 billion thanks to the inflationary premium placed on 3D movie tickets. Meanwhile, in 2011 attendance in North America was down a further 4.4% - the lowest number since 1995. Falling attendance is the cancer that many studio heads fear could eat away the traditional movie business from within. What it points to is the stuff of Hollywood nightmares: people don't love movies like they used to.

Just as in any self-respecting disaster movie, every pundit has an opinion on what's causing the threat of imminent destruction. It could be the quality of the movies themselves. Sequelitis - and its cousin, reboot fever - have worn down audiences pining for originality. "So far there is just nothing terribly compelling about what we're delivering as an industry," Michael Lynton, chief executive of Sony Pictures Entertainment, told the Los Angeles Times in March 2011. Or it could be the rise of the internet: online streaming, peer-to-peer piracy and web-produced content are hurting movie attendance and causing a slump in DVD sales.

Or it could be a symptom of Generation Xbox's changing tastes. When your core demographic is torn between spending $20 on a two-hour IMAX

3D movie or $60 on a videogame that will give them 40 hours of interactive play (plus the potential for unlimited online multiplayer socialising), it's pretty obvious why cinema attendance is plummeting faster than a base-jumping elephant. Videogames, a vibrant, youthful medium, are beating on the movie industry - culturally, artistically and in terms of popularity. To rework that old gamer meme: "Hollywood, All Your Base Are Belong To Us..." [sic]

Today the movie industry is running scared from videogames, just like it was back in 1982. Only this time Hollywood isn't nervously watching the rise of a brash, 8-bit upstart like Atari. Its competitor has evolved into a mature industry that's established itself as both a credible business and a standalone entertainment medium for more than three decades. Once upon a time, interactive entertainment was seen as a niche hobby. Today it's become a permanent feature in the media landscape.

That landscape is changing rapidly too. Those visionaries in Hollywood back in the '90s who warned about the rise of the "Information Super Highway" never imagined how revolutionary it would be. The internet, social media, online gaming and digital distribution have all shifted the playing field in unexpected ways - so much so that those born before Generation Xbox are still struggling to keep up. Hollywood knows that videogames are impossible to ignore. "Today you can walk into any president of a studio's office and if you have a really good videogame they won't dismiss it out of hand," says Alex Young, producer of *The A-Team* and *Die Hard 5*. "They'll take you as seriously as if you're walking in with a bestselling book or a huge comic book title. It's now perfectly legitimate."

At the same time, filmmakers are keenly aware of the need to appeal to a generation that has been weaned with a gamepad in its hands. Just as MTV revolutionised the visual aesthetics of Hollywood filmmakers in the '80s and '90s, videogames are doing much the same for today's cinema. From *Sucker Punch* to *Inception* to *Avatar*, movies are appealing to an audience that is comfortable sliding between the real and the virtual, both visually and conceptually.

Companies like French videogame giant Ubisoft are now facing a huge opportunity: the chance to take their interactive IP into other mediums. Today, a blockbuster videogame franchise like *Assassin's Creed* can spawn tie-in novels, comics and merchandise. But can it also support a movie? Ubisoft believe so. In 2009, not long after its acquisition of visual effects studio Hybride, Ubisoft dipped a toe in the water of film production, shooting live-action shorts for its *Assassin's Creed* franchise. In 2011 the company announced Ubisoft Motion Pictures, a Paris-based film division headed up by Jean-Julien Baronnet, former chief executive of Luc Besson's French movie studio EuropaCorp. Not long later, Ubisoft signed a deal with Sony for an *Assassin's Creed* movie.

Does Ubisoft's chief executive Yannis Mallat agree the relationship between the movie and game industries is changing? Very definitely. "Not only is it changing, more importantly, we are actively participating in this change, even modelling parts of it," he says. "On many levels, the gaming and movie industry have a lot in common. Technologically and creatively speaking, both mediums use similar processes to develop visually compelling stories. Recent advancements have made it possible for us to create visually enticing games akin to what you might see today in movies, especially when CGI is involved. We are no longer limited by the same technological drawbacks from 10 or even five years ago. Our creators now have at their disposals the technological support to bring their ideas to life on a more grandiose scale. The boundaries that use to define our respective industries are blurring and the similarities between the two can sometimes be astonishing!"

Even still, Ubisoft know that taking a videogame IP into Hollywood can be problematic. After all, they watched Jerry Bruckheimer and Walt Disney Pictures fail to turn the lucrative *Prince of Persia* franchise into a blockbuster worthy of *Pirates of the Caribbean* in 2010. Despite taking $335 million at the box office worldwide, *Prince of Persia: The Sands of Time* underperformed since, with marketing included, it cost around $300 million to make.

By establishing their own film division in Ubisoft Motion Pictures, the company hopes to retain control over its game brands as they head onto the big screen. They're not content to take film producers' money and run. They want a creative partnership. When a franchise like *Assassin's Creed* is worth north of $1 billion, why would they sign away creative control?

"By managing the production of our films, we'll be ensuring they will reflect the brands accurately, offer our fans new content while expanding beyond the games' primary target audience," Mallat explains. "Throughout this process, it is key that we keep ownership and retain control over the film content. And yes, we do expect to work with other studios on the development of our projects, and eventually collaborate on the pre-casting, pre-budget and script. It is this very collaboration with professionals from the movie industry which will enable us to further augment the content we develop in our games and fully take advantage of the next generation platforms."

Obviously, Ubisoft isn't about to turn into a major motion picture studio like Universal or Warner Bros. Producing a few short films or even a feature can't compare with launching international movies on a weekly basis. What they want to do, however, is meet the Hollywood studios on equal terms. For the videogame industry it's a momentous event, the culmination of 40 years of growth and evolution. For Hollywood it's inevitably terrifying. Trade gossip about the Ubisoft/Sony *Assassin's Creed* movie deal suggests that the games company has an unprecedented amount of control over the project - something that allegedly scared off other interested studios including DreamWorks, Universal and Warner Bros. To achieve that level of control there are unconfirmed reports that the videogame company has spent its own money bankrolling part of the development process. Whatever happens with the *Assassin's Creed* movie, it's clear that we're witnessing something unique: a foreshock, a tremor in the tectonic plates of the entertainment industry. It's a shakeup in which videogame companies are stepping into Hollywood, demanding to be taken seriously as equal partners.

Microsoft failed to achieve that with *Halo* in 2006. But in retrospect, the aborted *Halo* movie looks like an early reconnaissance into hostile territory; a first manoeuvre in a much bigger campaign. If the *Halo* deal had happened in 2011 instead of 2006 - following the incredible success of videogames *Halo 3: ODST* and *Halo: Reach* - the studios might have better appreciated the value of the brand. In the years since 2006, a lot has changed. The videogame industry is no longer the little brother of the movie biz. It's come of age.

When a videogame company finally jumps into the movie production arena and scores a hit, the era of crappy game-to-movie outings will finally be over. There is no reason why a decent movie can't be made from a videogame, regardless of the fact that both mediums privilege different modes of narrative and audience participation. Videogames now have rich enough worlds to support a Hollywood movie set in their universes: it's easy to imagine a film based on the fall of the planet Reach in *Halo*, for instance. They've also begun developing deep enough characters, like the cocksure hero Nathan Drake and his roguish mentor Sully from the *Uncharted* series, that you could base a three act drama around. It's not that videogames and movies are unsuited to each other. It's just that their marriage was forced too early, back in a period when games involved fat plumbers jumping over piranha plants.

Today's games offer filmmakers more than just a brand name (although, ironically, today's studios are more interested in brands than ever - witness

Transformers, *Battleship* and the mooted *Asteroids* movie). Comic book fans will already know how this story ends. After all, it was only once Marvel Studios established itself as a Hollywood player that the phrase "comic-book movie" stopped being something cinemagoers ran in terror from. Compared like-for-like with superhero blockbusters, videogame movies are currently stalled somewhere around 1998, waiting for *Blade* to happen. After that comes *X-Men*, *Spider-Man* and ultimately something as critically-acclaimed as *The Dark Knight*. Movies based on videogames will get there. It's just a matter of time.

What about Hollywood? Are the studios - and the mega-corporations behind them - totally blind to the shift that's happening in popular culture? Apparently not. Back in the '70s, Warner Communications led the charge of Hollywood into videogames and got its fingers burnt. Now, Time-Warner is taking another bite of the cherry with Warner Bros. Interactive Entertainment.

The division was founded in 2004 with Jason Hall as senior vice president. Hall, former chief executive of Monolith Productions, the creators of the *Matrix Online* game, found himself in a unique position. Arriving at Warner Bros. senior management board meetings dressed in a baseball cap and an Atari T-shirt, while his peers wore Hugo Boss, Hall was given the task of opening up a new revenue stream for the multi-faceted media corporation.

Unlike in the '70s when Warner blindly bought into an industry they knew nothing about and had no strategy for growing; or in the '90s when the company set up a videogames division simply to license its intellectual property while its dreams of interactive TV floundered, this time things were different. Warner Bros. didn't simply want to be a licensor, they wanted to expand their reach. They'd seen how much money EA had made from games based on Warner Bros.' *Harry Potter* movies and they realised they were missing out on a huge opportunity. "I think it was a natural evolution for the studio," says Hall. "The fact was the videogame business was growing at 20% a year. You can't be a media company and ignore that. At some point your shareholders look at you and say 'What are you doing?'. It was time for the studio to become more involved and just figure it out."

Torn between licensing out their movie properties for games and developing them in-house, Warner Bros. took Hall's advice: "My position was, 'No man, keep your IP and make games'. You're in the content creation business, you should be applying that to this.'" With a huge distribution network reaching all the major retailers already in place, it made sense for Warner Bros. to become a publisher themselves.

286 | GENERATION XBOX

And why only publish when you can develop too? It wasn't long until Warner Bros. Interactive began an aggressive array of acquisitions and turned the traditional narrative of movie studios entering the videogame sphere on its head: instead of simply letting developers license its movie IP to make games, Warner Bros. Interactive set out to become a full-blown game studio, following the EA model. "Unlike other movie studios that have dabbled and done a little bit of licensing, tried to buy a game studio and then back off, Kevin Tsjuihara [head of WB Home Entertainment] and the larger Warner organisation decided to actually commit to being a real player in this business," explains Greg Ballard, senior vice president of Warner Digital Games.

Commitment involved throwing a lot of money at the problem. Warner bought Monolith in 2005. Under Hall's successor, Martin Tremblay, it also snapped up videogame stalwarts like the troubled Midway, owners of the *Mortal Kombat*, *Wheelman* and *Spy Hunter* brands. It acquired developers like Snowblind Studios (creators of *Justice League Heroes*), Traveller's Tales (who made *LEGO: Batman*) and Rocksteady (who scored a hit with *Batman: Arkham Asylum* and *Batman: Arkham City*). Meanwhile, it also bought back the gaming rights to *The Lord of the Rings* franchise from EA and upped its stake in Eidos (a deal which also secured Warner the movie rights to the *Tomb Raider* franchise). In short, it has been very busy consolidating its position in the interactive arena.

"The movie-based games business the way we have known it is broken," Tremblay announced in 2010. "Quality is king now and quality is expensive, so it makes more sense than ever to own your own intellectual property instead of paying for a license." It was a high-risk strategy, but games have now become one of the high-growth areas within Time-Warner's Filmed Entertainment division.

Back in the '70s, when Warner first hatched the idea of using a videogame as an ancillary product for a movie release for *Superman*, nobody had any idea how to port the IP between platforms. "Stupid-Man", as the Atari programmers called it, bore little resemblance to the Warner movie or the D.C. comic it was based on. Thirty odd years later, the process has been super-charged. What began in the labs of Atari as a stunted, half-accidental experiment has evolved, in fits and starts, into a genuine transmedia strategy. Today, a property like *Mortal Kombat*, developed by Warner-owned NetherRealm Studios and published by Warner Bros. Interactive, is more than just a videogame. It's also part of a much bigger transmedia tapestry that includes a live-action online digital media series, *Mortal Kombat: Legacy*, produced by Warner Premiere and distributed via YouTube by Machinima.com; and plans for a feature movie reboot under the Warner Bros. Studios banner.

Yet in that story, the seed of something potentially much bigger can be seen. Machinima.com, the video portal and content creator that distributed the *Mortal Kombat: Legacy* series, is actually part of a shadow Hollywood movie system that's emerging from gaming culture. Machinima, a mash-up of "machine" and "cinema", was traditionally about videogame players shooting their own movies within the virtual, real-time 3D worlds of game engines. The pursuit was mostly just a hobby: creating user-generated content to be shared among friends and online gaming clan members. Occasionally, though, it hinted the possibility of a new kind of filmmaking, a bargain basement *Avatar* virtual production using borrowed game assets.

The video entertainment network Machinima.com grew out of the craze and is now targeting Generation Xbox directly by giving them access not only to trailers and other game-focused content, but also to original content. How popular is this? Well, in April 2011 the live-action *Mortal Kombat: Legacy* web series produced by Warner received around 5 million hits within its first week of airing. Zombie series *Bite Me*, the story of three gamers dealing with a real-life living dead apocalypse, was made by Machinima.com in partnership with Capcom, Microsoft and YouTube. It clocked up 13 million views in less than 6 months. In May 2011, Machinima.com streamed 660 million videos to 73 million unique users. Those are figures strong enough to make cable channel executives sweat.

At the same time, Machinima's users - hardcore gamers who are fans of titles like *Call of Duty* and *Halo* - are constantly creating, watching and commenting videos from their own play sessions, generating considerable free publicity for the IP owners. What Machinima.com has succeeded in becoming is not just a distribution channel but a space where Generation Xbox can meet, socialise, play and watch. This is interactive television of a sort that pioneers like Tom Zito could only feverishly dream of back in the '80s and '90s. It's also the kind of interactive entertainment that's helping to kill cinema attendance among the young.

Among those embedded in the trenches of this new convergence is Hall. When he left Warner Bros. Interactive in 2007, the muscular, six-foot-seven exec announced he was segueing into a job as a producer under his HDFilms banner. Back then, some scoffed. But today Hall is pushing the videogame-Hollywood convergence even further than he did while as an executive at Warner. Among his many projects is *The Jace Hall Show*, an anarchic, not-quite-reality-TV mix of gaming scoops, postmodern comedy and celebrity interviews. It can be seen on Xbox Live, Hulu, IGN.com and, of course, Machinima.com.

Hall reckons Generation Xbox has already changed the entertainment landscape. "To the consumer, the young consumer, content is content is content," he argues. "They don't see much distinction between where it's being delivered or how. With *Mortal Kombat*, yes they want to play the game. But they also want that content in every form that they're used to experiencing content: Where is my movie? Where is my TV show? It's all part of the same thing. We now have adults who grew up with *Pokémon* on their TV screens and their lunchboxes. They're used to this sort of ubiquitous presence of their content. Whereas a more traditionalist would view the content as segmented across different platforms, for the consumer they view it as one continuous thing."

It's not just continuity. They also want control. Generation Xbox has been brought up with a control pad in their hands. Not a TV remote to flick through channels, but a fully-fledged controller that will let them move through three-dimensional virtual space, access online content and interact with each other and what they're watching. Like the fans of Machinima.com, they don't just want to consume their entertainment they want to interact with it too. Passivity - sitting in the dark of a movie theatre - is so last century.

Transmedia, an ugly word for a fascinating process, is becoming the model around which videogame companies are rallying because they know they can facilitate the kind of experience fans desire. Gabe Newell is chief executive of Valve, the company behind the *Half-Life*, *Portal* and *Left 4 Dead* franchises. One of the original "Microsoft millionaires", he's a talented man who doesn't suffer fools gladly. So, when Valve first listened to Hollywood pitches for a *Half-Life* movie in the mid-2000s - including approaches by DreamWorks and Sony - Newell quickly realised that his time was being wasted. "Mostly people were just trying to vampire off of the success and popularity of the property, without any real understanding of what made it an interesting or successful property in the first place," he explains. "The sense that we had was that if we went down the traditional route of licensing a property to a Hollywood studio, we would be losing control at that point. The fans were going to be ill-served 90% of the time."

One movie pitch based on the company's *Half-Life* universe was so spectacularly unrelated to the property that Newell drew a line in the sand. "This writer was trying to convince us that it'd be cool to have this new modern cavalry with these Kevlar-armoured horses charging across this field. It had absolutely nothing to do with what made *Half-Life* an interesting entertainment experience for our customers. It was just bizarre." After that meeting, Newell decided, Hollywood had nothing to offer Valve. Problem was, that left Valve facing a dilemma. Not least of all because the business of being a videogame developer isn't as straight forward as it used to be. "It's pretty clear that our customers are cross-media consumers," Newell explains. "If they like a game, they want to see a movie; if they like a movie they want to be able to run around and shoot rockets off in those spaces. They are telling us we don't have the luxury of just being a games company anymore."

Around 2008, Valve began to look at other ways of getting into movie production themselves. New hires focused on people from the film and TV world and the company started experimenting with CG movie shorts. They eventually gave birth to a series of animated episodes introducing players to the characters of *Team Fortress 2*. The shorts were released online, including on Valve's digital distribution platform Steam. "It's not like we're trying to do a theatrical release, a 90-minute film the first thing out, which is the traditional way of measuring how you're doing, as well as to monetise your investment in that space," says Newell. "We have the luxury of moving in smaller steps in this direction of cross-media production."

With Steam able to collect and track user data and trends, Valve could instantly see the impact of the animated shorts. *Team Fortress 2*'s highest sales didn't come in its first week or month but 14 months after its first release (imagine a movie blockbuster that did that!). Building a franchise clearly has its advantages. So too does tapping into the enthusiasm of the fan community for that franchise via transmedia outings. This wasn't the traditional Hollywood blockbuster model of a big splash opening followed by a steady decline in sales. It was instead about maintaining an on-going relationship with the customer base via the franchise, a relationship that was about deepening and extending their enjoyment of it through regular updates, spin-offs and add-ons. It was about engagement and interactivity, not passive consumption.

"We started thinking of entertainment not as a one-shot opening week-end, blockbuster mentality," says Newell, "but a 'What have we done for our customers today? How are we entertaining them today, how can we keep that going?'" Using their precious brands as the basis for high-quality, in-house movies is one way Valve could potentially keep their customer base happy. Judging by the shorts, the idea of Valve making a CG movie based on its own IP doesn't seem far-fetched.

Around the same time, Valve were approached by The Purchase Brothers, a pair of Canadian commercials directors who had asset-stripped the 3D models and sound effects from *Half-Life 2* to make their own live-action short set in the game's universe called *Escape From City 17*. Instead of speed-dialling their lawyers, Valve flew the brothers down to Bellevue for talks. "I would have trusted the brothers to go and make a *Half-Life* movie way before I would have trusted somebody down in LA to do it," Newell says. Why? "Because they could demonstrate that they were coming at it from an enthusiasts' perspective and would be able to connect with other fans and enthusiasts".

What interested Valve wasn't necessarily the idea of a live-action movie that the short hinted at, but the way in which it had been put together. Valve, a company that has always appreciated the value of "modding" - where fans are encouraged to create additional levels or content for its games - instantly saw the significance.

For Newell, the future of entertainment is truly interactive. The next generation of entertainment companies will be those which are in partnership with their fan-base; and where the line between fans and creators blurs thanks to technology itself. "If Lucasfilm had taken all the assets they had created for *Star Wars: Episodes 1, 2* and *3* and released them to the fan community and said 'you guys go and make three 90-minute movies', in aggregate the community would have built better movies than George Lucas did," he argues. "I'm not being hyperbolic at all. I mean literally they would have made better, higher quality entertainment experiences than he did. The key is to connect the dots for the community in terms of giving them the tools that they need. If you can mod a game like *Half-Life 2*, there's no reason why you can't mod a movie like *The Phantom Menace*."

Newell isn't blind to the fact that most of the material resulting from that kind of asset dump would likely be terrible: "You'd have 40,000 Princess Leia slave porn videos," he says, only half-joking. But he also believes that at least some of the user-generated content would be brilliant. After all, some of Valve's most popular properties - from *Counter-Strike* to *Team Fortress* - started off as fan-created properties.

What does all this mean for the future of movies? "What's going to happen is that the Hollywood guys will start to realise that the creation of entertainment isn't a one-way experience where they have all the professional tools and giant budgets and everything flows downhill from there to the customers," Newell believes. "If they're collaborating and co-operating with their fanbases to create these entertainment experiences, you will see the same kinds of things occurring - most of it will be terrible but some of it will be brilliant."

Videogames, with their emphasis on interactivity, are pointing towards a new relationship between creators and their audiences. It's something that companies like Valve and Machinima.com are responding to in a variety of ways. "Games have forced us, as creative people, to recognise that we are in partnership with our communities, rather than Olympian Gods sending beams of entertainment down at them," says Newell.

Imagine what could happen if the movie industry took a similar approach? True, it's difficult to see the major motion picture dinosaurs being able to embrace such a change. But recent history has shown us what happens when traditional media companies don't keep up with the times. Who would have thought, even a decade ago, that Apple's iTunes would become the biggest distributor of media in the world?

The rise of a new kind of filmmaking, born out of the interactive technology of videogames, could break the chokehold that the major corporations currently have on the entertainment industry. Or, more likely, it could offer those same corporations a new revenue opportunity. Television, the VCR and the internet were all predicted to obliterate Hollywood, but they didn't. Videogames may just another bogeyman to keep Hollywood executives awake at night, while the real change happens at a much more organic level in the fabric of how we consume mass entertainment.

This much is certain: Generation Xbox, and the interactive entertainment it's consuming, is about to shake the entertainment industry to its core. When this earthquake is over, those big white letters on Cahuenga Peak that spell out H-O-L-L-Y-W-O-O-D may no longer be standing.

Don't think of it as Game Over. It's more like the next level...

REFERENCES

INTRODUCTION I THE END OF THE BEGINNING

"[Videogames] are genuine narrative forms...": Mark Kermode, "Guillermo del Toro: Guardian/BFI Interview," Guardian (21 November, 2006). Online at <http://www.guardian.co.uk/film/2006/nov/21/guardianinterviewsatbfisouthbank>.

"We see games as being...": Adam Sherwin, "Grand Theft Auto IV Embodies The Future of Entertainment," London Times (26 April, 2008). Online at <http://technology.timesonline.co.uk/tol/news/tech_and_web/gadgets_and_gaming/article3818900.ece>.

"I've been crushing them...": M.E. McQuiddy, "Dump Here Utilized," Alamogordo Daily News (25 September, 1983), 1.

Each truckload cost: Ibid., 1.

Although contemporary reports: New York Times Staff, "Atari Parts Are Dumped," New York Times (28 September, 1983), D4.

On the internet, a group: Shelley E. Smith, "Search On To Raise The 1983 Atari Titanic," Alamogordo Daily News (12 April, 2005), A1.

"There was overproduction because...": Emmanuel "Manny" Gerard, Interview with the author, 17 December 2009.

"If you want to make an interesting analogy...": Jordan Mechner, Interview with the author, 16 October 2010.

As one poster put it: See the forum thread "Atari's Landfill Adventures, I now have proof it's true," posted by "Spud" on 20 March 2005 at AtariAge.com. Online at <http://www.atariage.com/forums/topic/66637-ataris-landfill-adventures-i-now-have-the-proof-its-true/>.

In 2010, according to figures: Figures supplied directly from IHS Screen Digest on 9 August 2011, with thanks to Piers Harding-Rolls.

No wonder Bobby Kotick: Sandra Ward, "Game-Changing Hero Is Poised to Rule," Barron's Online (31 August, 2009). Online at < http://online.barrons.com/article/SB125150805017468583.html>.

It made entertainment history: Georg Szalai. "Activision's 'Black Ops' First-Day Game Sales Set $360 Mln Record," The Hollywood Reporter (11 November, 2010). Online at <http://www.hollywoodreporter.com/news/activisions-black-ops-day-game-44526>.

1 I E.T. PHONES HOME

Author interviews with Nolan Bushnell (14 May 2010); John Dunn (17 November 2009); Rob Fulop (19 May 2010); Emmanuel "Manny" Gerard (17 December 2009); Tom Holland (31 May 2011 via email); Eugene Jarvis (24 May 2011 via email); Ray Kassar (21 July 2011); George Kiss (31 March 2010); Andrew London (31 May 2011 via email); Frank O'Connell (23 March 2010); Steve Ritchie (25 May 2011 via email); Bud Rosenthal (26 May 2011 via email); Jewel Savadelis (14 April 2010); Howard Scott Warshaw (21 July 2009 and 1 October 2009; 3 July 2011 via email).

There isn't a company: Dave Pirie, "Man in The Machine," Time Out (22-28 October, 1982), 27.

He was the kind of guy: Rob Fulop, interviewed in the video documentary Once Upon Atari (Dir. Howard Scott Warshaw, 2003).

"So simple that any drunk...": Scott Cohen, Zap! The Rise and Fall of Atari (New York: McGraw-Hill, 1984), p.23.

"We've created a whole new...": Newsweek Staff, "King of Pong," Newsweek (17 December, 1973), 91.

Hooked on the game: This anecdote may be apocryphal. See Connie Bruck, Master of the Game: Steve Ross and the Creation of Time Warner (New York, London: Simon & Schuster, 1994), p.166 and Steven L. Kent, The Ultimate History of Videogames (New York: Three Rivers Press, 2001), p.104.

Since the average VCS game cartridge: Kent, p.107.

The Woodstock Generation: Bernice Kanner, "Can Atari Stay Ahead of the Game?", New York Magazine (16 August, 1982), 16.

"The biggest difference...": Tristan Donovan, Replay: The History of Video Games (Lewes: Yellow Ant, 2010), p.70.

Based on a comic book: George Anderson, "The Making and Selling of Superman," Pittsburgh Post-Gazette (15 December, 1978), 21.

In revenge they dubbed him: See John Hubner and William F. Kistner Jr. "What Went Wrong At Atari [Part 1]," InfoWorld, Vol. 5, Issue 48 (28 November, 1983), 158 and also Rusel DeMaria and Johnny L. Wilson, High Score!: The Illustrated History of Electronic Games (New York: McGraw-Hill, 2003), p.40.

The party trick: Tod Frye interviewed in the video documentary Once Upon Atari (Dir. Howard Scott Warshaw, 2003).

"We were like renegade Picassos...": Michael Schrage, "Video-Game Pros Zapped," Washington Post (23 December, 1985), A1.

With Atari's profits dwarfing: Aljean Harmetz, "Hollywood Shivers in a Crisis of Confidence," New York Times (20 December, 1981), D26.

"In the 35 years...": Ibid, D1.

Videogame revenue from coin-op: The figures, taken from Variety, Play Meter magazine and Replay magazine, are referenced in Montreal Gazette Staff, "Arcade Games A Bigger Draw Than The Movies," Montreal Gazette (27 July, 1981), 28.

"Hollywood," The Montreal Gazette gloated...": Ibid., 28.

Add in the numbers: Kent, p.128.

In 1981, in a desperate: Aljean Harmetz, "Is Electronic-Games Boom Hurting The Movies?" New York Times (6 July, 1981), C11.

"There just isn't that much...": Montreal Gazette Staff, "Arcade Games," 28.

"Videogames, per se, are becoming...": Harmetz, "Electronic-Games Boom", C11.

Atari had struck a secret deal: Tina Daniell, "Lucasfilm, Atari Join in Vid Game, Home Computer Effort," The Hollywood Reporter (7 June, 1982), 1.

The programmer, according to his Atari colleague: Dave Staugas interviewed in the video documentary Once Upon Atari (Dir. Howard Scott Warshaw, 2003).

"A certifiable genius": Steven Spielberg in video interview recorded for Atari circa late 1982. A clip of this interview appears on the Once Upon Atari documentary's website. Online at <http://www.onceuponatari.com/>.

"I was making Jaws": Tom Chick, "A Close Encounter with Steven Spielberg," Yahoo Games: Celebrity Byte (8 December, 2008). Previously online at <http://videogames.yahoo.com/celebrity-byte/steven-spielberg/1271249/3>, now a dead link.

In 1984 Kenneth Lim: Loretta Noffsinger, "Atari, Lucasfilm Video Games Aimed at Reviving Market," The Palm Beach Post (9 May 1984), 86.. See also Andrew Pollack, "The Game Turns Serious At Atari," New York Times (19 December, 1982), S3, 1.

"The implications for the entertainment industry": Aljean Harmetz, "Home Video Games Nearing Profitability of the Film Business," New York Times (4 October, 1982), A1.

"[Videogame companies] have licensed everything...": Aljean Harmetz, "Makers Vie For Millions in Home Video Games," New York Times (13 January, 1983), C17.

Paramount, whose parent company: Aljean Harmetz, "Movie Themes Come to Videogames", New York Times (1 July, 1982), D1.

"Hollywood is cashing in": Ibid., D1.

In June 1982, Universal: Hollywood Reporter Staff, "MCA Inc. Joins Majors in Home Video Game Distrib'n," The Hollywood Reporter (9 June, 1982), 4.

"I think of Steve": Tony Schwartz, "Steve Ross On The Spot - Can The Wizard of Warner Rebound?," New York Magazine (24 January, 1983), 27.

"He was like a Frank Capra movie": Bruck, p.195.

When Spielberg told him: Schwartz, 27.

"I had been told, 'Watch out...'": Bruck, p.179.

By the beginning of 1983 the industry: Harmetz, "Makers Vie For Millions," C17.

"I was thrown out of Sid's office,": Bruck, p.179.

There were parties where $30,000: Michael Rubin, Droidmaker: George Lucas and the Digital Revolution (Gainesville, Florida: Triad Publishing, 2006), p.296.

As Atari's Skip Paul later told: Bruck, p.199.

In comparison theatrical releases: Harmetz, "Movie Themes," D1.

Pac-Man alone took in an estimated: Time Staff, "Pac-Man Fever," Time (5 April, 1982), 48.

"I think of myself as a very quick...": Schrage, A2.

"They said that it was a lovely...": Bruck, pp.179-180.

"It wasn't a game...": Ibid., p.180.

The company was overproducing cartridges: John Hubner and William F. Kistner Jr., "What Went Wrong At Atari [Part 2]," InfoWorld, Vol. 5 Issue 49, (5 December, 1983), 145-148.

The media conglomerate's stock: Alexander L. Taylor III, Dick Thompson and Susanne Washburn, "Pac-Man Finally Meets His Match," Time (20 December, 1982), 62.

"Americans are mazed out...": William McWhirter, "The Zinger of Silicon Valley," Time (6 February, 1984), 51.

"A lot of people handled...": Schrage, A1.

2 I HERE BE DRAGONS

Author interviews with Don Bluth (13 January 2010); Jim Garber (11 March 2010); Gary Goldman (13 January 2010; 22 January 2010 and 19 July via email); Peter Langston (28 March 2011 via email); Frank O'Connell (23 March 2010); Tom O'Mary (28 January 2010); John Pasierb (22 March 2010); Victor Penman (15 January 2010); David Riordan (29 March 2010); Bill Van Workum (14 April 2010).

Dragon's Lair is this summer's hottest: Cathleen McGuigan and Peter McAlevey, "Mini-Movies Make the Scene," Newsweek, (8 August, 1983), 79.

"We took our vacation money...": Richard Harrington, "For Don Bluth, 'All Dogs' Has Its Day," Washington Post (19 November, 1989), G1.

"They were angry with us...": Stephan Talty, "Escape From The Magic Kingdom," Empire (August, 1989), 26.

The talking car impressed: Dot Eaters Staff, "Laser Daze," The Dot Eaters.com. Online at <http://www.thedoteaters.com/p2_stage6.php>.

No one knew what a laser was: Rick Dyer, Interview with John Culea, News 8 circa 1984. Online at <http://www.youtube.com/watch?v=Z2LZaNnUp_g>.

"Too late" to break into the new medium: Kathryn Harris, "Video Games: Is It Too Late To Play?," Los Angeles Times (21 November, 1982), F3.

"It occurred to me that the games...": Dave Pirie, "Man in The Machine," Time Out (22-28 October, 1982), 27.

"Though [TRON is] certainly very impressive...": Janet Maslin, "Review of TRON," New York Times (9 July, 1982), C8.

Disney was hit hard: The Associated Press, "Stock Decline After Screening of 'TRON' Irks Disney Studio," New York Times (9 July, 1982), C8.

" I don't think there's any question...": Bruce Chadwick, "Reviews Are Mixed For Movie-Based Games," Miami Herald (24 February, 1983), D11.

"Where does the future...": Charles Solomon, "Will The Real Walt Disney Please Stand Up," Film Comment, (July/August, 1982), 49.

"The Secret of N.I.M.H. is not only a wonderful film...": The review in the Minneapolis Star & Tribune is cited in John Cawley, The Animated Films of Don Bluth (New York: Image Publishing, 1991), p.54.

It took four months, 50,000 drawings: Francesca Landau and Phil Edwards, "Dragon's Lair: Animator Don Bluth Re-defines the Video Arcade Game," Starburst Vol. 5, No. 8 (April, 1984), 28.

It was, he decided, a dinghy: Cawley, p.57.

The rest of the manufacturing process: Jay Arnold, "New Breed Arcade Games Make Players A Part of the Action," Baltimore Sun (22 August, 1983), B7.

There were hundreds of people: Edge Staff, "The Making of Dragon's Lair," Edge Retro (March, 2003), 60.

"Yes Rick", he confirmed in amazement: Ibid., 60.

Earning between $200 and $400 a day: Jefferson Graham, "Bluth's 'N.I.M.H.' Still In Red; Vidisc [sic] Game Pulls in $25 mil," The Hollywood Reporter (18 July, 1983), 8. Also Les Paul Robley, "The Making of Dragon's Lair," American Cinematographer (November, 1983), 74-78.

Audiences swelled to such numbers: See Cawley, p.63. Also Aljean Harmetz, "Hollywood Playing Harder at the Video Game," New York Times (2 August, 1983), C11.

The New York Post guided readers: The New York Post article is cited by Cawley, p.67.

In a Boise, Idaho arcade: Harmetz, "Hollywood Playing Harder," C11.

"The cozy relationship between...": Ibid., C11.

"If Walt Disney was alive today...": Dick Kleiner, "Don Bluth Animates Arcade Games," The Rock Hill Herald (23 June, 1984), 13.

In its first five weeks of release: Harmetz, "Hollywood Playing Harder," C11.

In a year, Cinematronics had shipped: Tony Crawley, "Space Ace," Starburst (June, 1984) 20-21.

And it far out-grossed: Graham, 8.

"I couldn't get those kids excited...": Eric Zorn, "Coming Soon to a Laser Game Near You," Chicago Tribune (15 March, 1984), A3.

"Classical animation is going...": Ibid., A3.

"No more computer-generated dots...": Harmetz, "Hollywood Playing Harder," C11.

"We're in the visuals market...": Les Paul Robley, 78.

"Dragon's Lair is the follow up...": Graham, 8. Gary Goldman at Don Bluth Productions points out that *The Secret of N.I.M.H.* has made its costs back and generated a handsome profit for investors via worldwide video/DVD sales. The film's final cost in 1982 was $6.3 million. The P&A (Prints and Advertising) costs were paid back to the investors, Aurora Productions, within the first 90 days of the film's release. It took less than 25% of the video revenues to pay off the balance of the film's negative cost to the investor.

Eastwood himself recorded: Scott Mace, "Computer Games Meet The Videodisc," InfoWorld Volume 5, Number 50 (12 December, 1983), 90-91.

"We'll never find exactly what...": Harmetz, "Hollywood Playing Harder," C11.

Until the fever for videodisc games: Charles Storch, "Videodisc-player Shortage Zaps Arcade Gamemakers," Chicago Tribune (14 October, 1983), C1-C3.

3 I WELCOME TO SILIWOOD

Author interview with Barry Alperin (7 June 2010; 15 July 2011 via email); Deke Anderson (4 June 2010); Nolan Bushnell (14 May 2010); Rob Fulop (19 May 2010; 25 May 2010 via email); Andras Jones (22 June 2010); Ken Melville (20 and 21 March 2010, 7 July 2011 via email); Ed Neumeier (3 March 2010); Jim Riley (30 July 2009 and 23 September 2010; 24 July 2011 via email); David Riordan (26 March 2010, 29 June 2010; 28 July 2011 via email); Ralph Winter (22 July 2010 via email); Tom Zito (30 August 2010).

Within 12 months of its 1985 launch: Heather Chaplin and Aaron Ruby, Smartbomb: The Quest for Art, Entertainment, and Big Bucks in the Videogame Revolution (Chapel Hill: Algonquin Books, 2005), p.78.

By 1988 Nintendo was: Eugene F. Provenzo, Video Kids: Making Sense of Nintendo (Cambridge, MA: Harvard University Press, 1991), p.13.

"Here's the real Bob Woodward": Tom Shales, Tom Zito and Jeannette Smyth, "When Worlds Collide: Lights! Cameras! Egos!", Washington Post (11 April, 1975). Online at <http://www.washingtonpost.com/wp-srv/style/longterm/movies/features/dcmovies/postinfilm.htm>.

Moses Znaimer, the Canadian TV producer: Barbara Isenberg, "Secrets of the Play That Refuses to Close," Los Angeles Times (12 February, 1989). Online at <http://articles.latimes.com/1989-02-12/entertainment/ca-3037_1_producers>.

The New York Times critic suggested: Mel Gussow, "The Stage: Tamara," New York Times, (3 December, 1987). Online at <http://www.nytimes.com/1987/12/03/theater/the-stage-tamara.html>.

"There are certain human...": Next Generation Staff, "Is This The End of FMV As We Know It?" Next Generation, (October, 1995), 8.

"Bob Jacob really wanted to make movies...": Adam Bormann, "Interview with Past Cinemaware Employees," Just Adventure. com. Online at <http://www.justadventure.com/Interviews/Cinemaware/Cinemaware_Interview.shtm>.

"We are redefining, in some ways...": Ronald T. Farrar, Mass Communication: An Introduction to the Field, Second Edition (New York: McGraw-Hill, 1997), p.232.

4 | THE NEW HOLLYWOOD

Author interviews with Bob Bejan (24 June 2010); Christopher Bradley (7 April 2010); Noah Falstein (14 July 2010); Paul Franklin (13 May 2011); Tracey Fullerton (26 August 2010); Bob Gale (16 July 2010); Daniel Kaufman (10 February 2010); John Lafia (3 June 2010); Ken Melville (20 and 21 March 2010, 7 July 2001 via email); Ed Neumeier (3 March 2010); Jim Riley (24 July 2011 via email); David Riordan (29 June 2010); Greg Roach (20 July 2010; 7 August and 22 October 2010 via email); Joshua Solomon (5 March 2010); Ken Soohoo (18 June 2010); Jason Vandenberghe (16 October 2010); Strauss Zelnick (30 June 2010); Tom Zito (30 August 2010).

"If traditional film is a river...": Marilyn A. Gillen, "Ties With WEA Spur Growing Hyperbole," Billboard (12 November, 1994), 90.

"It's going to be a whole new kind....": John Tierney, "Movies That Push Buttons," New York Times (3 October, 1993). Online at <http://www.nytimes.com/1993/10/03/movies/movies-that-push-buttons.html>.

"The silver disk," warned": Steve Lohr, "The Silver Disk May Soon Eclipse the Silver Screen," New York Times (1 March 1994). Online at <http://www.nytimes.com/1994/03/01/business/the-silver-disk-may-soon-eclipse-the-silver-screen.html>.

"Games are part of a rapidly...": Philip Elmer-DeWitt, John F. Dickerson and David S. Jackson, "The Amazing Video Game Boom," Time (27 September, 1993), 66.

Elsewhere MCA, Universal Studio's parent: Andrew Pollack, "Where Electronics and Art Converge," New York Times (15 September, 1991), F1.

"They just sense that there's money here...": Charles Fleming, "A Marriage Made in Hollywood," Newsweek (27 June, 1994), 45.

"Hollywood agencies already have...": Ibid., 45.

"For multimedia's emerging superstars...": Amy Harmon, "For Multimedia's Emerging Superstars, are Hollywood Talent Agents. . . : The 10% Solution?" Los Angeles Times (12 June, 1994). Online at <http://articles.latimes.com/1994-06-12/business/fi-3443_1_hollywood-talent-agents>.

"People used to ask...": Elmer-DeWitt, Dickerson and Jackson, 72.

Hailed as "The Bard of CD-ROM": See Sabine Durrant, "Bard of the CD-ROM," The Independent (11 June, 1993). Online at < http://www.independent.co.uk/arts-entertainment/outside-edge--bard-of-the-cdrom-sabine-durrant-talks-to-greg-roach-the-bard-of-cdrom-1490900.html >. See also Mark Trumball, "The Viewer Is in the Driver's Seat In This Movie for the 21st Century," Christian Science Monitor (21 July, 1994), 1.

It was clear after two viewings: Roger Ebert, "Review of Mr Payback," Chicago Sun-Times (17 February, 1995). Online at <http://rogerebert.suntimes.com/apps/pbcs.dll/article?AID=/19950217/REVIEWS/502170304/1023>.

"Ultimately I don't think...": Tierney.

"It's deadly to be a so-called...": Alan Citron, "Taking High-Tech Road to 'New Hollywood,'" Los Angeles Times (22 June, 1993). Online at <http://articles.latimes.com/1993-06-22/business/fi-5668_1_hollywood-executives>.

"If you take live-action footage...": Peter M. Nichols "Home Video," New York Times (10 December, 1993). Online at < http://www.nytimes.com/1993/12/10/arts/home-video-290893.html>.

"I flew to Washington...": Zito interviewed in the 1995 documentary Dangerous Games. Online at <http://www.youtube.com/watch?v=jc-TdbpU-4k>.

In contrast to what the Senators...: Ironically, Night Trap was much supposed to be more violent. Jim Riley, the co-creator, writer and director of Night Trap explains: "Night Trap was originally conceived as an interactive teenage horror movie.

Wealthy girl has a slumber party for her friends at their Lake Tahoe mansion. They're attacked by ninja style burglars and are saved, or not, by the high tech surveillance and trap systems controlled by the user. At the time, everyone was concerned about 'reproducible violence' issues, so I changed the villains to vampires. The consensus was that vampires were okay but they couldn't bite, so we ended up with these silly black blobs, covered in black trash bags (literally), hobbling around after the girls using the "trocar" to get their blood. Ironically, *Night Trap* was still considered one of the most violent videogames for it's time - mostly because it was real. You can blow a guy's head off with a shotgun, but the minute it's a real image, different rules apply." Interview with the author, 24 July 2011 via email.

"We don't even consider Digital Pictures...": Tom Zito, "Senate Demagoguery: Leave My Company's Video Game Alone," Washington Post (17 December, 1993), A25.

He was, as author and journalist: J.C. Hertz, "Rendering Refusenik," Wired (February, 1996), no page reference.

5 | IT'S A-ME, MARIO

Author interviews with Paul W.S. Anderson (4 August 2009); Keith Boesky (16 December 2010); Jeff Goodwin (16 September 2010); Annabel Jankel (7 June 2009; 12 August 2011); Roland Joffé (9 July 2011); Larry Kasanoff (3 September 2010); Moe Lospinoso (21 September 2010); Howard Lincoln (7 October 2010); Peter Main (14 and 15 October 2010, via email); Rocky Morton (5 August 2011); Todd Moyer (7 October 2010); Mojo Nixon (7 July 2010); Chris Roberts (15 October 2010); John Tobias (26 October 2010); Ken Topolsky (15 September 2010), Alex Young (18 July 2011).

It was an instant, unexpected hit...: David Sheff, Game Over: Press Start to Continue - The Maturing of Mario (Wilton, CT: CyberActive, 1999), p.111.

Sales of the NES console were awesome: Sheff, p.172.

Mario became a pop culture icon...: Susan Moffatt, "Can Nintendo Keep Winning?", Fortune (5 November 1990). Online at < http://money.cnn.com/magazines/fortune/fortune_archive/1990/11/05/74307/index.htm>.

Nintendo were pocketing more gold coins...: Sheff, p.349.

"Game industry experts...": Moffatt.

"By 1992, Nintendo were profiting more": Sheff, p.5.

The case would become known: Kent, p.199.

"If you own King Kong...": Sheff, p.118.

In comparison, Super Mario Bros. 3 grossed: Sheff, p.191.

Like Heaven's Gate, it wasn't just: Figures are from Box Office Mojo.com.

"Super Mario Bros. is 1993's answer...": Lawrence Cohn, "Review of Super Mario Bros." Variety (31 May, 1993). Online at <http://www.variety.com/review/VE1117900877/>.

Mojo Nixon described it as 'a cross...'": Spy Magazine Staff, "The Hot Summer Movie Thing," Spy (June, 1993), 32-43.

"It was like being directed...": John Leguizamo, Pimps, Hos, Playa Hatas and all the Rest of My Hollywood Friends: My Life (New York: HarperCollins, 2006), p.93.

"The worst thing I ever did?...": Simon Hattenstone, "The Method? Living it out? Cobblers!" Guardian (3 August, 2007). Online at <http://www.guardian.co.uk/film/2007/aug/03/2>.

To keep himself sane during filming": Leguizamo., p.94.

"Oh well, he's just an extra...": Ibid., p.94.

"I wasn't terribly involved because...": Edge Staff, "Miyamoto: The Interview," Edge (November, 2007). Online at <http://www.next-gen.biz/features/miyamoto-interview>.

"Mortal Kombat reminded me of movies...": Douglas Eby, "Mortal Kombat: From Game To Film," Cinefantastique (June, 1995), 8.

He became infamous in 1998: Anita M. Busch, "In The Line Of Fire," Entertainment Weekly (10 April, 1998). Online at <http://www.ew.com/ew/article/0,,282635,00.html>.

It was candy-coloured, frenetic: Figures are from Box Office Mojo.com.

Mortal Kombat cost $20 million to produce: Martin Picard, "Video Games and Their Relationship with Other Media," in Mark J.P. Wolf ed., The Video Game Explosion: A History From Pong to PlayStation and Beyond (Westport, CT: Greenwood Press, 2008), p.295.

That was just the tip of the iceberg: Steven Smith, "Hollywood's Holy Grail," Los Angeles Times (22 August, 1997). Online at <http://articles.latimes.com/1997/aug/22/entertainment/ca-24695>.

"It's a lot more than a movie...": Douglas Eby, "Mortal Kombat: The Movie," Cinefantastique (August, 1995), 42.

"Star Bores" joked": Owen Gleiberman, "Star Bores: Review of Wing Commander," Entertainment Weekly 477 (19 March, 1999), 76.

By 2010 the multi-platform videogame: Dave McNary, "Lara Croft to Return to the Big Screen," Variety (7 March, 2011). Online at <http://www.variety.com/article/VR1118033503>.

"I warmed to Lloyd instantly...": Alan Jones, Lara Croft Tomb Raider: The Official Film Companion (London: Carlton Books, 2001), p.20.

"We pursued the movie rights...": Jones, pp.19-20.

"My sense is, of all the people...": Christine Spines, "Tomb With A View," Premiere (US) (July, 2011), 36.

"Larry [Gordon] and I were dumbfounded...": PC Gamer Staff, "From Die Hard To Tomb Raider: An Interview with Steven E. De Souza," PC Gamer (March, 2000), 4.

She was also forced to squeeze: Spines, 40.

"Like every woman, I'd go 'Ugh, her!...": Stephen Short and Chris Taylor, "Watch Out, Indiana. Here Comes Lara Croft," Time (26 March, 2001). Online at <http://www.time.com/time/magazine/article/0,9171,999542,00.html>.

"I see Lara as like a creature...": Jones, pp.35, 39.

"It's just like finding Sean Connery...": David Gritten, "She's Game For The Adventure Of Her Career," Los Angeles Times (21 January, 2001). Online at <http://articles.latimes.com/print/2001/jan/21/entertainment/ca-14879>.

When Tomb Raider finally hit cinemas: Figures are from Box Office Mojo.com

"Tomb Raider will go down in history ...": Charles Herold, "Game Theory: Making The Leap From A Game To The Movies," New York Times (21 June, 2001). Online at <http://www.nytimes.com/2001/06/21/technology/game-theory-making-the-leap-from-a-game-to-the-movies.html>.

6 I A TALE OF TWO EMPIRES

Author interviews with Hal Barwood (27 July 2010; 13 February 2011 via email); John Batter (11 August 2011); Mark Cerny (8 April 2011); Noah Falstein (14 and 29 July 2010); Ron Gilbert (13 July 2011 via email); Patrick Gilmore (23 February 2011); Bing Gordon (18 November 2010 via email); Matt Hall (26 February 2011); Peter Hirschmann (16 February 2011; 26 July 2011); Daniel Kaufman (10 February 2011); Peter Langston (25 March, 2011 via email); David Riordan (29 March 2010); Max Spielberg (23 March 2011 via email); Richard Wyckoff (4 April 2011 via email).

In the mid-90s he reputedly still: Nicole LaPorte, The Men Who Would Be King: An Almost Epic Tale of Moguls, Movies and a Company Called DreamWorks (New York: Houghton Mifflin Harcourt Publishing, 2010), p.244.

"Move Over Sega - Here Come the Conglomerates": Amy Harmon, "Move Over Sega - Here Come the Conglomerates," Los Angeles Times (21 June, 1994). Online at <http://articles.latimes.com/1994-06-21/business/fi-6674_1_video-game-publishers>.

By 1998, Forbes magazine was: Forbes Staff, "Say Good-Bye to Hollywood," Forbes (30 May, 1998). Online at <http://www.forbes.com/1998/05/30/side1_print.html>.

"Every failed talent in Hollywood...": Amy Harmon, "Help Wanted: Talent's Rare, Experience Short on Interactive Frontier," Los Angeles Times (24 March, 1995). Online at <http://articles.latimes.com/1995-03-24/business/fi-46610_1_dreamworks-interactive>.

"Just because a bunch of Hollywood guys...": Ibid.

"You take the property content owners...": Ibid.

"[We're] not a technology company": Amy Harmon, "Disney to Get Interactive With Start of New Division," Los Angeles Times (5 December, 1994). Online at <http://articles.latimes.com/1994-12-05/business/fi-5216_1_video-game-industry>.

"The whole thing is the game...": Marilyn A. Gillen and Eileen Fitzpatrick, "'Jurassic' Video Game Arrives in 3DO," Billboard (21 May, 1994), 4.

The deal would create: BusinessWeek Staff, "Hollywood's Digital Godzilla," BusinessWeek Online (3 April, 1995). Online at <http://www.businessweek.com/archives/1995/b341844.arc.htm>.

Paul Allen, one of Bill Gates's closest: LaPorte, pp.72-73.

"It really will be the meeting of...": Journal Record Staff, "High Technology Briefs," The Journal Record (23 March, 1995). Online at < http://findarticles.com/p/articles/mi_qn4182/is_19950323/ai_n10077805/>.

"The wide line dividing this technology...": Ibid.

He, Steven Spielberg, the movie industry's: David A. Kaplan and Corie Brown, "Good-bye Pac-Man: Steven Spielberg Unveils The Video Arcade of the Future," Newsweek, (10 March, 1997), 98.

He earned just $150,000: Michael Rubin, Droidmaker: George Lucas and the Digital Revolution (Gainesville, Florida: Triad Publishing Co, 2006), p.77.

After Star Wars came out: Rubin, p.77.

In its first thirty years: Andy Greenberg, "Star Wars' Galactic Dollars," Forbes.com (24 May, 2007). Online at <http://www.forbes.com/2007/05/24/star-wars-revenues-tech-cx_ag_0524money.html>.

"I had visions of R2D2 mugs...": Rubin, p.78.

"It was really an extraordinary dream...": Rubin, p.81.

Atari gave Lucasfilm Games a $1 million: Rob Smith, Rogue Leaders: The Story of LucasArts (London: Titan Books, 2009), p.12.

Mostly, though, he left them to: Ibid., p.25.

During one of his rare visits to the division: Ibid., p.25.

"How can we invent new storytelling...": Rubin, p.418.

The team were encouraged to think: Jack Powell, "New Lucasfilm Games: Antic's Sneak Preview," Antic (December, 1985), 20.

It was described by one former: LaPorte, p.206.

As Nicole LaPorte recounts: Ibid., p.100.

Spielberg later described the sale: John Gaudiosi, "Spielberg Makes Videogames To Keep His Family Happy," Reuters.com (14 May, 2009). Online at <http://www.reuters.com/article/2009/05/14/us-videogames-spielberg-tech-life-idUSTRE54D2H4200 90514?feedType=RSS&feedName=technologyNews>.

"E.T. meets North By Northwest": N'Gai Croal, "Wii Can't Wait to Play: Steven Spielberg Makes His Return To Videogames," Newsweek (16 July, 2007). Online at <http://www.newsweek.com/2007/07/15/wii-can-t-wait-to-play.html >.

"The challenge is, can the game...": Ibid.

7 I GENERATION XBOX

Author interviews with Paul W.S. Anderson (4 August 2009); John Batter (11 August 2011); Neill Blomkamp (17 November 2010); Uwe Böll (19 July 2011); Phil Campbell (8 October 2010); Lev Chapelsky (23 November 2010); Lorenzo DiBonaventura (22 January 2011); Alex Garland (23 November 2010); Bing Gordon (18 November 2010 via email); Navid Khonsari (26 October 2010); Larry Shapiro (20 October 2010); Jason Vandenberghe (16 October 2010); Alex Young (18 July 2011); Neil Young (5 January 2011).

"I remember the day when..." Alex Wiltshire, "Interview: Lev Chapelsky," Edge (May, 2009). Online at <http://www.next-gen. biz/features/interview-lev-chapelsky?page=1>.

"But, typical Hollywood...": Ibid.

It had built its rep by releasing: Patrick Hruby, "The Franchise: The Inside Story of How Madden NFL Became a Videogame Dynasty," ESPN: Outside The Lines, 6 August 2010. Online at <http://sports.espn.go.com/espn/eticket/story?page=100805/ madden>.

It also took flak over: Randall Stross, When a Video Game Stops Being Fun," New York Times (21 November, 2004). Online at <http://www.nytimes.com/2004/11/21/business/yourmoney/21digi.html>.

"Right now, videogames [are]...": Roger Vincent and Alex Pham, "EA Makes a Play for L.A.," Los Angeles Times (6 August, 2003). Online at <http://articles.latimes.com/2003/aug/06/business/fi-ea6>.

"You see," explained Rockstar's COO: Logan Hill, "Why Rockstar Games Rule: The Badboys of Rockstar Games," Wired (July, 2002). Online at <http://www.wired.com/wired/archive/10.07/rockstar_pr.html>.

"We always wanted to be like...": Carsten Görig, "Grand Theft Auto Is A Version of Gangster Fiction: Interview with Dan Houser," Spiegel Online (30 April, 2008). Online at <www.spiegel.de/international/business/0,1518,550771,00.html>.

Rockstar had finally achieved the dream: Design Museum Staff, "Rockstar Games: Multimedia Designers" (2002). Online at <http://designmuseum.org/design/rockstar-games>.

"To me, [the '80s is] still hands-down...": Edge Staff, "Grand Theft Auto: The Inside Story," Edge (March, 2008). Online at <http://www.next-gen.biz/features/grand-theft-auto-inside-story>.

Their father, Wally, was: Rob Waugh, "Grand Theft Auto: The Reckoning," Mail Online (24 August 2007). Online at <http:// www.dailymail.co.uk/home/moslive/article-477505/Grand-Theft-Auto-The-reckoning.html>.

"We believed that the business was...": See "Rockstar Games: Multimedia Designers".

"I think the videogame industry...": Hill.

"Controlling a character in a world...": Chris Morris, "Dan Houser's very extended interview about everything Grand Theft Auto IV and Rockstar," Variety (19 April, 2008). Online at <http://weblogs.variety.com/the_cut_scene/2008/04/dan-hous-ers-ver.html>.

When they were supposed to be in a car: Andy Grieser, "The Body Behind Vice City's Tommy Vercetti: Jonathan Sale Interview," ESCmag (9 June, 2003). Online at <http://www.escmag.com/v5/features/feature.cfm?fv=5>.

I'll be honest," Sam Houser told Edge: See "Grand Theft Auto: The Inside Story".

"[Ray Liotta] was a very interesting guy...": Ibid.

"He made some comments later on...": Ibid.

Talking to Edge in 2008 he claimed: Ibid.

According to EA's CEO John Riccitiello: Chris Nuttall and Matthew Garrahan, "Game On for Comic 'Iron Man' Faces Big Screen Test," Financial Times (27 April, 2008). Online at <http://www.ft.com/cms/s/0/bec02d88-1482-11dd-a741-0000779fd2ac.html#axzz1SYNkyFg5>.

Iron Man's breathtaking $100m: Brooks Barnes, "Iron Man Tops $100m in Opening Weekend," New York Times (5 May, 2008). Online at <http://www.nytimes.com/2008/05/05/technology/05iht-film.1.12567303.html>; also Curt Feldman, "Grand Theft Auto IV steals sales records," CNN.com (8 May, 2008). Online at <http://articles.cnn.com/2008-05-08/tech/gta.sales_1_ea-sales-grand-theft-auto-iv>.

"Videogame makers," as Dan Houser: Scott Alexander, "Grand Theft Autonomy," Playboy (June, 2008), 47.

Combined sales of the first two Halo: Ben Fritz, "Halo Stomps into Studios," Variety (6 June, 2005). Online at <www.variety.com/article/VR1117923988?refCatId=1009>.

According to Variety Microsoft wanted: Marc Graser, "Halo: The Care and Feeding of a Franchise", Variety (4 September, 2010). Online at <http://www.variety.com/article/VR1118023688?refCatId=1009>.

The first movie based on Capcom's: Figures are from Box Office Mojo.com.

As star Milla Jovovich put it: Mark Salisbury, "Dead Residents: On the Set of Resident Evil," Total Film (August, 2001), 8.

House of the Dead was made for $12 million: Figures from Box Office Mojo.com.

But on DVD it shipped 1.48 million rental units: John Gaudiosi, "BloodRayne DVD to Ship With Full Video Game," Home Media Magazine (3 April, 2006). Online at <http://www.homemediamagazine.com/news/bloodrayne-dvd-ship-with-full-video-game-8876>.

According to Home Media Magazine: Ibid.

"House of the Dead is a brainless shooter...": Ellie Gibson, "Uwe Böll Bites Back," Eurogamer.net (15 February, 2006). Online at <http://www.eurogamer.net/articles/i_uweboll_multi>.

"The reality is that a lot of the videogame companies...": Ibid.

According to the New York Times the software: Laura M. Holson, "Hollywood Hardball," New York Times (10 June, 2005). Online at <http://www.nytimes.com/2005/06/10/business/media/10halo.html>.

"We don't understand Hollywood...": John Gaudiosi, "Microsoft Eying TV, Movie Deals, Signs with CAA," The Hollywood Reporter (5 March, 2002), 3.

It grossed $211 million worldwide: Figures from Box Office Mojo.com.

The Halo: Legends anime series: DVD sales from The-Numbers.com.

Similarly, Halo novels and comics are big business: Graser.

"We have a lot in common with...": Ibid.

"[Microsoft] are just trying to figure out...": WorstPreviews.com Staff, "Peter Jackson Gives 'Halo' Update," WorstPreviews.com (26 July, 2009). Online at <http://www.worstpreviews.com/headline.php?id=14401>.

8 | EMOTION IN MOTION

Author interviews with: Tameem Antoniades (16 December 2010); David Cage (24 January 2011); Phil Campbell (8 October 2010; 24 January 2011 via email); Robert Davidsen (23 January, 9 February 2011 via email); Guillaume de Fondaumière (26 November 2010); Jon Landau (13 July 2011); Pascal Langdale (2 December 2010); Chris Lee (30 November 2010); Chuck Mongelli (8 August 2011); Jim Riley (23 September 2010; 24 July 2011 via email); Remington Scott (24 November 2010; 24 December 2010 via email).

"I think the real indicator...": Anthony Breznican, "Spielberg, Zemeckis Say Video Games, films Could Merge," USA.com (16 September, 2004). Online at <http://www.usatoday.com/tech/products/games/2004-09-16-game-movie-meld_x.htm>.

"My son was 5 years old...": Kevin O'Hannessian, "A Conversation With 'Heavy Rain' Creator David Cage Continues," Fast Company.com (23 February, 2010). Online at <http://www.fastcompany.com/1558728/david-cage-heavy-rain-sony-playstation-video-games-interactive-drama>.

"It feels like what movie moguls...": Chris Nuttall and Matthew Garrahan, "Game On for Comic 'Iron Man' Faces Big Screen Test," Financial Times (27 April, 2008). Online at <http://www.ft.com/cms/s/0/bec02d88-1482-11dd-a741-0000779fd2ac.html#axzz1SYNkyFg5>.

"We're going to get three sets of data...": Richard Sandomir, "A Big Hitter Aims for a Video Homer," New York Times (10 April, 1995). Online at <http://select.nytimes.com/gst/abstract.html?res=F6061FFD3F5A0C738DDDAD0894DD494D81>.

"The key to creating human beings...": Jody Duncan, "Flesh For Fantasy", Cinefex (July, 2001), 43.

"I needed cutting edge computer graphic artists...": Jeff L. Peterson, "Once Upon a Time in the Future: Final Fantasy" Cinefantastique (August, 2001), 11.

People certainly took notice: in 1999 UK trade paper: Screen International Staff, "Synthespians to Invade Hollywood," Screen International (6 August, 1999), 1.

"It was their idea and we complied...": Anthony C. Ferrante, "The Fantasy Becomes Real," Fangoria (August, 2001), 57.

"I am very troubled by it...": Rick Lyman, "Movie Stars Fear Inroads By Upstart Digital Actors," New York Times (8 July 2001). Online at < http://www.nytimes.com/2001/07/08/us/movie-stars-fear-inroads-by-upstart-digital-actors.html>.

"It really is a silly idea...": Duncan, 43.

"This one lone character had the emotional...": Andy Serkis, The Lord of the Rings Gollum: How We Made Movie Magic (London: Collins, 2003), p.85.

As Wired put it in 2009: Hugh Hart, "Virtual Sets Bring Holodeck to Hollywood," Wired (31 March 2009). Online at <http://www.wired.co.uk/news/archive/2009-03/30/virtual-sets-bring-holodeck-to-hollywood->.

"If we make this," they told him: James Cameron speaking at Ubisoft's E3 2009 Press Conference. Video online at <http://incontention.com/2009/06/02/james-cameron-talks-avatar-at-e3/>.

"I liken the experience of making Avatar...": Jody Duncan and Lisa Fitzpatrick, The Making of Avatar (New York: Abrams, 2010), p.116.

According to a report from CNN: Jo Piazza, "Audiences Experience Avatar 'blues'," CNN.com (11 January, 2010). Online at <http://articles.cnn.com/2010-01-11/entertainment/avatar.movie.blues_1_pandora-depressed-posts?_s=PM:SHOWBIZ>.

"Actors," said the director: Douglas Wolk, "James Cameron and Peter Jackson Explore the Future of Film," Rolling Stone (27 July, 2009). Online at <http://www.rollingstone.com/movies/news/james-cameron-and-peter-jackson-explore-the-future-of-film-20090727>.

"After all," claimed producer Jon Landau: Daniel Terdiman, "Lights, Camera, Videogames," CNet News (7 September, 2006). Online at <http://news.cnet.com/Lights,-camera,-video-games/2100-1025_3-6113481.html>.

"What we are doing, virtual production...": Ibid.

"When people see a movie that's really immersive...": BusinessWeek staff, "Syncing Hollywood and Gamers," BusinessWeek. com (13 February, 2006). Online at <http://www.businessweek.com/magazine/content/06_07/b3971076.htm?chan=tc>.

Digital Acting staff, "James Cameron Performance Capture re-invented Avatar -Interview," Digital Acting.com (8 February, 2010). Online at <http://www.digitalacting.com/2010/02/08/james-cameron-performance-capture-re-invented-avatar/>.

EPILOGUE | THE NEXT LEVEL

Greg Ballard (8 April 2011), Jace Hall (15 April 2011), Yannis Mallat (12 October 2009; 9 September 2011), Gabe Newell (23 June 2009), Alex Young (18 July 2011).

In 2010, US box office attendance sank: See BBC News Staff, "US cinema attendance 5% down on 2009," BBC News Online (30 December, 2010). Online at <http://www.bbc.co.uk/news/entertainment-arts-12093041>; see also Richard Verrier, "Worldwide movie box-office receipts rise in 2010," Los Angeles Times (24 February, 2011). Online at <http://articles.latimes.com/2011/feb/24/business/la-fi-0224-ct-mpaa-stats-20110224>. For 2011 figures see Pamela McClintock, "Box Office Shocker: Movie Attendance Falls to Lowest Level in 16 Years," The Hollywood Reporter (29 December 2011). Online at <http://www.hollywoodreporter.com/news/movie-attendance-down-mission-impossible-box-office-276699>.

"So far there is just nothing terribly...": Richard Verrier and Ben Fritz, "Movie industry hits ticket sales decline on the nose: It's put out some stinkers," Los Angeles Times (30 March, 2011). Online at <http://articles.latimes.com/2011/mar/30/business/la-fi-ct-cinemacon-20110330/2>.

"Trade gossip about the Ubisoft/Sony Assassin's Creed movie deal...": Claude Brodesser-Akner, "Why a Killer Deal to Turn the Hit Video Game Assassin's Creed into a Movie had Shocked Hollywood," New York Magazine (3 November 2001) Online at <http://nymag.com/daily/entertainment/2011/11/assassins_creed_movie_sony_ubi.html>.

Despite taking $335 million: Brooks Barnes, "An Action Star Is Born? Not Just Yet in 'Prince'," New York Times (31 May, 2010). Online at <http://www.nytimes.com/2010/06/01/movies/01box.html>.

"The movie-based games business the way...": Ben Fritz, "Video Games Based on Movies Take A New Hit," Los Angeles Times (15 June, 2010). Online at <http://articles.latimes.com/2010/jun/15/business/la-fi-ct-moviegames-20100615>.

Well, in April 2011 the live-action Mortal Kombat: Legacy: See Marc Graser, "New Weapon For Kombat," Variety (18 April, 2011). Online at <http://www.variety.com/article/VR1118035561> and Andrew Hampp, "Gamer Channel Machinima Offers New Model for YouTube's Premium Strategy," Advertising Age (16 May, 2011). Online at <http://adage.com/article/news/machinima-offers-model-youtube-s-premium-strategy/227572/>.

BIBLIOGRAPHY

A

Alexander, Scott. "Grand Theft Autonomy," Playboy (June, 2008), 47.

Anderson, George. "The Making and Selling of Superman," Pittsburgh Post-Gazette (15 December 1978), 21.

Arnold, Jay "New Breed Arcade Games Make Players A Part of the Action," Baltimore Sun (22 August, 1983), B7.

B

Barnes, Brooks. "Iron Man Tops $100m in Opening Weekend," New York Times (5 May, 2008). Online at <http://www.nytimes.com/2008/05/05/technology/05iht-film.1.12567303.html>.

Bernice Kanner, "Can Atari Stay Ahead of the Game?", New York Magazine (16 August, 1982), 16-18.

Bissell, Tom. Extra Lives: Why Video Games Matter (New York: Pantheon Books, 2010)

Bormann, Adam. "Interview with Past Cinemaware Employees," Just Adventure.com. Online at <http://www.justadventure.com/Interviews/Cinemaware/Cinemaware_Interview.shtm>. No date.

Breznican, Anthony. "Spielberg, Zemeckis Say Video Games, films Could Merge," USA.com (16 September, 2004). Online at <http://www.usatoday.com/tech/products/games/2004-09-16-game-movie-meld_x.htm>.

Brodesser-Akner, Claude. "Why a Killer Deal to Turn the Hit Video Game Assassin's Creed into a Movie has Shocked Hollywood," New York Magazine, November 2011. Online at <http://nymag.com/daily/entertainment/2011/11/assassins_creed_movie_sony_ubi.html>.

Brookey, Robert Alan. Hollywood Gamers: Digital Convergence in the Film and Video Game Industries (Bloomington and Indianapolis: Indiana University Press, 2010).

Brown, Eryn. "Electronic Arts Makes Itself a Hollywood Home," New York Times (5 October, 2003). Online at <http://www.nytimes.com/2003/10/05/business/business-electronic-arts-makes-itself-a-hollywood-home.html>.

Bruck, Connie. Master of the Game: Steve Ross and the Creation of Time Warner (New York, London: Simon & Schuster, 1994).

Busch, Anita M. "In The Line Of Fire," Entertainment Weekly (10 April, 1998). Online at <http://www.ew.com/ew/article/0,,282635,00.html>.

BusinessWeek Staff, "Hollywood's Digital Godzilla," BusinessWeek.com (3 April, 1995). Online at <http://www.businessweek.com/archives/1995/b341844.arc.htm>.

BusinessWeek staff, "Syncing Hollywood and Gamers," BusinessWeek.com (13 February, 2006). Online at <http://www.businessweek.com/magazine/content/06_07/b3971076.htm?chan=tc>.

C

Cawley, John. The Animated Films of Don Bluth (New York: Image Publishing, 1991).

Chadwick, Bruce. "Reviews Are Mixed For Movie-Based Games," Miami Herald (24 February, 1983), D11.

Chaplin, Heather and Ruby, Aaron. Smartbomb: The Quest for Art, Entertainment, and Big Bucks in the Videogame Revolution (Chapel Hill: Algonquin Books, 2005).

Chick, Tom. "A Close Encounter with Steven Spielberg," Yahoo Games: Celebrity Byte (8 December 2008). Previously online at <http://videogames.yahoo.com/celebrity-byte/steven-spielberg/1271249/3>, now a dead link.

Citron, Alan. "Taking High-Tech Road to 'New Hollywood'," Los Angeles Times (22 June, 1993). Online at <http://articles.latimes.com/1993-06-22/business/fi-5668_1_hollywood-executives>.

Cohn, Lawrence. "Review of Super Mario Bros." Variety (31 May, 1993). Online at <http://www.variety.com/review/VE1117900877/>.

Cohen, Scott. Zap! The Rise and Fall of Atari (New York: McGraw-Hill, 1984).

Crawley, Tony. "Space Ace," Starburst (June, 1984) 20-21.

Croal, N'Gai. "Wii Can't Wait to Play: Steven Spielberg Makes His Return To Videogames," Newsweek (16 July, 2007). Online at <http://www.newsweek.com/2007/07/15/wii-can-t-wait-to-play.html >.

Culea, John. "Interview with Rick Dyer," News 8 circa 1984. Online at <http://www.youtube.com/watch?v=Z2LZaNnUp_g>.]

D

Daniell, Tina. "Lucasfilm, Atari Join in Vid Game, Home Computer Effort," The Hollywood Reporter (7 June, 1982), 1.

DeMaria Rusel and Johnny L. Wilson. High Score!: The Illustrated History of Electronic Games (New York: McGraw-Hill, 2002).

Design Museum Staff, "Rockstar Games: Multimedia Designers" (2002). Online at <http://designmuseum.org/design/rockstar-games>.

Digital Acting staff, "James Cameron Performance Capture re-invented Avatar -Interview," Digital Acting.com (8 February, 2010). Online at <http://www.digitalacting.com/2010/02/08/james-cameron-performance-capture-re-invented-avatar/>.

Digital Pictures. Dangerous Games (2005). Online at <http://www.youtube.com/watch?v=jc-TdbpU-4k>.

Donovan, Tristan. Replay: The History of Video Games (Lewes: Yellow Ant, 2010).

Dot Eaters Staff, "Laser Daze," The Dot Eaters.com. Online at <http://www.thedoteaters.com/p2_stage6.php>. No date.

Duncan Jody, and Fitzpatrick, Lisa. The Making of Avatar (New York: Abrams, 2010).

Duncan, Jody. "Flesh For Fantasy", Cinefex (July, 2001), 43.

Durrant, Sabine. "Bard of the CD-ROM," The Independent (11 June, 1993). Online at < http://www.independent.co.uk/arts-entertainment/outside-edge--bard-of-the-cdrom-sabine-durrant-talks-to-greg-roach-the-bard-of-cdrom-1490900.html >.

E

Ebert, Roger "Review of Mr Payback," Chicago Sun-Times (17 February, 1995). Online at <http://rogerebert.suntimes.com/apps/pbcs.dll/article?AID=/19950217/REVIEWS/502170304/1023>.

Eby, Douglas. "Mortal Kombat: From Game To Film," Cinefantastique (June, 1995), 8-11.

Eby, Douglas. "Mortal Kombat: The Movie," Cinefantastique (August, 1995), 42.

Edge Staff, "Grand Theft Auto: The Inside Story," Edge (March, 2008). Online at <http://www.next-gen.biz/features/grand-

theft-auto-inside-story>.

Edge Staff, "Miyamoto: The Interview," Edge (November, 2007). Online at <http://www.next-gen.biz/features/miyamoto-interview>.

Edge Staff, "The Making of Dragon's Lair," Edge Retro (March, 2003), 56-60.

Elmer-DeWitt, Philip, Dickerson, John F. and Jackson, David S. "The Amazing Video Game Boom," Time (27 September, 1993), 66-73.

F

Farrar, Ronald T. Mass Communication: An Introduction to the Field, Second Edition (New York: McGraw-Hill, 1997).

Feldman, Curt. "Grand Theft Auto IV steals sales records," CNN.com (8 May, 2008). Online at <http://articles.cnn.com/2008-05-08/tech/gta.sales_1_ea-sales-grand-theft-auto-iv>.

Ferrante, Anthony C. "The Fantasy Becomes Real," Fangoria (August, 2001), 54-57.

Fleming, Charles. "A Marriage Made in Hollywood," Newsweek (27 June 1994), 45.

Forbes Staff, "Say Good-Bye to Hollywood," Forbes (30 May, 1998). Online at <http://www.forbes.com/1998/05/30/side1_print.html>.

Fritz, Ben. "Halo Stomps into Studios," Variety (6 June, 2005). Online at <www.variety.com/article/VR1117923988?refCatId=1009>.

Fritz, Ben. "Video Games Based on Movies Take A New Hit," Los Angeles Times (15 June, 2010). Online at <http://articles.latimes.com/2010/jun/15/business/la-fi-ct-moviegames-20100615>.

G

Gaudiosi, John. "BloodRayne DVD to Ship With Full Video Game," Home Media Magazine (3 April, 2006). Online at <http://www.homemediamagazine.com/news/bloodrayne-dvd-ship-with-full-video-game-8876>.

Gaudiosi, John. "Microsoft Eying TV, Movie Deals, Signs with CAA," The Hollywood Reporter (5 March, 2002), 3.

Gaudiosi, John. "Spielberg Makes Videogames To Keep His Family Happy," Reuters.com (14 May, 2009). Online at <http://www.reuters.com/article/2009/05/14/us-videogames-spielberg-tech-life-idUSTRE54D2H420090514?feedType=RSS&feedName=technologyNews>.

Gibson, Ellie. "Uwe Böll Bites Back," Eurogamer.net (15 February, 2006). Online at <http://www.eurogamer.net/articles/i_uweboll_multi>.

Gillen, Marilyn A. "Ties With WEA Spur Growing Hyperbole," Billboard (12 November, 1994), 90.

Gillen, Marilyn A. and Fitzpatrick, Eileen. "'Jurassic' Video Game Arrives in 3DO," Billboard (21 May, 1994), 4.

Gleiberman, Owen. "Star Bores: Review of Wing Commander," Entertainment Weekly (19 March, 1999), 76.

Görig, Carsten. "Grand Theft Auto Is A Version of Gangster Fiction: Interview with Dan Houser," Spiegel Online (30 April, 2008). Online at <www.spiegel.de/international/business/0,1518,550771,00.html>.

Graham, Jefferson. "Bluth's 'N.I.M.H.' Still In Red; Vidisc [sic] Game Pulls in $25 mil," The Hollywood Reporter (18 July, 1983), 8.

Graser, Marc. "Halo: The Care and Feeding of a Franchise", Variety (4 September, 2010). Online at <http://www.variety.com/article/VR1118023688?refCatId=1009>.

Graser, Marc. "New Weapon For Kombat," Variety (18 April, 2011). Online at <http://www.variety.com/article/VR1118035561>.

Greenberg, Andy. "Star Wars' Galactic Dollars," Forbes.com (24 May, 2007). Online at < http://www.forbes.com/2007/05/24/star-wars-revenues-tech-cx_ag_0524money.html>.

Grieser, Andy. "The Body Behind Vice City's Tommy Vercetti: Jonathan Sale Interview," ESCmag (9 June, 2003). Online at <http://www.escmag.com/v5/features/feature.cfm?fv=5>.

Griffin, Nancy and Masters, Kim. Hit & Run: How Jon Peters and Peter Guber Took Sony for a Ride in Hollywood (New York: Simon & Schuster, 1996).

Gritten, David. "She's Game For The Adventure Of Her Career," Los Angeles Times (21 January, 2001). Online at <http://articles.latimes.com/print/2001/jan/21/entertainment/ca-14879>.

Gussow, Mel. "The Stage: Tamara," New York Times, (3 December, 1987). Online at <http://www.nytimes.com/1987/12/03/theater/the-stage-tamara.html>.

H

Hampp, Andrew. "Gamer Channel Machinima Offers New Model for YouTube's Premium Strategy," Advertising Age (16 May, 2011).

Harmetz, Aljean. "Hollywood Shivers in a Crisis of Confidence," New York Times (20 December, 1981), D1, D26.

Harmetz, Aljean. "Home Video Games Nearing Profitability of the Film Business," New York Times (4 October, 1982), A1, C15.

Harmetz, Aljean. "Is Electronic-Games Boom Hurting The Movies?" New York Times (6 July, 1981), C11.

Harmetz, Aljean. "Makers Vie For Millions in Home Video Games," New York Times (13 January, 1983), C17.

Harmetz, Aljean. "Movie Themes Come to Videogames," New York Times (1 July, 1982), D1.

Harmon, Amy. "Disney to Get Interactive With Start of New Division," Los Angeles Times (5 December, 1994). Online at <http://articles.latimes.com/1994-12-05/business/fi-5216_1_video-game-industry>.

Harmon, Amy. "For Multimedia's Emerging Superstars, are Hollywood Talent Agents. . . : The 10% Solution?" Los Angeles Times (12 June, 1994). Online at <http://articles.latimes.com/1994-06-12/business/fi-3443_1_hollywood-talent-agents>.

Harmon, Amy. "Help Wanted: Talent's Rare, Experience Short on Interactive Frontier," Los Angeles Times (24 March, 1995). Online at <http://articles.latimes.com/1995-03-24/business/fi-46610_1_dreamworks-interactive>.

Harmon, Amy. "Move Over Sega - Here Come the Conglomerates," Los Angeles Times (21 June, 1994). Online at <http://articles.latimes.com/1994-06-21/business/fi-6674_1_video-game-publishers>.

Harrington, Richard. "For Don Bluth, 'All Dogs' Has Its Day," Washington Post (19 November, 1989), G1-3.

Harris, Kathryn. "Video Games: Is It Too Late To Play?," Los Angeles Times (21 November, 1982), F3.

Hart, Hugh. "Virtual Sets Bring Holodeck to Hollywood," Wired (31 March, 2009). Online at <http://www.wired.co.uk/news/archive/2009-03/30/virtual-sets-bring-holodeck-to-hollywood->.

Hattenstone, Simon. "The Method? Living it out? Cobblers!" Guardian (3 August, 2007). Online at <http://www.guardian.co.uk/film/2007/aug/03/2>.

Herman, Leonard. Phoenix: The Fall & Rise of Videogames (Union, NJ: Rolenta Press, 1997 second edition).

Herold, Charles. "Game Theory: Making The Leap From A Game To The Movies," New York Times (21 June, 2001). Online at

<http://www.nytimes.com/2001/06/21/technology/game-theory-making-the-leap-from-a-game-to-the-movies.html>.

Hertz, J.C. "Rendering Refusenik," Wired (February, 1996), 15.

Hertz, J.C. Joystick Nation: How Videogames Gobbled Our Money, Won Our Hearts And Rewired Our Minds (London: Abacus Books, 1997).

Hill, Logan. "Why Rockstar Games Rule: The Badboys of Rockstar Games," Wired (July, 2002). Online at <http://www.wired.com/wired/archive/10.07/rockstar_pr.html>.

Hollywood Reporter Staff. "MCA Inc. Joins Majors in Home Video Game Distrib'n," The Hollywood Reporter (9 June, 1982), 4.

Holson, Laura M. "Hollywood Hardball," New York Times (10 June, 2005). Online at <http://www.nytimes.com/2005/06/10/business/media/10halo.html>.

Howard Scott Warshaw (director). Once Upon Atari documentary (2003).

Hruby, Patrick. "The Franchise: The Inside Story of How Madden NFL Became a Videogame Dynasty," ESPN: Outside The Lines (6 August, 2010). Online at <http://sports.espn.go.com/espn/eticket/story?page=100805/madden>.

Hubner, John and Kistner Jr., William F. "What Went Wrong At Atari [Part 2]," InfoWorld (5 December, 1983), 145-148.

Hubner, John and William F. Kistner Jr. "What Went Wrong At Atari [Part 1]," InfoWorld (28 November, 1983), 151-152, 157-158.

I

Isenberg, Barbara. "Secrets of the Play That Refuses to Close," Los Angeles Times (12 February, 1989). Online at <http://articles.latimes.com/1989-02-12/entertainment/ca-3037_1_producers>.

J

Jones, Alan. Lara Croft Tomb Raider: The Official Film Companion (London: Carlton Books, 2001).

Journal Record Staff, "High Technology Briefs," The Journal Record (23 March, 1995). Online at < http://findarticles.com/p/articles/mi_qn4182/is_19950323/ai_n10077805/>.

K

Kanner, Bernice. "Can Atari Stay Ahead of the Game?" New York Magazine (16 August, 1982), 16-18.

Kaplan, David A. and Brown, Corie. "Good-bye Pac-Man: Steven Spielberg Unveils The Video Arcade of the Future," Newsweek, (10 March, 1997), 98.

Kathryn Harris, "Video Games: Is It Too Late To Play?" Los Angeles Times (21 November, 1982), F1-F3.

Kent, Steven L. The Ultimate History of Videogames (New York: Three Rivers Press, 2001).

Kermode, Mark. "Guillermo del Toro: Guardian/BFI Interview," Guardian (21 November, 2006). Online at <http://www.guardian.co.uk/film/2006/nov/21/guardianinterviewsatbfisouthbank>.

Kimmel, Daniel M. The Dream Team: The Rise and Fall of DreamWorks: Lessons from the New Hollywood (Chicago: Ivan R. Dee, 2006).

Kleiner, Dick. "Don Bluth Animates Arcade Games," The Rock Hill Herald (23 June, 1984), 13.

Kushner, David. Masters of Doom: How Two Guys Created An Empire and Transformed Pop Culture (London: Piatkus, 2004).

L

Landau, Francesca and Edwards, Phil. "Dragon's Lair: Animator Don Bluth Re-defines the Video Arcade Game," Starburst (April, 1984), 26-28.

LaPorte, Nicole. The Men Who Would Be King: An Almost Epic Tale of Moguls, Movies and a Company Called DreamWorks (New York: Houghton Mifflin Harcourt Publishing, 2010).

Leguizamo, John. Pimps, Hos, Playa Hatas and all the Rest of My Hollywood Friends: My Life (New York: HarperCollins, 2006), p.93.

Lohr, Steve. "The Silver Disk May Soon Eclipse the Silver Screen," New York Times (1 March, 1994).

Lyman, Rick. "Movie Stars Fear Inroads By Upstart Digital Actors," New York Times (8 July, 2001). Online at <http://www.nytimes.com/2001/07/08/us/movie-stars-fear-inroads-by-upstart-digital-actors.html>.

M

Mace, Scott. "Computer Games Meet The Videodisc," InfoWorld (12 December, 1983), 88-93.

Maslin, Janet. "Review of TRON," New York Times (9 July, 1982), C8.

Matt Leone, "The Story Behind LMNO," 1Up.com (2 November, 2010). Published online at <http://www.1up.com/features/story-steven-spielberg-lmno>.

McClintock, Pamela. "Box Office Shocker: Movie Attendance Falls to Lowest Level in 16 Years," The Hollywood Reporter (29 December 2011).

McGuigan, Cathleen and McAlevey Peter. "Mini-Movies Make the Scene," Newsweek, (8 August, 1983), 79.

McNary, Dave. "Lara Croft to Return to the Big Screen," Variety (7 March, 2011).

McQuiddy, M.E. "City to Atari: 'E.T.' Trash Go Home". Alamogordo Daily News (27 September, 1983), 1.

McQuiddy, M.E. "Dump Here Utilized," Alamogordo Daily News (25 September, 1983), 1.

McWhirter, William. "The Zinger of Silicon Valley," Time (6 February, 1984), 50-51.

Moffatt, Susan. "Can Nintendo Keep Winning?", Fortune (5 November, 1990). Online at <http://money.cnn.com/magazines/fortune/fortune_archive/1990/11/05/74307/index.htm>.

Montfort, Nick and Bogost, Ian. Racing The Beam: The Atari Video Computer System Cambridge, MA: MIT Press, 2009).

Montreal Gazette Staff (1981). "Arcade Games A Bigger Draw Than The Movies," The Gazette Montreal (27 July, 1981), 28.

Morris, Chris. "Dan Houser's very extended interview about everything Grand Theft Auto IV and Rockstar," Variety (19 April, 2008). Online at <http://weblogs.variety.com/the_cut_scene/2008/04/dan-housers-ver.html>.

N

New York Times Staff. "Atari Parts Are Dumped," New York Times (28 September, 1983), D4.

Newsweek Staff. "King of Pong," Newsweek (17 December, 1973), 91.

Next Generation Staff, "Is This The End of FMV As We Know It?" Next Generation, (October, 1995), 6-10.

Nichols, Peter M. "Home Video," New York Times (10 December, 1993). Online at < http://www.nytimes.com/1993/12/10/arts/home-video-290893.html>.

Noffsinger, Loretta. "Atari, Lucasfilm Video Games Aimed at Reviving Market," The Palm Beach Post (9 May 1984), 86.

Nuttall, Chris, and Garrahan, Matthew. "Game On for Comic 'Iron Man' Faces Big Screen Test," Financial Times (27 April, 2008). Online at <http://www.ft.com/cms/s/0/bec02d88-1482-11dd-a741-0000779fd2ac.html#axzz1SYNkyFg5>.

O

O'Hannessian, Kevin. "A Conversation with 'Heavy Rain' Creator David Cage Continues," Fast Company.com (23 February, 2010). Online at <http://www.fastcompany.com/1558728/david-cage-heavy-rain-sony-playstation-video-games-interactive-drama>.

P

PC Gamer Staff, "From Die Hard To Tomb Raider: An Interview with Steven E. De Souza," Pc Gamer (March, 2000), 4.

Peterson, Jeff L. "Once Upon a Time in the Future: Final Fantasy" Cinefantastique (August, 2001), 8-11.

Piazza, Jo, "Audiences Experience Avatar 'blues'," CNN.com (11 January, 2010). Online at <http://articles.cnn.com/2010-01-11/entertainment/avatar.movie.blues_1_pandora-depressed-posts?_s=PM:SHOWBIZ>.

Picard, Martin. "Video Games and Their Relationship with Other Media," in Mark J.P. Wolf ed., The Video Game Explosion: A History From Pong to PlayStation and Beyond (Westport, CT: Greenwood Press, 2008), pp.293-300.

Pirie, Dave. "Man in The Machine," Time Out (22-28 October, 1982), 27.

Pollack, Andrew (1982). "The Game Turns Serious At Atari," New York Times (19 December, 1982), S3,1.

Pollack, Andrew. "Where Electronics and Art Converge," New York Times (15 September, 1991), F1.

Poole, Steven. Trigger Happy: The Inner Life of Videogames (London: Fourth Estate, 2000).

Powell, Jack. "New Lucasfilm Games: Antic's Sneak Preview," Antic (December, 1985), 20.

Provenzo, Eugene F. Video Kids: Making Sense of Nintendo (Cambridge, MA: Harvard University Press, 1991).

R

Reid, T.R. (1983). "Inventing Pac-Man's Rivals Can Make You a Millionaire at 25," Washington Post (20 February, 1983).

Robley, Les Paul. "The Making of Dragon's Lair," American Cinematographer (November, 1983), 74-78.

Rubin, Michael. Droidmaker: George Lucas and the Digital Revolution (Gainesville, Florida: Triad Publishing, 2006).

S

Salisbury, Mark. "Dead Residents: On the Set of Resident Evil," Total Film (August, 2001), 8.

Sandomir, Richard. "A Big Hitter Aims for a Video Homer," New York Times (10 April, 1995). Online at <http://select.nytimes.com/gst/abstract.html?res=F6061FFD3F5A0C738DDDAD0894DD494D81>.

Schrage, Michael. "Video-Game Pros Zapped," Washington Post (23 December, 1985), A1-2.

Schwartz, Tony. "Steve Ross On The Spot-Can The Wizard of Warner Rebound?," New York Magazine (24 January, 1983), 22-32.

Screen International Staff, "Synthespians to Invade Hollywood," Screen International (6 August, 1999), 1.

Serkis, Andy. The Lord of the Rings Gollum: How We Made Movie Magic (London: Collins, 2003).

Shales, Tom, Zito, Tom, and Jeannette Smyth, "When Worlds Collide: Lights! Cameras! Egos!", Washington Post (11 April, 1975). Online at <http://www.washingtonpost.com/wp-srv/style/longterm/movies/features/dcmovies/postinfilm.htm>.

Sheff, David. Game Over: Press Start to Continue - The Maturing of Mario (Wilton, CT: CyberActive, 1999).

Sherwin, Adam. "Grand Theft Auto IV Embodies the Future of Entertainment". London Times, 26 April 2008. Online <http://technology.timesonline.co.uk/tol/news/tech_and_web/gadgets_and_gaming/article3818900.ece>

Short, Stephen and Taylor, Chris. "Watch Out, Indiana. Here Comes Lara Croft," Time (26 March, 2001). Online at <http://www.time.com/time/magazine/article/0,9171,999542,00.html>.

Smith, Rob. Rogue Leaders: The Story of LucasArts (London: Titan Books, 2009).

Smith, Shelley E. "Search On To Raise The 1983 Atari Titanic," Alamogordo Daily News (12 April, 2005), A1.

Smith, Steven. "Hollywood's Holy Grail," Los Angeles Times (22 August, 1997). Online at <http://articles.latimes.com/1997/aug/22/entertainment/ca-24695>.

Solomon, Charles. "Will The Real Walt Disney Please Stand Up," Film Comment, (July/August, 1982), 49-54.

Spines, Christine. "Tomb With A View," Premiere (July, 2011), 35-40, 101.

Stayton, Richard. "The Bros. Mario Get Super Large," Los Angeles Times (16 August, 1992). Online at < http://articles.latimes.com/print/1992-08-16/entertainment/ca-6865_1_koopa-square-dennis-hopper-rocky-morton>.

Stephan Talty, "Escape From The Magic Kingdom," Empire (August, 1989), 26-27.

Storch, Charles. "Videodisc-player Shortage Zaps Arcade Gamemakers," Chicago Tribune (14 October, 1983), C1-C3.

Stross, Randall. "When a Video Game Stops Being Fun," New York Times (21 November, 2004). Online at <http://www.nytimes.com/2004/11/21/business/yourmoney/21digi.html?pagewanted=print&position=>.

Super Mario Bros. The Movie Archive. Online at < http://www.smbmovie.com/>.

Szalai, Georg. "Activision's 'Black Ops' First-Day Game Sales Set $360 Mln Record" The Hollywood Reporter (11 November, 2010). Online at <http://www.hollywoodreporter.com/news/activisions-black-ops-day-game-44526>.

T

Taylor III, Alexander L., Thompson, Dick and Washburn, Susanne. "Pac-Man Finally Meets His Match," Time (20 December, 1982), 62.

Terdiman, Daniel. "Lights, Camera, Videogames," CNET.com (7 September, 2006). Online at <http://news.cnet.com/Lights,-camera,-video-games/2100-1025_3-6113481.html>.

The Associated Press, "Stock Decline After Screening of 'TRON' Irks Disney Studio," New York Times (9 July, 1982), C8.

Tierney, John. "Movies That Push Buttons," New York Times (3 October, 1993). Online at <http://www.nytimes.com/1993/10/03/movies/movies-that-push-buttons.html>.

Time Staff, "Pac-Man Fever," Time (5 April, 1982), 48.
Trumball, Mark. "The Viewer Is in the Driver's Seat In This Movie For The 21st Century," Christian Science Monitor (21 July, 1994), 1.

V

Verrier, Richard and Fritz, Ben. "Movie industry hits ticket sales decline on the nose: It's put out some stinkers," Los Angeles Times (30 March, 2011). Online at <http://articles.latimes.com/2011/mar/30/business/la-fi-ct-cinemacon-20110330/2>.

Vincent, Roger and Pham, Alex. "EA Makes a Play for L.A.," Los Angeles Times (6 August, 2003). Online at <http://articles.latimes.com/2003/aug/06/business/fi-ea6>.

W

Ward, Sandra. "Game-Changing Hero Is Poised to Rule," Barron's Online (31 August, 2009). Online at <http://online.barrons.com/article/SB125150805017468583.html>.

Waugh, Rob. "Grand Theft Auto: The Reckoning," Mail Online (24 August, 2007). Online at < http://www.dailymail.co.uk/home/moslive/article-477505/Grand-Theft-Auto-The-reckoning.html>.

Wiltshire, Alex. "Interview: Lev Chapelsky," EDGE (20 May, 2009). Online at <http://www.next-gen.biz/features/interview-lev-chapelsky?page=1>.

Wolf, Mark J.P., ed., The Video Game Explosion: A History From Pong to PlayStation and Beyond (Westport, CT: Greenwood Press, 2008)

Wolk, Douglas. "James Cameron and Peter Jackson Explore the Future of Film," Rolling Stone (27 July, 2009). Online at <http://www.rollingstone.com/movies/news/james-cameron-and-peter-jackson-explore-the-future-of-film-20090727>.

WorstPreviews.com Staff, "Peter Jackson Gives 'Halo' Update," WorstPreviews.com (26 July, 2009). Online at <http://www.worstpreviews.com/headline.php?id=14401>.

Z

Zito, Tom. "Senate Demagoguery: Leave My Company's Video Game Alone," Washington Post (17 December, 1993), A25.

Zorn, Eric. "Coming Soon to a Laser Game Near You," Chicago Tribune (15 March, 1984), A1, A3.

ACKNOWLEDGEMENTS

Writing a narrative history of this sort wouldn't be possible without the generosity of those who agreed to be interviewed. More than a hundred games developers, filmmakers, actors and executives were kind enough to talk to me on the phone, in person and by email. I hope I've done justice to their stories.

Some sections of this history were originally written for Edge magazine's retrospectives on the making of classic videogames. My thanks to Future Publishing for letting me incorporate the material here. Meanwhile, I'm grateful to everyone at both Total Film and Edge magazines for their support during the lengthy writing process - in particular Jane Crowther, Ian Evenden, Jamie Graham, Jason Killingsworth, Matthew Leyland and Tony Mott.

I'd also like to thank Daniel Etherington - the best *Planetside* tank driver I've ever had the pleasure to ride with and a formidable bullet magnet in *Call of Duty* - for his feedback on early drafts; the staff at the British Film Institute Library in London (in particular Sean Delaney) for all their assistance; and all those publicists who arranged interview access for me.

It was crucial to find the right publisher for *Generation Xbox* - someone who understood the remarkable place we find ourselves in: where a medium born in the 19th century is blending with one forged in the 20th, to create the future of entertainment. Tristan Donovan at Yellow Ant recognised the importance of this constantly evolving area and has been a great collaborator.

A big thank you to my family: my fantastic wife Louise and wonderful daughters Isobel and Alice for all their love and patience during the three years it took to take this project from inception to publication. Thanks also to my extended family: the Grisottis, McDonalds, Russells and Whitehouses for all their support; and to John and Anna Groombridge, for many debts still unpaid. Last but not least, my thanks to Nev Pierce: a tireless and perceptive sounding board for many of the ideas in this book and a great friend.

INDEX

ABOUT THE AUTHOR

Jamie Russell is a contributing editor for Total Film magazine and regularly writes for Edge, the world's most respected videogames publication. He has also contributed to The Guardian, The Scotsman, Radio Times, Sight & Sound, FHM and the BAFTA magazine.

He's happiest writing about zombies, first-person shooters and William S. Burroughs. One day he plans to combine all three obsessions in the same feature article.

Jamie has written several books, including Book of the Dead: The Complete History of Zombie Cinema. He had a Ph.D in English Literature but he only calls himself Dr when talking to bank managers. He lives in Shropshire with his wife, two daughters and a growing collection of games consoles.

ALSO BY JAMIE RUSSELL

Queer Burroughs
The Pocket Essential Beat Generation
The Pocket Essential Vietnam War Movies
Book of the Dead: The Complete History of Zombie Cinema

ALSO PUBLISHED BY YELLOW ANT

Replay: The History of Video Games by Tristan Donovan

Made in the USA
San Bernardino, CA
15 December 2012